THE MAKING OF MODERN THEOLOGY
NINETEENTH- AND TWENTIETH-CENTURY TEXTS

This major series of theological texts is designed to introduce a new generation of readers—theological students, students of religion, professionals in ministry, and the interested general reader—to the writings of those Christian theologians who, since the beginning of the nineteenth century, have had a formative influence on the development of Christian theology.

Each volume in the series is intended to introduce the theologian, to trace the emergence of key or seminal ideas and insights, particularly within their social and historical context, and to show how they have contributed to the making of modern theology. The primary way in which this is done is by allowing the theologians chosen to address us in their own words.

There are three sections to each volume. The Introduction includes a short biography of the theologian, and an overview of his or her theology in relation to the texts which have been selected for study. The Selected Texts, the bulk of each volume, consist largely of substantial edited selections from the theologian's writings. Each text is also introduced with information about its origin and its significance. The guiding rule in making the selection of texts has been the question: In what way has this particular theologian contributed to the shaping of contemporary theology? A Select Bibliography provides guidance for those who wish to read further both in the primary literature and in secondary sources.

Series editor John W. de Gruchy is Professor of Christian Studies at the University of Cape Town, South Africa. He is the author of many works, including *Church Struggle in South Africa,* and *Theology and Ministry in Context and Crisis.*

Volumes in this series

1. Friedrich Schleiermacher: Pioneer of Modern Theology
2. Rudolf Bultmann: Interpreting Faith for the Modern Era
3. Paul Tillich: Theologian of the Boundaries
4. Dietrich Bonhoeffer: Witness to Jesus Christ
5. Karl Barth: Theologian of Freedom
6. Adolf von Harnack: Liberal Theology at Its Height
7. Reinhold Niebuhr: Theologian of Public Life

Karl Rahner, 1904–84

THE MAKING OF MODERN THEOLOGY

Nineteenth- and Twentieth-Century Texts
General Editor: John W. de Gruchy

KARL RAHNER

Theologian of the Graced Search for Meaning

GEFFREY B. KELLY
Editor

Fortress Press
Minneapolis

KARL RAHNER
Theologian of the Graced Search for Meaning
The Making of Modern Theology series

Copyright © 1992 Augsburg Fortress. All rights reserved. Except for brief quotations in critical articles or reviews, no part of this book may be reproduced in any manner without prior written permission from the publisher. Write to: Permissions, Augsburg Fortress, 426 S. Fifth St., Box 1209, Minneapolis, MN 55440.

The publishers gratefully acknowledge permission of the Crossroad Publishing Co. and Darton, Longman and Todd Ltd to reproduce in this volume copyrighted excerpts of the works of Karl Rahner as specified in the source lines preceding each selection.

Interior design: Colin Reed
Cover design: Neil Churcher
Cover photo: Andes Press Agency

Library of Congress Cataloging-in-Publication Data

Rahner, Karl, 1904–1984
   [Selection. English. 1992]
   Karl Rahner : theologian of the graced search for meaning /
Geffrey B. Kelly, editor.
      p. cm. — (The Making of modern theology)
   Includes bibliographical references and index.
   ISBN 0-8006-3400-4
   1. Theology, Doctrinal. I. Kelly, Geffrey B. II. Title.
III. Series.
BT75.2.R322513 1992
230'.2—dc20   92-21018
                                                      CIP

The paper used in this publication meets the minimum requirements of American National Standard for Information Sciences—Permanence of Paper for Printed Library Materials, ANSI Z329.48-1984 ∞™

Manufactured in the U.S.A.   AF 1–3400

96   95   94   93   92   1   2   3   4   5   6   7   8   9   10

CONTENTS

PREFACE

Not long after I had accepted the invitation of John de Gruchy, general editor of this series, to edit this book, I began to wonder what I had gotten myself into. As soon as I had commenced the work of reading anew some of the popular books by Rahner and of absorbing as comprehensively as possible the massive collection of his writings, questions began to disturb my peace: How would I ever finish studying all these books and articles, numbering into the thousands? How would I ever make selections from this vast literature that would capture the essence of Rahner's contribution to modern theology in the few hundred pages allotted? I was further dismayed when, on asking people to let me know what their favorite Rahnerian piece was, I discovered such a widely flung variety that, early on, I knew my selections would not please everybody. Rahner wrote on nearly every aspect of religious thought. His influence extended into nearly every branch of theology and spirituality. I soon realized that inevitably people were going to be disappointed not to find here selections from their favorite article, book, meditation, or even prayer.

As for the selections themselves, I had to cope with the encyclopedic interests of Rahner and the unlimited variety of his contribution to "the making of modern theology," the general theme of this series. Because Rahner is so often compared to Thomas Aquinas, the theological genius of the thirteenth century, I conceived of the idea of setting up a mini-*Summa Theologica* in which I would arrange lengthy excerpts—or, where possible, whole articles, sermons, or prayers—under headings that show not only the versatility of Rahner's theological and spiritual interests but also the extent and depth of his influence on twentieth-century theology, especially Catholic theology. The headings I chose were these: prayer and the spiritual life; grace and freedom; revelation and the development of dogma; the doctrine of God; Christology; the Holy Spirit; church; sacrament and symbol; Christian faith, praxis, and martyrdom; and, finally, theological methodology. This arrangement is not without its flaws. Nonetheless, I believe my selections from Rahner on these varied topics will illustrate to a new generation of readers Rahner's creative genius, his prowess as a theologian and spiritual writer, and his consequent influence on modern religious thought.

Because this book is directed to a general readership as well as the more specialized student of Rahner's religious thought, the introduction to each chapter sets the ensuing cluster of texts within the framework of Rahner's theological, pastoral concerns. The introduction to each selection, in turn, not only traces the original setting of the piece, but also shows how the text in question illustrates Rahner's creative contribution to contemporary theology. To make Rahner more accessible to the world beyond academe and his literary legacy more comprehensible to that wider world, the first section of the Introduction portrays Rahner in biographical context. My intention there is to help readers appreciate Rahner as a Jesuit theologian, a teacher and lecturer, a courageous priest, and a servant of his church and of people everywhere who looked to him for guidance and inspiration. With this same aim in mind, the second section of the Introduction examines at length Rahner's way of doing theology. That section serves as an interpretive key to assist students of Rahner's religious thought in reading his works even beyond the selections that form the major portion of this book.

Despite the complexities of writing about an author of such renown and productivity, I have always wanted to explore Rahner's theology and spirituality in greater depth. Like so many Catholic theologians I consider him among my most important formative influences. For me personally, he kept alive the "Catholic" dimension of my theological interests, as time and again he retrieved coherence and meaning for Catholic doctrine in the face of that ecclesiastical narrow-mindedness that continues to weaken the credibility of the church leadership for so many thinking Catholics. Rahner has made doing theology in the service of faith and of the church seem an attractive and worthwhile vocation. My other great influence has been the German Lutheran theologian and martyr Dietrich Bonhoeffer, about whom I have written several books, monographs, and articles.

I first met Rahner and joined the ranks of his devotees while I was working on my dissertation on Bonhoeffer at the Catholic University of Louvain in Belgium, during the academic year 1971–72. Rahner had been invited to the University of Louvain to deliver a series of lectures on the "Resurrection of Jesus Christ as a Dogmatic Problem." I had been asked to be his "runner," note taker, and sometimes translator. We budding theologians had been promised colloquium time with the "master," but all of us held him in such awe that we could not help

viii

but wonder if the great theologian would tolerate "fools" like us. We worried and even joked about whether we would be able to ask intelligent enough questions. As it turned out, Rahner showed an unusual deference to those of us not fully accepted in the world of theological debate. Every question was taken with utmost seriousness; his mind could make connections few of us would have imagined. Our hopes to serve the church with all the critical acumen our theological training at Louvain was preparing us for seemed to intrigue and delight him. Our concerns quickly seemed to become his concerns. It was only the learned exegetes and professors of dogmatics of the university whom he treated with a sharpness, wit, and repartee that struck us as theological jousting with real barbs. Rahner was feisty, even gruff, with those who would try to spring intellectual traps, question his credentials in exegesis, or test his orthodoxy. In contrast, he seemed gentle and helpful with those who lacked the expertise of the professors but who wanted to explore deeper and at times hidden dimensions of dogmatic and exegetical problems. We were lost in admiration at the keenness of mind of this renowned theologian who had only recently retired from active teaching. Just as Bonhoeffer admitted after his first meeting with Karl Barth, I found myself wishing then that I had met Rahner sooner. In a way, I envied those who had opted for the University of Münster and who had been able to experience his greatness and guidance over the entire course of their doctoral studies.

My initial desire to write a lengthy interpretation of Rahner's theology and spirituality, however, originated at the practical level in my seminars on his theology at La Salle University. In those high-powered sessions with religion majors at the undergraduate level and with teachers of religion and future theologians at the graduate level, I would typically intersperse my own analysis with study of and shared research on the widest possible selection of Rahner's writings. My students clamored for secondary literature that could not only clarify his more profound theological essays with their long, at times involuted, Germanic sentences, but also provide an interpretive key to these texts. I was fortunate to have nearby, at the Washington Theological Union, the Augustinian scholar Michael Scanlon, who was able to fulfill this need with his lectures, which combined insightful interpretation with wit and eloquence. In many ways, Mike's lectures at La Salle are foundational for my own analysis, particularly in his observations on Rahner's connections with Augustine's "restlessness of heart" and with his strengths in the theological anthropology that is context and foundation for so many of Rahner's reflections. While I take responsibility for my own analysis of Rahner's life and thought here, I would be remiss if I did not acknowledge the boost Mike gave to my seminars in our common quest to appreciate Rahner's creative contribution to contemporary theology.

Having neither studied under Rahner nor written a dissertation on him, and having never been drawn into the cross fire of the spirited debates among his interpreters, I could enter the exciting circles of Rahner scholarship only vicariously. I consider myself fortunate to have had access to so many compelling analyses of Rahner's theological legacy. My indebtedness to these writers should be clear from the quotations interwoven in the introductory section and the documentation listed at the end of the book. These authors of the secondary literature include close friends of Rahner and theologians who have themselves exemplified the Ignatian spirituality that is the soul of Rahner's theology. It is risky to name only a few among so many. But to the extent this book is successful in helping readers appreciate Rahner's contribution to modern religious thought, I must acknowledge the insightful contributions to my own interpretation by Herbert Vorgrimler, Leo O'Donovan, Harvey Egan, William Dych, Anne Carr, Robert Kress, and Francis Schüssler Fiorenza. I trust that I have not subjected these writers to the same distortions I detected in some of the earlier secondary literature on Rahner.

That this project reached completion with any degree of coherence, given the nature of interpreting a religious writer of Rahner's stature and the problem of sifting through bibliographical items numbering in the thousands, is due to a wide network of colleagues and personal friends who have graciously given of their time and talent to help me. In particular, I am indebted to Michael Scanlon of the Washington Theological Union and to Bernard Prusak and Anthony Godzieba of Villanova University for reading the manuscript and for their constructive suggestions on how to improve the text. I profited too from the gentle encouragement of my departmental chairman, David Efroymson, who was instrumental in my obtaining release time for one semester so that the project could move beyond the initial research phase. In preparing the manuscript, I was soon made aware of my illiteracy with computers. That was remedied by Dr. John O'Neill of La Salle's Mathematics and Computer Science Department. John spent many evenings patiently teaching me the basics of word processing and even more hours retrieving materials I had lost through overloading two disks. To John I owe my being able to complete the manuscript with only a minimum of deadline breakage.

Speaking of deadlines, these were set and the task of meeting them was made easier by J. Michael West, my editor at Fortress Press. Michael shepherded the manuscript from its arrival on his desk in less-than-polished form through to its publication. Michael's organization of the time lines and format and his valuable suggestions on the arrangement of the text have been unfailingly helpful. His interest and encouragement in every phase from yellow pads to computer disks kept my spirits up at times when the project never seemed to have an end. To my copy editor, W. Hank Schlau, I am indebted for his scrutiny of the manuscript and for his hundreds of questions that were like a "thousand points of light" during the final months of the book's gestation. If any mistakes escaped his sharp eyes, these were picked up by Betty Coyne, to whom I am grateful for her patient work with me across a cluttered dining room table during the proofreading phase.

This book, unfortunately, had to be completed under the most difficult of all circumstances, the serious illness of my nine-year-old daughter, Susan, who suffers from a brain tumor. Many people made it possible not only for our family to cope with the surgeries and various therapies Susan has required but also for me to continue work on this project. It is impossible to list here all the people of this community of support. But some were particularly helpful in terms of this project as it impinged on the greater need to care for my family. Hence I am grateful to the Reverend John McLoughlin, who not only had contributed many insights in our shared seminar research on Rahner but who likewise kept after me "to provide for my students" by finishing the book. John, I might add, also helped to keep up our courage during the worst moments of Susan's illness, often appearing at our home with presents and a warm personality that never failed to cheer Susan and us. Visits from "Uncle Father John" were a highlight in the early phases of my work on the text. My family and I are also deeply indebted to the Sisters of Ancillae Assumpta Academy of Wyncote, who have welcomed Susan into their midst and given her the loving care and spiritual nurture that have, more than anything else, helped her overcome the handicaps of her disease and continue the struggle in such good spirits. These Sisters, from the order of the Handmaidens of the Sacred Heart, and their skilled staff at Ancillae have in so many ways exemplified what I have tried to convey here of the spirituality of Karl Rahner. Although I am not able to name all of them here, Sisters Liz, Maureen, Kathy, and Connie stand out for the way they made the Rahnerian "joy of finding God in all things" real for Susan and for our entire family.

Finally, I am most of all grateful to Sister Jean Burns of the Religious Sisters of Mercy, a teacher of theology at Gwynedd-Mercy College and one of my students in La Salle's Graduate Religion Program. Sister Jean not only assisted in preparing and correcting the manuscript but also motivated me to continue work on the "Rahner project" whenever my spirits flagged. It was Sister Jean who made the book's completion possible by caring for the children and, in many ways, conspiring with my wife, Joan, to free me for the time needed to finish the project, as much as any project dealing with Rahner's theology can ever be "finished." With gratitude and affection I dedicate this book to Sister Jean; to Sisters Liz, Maureen, Kathy, Connie, and the Handmaidens of the Sacred Heart of Ancillae; to Passionist Father John McLoughlin and Augustinian Father Mike Scanlon; and to my wife, Joan, for her patience as this project "never seemed to end."

EDITOR'S NOTE

Some phrases in the Selected Texts as well as in the Rahnerian passages cited in the Introduction have been slightly altered to make them accord more with Rahner's German texts or to make explicit the gender-inclusive language often taken for granted in the original German.

INTRODUCTION

I. KARL RAHNER: AN OUTLINE OF HIS LIFE

Even before his death at Innsbruck on March 30, 1984, Karl Rahner had been hailed as *the* religious thinker who had contributed more than any other to the renewal of Catholic theology in the twentieth century. His influence on systematic theology was such that in a poll taken in 1978 among North American theologians representing seventy-one different denominations, Rahner was named after Paul Tillich and Thomas Aquinas as the greatest influence on their thinking, even ahead of St. Augustine and Martin Luther.[1] Indeed, Rahner's sheer productivity seems awesome. There are over four thousand entries in his bibliography, including the massive sixteen volumes of his *Schriften zur Theologie* (translated into English in twenty-two volumes as *Theological Investigations*), covering nearly every aspect of religious thought in a manner that is at once thoroughly contemporary and faithful to the Christian tradition. Critics have both admired the depth and marveled at the extent and complexity of his writings. Rahner's style of "transcendental" reflection often took involuted twists and turns in his search for truth and for the proper nuances to express that truth.

Yet, for all that, there is a remarkable simplicity to the Rahnerian system that holds his theological legacy together, namely, the incarnational principle that God and the human must always be found together. His reflections were "always in the service of human hearts that had been addressed in time by grace."[2] The question of God that courses throughout Rahner's entire theological legacy unfolds at the same time into the question of what humans are called by God to become. Rahner's genius was to link the human search for fulfillment with the restlessness implanted in the individual's heart by God and to correlate God's trinitarian presence in historical, somatic reality with what he affirmed to be the signs of God's grace investing human life with dignity and beatific destiny. To those who knew him, Rahner's life and theology seemed an echo of Augustine's prayer: "Our hearts are made for you, O God, and they are restless until they rest in you!"

Karl Rahner was born on March 5, 1904, in the Black Forest city of

1

Freiburg-im-Breisgau, Germany. He was the fourth of seven children in the family of Karl (1868–1934) and Luise Trescher (1868–1976) Rahner. He described his upbringing as typical of a traditionally pious but "perfectly normal Christian family—Catholic but not bigoted."[3] His father was a professor in the local teachers college. Rahner remembered him as a good provider who had to tutor pupils after school hours in order to pay for the solid education all his children received. The Catholic ambience of their home seemed to him to have been primarily due to the effort of his mother, whom he once likened to the valiant woman of the wisdom literature. He recalled that his family was far from being shaped in "a narrowly clerical way."[4] In fact it was his secondary-school religion teacher who first informed his parents that Karl intended to follow in his brother Hugo's steps and enter the Society of Jesus upon graduation. That the teacher did not think much of the decision is evident from a remark of his that later gave Karl and many of his future students a chuckle: "He's too withdrawn and grumpy. He should become something else."[5] His teacher may have mistaken for grumpiness what a close friend, Herbert Vorgrimler, listed as a characteristic of the people from that section of Germany, who "are supposed to be reserved, introspective, and ready to work like horses; they are considered to have a deep sense of humor, but no spontaneous and clearsighted joy in life—only a melancholy irony."[6] The same commentator mentions that Rahner was considered only an average student, one thoroughly bored by the lessons he was asked to master at school.

JESUIT TRAINING

However that may be, Karl began his novitiate in the North German Province of the Jesuits on April 20, 1922, at the age of eighteen. During the novitiate period at Feldkirch in the region of Varalberg, 1922–24, Rahner deeply encountered the Ignatian spirituality that became part of his life's inspiration and that enlivened his later writings on prayer and the spiritual life. He even began to compose the first of his articles on spirituality for publication in the novitiate magazine.

In particular, Rahner began to experience then what has been called the "Ignatian mysticism of joy in the world" and of "finding God in all things." These Ignatian insights would become lasting dimensions of his spirituality and form an attractive foundation for his lifelong concentration on what he would confess to be at the core of his religious commitment—dedication to the "holy mystery" that in Jesus Christ has entered into a special communion with people in their concrete history.

Rahner's subsequent conjoining of God's revealed love for creation with human concerns and with experiential search for meaning, at the roots of Ignatian spirituality and illuminated in the story of Jesus, provided a strong guideline in his attempt to retrieve and thematize what he believed to be the signs of God's presence in human history. The unity between the divine and the human that he conveyed throughout his writings derived from his strong conviction that God has created, sustained, and loved a "world of grace."[7]

Rahner's Ignatian exultation in this mysterious communion of God with the world had its counterpart in what has been designated as Ignatian "indifference" toward the various modes of God's self-manifestation and of God's call in Christ to be both more Christian and more human. This is not the cold, uncaring apathy one might infer from current usage of the term. Rather, Ignatian "indifference," in a seemingly paradoxical way, derives from one's spiritual "enthusiasm," etymologically from one's "being in God" to the extent that one is so overwhelmed by God's presence within that one is ready to do anything, to go anywhere, to suffer any deprivation in order to help bring about God's reign in Christ throughout the world. Everything can, then, become bearer of God's presence, even the ordinary events of a humdrum existence. In a word, as a Christian, one should be willing to be led by God's Spirit into any desert and temple, onto any Calvary and mountaintop of the world. God's nearness is unrestricted. All being can be revelatory of God; hence one can be "indifferent" in the sense of having confidence that one can experience the joy that flows from communion with God in any and all things. Or, as the Jesuit poet Gerard Manley Hopkins expressed it in words that could also describe Rahner's outlook on God's all-pervasive, incarnationally graced nearness: "The world is charged with the grandeur of God."[8]

PHILOSOPHICAL FOUNDATIONS

After having made his first profession as a Jesuit on April 27, 1924, Rahner began his philosophical studies, first in Feldkirch from 1924–25, then at Berchmanskolleg in Pullach outside Munich from 1925–27. This scholasticate was followed by a period of regency, or initiation into the practical life of a Jesuit, in Rahner's case, as teacher of Latin in the juniorate in Feldkirch. One of his students of that time was Alfred Delp, a young Jesuit who was later to be executed by the Nazis because of his role in the Kreisau Circle, an ecumenical group opposed to Hitler's war policies and the criminal government then in power in Germany.

In 1929 Rahner began four years of theological studies at Valkenberg, Holland. Between the third and fourth years of this theologate, on July 26, 1932, Rahner was ordained to the priesthood by Cardinal Faulhaber in Munich. After he had spent a year of tertianship, or spiritual retreat, in St. Andrä in the Lavant Valley, Rahner's superiors sent him in 1934 to the University of Freiburg, there to obtain the doctorate in philosophy, a prelude to his becoming a teacher of the history of philosophy. Each of these moves had significance for the development of the philosophical-theological foundations of Rahner's religious thought.

During his scholasticate years at Pullach, Rahner first began to study seriously the philosophy of Immanuel Kant and Joseph Maréchal. The latter, called the "Father of Transcendental Thomism," was a Jesuit philosopher on the faculty of philosophy at Louvain, Belgium. He was to exercise a most profound influence on Rahner's earliest philosophical development, particularly in the way Rahner became adept at opening Catholic dogmatics not only to Kant's critical assessment of the process of knowing, but also, beyond Kant, to the Maréchalian contention that it is God's real existence in the world that elicits from people the enduring drive to know and to love in an unlimited way. Maréchal himself had argued in the fifth volume of his monumental study of metaphysics, *Le thomisme devant la philosophie critique*, that Kant's transcendental reflection on human knowledge appeared to terminate in the dead-end of unexplored judgments about God, one's soul, and the world. Maréchal wanted to bridge the apparent gap Kant had left in his analysis of how one "objectifies" reality.

For Kant, in contrast, the knower unites all empirical data with categories of understanding and the given forms of space and time; this is done when the knower, using speculative reason, makes an objective, categorical judgment. Kant conceded that for life to make more complete sense the objectified judgments that ensued needed in turn to be organized into a more coherent, intelligible whole by means of the "regulative ideals" of God, soul, and the world. Kant also concluded, however, that these ideals are neither a condition for the validity of the objective judgment nor a constitutive element in the judgment itself. In short, the mind's dynamic thrust toward truth seemed, in the Kantian analysis, unsupported in any real way by the so-called regulative ideals. Genuine objective knowledge seemed to depend only on the subjective realm of human experience where, for Kant, the raw data of one's senses are refracted through the forms and categories of one's speculative reason. For the sake of the purity of one's search for truth, Kant argued that one had to be agnostic about the existence of God. The idea

4

of God became, then, a postulate of one's "practical reason," necessary for one's everyday life, but ultimately a matter of pure faith.[9]

The Maréchalian critique of Kant would not only dramatically open up Rahner's own reading of Aquinas's metaphysics but also fire the beginnings of Rahner's synthesis of philosophical anthropology with traditional dogmatics. The application of this to Catholic theology would come later. To get "beyond Kant," Maréchal integrated the insights of Fichte, Blondel, and Rousselot into his own synthesizing dialogue between Thomism and critical idealism. In particular, Maréchal was impressed by the way Fichte had attempted to overcome the split between the Kantian speculative reason—the agent of knowing—and practical reason, where the regulative ideals of God, soul, and world could be applied for the sake of articulating a more coherent contextual whole for reality. Fichte had suggested that the intuiting of one's spiritual activity in knowing and willing is animated by the "infinite absolute" to which one's energies of mind and will are attracted. Hence God, in Fichte's perspective, is foundational in a real sense for the knowledge that Kant reserved to speculative reason alone. The God-inspirited dynamism of the human mind would constitute for both Maréchal and Rahner a vital part of the bridge they needed to cross over from Kantian idealism into the realism of Thomistic metaphysics.

Maréchal had likewise noted how Maurice Blondel had turned the Fichtean dynamism of mind into an affirmation that the human will is geared to concrete choices of action, not by reason alone, but primarily by its innate orientation to God. Maréchal was also in agreement with the way Pierre Rousselot was able to apply the Blondelian analysis to Thomism in his own effort to rescue Aquinas from the neoscholastics then closed off from the wider philosophical world in their rigid, Vatican-controlled authoritarianism. It seemed clear to Rahner that, in analyzing the act of knowing, Maréchal had succeeded in focusing on the goal or end of the human person's dynamic orientation to the infinite affirmed as real and as the principal a priori condition for any speculative judgment in the Kantian sense. Through Maréchal, Rahner would himself be led to ground all philosophical affirmations about being and reality in the dynamism of the human mind that is inspirited, supported, and led by the infinite, final cause of all order in the mind as in the world.[10] Because of this Rahner would be convinced that we all live in a world of grace in which God is the ultimate source of every human longing and the attractive horizon of our search for truth and meaning.

In many ways Rahner's doctoral work at Freiburg stamped him as the successor to Maréchal; this was particularly so because Rahner was able to take the idealism of Hegel and the phenomenal ontology of Martin Heidegger and add them to the creative synthesis that was called Transcendental Thomism. Rahner was fortunate in being allowed to enroll in the highly restricted seminars of Heidegger. He was moving then in the company of others who had likewise been influenced by Maréchal; this group included John Baptist Lotz, Bernard Welte, Max Müller, and Gustav Siewerth, later to become well-known philosophers in their own right. Erich Pryzara called them "The Catholic Heidegger School."[11] Because of the opening Maréchal had made in traditional neo-scholastic philosophy, they were, as Rahner recalled, "naturally more in tune with Martin Heidegger's thought from the beginning."[12] Later in life, when asked to say something about these philosophical influences on his religious thinking, Rahner did not seem very ready to acknowledge the dominance of Heidegger. In fact, he remembered more the direction given his thought by Maréchal. Heidegger, he acknowledged, taught him how to think creatively. "Certainly, I learned a variety of things from him, even if I have to say that I owe my most basic, decisive, philosophical direction, insofar as it comes from someone else, more, in fact, to the Belgian philosopher and Jesuit, Joseph Maréchal. His philosophy already moved beyond the traditional neo-scholasticism. I brought that direction from Maréchal to my studies with Heidegger and it was not superseded by him."[13] He also recalled that he did not have the advantage of being inspired by a great master to whom he would be "bound in a blazing discipleship."[14]

It is important to keep these observations in mind when one analyzes the philosophical-theological foundations for Rahner's unique way of doing theology. Rahner is more than the sum of his early philosophical influences. He himself confesses a deeper, lifelong indebtedness to the Ignatian spirituality that seems to give such a special direction to both the substance and the mode of his theological reflections. That is why when asked if Ignatius of Loyola had molded his religious experience, he replied:

> I do think that in comparison with other philosophy and theology that influenced me, Ignatian spirituality was indeed more significant and important. There, too, to be honest, I cannot say that individual Jesuits, spiritual directors, retreat masters, and so forth made an overpowering impression on me. . . . But I think that the spirituality of Ignatius himself, which one learned through the practice of prayer and religious formation, was more significant for me than all learned philosophy and theology inside and outside the order.[15]

6

DOCTORAL DISSERTATION

Rahner's dissertation at Freiburg, *Geist im Welt*, later published in English as *Spirit in the World*, was, on the surface, a historical study of Aquinas's metaphysics of the mind's act of judgment. Rahner went beyond this, however, to bring the Maréchalian interpretation of Aquinas into critical dialogue with Kant and Heidegger. Rahner seemed fascinated by the congruence between Heidegger's concept of *Dasein*, or being-in-the-world, and Aquinas's concept of the dynamism of the human mind. For Heidegger, one attains awareness of the self by posing the fundamental question of being, a question of the search for the truth or meaning in a world dominated by the sensate. One's judgments are on and about the world. Yet each judgment, as Rahner, following Aquinas, points out, must go through a process of abstraction and the conversion of what one perceives into an image or phantasm. The process of "abstraction" demands, in turn, an application of universal conceptual forms that are more than any individual object to be known.

This, for Rahner, has to place the knower into a real contact with the absolute of being, which is more than any finite concept one might form. Heidegger's contention that to question the meaning of one's being must in some way be directed by a preliminary grasp or judgment (*Vorgriff*) of the world's horizon of being was adapted by Rahner into an affirmation that true knowledge of oneself and the meaning of one's existence demanded a preconceptual, pregrasp (*Vorgriff*) of *infinite* being or of God. Rahner thus bypassed Heidegger's refusal to affirm anything beyond finite and historical being and Heidegger's as well as Kant's agnosticism on the question of God. Rahner argued, on the contrary, that the dynamism of the human mind was inspirited by the dynamism of God's own infinitude, the limitless horizon that was God's own being providing the "whither" of all human search for meaning. With one's rootedness in the world of the material, the sensate, one could, following Rahner's argument, attain the absolute in some way because the absolute of being was already implanting a restlessness within the human spirit and offering a horizon of unlimited attraction.[16]

TEACHER OF THEOLOGY

Rahner's doctoral dissertation, submitted at the University of Freiburg in 1936, and now considered a tour de force in Transcendental Thomism, was surprisingly enough rejected by his mentor, Martin Honecker. It was too much Heidegger and not Catholic enough—in the narrow-minded, neo-scholastic understanding of that term—for Honecker, Chairman of Catholic Philosophy at Freiburg. Rahner had succeeded in formulating a Christian anthropology with a unique synthesis of Aquinas, Heidegger, and Kant. Honecker wanted something more traditional, predictable, and safe. It is ironic that today Honecker is known principally for his having failed Rahner and deprived him of the doctorate in philosophy. Rahner simply states: "I was flunked by the Catholic Honecker for being too inspired by Heidegger."[17] But Rahner noted, too, that the rejection did not disturb him for too long. In fact, he was quickly reassigned to teach theology at Innsbruck. The "failure" in philosophy thus became theology's gain. His rejected dissertation was, nonetheless, published without his having received the doctorate and has since then been through several editions and has been translated into several languages. There was little jolt either to his career or to his self-esteem, even apart from any invocation of his Ignatian "indifference" to such a setback.

At Innsbruck, Rahner was able to complete work on his doctorate in theology by December 1936. His dissertation is on the birth of the church from the pierced side of Christ and is entitled *E Latere Christi: Der Ursprung der Kirche als zweiter Eva aus der Seite Christi des zweiten Adam. Eine Untersuchung über den typologischen Sinn von Jo 19, 34* (From the side of Christ: The origin of the church as second Eve from the side of Christ the second Adam. An examination of the typological meaning of John 19:34). It is based on patristic texts and is significant for Rahner's early attention to the symbolic meaning that Jesus' actions in the Gospel offer for churches and the Christian life. We see here, too, evidence of his familiarity with the writings of the fathers of the church and of his ability to do historical theology. This talent is brought out further in volume 11 of his *Theological Investigations,* which contains his early studies on the history of the sacrament of penance.

With his doctorate in tow, Rahner was officially appointed as *Privatdozent* or lecturer in the faculty of theology of the University of Innsbruck on July 1, 1937. He modestly described the appointment as merely filling a need in the ranks: "My religious superiors were of the opinion that I wouldn't do it any worse than many others."[18] Soon enough his skills as a creative theologian began to be acknowledged when in the summer of 1937, Rahner presented a series of lectures on the "Foundations of a Philosophy of Religion" to the Salzburg Summer School. These lectures were later published in 1941 under the title of *Hörer des Wortes* (*Hearers of the Word*). Here, too, Rahner continued his Thomistic-metaphysical dialogue with Heidegger's phenomenological ontology. As in his *Spirit in the World*, Rahner turned Heidegger's insistence on the pregrasp of being into a pregrasp of and by the horizon of meaning that elicits from one's own spirit not only the longing for fulfillment but also the search for one's own rootedness in the absolute being of God in a way that could only enhance the freedom to be and to become that was Heidegger's philosophical trademark. Rahner views this being grasped by absolute being as part of a process of transformation in which in some way one shares in God's own life. "You have seized me. I have not 'grasped' you. You have transformed my being right down to its very last roots and made me a sharer in your own being and life," he would write in his classic book on prayer, *Encounters with Silence*.[19]

Rahner depicts the human subject, therefore, as primarily spirit that in the act of knowing has already experienced a prior identity with and attraction toward absolute being, the inspiriting source and ultimate object of one's drive to be a knower of truth and a doer of good in the world. This is a communion of God with one's very being, which is in turn a condition for making possible the union between knower and known so vital to the Thomistic understanding of knowledge and to Rahner's description of a characteristic of both knowledge and freedom, the subject's being present unto itself. Rahner's description of this process of knowing and being known will become foundational for his theology of revelation and be reminiscent of Augustine's claim that "God is more intimate to me than I am to myself." With Rahner, as with Augustine, the intimacy of the union leads one to a mystical ecstasy in which one's self is enhanced and one has an intimation of eternal beatitude. Later Rahner would use this to explain how Christ as a human subject is able to grow in knowledge of himself and of his world through ever more intensely being present unto himself—in short, knowing himself in every act of knowing and choosing himself in every act of willing.[20]

WAR YEARS

By 1938, in the wake of the Nazi annexation of Austria, Rahner's teaching career at Innsbruck was in jeopardy. The Nazis closed the faculty of theology at the university in October 1939. Rahner and others continued to teach theology at the Jesuit residence until that too was suppressed. The Jesuit residence was expropriated and the Jesuits themselves expelled from the Tyrol. Rahner attributed the moves to the antipathy of Höfer, Nazi district leader for the Tyrol, surmising that, for him, "The idea of a Jesuit theological faculty was absolutely intolerable. So he quickly dissolved it. The Canisianum, the seminary for diocesan priests that we ran in Innsbruck, was expropriated.... We were thrown out of Innsbruck on short notice. And then we received the district prohibition order."[21] Under these difficult circumstances Rahner remained in Austria, where he had made his final profession as a Jesuit on August 15, 1939. Fortunately, he was invited by Cardinal Innitzer, the archbishop of Vienna, to work in the Pastoral Institute there with the title of "curial counsellor." He was thus enabled to continue his lecturing both at the institute and at the Franciscan church throughout most of the war years. He often left Vienna in order to give talks in Leipzig, Dresden, Strasbourg, and Cologne, continuing his exploratory work on Christian anthropology, dogmatic theology, and the special questions that continued to interest him, especially mysticism.

One event that stands out during his work in Vienna was the refutation, commissioned by Cardinal Innitzer and written by Rahner, of the lengthy diatribe against pastoral, theological, and liturgical innovations issued by Archbishop Conrad Gröber of Freiburg to the German and Austrian episcopate. Among Gröber's seventeen complaints against the Viennese activists were the following: decline of interest in neo-scholasticism and natural law; too much Protestant influence in Catholic dogmatics; overemphasis on the liturgy and the attempt to make Communion part of the essence of the Mass; advocacy of the vernacular; failure to affirm that the church is a "perfect society"; overemphasis on mysticism and the more Protestant concept of universal priesthood; too much deference to the ecumenical movement; and an exaggerated use of Paul's metaphor of the mystical body to justify that movement. In short, the document was a laundry list of denunciations reflecting the Tridentine, bulwark mentality and theological insecurity of its author. Rahner's fifty-three-page refutation was both scholarly and compelling as he pointed out to the archbishop that the Catholic tradition was ill-served by closed-minded hostility to processes of development that were clearly called for in a church not only searching for truth but also in touch with the dynamism of its origins in Christ. One sentence of Rahner's reply stands out for its perceptiveness in pointing out the danger of alienating younger generations of Catholics from their own tradition if officials of the church stifle innovation and development: "It is only when there is an honest attempt at finding new ways and means that the will to maintain tradition is likely to be effective also in the future."[22]

Rahner was thus active through much of the war, but by the summer of 1944 intense pressure from the Gestapo rendered his pastoral work impossible, even dangerous, and he left Vienna to do pastoral care in a parish ministry in rural Lower Bavaria. His firsthand experience of the misery experienced in Munich during the destructive bombings in the last months of the war led him to undertake extensive relief work in the bombed-out city. This is reflected in his 1946 Lenten lectures in St. Michael's Church, "On the Need and Blessing of Prayer." According to one student of Rahner's thought, this series of lectures is regarded "as a modern spiritual classic."[23] Rahner himself recollected later that this disturbing period in German history was like an exile for him. He had little to eat, but still, he was "one of those spared the most frightening horrors of those days."[24] After the American occupation was in place, in August 1945, Rahner was assigned to Berchmanskolleg in Pullach near Munich where he was able to resume teaching dogmatic theology to young Jesuits and giving courses in Catholic dogmatics as part of an adult education program.

POSTWAR CAREER AT INNSBRUCK

In August 1948, Rahner was again appointed to the Canisianum, the Jesuit theological faculty at Innsbruck, where he had to lecture in Latin on dogmatic tracts on the doctrines of creation and sin, grace, justification, the theological virtues, and the sacraments. Less than a year later, on June 30, 1949, he was nominated and approved as Ordinarius Professor of Dogmatics at the theological faculty of the University of Innsbruck. Those postwar years were to become an exciting new beginning to his career as a Jesuit theologian. Because of Rahner, Innsbruck became an international center of attraction for young theologians from around the world. Students enrolled in his seminars not only for the glamor of having been taught by Rahner but also, for some, to have him direct their own theological research. Some of these doctoral students have achieved fame in their own right even as they acknowledge the influence of Rahner on their later development. Rahner's Innsbruck lectures likewise provided the original setting for the many papers and essays that were later incorporated into his *Theological Investigations*. A former student and colleague, Herbert Vorgrimler, describes this phase of Rahner's life as one "in which with an almost inconceivable intensity of work and movement he began projects, seized initiatives and transformed his modest study and bedroom in Sillsasse, Innsbruck, into a unique production line."[25]

As a teacher, Rahner was personally attractive and intellectually challenging to his students. One of those students, Robert Kress, recalls a feature of Rahner's classes in those postwar years. This was the

"Free Theological Colloquy." "On Friday evenings after supper Rahner and whoever wished to come would assemble in a classroom. He would accept any and all questions from the audience and then think aloud for two hours."[26] Kress remembers Rahner as anything but a dull lecturer. Not unlike a preoccupied bear tracing and retracing his steps, Rahner paced back and forth on the elevated roomwide platform before 250 and more students, thinking his theological thoughts aloud in a deep, rumbling voice.... His lectures, however, were also filled with witty and arty turns of phrases as well as homey and earthy metaphors. In the fitting contexts, Rahner could refer to the prevalent textbook theology as *"Wald und Wiesen Theologie"* ("theology of the woods and meadows") or *"laundläufige"* (which on his lips, evoked the connotations of a thoroughly dull and unexciting landscape).... During his days under siege by Roman and other authorities, he could still jest that, like Peter Olivi in an earlier age, he had indeed been aimed at by his detractors, but their big cannons had missed.... His writings are also replete with sarcastic observations.... Theologians, of course, are not spared, and, above all, not Rahner himself. In "Dialogue on Sleep, Prayer, and Other Things" between a doctor and pastor, Rahner has the former assert that "I have always thought that theologians do most for sleep through their lectures and writings."[27]

In a short while, Rahner's time became more and more taken up with outside lectures. This was in keeping with the spread of his fame as an innovative theologian in a church in which many members were beginning to hunger for more than prosaic repetitions of neo-scholastic conundrums in their religious education. It is impossible here to enumerate all the speaking appearances that Rahner made in nearly every theological center around the world during his long career as a theologian. One engagement that should be singled out, however, is his lecture at the first conference of Protestant and Catholic theologians held in Bad Driburg, Westphalia, in 1948. The discussion group that emanated from this conference became known as the Jaeger-Stählin Group, named after Jaeger, archbishop of Paderborn, and Stählin, the Protestant bishop of that district. Rahner soon became active in this unique participation of Catholics in the budding ecumenical movement at a time when such exchanges were frowned upon by the Vatican and before ecumenical reunion became a theme at the Second Vatican Council. The group's annual conference became the prototype of the Secretariat for Promoting Unity of the Christian Churches, set up in Rome in 1960.[28] Many of the participants later became members of that

Vatican secretariat. Rahner's theology would, as a consequence of his association with this group, have a strong ecumenical opening to other Christian denominations, as he began to incorporate the groundwork and motivation for a dogmatics more amenable to the Reformed tradition. Despite his dedication to this ecumenical activity and the demands on his time as a lecturer beyond the academic world of which he had become the center, Rahner's primary commitment was to the students of theology at Innsbruck. The lecture halls continued to be crowded when he was at the podium.

Vorgrimler likewise notes the enriching effect on Rahner's theology and teaching of his involvement with two other discussion groups at that time. The first of these was the special institute to foster the encounter of natural science and faith set up by the Görresgesellschaft for the Advancement of Science. As an active member, Rahner was often invited to present papers at the group's annual meetings. The second of these groups also worked to counteract the seeming alienation between science and faith. This was the Paulusgesellschaft, an association that met periodically to promote dialogue between scientists and academics on a variety of topics of interest, including fields where scientific technology intersected with the so-called domain of religion. Later, this group would initiate a Christian-Marxist dialogue in which both Rahner and one of his most distinguished students, Johann Baptist Metz, took part. Rahner's activities in these circles left many with the impression that he was a leftist theologian quite willing to challenge his peers to self-criticism. Although known as staunchly Roman Catholic in all these circles, he was neither defensive about nor protective of traditional Catholic positions on issues. In fact, he impressed the members of these groups with his ability to understand other viewpoints with a critical appreciation of different approaches in the pursuit of truth. For their part, they esteemed his "critical detachment from his own system [and his] concern for renewal and openness to others."[29] For his part, Rahner's participation in these scholarly, interdisciplinary societies was part of an ongoing effort to prevent Roman Catholicism from enclosing itself within a smug, cultural ghetto.

THEOLOGICAL WRITINGS

Rahner's renown as a theologian had thus leaped beyond Innsbruck, and with the publication of the first collections of his hitherto scattered articles, his stature as a creative thinker in the Catholic tradition grew even more. The first of these *Schriften zur Theologie* (Writings on theology—called *Theological Investigations* in their English translation) appeared in 1953 through the efforts of Dr. Oscar Bettschart of the Benziger Publishing House in Einsiedeln. Bettschart found the articles highly suited to the achievement of one of his goals, the renewal of theology among German-speaking peoples. Surprisingly for both Rahner and Bettschart, the first three volumes sold more than sixteen thousand copies each. Other volumes appeared in fairly regular sequence for the next thirty years.[30] These "writings" cover nearly the whole terrain of theology and spirituality, not in any systematic way, but in the Rahnerian manner of critically probing into issues and asking questions of contemporary meaning in an honest search for truth or in reflection on church praxis. At least one writer has claimed that Rahner's biography can be traced in these *Theological Investigations*.[31] Rahner refused to call these "writings" scholarly. Rather, he insisted that his "publications address individual questions. I only attempt to clarify those individual questions that modern readers are interested in understanding better. I would say that I have always done theology with a view to kerygma, preaching, pastoral care."[32]

The articles that dealt directly with pastoral care had been excluded from the first three volumes of his *Schriften zur Theologie*, along with several articles on church praxis. These he collected in 1959 for inclusion in the massive, 561-page volume, *Sendung und Gnade* (translated into English and organized into three volumes as *Mission and Grace*, 1963–66). Because of its strong foundational analysis of the role of Christians in the modern world as well as the basic questions of church praxis and the practical aspects of pastoral care, this volume attracted wider attention than his earlier *Theological Investigations* and was read by many bishops at Vatican II.[33] It led moreover to Rahner's being asked by Herder Publishing House in Freiburg to prepare a *Handbuch der Pastoraltheologie* (Handbook of pastoral theology). Assisted by Heinz Schuster, a student whose dissertation on practical theology he had directed, he took over the editorial direction of the handbook in 1960. Rahner conceived of this work in a fundamentally different way from the current views on pastoral care. These had emphasized the pastoral work itself without, as he himself advocated, plunging seriously into the historical foundations of practical theology and church strategy. Pastoral theology should, he felt, be dictated by one's renewed understanding of church and the most pressing existential needs woven into the historical situation. Rahner overcame his main opponents and even incorporated these "opposition theologians" into the editorship. With their help he published the four volumes of the handbook between 1964 and 1969, followed by a lexicon in 1972.[34] Rahner himself wrote several articles attempting to establish a solid theological foundation for the "practical theology" to which the handbook was directed. His work on the handbook is, in fact, further evidence that in all of his literary accomplishments as a dogmatic theologian he remained convinced that his dogmatics were in service to praxis and hence aligned in some way with pastoral theology.

Another series, which was in progress at the time of Rahner's involvement as a theological expert at Vatican II and his work on the *Handbuch der Pastoraltheologie,* further reinforced Rahner's growing world reputation. In 1955 Herder Publishing House of Freiburg persuaded Rahner to become editor of the *Lexikon für Theologie und Kirche* (Lexicon for theology and church). Attracted by the thought of a work that allowed him to oversee a restating of everything important in theology as it related to church, Rahner accepted. From 1956 on, therefore, he devoted half of his working hours to this unique compendium. Because the church authorities who sponsored the *Lexikon* viewed it as primarily addressed to clergy and to be used in their theological education, they were particularly concerned that its content be confined to what was already the Catholic church's so-called generally accepted teaching with only some small openings to the new questions then prickling their theological flanks. Bishop Buchberger of Regensburg and Archbishop Seiterich of Freiburg agreed to oversee the project as long as they had veto powers. Rahner, along with his coeditor, Herbert Vorgrimler, shepherded the ten volumes with their thirty thousand articles by 2400 authors through to completion between 1957 and 1965. The authors included nearly every reputable Catholic and Protestant scholar in the fields covered, including cardinals, bishops, and abbots. The index and three volumes on Vatican II followed shortly thereafter. Although Rahner personally authored 134 of the thirty thousand articles and heavily influenced the choice of authors and the editing, the *Lexikon* was not intended to be merely a forum for his theology. Yet it opened up Catholic theology in a way that reflects Rahner's concern, like that of Paul Tillich, to correlate the dogmatics of the church with the existential questions thinking persons were addressing to church teachings in the light of their own critical appraisal of faith. Because of Rahner's more open approach to traditional church dogmatics, some articles—including Rahner's own article on eschatology—were attacked by church authorities in an earlier phase of the *Lexikon* for being too existential in language and for dealing in matters beyond the church's so-called assured teaching.[35]

While halfway through the *Lexikon*, Rahner, with his coeditor, Adolf Darlap, had already begun work on the multivolumed *Sacramentum Mundi: Lexikon für die Praxis*. This appeared in six languages, including the English translation, *Sacramentum Mundi: An Encyclopedia of Theology* (edited by Rahner with Cornelius Ernst and Kevin Smyth), between 1967 and 1969. It had a clearly international character. Explaining the difference between the *Lexikon für Theologie und Kirche* and this new *Lexikon,* Rahner wrote in the preface to *Sacramentum Mundi* that he wanted to incorporate developments in the understanding of faith based on contemporary scholarship and that, therefore, the new encyclopedia would have "a strongly marked orientation to the future—its historical dimension—and [be] ... marked by its openness for the other Christian churches, the non-Christian religions and for the world in general—its social dimension." He then stated as his goal that he wanted this encyclopedia to be accessible to inquiring, open-minded, ordinary people, "to furnish the truths which should be the constant and vital possession of believers as they try to answer for their faith and their hope and the promise which it contains."[36] Rahner himself contributed sixty-eight articles to this encyclopedia.

During this same period Rahner approached the New Testament scholar Heinrich Schlier with the idea of producing a new series of books on Catholic theology. These would foster inquiry in the Catholic church based on Rahner's contention that many questions long thought settled by ecclesiastical fiat were, in fact, still open matters for public discussion. Schlier, who had studied under Bultmann, Barth, and Heidegger and had thus acquired strengths in historical-critical biblical scholarship of both the Protestant and Catholic traditions, joined Rahner in this venture. Their ongoing project has opened up far-reaching theological discussions on several "disputed questions," a term used as the title of the series (*Quaestiones Disputatae*, 1958–). The rationale for the series is stated in the very first volume; there Rahner describes the wide scope of what he wished to open up for investigation: "There could be room in this series for all that a person seeks to clarify as a Christian, in order to be a better Christian, provided that such clarification is carried out with the objectivity and conceptual strictness which makes reflection a scholarly investigation."[37] He added that he hoped through the series to widen the theological horizons of both priests and lay people. Rahner himself published eight books in the series and coauthored an additional eight. He persuaded Herbert Vorgrimler to assume theological editorship of the series in 1964. Together they either organized or actually produced a hundred volumes. The last of those volumes, entitled *Unity of the Churches—An Actual Possibility,* was produced by Rahner and the Protestant scholar Heinrich Fries. The book is about the potential of the ecumenical question for renewal of church and theology. It was highly regarded in those ecumenical circles still viable, but was denounced by Cardinal Joseph Ratzinger, prefect of the Sacred Congregation for the Doctrine of the Faith, as a distortion of the question for the sake of a shortsighted political accommodation.[38] Ratzinger accused Rahner and Fries of "theological acrobatics" and being out of touch with reality, in this case the reality of the Catholic church's "unchangeable" teachings. This critique by Ratzinger, needless to say, increased the book's impact and popularity.

TROUBLES WITH ROME

Ratzinger's denunciation of one of Rahner's last books was not the first attack on his work by church authorities. In fact, his skirmishes with the Catholic church officialdom on a number of theological issues had a history dating to the postwar era. Vorgrimler traces Rahner's troubles with official church circles to his outspokenness "to the point of rudeness."[39] It is well known that Rahner's frankness, coupled with his passion for truth and a detestation of self-righteous clericalism and pompous claims to certitude, led him to challenge church authorities to openness in many areas where ecclesiastical cloture on inquiry had already been invoked. His efforts were not always kindly received by church authorities. As Vorgrimler notes, Rahner was at the height of his theological career at a time when the mood in Germany was already shifting toward a critical reappraisal of the past. In a Germany just beginning to rebound from being held in thrall by a criminal, terroristic government, this included a scrutiny of the church, accused by such a respected writer as Ida Görres of "clerical fascism."[40] Rahner's own efforts to retrieve the core truths of the church's dogmatic past seemed aimed at goading the church to be faithful to its own mission as witness to Christ's freedom in the search for contemporary meaning. In this he was animated by his intense love for Catholicism and a desire to rescue the Catholic church from its own bent toward absolutism and arrogant rigidity.

In reaction to Rahner's efforts at rethinking so many officially defined, seemingly "unchangeable" Catholic dogmas, church authorities had initiated a quiet campaign either to silence him or to offset his annoying questions and their implied critique of Vatican-approved theology. To begin, some bishops questioned Rahner's orthodoxy in the aftermath of Pius XII's encyclical *Humani Generis* (On the Origin

17

of the Human Species), and pressured his superiors to scrutinize his writings more suspiciously and to prohibit his speaking on certain controversial topics. Further, he was denied permission to publish his five hundred-page manuscript on the problems of contemporary Mariology. Although it had the potential to allay much of the anxiety of Protestant theologians eager to engage in ecumenical discussions but concerned over what they considered Roman Catholicism's mariological distortions of God's word in the Bible, the work remains unpublished to this day. The work is vintage Rahner in that he probes critically into the meaning of Marian dogmas, particularly the then recently declared dogma of Mary's assumption into heaven. He attempts to retrieve the core significance of the declaration in terms of asking whether the meaning of the dogma is not more its symbolizing the destiny of all people called to a "resurrection in death" or bodily consummation in death. His efforts at toning down what appeared to be Vatican pietistic and devotional excesses in Mariology did not endear him to the Roman censors.

Rahner's next venture in rethinking what Catholics had come to take for granted came in his essays on concelebration of the Eucharist or Lord's Supper. So critical was he of the Catholic church's tendency at the time to see in the multiplication of the services a crude multiplication of grace (and in some instances the multiplication of monetary stipends for the clergy) that Pope Pius XII seemed to have Rahner directly in mind in his public denial of Rahner's contention that one Mass concelebrated by a hundred priests with devotion was "the same as a hundred Masses celebrated by a hundred priests." The pope added that Christ's actions were as many as the number of priests celebrating. To the pope the actions of the individual priests offering private Masses were obviously several levels of worth above those of the faithful present at the one Mass of a bishop or a priest. Concelebration seemed to flatten out the distinctions between priests and laity with regard to the efficacy of the Mass or the one "Lord's Supper." Rahner was thus placed in the unenviable position of being in open contradiction with the pope.[41] For his stand on this issue, Rahner earned another prohibition from the "Holy Office" (then known as the Holy Office of the Inquisition and now as the Sacred Congregation for the Doctrine of the Faith), this time never to speak again on concelebration. Rahner's vindication on this issue would come later at Vatican II. As he reported in a radio interview describing an exchange with Pope Paul VI after the council: "I said to him, 'Look, Holy Father, ten years ago the Holy Office forbade me to say another word about concelebration, and today you concelebrate yourself.' He chuckled ever so quietly and said, 'There is a time to weep and a time to laugh.' What that is supposed to mean in the context is not so clear to me, but he apparently meant to say that times and mentalities change, even in the church of God, and there is no escaping that."[42]

For the moment, however, Rahner's life seemed, in terms of church determination to silence and punish him, more a time for "weeping." This prohibition portended further moves against him. For example, his 1960 article on the virgin birth, in which he tried to redirect the Catholic church's viewpoint away from the biological or physical aspects of Mary's virginity toward the nucleus of symbolic meaning in the doctrine, stirred up the rumors of his being investigated and of an impending trial for theological error. Fortunately, Cardinal Döpfner interceded for him at the Vatican.[43] Not only were there no proceedings against him, but he was named a consulter for the council's preparatory commission on the sacraments.

If this was a truce, it did not last. Following his talk "Do Not Stifle the Spirit!" delivered at the Austrian Catholics' Day in Salzburg, June 1, 1962, he was again in trouble with the Roman curia. In that talk he had declared that "the spirit of true obedience is present not so much where the official machinery of the church is running smoothly and without friction, not so much where a totalitarian regime is being enforced, but rather where the non-official movements of the Spirit are recognized and respected by the official church in the context of a universal striving for the will of God."[44] He was informed less than a week later that from then on everything he wrote had to pass Vatican censorship. Rahner alerted Cardinals König and Döpfner as well as Bishop Volk and Prelate Höfer, first secretary at the Federal German embassy to the Holy See, of this development. In a meeting with the pope, Cardinal König requested official protection for Rahner. Rahner wrote to Vorgrimler asking him not to make the story public, adding: "I must keep my powder intact and dry."[45] He knew the move against him came from the Holy Office. He reiterated his determination to fight this censorship, as is borne out in a letter of June 15 to Vorgrimler:

> I told the General [Jean Baptiste Janssens, S.J.] (and he did not contradict me) that I had no intention of submitting anything to the Roman censorship but would rather write nothing at all; nor would I keep quiet about the matter, but would describe it all quite candidly, and those who had aspersions cast on them as a result would be others than me.... I'm not really concerned about myself. I would even be happy to spend a couple of years writing quietly for myself and publishing it later. But my feeling is that we should not make things too

easy for these terrible bigwigs. If they come up against resistance they will at least be more careful next time and think harder.[46]

He even asked Vorgrimler to ascertain whether a protest could be sent from the laity demanding the abolition of the censorship, pointing out that "this unjust measure...harmed and damaged the reputation of the church in Germany."[47] Volk suggested that Cardinals Döpfner, König, and Frings send an official letter asking for the removal of the Vatican gag on Rahner. By then the news was out that Rahner had been forbidden to speak and publish. Petitions in his defense were drawn up among members and friends of the Paulusgesellschaft and passed through diplomatic channels to the pope. No less a political figure than Konrad Adenauer joined the protest on Rahner's behalf.

VINDICATION AT THE COUNCIL

To dissipate the tensions, both political and ecclesiastical, created by this inquisitorial move against the most prominent theologian in Germany, Pope John XXIII, in October 1962, appointed Rahner to be one of the theological experts at the coming council. The appointment, widely interpreted as a strong vindication of Rahner, paved the way for his fulfilling the role of theological adviser to Cardinal König during the conciliar sessions. Through König, Rahner was granted access to even more significant work—the work to be done by the theological commission to study revelation, a topic that in the preliminary discussions threatened to polarize the assembled bishops. On May 28, 1963, Rahner was informed that the Holy Office had reversed itself on the matter of censorship; from that time on, it would leave censorship of Rahner in the hands of his Jesuit superiors, as it had been before the Vatican move against him. Rahner was never free from the conservative sniping at his theology. But he never again had to face the prohibitive censorship of the Holy Office. His contempt for his critics is clear from the letter to Vorgrimler cited above.[48]

Despite his awareness of the shadows of suspicion cast by Rome on his writings, Rahner continued to offer courageous, carefully nuanced dissent on Vatican documents that he viewed as based on shaky theological premises. These included the encyclical *Humanae Vitae* (1968), which contains the celebrated prohibition of all forms of "artificial" means of birth control, and the Sacred Congregation for the Doctrine of the Faith's instruction entitled *Inter Insigniores*, which in 1976 excluded women from the priesthood. Rahner's commentary on this Vatican instruction amounted to a counterdeclaration that because the prohibition of the priesthood to women was not clearly grounded in the certitude of Christian revelation, it was in principle both reformable in the future and susceptible to the possibility of being erroneous in its fundamental conclusions. In which case, he noted, a theologian had "the right and duty of critically examining this Roman Declaration, even to the point of regarding it as objectively erroneous in its basic thesis."[49]

At the council, though, Rahner's creative contribution to the schema on revelation now marched apace with his assignment in February 1963 to be one of the seven theologians who would develop *Lumen Gentium*, the dogmatic schema on the church. Soon, he became regarded "as 'the most powerful man' at the council."[50] Indeed, traces of Rahner's influence can be found in all but four of the conciliar texts.[51] Later, he and Vorgrimler collaborated on a paperback edition of the sixteen conciliar texts, the *Kleine Konzilskompendium*, which appeared in December 1966.[52]

Rahner was able to bring to the conciliar discussions his own openness to the Reformed tradition and to other religions, and that helped the council in shaping a wider understanding of the church's role in society. He desired, in accord with one of the major themes at the council, that the church cease its ecclesiastical apartheid and truly become a church in the modern world. Rahner contended that the kingdom of God was coming to be not only in the church but in the world itself, "wherever obedience to God occurs, . . . and this does not take place solely in . . . metahistorical religious subjectivity."[53] In 1970, he would write a passage that poetically describes God's involvement in history as a liturgy that celebrates both human freedom and divine concern: "The world and its history is the terrible and sublime liturgy, breathing death and sacrifice, that God celebrates for God's self and allows to be held throughout the free history of people, a history which God sustains through the sovereign disposition of God's grace."[54] This lyrical assessment of church and world is on a par with Rahner's more open attitude in his later years toward church mission *to* and church structure *in* the world. At Vatican II he argued that the church was the sacrament of the world's salvation. It is the socially embodied faith of people whose reconciliation with God is a paradigm for the reconciliation of all peoples to God. But toward the last years of his life, his notion of a world church became more accentuated.

For Rahner that notion was the most fundamental ecclesial significance of Vatican II. He saw the church shedding its Western, Latinized, neo-scholastic image in favor of a more positive openness to world, world religions, and ultimately to God's universal salvific revelation.

He likened this to the early church's outreach to the Gentile world. The freshness of approach was also translated into a sweeping survey of church office and structure in an effort to have the church take into account its role in an ever-changing sociopolitical future. In the years after the council, he agitated, therefore, for a church that would be declericalized but not divested of leadership, ecumenical but not simplistic, moral without being moralizing, democratized without being further bureaucratized, and committed to a critically balanced relationship with the world.[55] His hope in this regard seemed pegged to the ecumenical movement. Because of this one can understand why *Unity of the Churches—An Actual Possibility*, which was his last ecumenical work and was written in collaboration with the Protestant scholar Heinrich Fries, was both a "cry of distress" and a call for hope and practical measures, both dogmatic and sacramental, to rethink the terms for reunion and even to achieve it. The book, although disapproved by the Sacred Congregation for the Doctrine of the Faith, prompted German scholar Eberhard Jüngel to assert "that all celebrations of the 500th anniversary of Luther's birth would have missed the mark if the challenge of this book were overlooked."[56]

APPOINTMENTS TO MUNICH AND MÜNSTER

During the council Rahner was honored with an invitation to become the successor to Romano Guardini in the Chair for Christianity and the Philosophy of Religion at the University of Munich. The difficult decision to leave Innsbruck was eased by the prospects of greater freedom from Roman censorship and the promise of having young assistants in Munich who could assume some of the more vexing burdens of ordinary academic work. His superiors cleared the way in May 1963 and Rahner was able to begin lecturing in Munich in May 1964. His Munich lectures later became the framework and core of his only major systematic work, *Grundkurs des Glaubens* (translated as *Foundations of Christian Faith*). Unfortunately, Rahner's style, subject matter, and complexity of thought did not attract the large number of students that had been expected to enroll in his courses. Vorgrimler reports that in the Munich phase of his career Rahner was simply overextended. Doubtless, his work in Munich was less than satisfying to him personally. But he was also frustrated in that he was unable to obtain from the Munich theological faculty the cooperation that would have permitted him to accept doctoral students, many of whom were in Munich expressly to qualify in theology and to profit from his theological expertise and guidance.[57]

That refusal and the awareness that his work in Munich was not so fulfilling as he had hoped led to Rahner's considering a move to the University of Münster. He had already received an attractive offer from Münster that he had declined because of his commitment to Munich. Now the theological faculty there, with his former student Johann Metz as dean, urged him to reconsider that earlier invitation. Before accepting this new offer, however, Rahner asked for two concessions. The first was, in Rahner's words, "if in the next few years it were possible to begin a thorough reform of theological study with the people there along the lines of my ideas." The second was that this plan for reform "be coupled in some way with . . . a call," to avoid the impression that his leaving Munich was due to failure there.[58] Rahner received this "call" and on April 1, 1967, he was named Ordinarius Professor of Dogmatics and the History of Dogma at the Catholic theological faculty.

Rahner's stay in Münster at the twilight of his teaching career was a very fulfilling period for Rahner. Here he was able to give seminars in dialogue with Metz, who had already begun to formulate his "political theology." Later he would defend Metz against Cardinal Joseph Ratzinger, who had rejected Metz for the position of Professor of Catholic Theology at Munich. Asked to evaluate Metz's controversial political theology, Rahner replied: "I am not a representative of political theology, but I believe that the kind of political theology which Metz represents is thoroughly orthodox. . . . If I were a bishop, I also ought to let those theologians speak out whose theology does not appeal to me, even if I believe that I have pertinent objections, provided, of course, that one could not claim that such a theology was no longer Catholic." He added that one could interpret Ratzinger's rejection of Metz as a symptom of officialdom's backward movement in the Catholic church.[59]

THE JESUIT PRIEST

In controversies like those provoked by Johann Metz, Rahner's advocacy of freedom to dissent from noninfallible, quasi-authoritarian (but not authoritative) teachings of the hierarchical magisterium was encouraging to those more vulnerable to Roman censure. It would not be a fully accurate reading of Rahner, however, to depict him solely in these heady theological jousts with a church bureaucracy, parrying the stale formulas endorsed by centuries of unquestioning acceptance or challenging the orthodoxic claims of the Roman curia. The esteem in which Rahner was held throughout his theological career had a more important underpinning in his Christian faith and the Ignatian spirituality in which that faith was expressed. Students in universities and seminaries have often been staggered by the depth of Rahner's theological reflections and even frustrated in their attempts to unscramble the various nuances and insights that are the hallmarks of his theological genius. Nonetheless, those who knew him best found in him not just a brilliant thinker but also a trusted guide, loyal friend, and a priest of astounding simplicity.

One student who became a personal friend, James Bacik, came to look on Rahner as "an old shoe in his Jesuit residence" who deliberately refused to be the center of attention. Bacik's most lasting impression of Rahner is of a priest who was fascinated by "the common ordinary things of life" and who "liked earthy people and avoided individuals who tended to be pompous." Asked by Bacik what his greatest religious experience was, Rahner replied, "Immersion in the incomprehensibility of God and the death of Christ," while quickly adding that this occurred not in prayer and meditation but "in life, in the ordinary things."[60]

Fellow Jesuit Harvey Egan found Rahner's most endearing qualities to be "his childlike curiosity and the simplicity, holiness, and priestliness of his Jesuit and theological life." Examples abound of Rahner's "uncanny ability" to find "money, food, clothing, and shelter for the needy and downtrodden who sought him out." Egan describes the two of them shopping in a supermarket and then spending two hours driving to deliver the food to a poor widow and, finally, finding her a home to live in. Rahner's outreach to people in need included missionaries working with the poor in foreign lands. Not long before his death, at an academic convocation to celebrate his eightieth birthday, he made a passionate, public appeal for money to provide a motorcycle for a priest in the African missions. Rahner was, as one student told Egan, "a professor to whom I can confess."[61]

Rahner's close friend and colleague Herbert Vorgrimler notes Rahner's generous availability to people of all stations in life and with all sorts of problems and concerns. Often this took the form of letters in which "he was indefatigably ready to cope with questions from the whole range of pastoral care." Several of these letters have been incorporated into a book, *Mein Problem—Karl Rahner antwortet jungen Menschen* (My problem—Karl Rahner replies to young people), in which one can see firsthand how Rahner, even while nearing his eightieth birthday, would take the time to address with characteristic wisdom and patience the myriad problems of young people in Vienna.[62] Rahner's willingness to be approached in the parlors of the Jesuit house by a multitude of people was legendary. Vorgrimler reports that despite the fact that these visitors ate up the little time left Rahner in the midst of an intensely busy schedule, he was always gracious, even to the panhandlers among them. The following passages from Rahner's letters are typical: "Again all good wishes. I must go back to the parlor. Early today I needed all my human and Christian eloquence to talk someone out of committing suicide. I wonder whether I have succeeded? And what I should have done this morning, the Hamburg lecture, is still not done" (March 11, 1962). "I'm always caught between two possibilities (I've just given 20 DM again to a man who is perhaps a swindler): either to fall for someone or not to help a really poor devil" (January 2, 1965). An intriguing aspect of his life in the Jesuit communities was his soliciting funds and collecting food to feed these "parlor people."[63]

Albert Görres, the noted psychotherapist, declared in an article written just before Rahner's death that Rahner's caring nature as a Jesuit priest was his most impressive quality. Görres confessed his own admiration for the man who, with such a worldwide renown, found delight in strangers' asking him for personal help and who could create wedges in time in his exhausting schedule whenever anyone approached him. Görres concluded that, as a Jesuit priest, Rahner was ultimately a healer who could find "helpful thoughts for countless battered heads and wounded hearts, for legions of people who had been (at least in their view) harmed by the church and disappointed by God, thoughts which again opened up an approach to the lost God which had been obstructed, to God's sometimes frightening creation, to his difficult gospel, and not least to his burdensome church, and showed them love. He comforted the sorrowing, taught the ignorant, and showed the right way to the doubters and those who had gone astray. He reconciled those who were not at peace and in all this achieved all that pastoral help can achieve."[64]

Few eulogies have captured so well the spirit of the man. In sum, what people would come to praise in the achievement of Karl Rahner the theologian was a carryover from the spirituality of a deeply dedicated Christian. Rahner was led in all simplicity to apply the gospel of Jesus Christ to his vocation as a Jesuit priest whether in the classroom, the confessional, the parlor, or the streets, whether it was a teaching experience with the brilliant or pastoral care for the hurting who came to him for help. As priest and theologian, Rahner's encounter with people was in a real way his encounter with the God whose attractive presence to him embraced even the ordinary things and the "little people."

RETIREMENT YEARS

Having reached the mandatory retirement age of sixty-eight and experiencing a decline in his physical strength, Rahner retired from active teaching at Münster in September 1971 and moved back to Munich, where at first he resided with the staff of *Stimmen der Zeit*. His expertise in so many matters pertaining to theological renewal still made his presence and participation in the joint synods of West German dioceses especially desirable. In the preparatory work for one such synod, that of Würzburg in 1971, his clash with the canonist, Professor Heinrich Flatten, and Cardinal Höffner of Cologne inspired Rahner to publish one of his feistiest and most controversial books, *Strukturwandel der Kirche als Aufgabe und Chance* (Structural change in the church as task and opportunity, translated into English as *The Shape of the Church to Come*).[65] This book contains his sharpest attack on conservative elements in the Catholic church and their closed-minded attitude toward structural change and toward the pursuit of theological meaning in prior dogmatic and moral declarations emanating from ecclesiastical authorities.

In August 1973, he became "writer in residence" at the Jesuit scholasticate, Berchmanskolleg, which was nearer the university. This allowed him to work as a consultant to the younger scholastics as well as to the faculty and students of the university. The period from 1971 until his death in 1984 was hardly a withdrawal into an inactive retirement. Rahner's literary production continued to the extent that he accomplished in those final years more than some theologians would hope to produce in an entire lifetime. Four more volumes of his *Schriften zur Theologie* (*Theological Investigations*) were published. He also expanded the *Kleines theologisches Wörterbuch* (translated as *Theological Dictionary*) that he had coauthored with Vorgrimler and Kuno Füssel. In addition, he wrote essays on prayer and on the love of neighbor and love of Jesus. These essays were edited by Metz in 1977 and published in two volumes in English as *The Courage to Pray* (1981) and *The Love of Jesus and the Love of Neighbor* (1983). Anthologies and autobiographical reflections likewise occupied these last years.

Even with his heavy commitment to publishing, Rahner continued to serve on the International Theological Commission founded by Pope Paul VI in 1969. There he maintained his outspoken ways, not hesitating to champion the rights of the individual theologian and to argue both for the recognition of pluralism within the Catholic tradition and for an attitude of tolerance toward dissent from noninfallible teachings. Karl-Heinz Weger calls Rahner's critical attitude toward official Catholic church teaching the "scarlet thread running through his theology—his desire to translate faith into the present and in this way to make it intelligible to modern man from within, that is, from man's point of view."[66] Rahner, however, resigned from the theological commission in 1974 before his five-year term was completed, later giving as reason: "It bored me and struck me as too inefficient." The commission had deviated into what he called "a theologians' club where theologians intelligently dialogued with one another." Some of these theologians were, in his opinion, "malicious and arrogant." He was, moreover, miffed because the "Congregation of Faith" had repeatedly ignored the theological commission in important questions.[67] For him, the International Theological Commission had ceased to serve the church in any meaningful way.

In these final years one can also observe the continuity with Rahner's earliest theological endeavor, what Leo O'Donovan has called "a courageous effort to indicate, somewhat less inadequately, the origin and ground and goal of human life in our universe."[68] To the end, Rahner maintained as the center of his theology the "trinitarian radicalization" of his monotheistic faith, that is, the search to understand and appreciate the mutual love of Jesus and his Father, to whom all are led by God's Spirit in a communion made possible by Jesus. Even within the recognizable constants of this theology, however, one can at the same time detect variations in Rahner's later reflections.

His Christology, for example, became much more an "ascending from below," focusing on the manner in which Jesus embodied the human search for meaning in a concrete history encountering God's graced presence at every turn. For Rahner, though, it was never a choice between either a Logos Christology or a historical Jesus. The shift in emphasis with the implied distinction between Christologies from above and from below can be misleading. A Logos Christology, stressing Christ depicted as God's word from eternity, needs its validation in the Jesus who is historically for us if it is not to die a death of mythological abstraction. According to O'Donovan, the most significant aspect of Rahner's later Christology is the way in which his writings lead to unique reflections on the meaning of Jesus for today's faith and for the solidarity Jesus has achieved between his Father God and his brothers and sisters throughout history. O'Donovan singles out Rahner's strong reliance in his later theology on the cross of Jesus and the meaning of Jesus' suffering and death as a final and perduring act of Jesus' solidarity with his people.[69] It was a reflection seemingly intensified as Rahner's life itself edged closer to death.

Rahner's final writings likewise tended to stress a pneumatology in which, as always with him, grace was identified with God's gift of the Holy Spirit for the renewal of people and of society. He associated God's actions in the world with the "outpouring" of the Holy Spirit. More and more he declared this divine presence acting in and on the world as the inner heart of God's communication of God's self beyond the Judaic and Christian experience and, therefore, in a human transcendentality even more radicalized. One can agree with Michael Scanlon that "the heart of the Rahnerian system is a universal Pneumatology within which... his sapiential Christology is grounded."[70] This deference to the Spirit in Rahner's theology engendered in him a greater sense of the freedom that is a key to his ecclesiology and that is the spark of his boldness in criticizing the church for stifling the Spirit's creative movements. Scanlon cites Rahner to the effect that one's understanding of faith must become detached from its constricted moorings in Judaism and Hellenism "in order to become, as it ought to be, a dialogue with the world."[71]

Because of his attunement to where the Spirit could be leading Christians in their efforts to grasp the meaning of creation beyond the narrow vistas of Jerusalem, Athens, and Rome, much of Rahner's earliest ambivalence toward the world and its proclivity to sin, which is also part of human experience, seems to have been replaced within his twilight years by a positive hope for the final, universal salvation of the world. Rahner views the church as a symbol of this possibility. He insists that in all the church's sacramental activity, "we should think not so much that God is 'breaking into' a profane world at particular points but rather that the most interior and always present grace of a world endowed with God's own self is 'breaking out' into history."[72] Like Ignatius before him, Rahner had found "God in all things" to the point that he saw even more clearly what in his early writings on grace had thrilled so many of his readers, namely, how, despite all the distortion that is the product of human malevolence and weakness of vision, God had indeed cared for this world, making of it a means of God's grace. Rahner's growing communion with God in these final years had inspired a deeper sensitivity to God's presence continuing to create the restless yearning for union with the holy mystery that had been the spark of his theological investigations. The joy and freedom engendered by his ever-growing realization of God's nearness confirmed Rahner in his conviction that the meaning of life was bound up into the experiences, history, and sacramental life that are God's world of grace. Throughout his spiritual writings and with greater vehemence in the latter part of his life, Rahner portrays God as inspiriting the world to shape human destiny and to liberate people to see God in all things in order to know in that freedom that their search for meaning can only end in God.

It was not unexpected, therefore, that Rahner's final years be marked by a careful and continuing focus on freedom in the face of the ever-new horizons of history and sociality in one's quest for God. Freedom became in his writings much more a sharing of one's capacity to shape the future in solidarity with the aspirations of a people trusting in and loving their God. Accepting God in all faith and freedom was, according to Rahner, a risky venture in which one's past, present, and future converged in the "unrepeatable history of the freedom of God and of humanity in an unrepeatable dialogue."[73] Because the unity of this history still lay at that imperfect, unrealized state, shrouded in the mystery of one's own freedom as well as in the freedom of God, Rahner insisted that a person's future was destined to remain unforeseeable and, thereby, radically open to God and faith. Affirming oneself and others in such openness and making choices in congruence with the gospel were for Rahner ways in which individuals "realize what it means to be human and to be related to God."[74] Rahner had a profound sense of the historical dimensions of an individual's encounter with God. This led him to urge Christians to promote a renewed consciousness of their own faith and the church to abandon its bourgeois, clericalized mentality in order to renew its awareness of and sensitivity to its mission in a largely non-Christian world. Rahner continued to insist that in this new opening to the future, the church, like Christ, must be a symbol of "the interdependence of all human beings on all others."[75]

FINAL DAYS

Rahner's last writings manifest, too, a sense of the cross of Christ and its stark reminder of the inevitable sorrows and unforeseen failures that bedevil human history. Life for him had become an existence in the shadow of the cross and of death, although lived with his characteristic hope in a future beyond that absolute horizon that is life's paradoxical end and beginning. Concerning his own future, limited by illness and troubled by the obvious signs of "being pushed along the rails of death," Rahner spoke of his feelings in an extensive interview with Meinold Krauss. He still declared his desire to struggle without any illusion, hoping "against all hope." When pressed on how at that ultimate stage of his life he saw his future, he replied in words that might fittingly become a summary of his life:

I have this hope, even if I cannot actually imagine what eternal life will really be like. I know through the good news of the Christian message and I know from Jesus Christ that the absolute, everlasting, holy, eternally good God has promised himself to me as my future. And because of that, I have a good hope, an unconditional hope that is still subject to temptation as long as I am here on earth and have negative experiences with life, with society, with people, and so on. That is self-evident. But till death's door I'll hold doggedly fast, if I may say so, to the belief that there is an eternal light that will illumine me.[76]

To the end Rahner retained his remarkable clarity of mind. On February 11 and 12, 1984, he spoke at the Catholic Academy of Freiburg. Shortly afterward, he gave lectures, first in England and then in Budapest, Hungary, as part of a dialogue with Marxists sponsored by the Budapest Academy of Sciences. In the beginning of March he was honored by the Jesuits of Innsbruck, the theological faculty of the university, the District of Tyrol, and the city of Innsbruck itself. At the celebrations these institutions announced the founding of a Karl Rahner Prize for the promotion of theological development. This was to be the last public ceremony Rahner was able to attend. Three days later, on March 8, he had difficulty in breathing and was suffering from nosebleeds. He was ordered to the sanatorium in Rum near Innsbruck where he remained under close medical supervision from March 9 until March 29.

Although fatally ill, Rahner found the strength to dictate a letter to Cardinal Juan Landazuri Ricketts, archbishop of Lima, and through him to the Peruvian bishops asking them to extend their protection and understanding to Gustavo Gutiérrez, whose life was said to be in danger and whose liberation theology was then under Vatican suspicion and scrutiny. In this letter Rahner said he was "fully convinced that a condemnation of Gustavo Gutiérrez would have dire consequences for the climate necessary to ensure the continuation of a theology which is at the service of evangelization."[77]

On March 29, Rahner, still alert, was transferred to the University Medical Clinic of Innsbruck. His condition soon worsened and just before midnight on March 30 he died as peacefully as he had seemed to envisage his encounter with death in one of his memorable prayers:

Then you will say the last word, the only word that abides and that one never forgets. Then, when all is silent in death and I have learned and suffered my last. Then will begin the great silence in which you alone resound, you who are word from eternity to eternity. Then all human words will be dumb. Being and knowing, knowing and experiencing will be all the same: "I will know as I am known," will understand what you have always said to me, namely yourself. No human word, no image and no concept will ever stand between me and you; you yourself will be the one joyful word of love and life that fills all the spheres of my soul.[78]

Rahner's lifelong search for truth and meaning had ended.

II. THE GRACED SEARCH FOR MEANING: RAHNER'S WAY OF DOING THEOLOGY

Even his most enthusiastic students admit that Karl Rahner is not always an "easy read." Rahner's writings have a complexity that comes from the depth of his ability to recognize the original vision of the gospel and the hidden wisdom that may have been buried beneath centuries of dogmatic formulas. Rahner had a genius for ferreting out the essential of religious truth from the peripheral of how that truth came to be expressed and imposed authoritatively. His theological endeavor to retrace, rethink, and restate the truths Christians are called to believe in drew from him an extraordinary ingenuity in which he confronted, as few other Catholic theologians before him, the intricate nature of credal statements and his church's dogmatic pronouncements in their historical-critical setting and in their philosophical, anthropological, and spiritual foundations. Rahner's probing, questioning, and rephrasing of the tradition made many people rather uncomfortable— especially those whose authority seemed to rest on their hierarchical status and their claim to having been gifted by God with the ability to preserve the "deposit" of church teachings with inerrancy and immutability.

For Rahner, Christian theology had to be not a static repetition of correct formulas, but, as Augustine had suggested, a faith seeking understanding. Hence, he challenged his readers to examine their faith critically to determine if their attitudes and praxis were in fidelity to the teachings of Jesus Christ. He urged the hierarchical magisterium not to reduce faith to a mere blind affirmation of official teachings coupled with the minimum requirements of church attendance. Rahner managed also on historical and philosophical grounds to chastise the Vatican watchdogs of orthodoxy for their simplistic, disquieting prohibitions against dissent. He characterized their addiction to an authoritative status quo as a distortion of the processes whereby truth is attained. Likewise, his lifelong advocacy of the freedom for theologians to search for new meanings and new formulations of traditional teaching was tantamount to a plea to recognize the creative presence of the holy mystery within a church moving people to understand more fully their gift of faith. His own theological investigations into all aspects of the Christian tradition involved his leading the church's official governing body on the tortuous path of a daring and, at times, upsetting intellectual inquiry into the sources and documented expressions that critically qualify their claims to teach only what is true and to be the guardians of that truth. One of the major tasks he faced, therefore, was to prod his church, its leaders and people, to have a sense of the depth and complexity of faith's meaning and to have a grasp of the priority that must be given to the gospel demands if the church leaders and people are to be faithful to their Christian vocation.

The complexity of that task is often evident in Rahner's own highly nuanced, even ponderous prose, which, when analyzed for its intent, compelling logic, and innate wisdom, can goad both bishops and theologians to reshape a more plausible understanding of revelation and the Christian tradition. Rahner's search for the contemporary theological meaning of church documents is, at the same time, an articulation of what must be affirmed as perennial truth under the ever-changing garments of history, culture, and language. It is inaccurate to call his theological work a mere updating and clarification of immutable magisterial truth. In many instances he was trying to tease the original insight out of historically conditioned ecclesiastical proclamations and dogmatic formulizations absolutized by centuries of unquestioning acceptance. With Rahner's original intent in view, then, this section will identify the various elements in Rahner's intricately worded theological analyses. These operative elements will be tracked to their philosophical, christological, and mystical foundations, and that, in turn, will help draw out what appears to be his method in doing theology.

It is clear what Rahner intended theology to do. How he did theology is the main subject of this section, which will offer both proper guidelines and interpretive keys to appreciating Rahner at every level of his innovative contribution to modern theology. It may be presumptuous to claim that I will be presenting here in its totality a study of Rahner's theological methodology. Indeed, those who knew him best found him to be diffident about describing in detail how he did theology. Not surprisingly, he once wondered out loud if he really had a method in theology.[79] Rahner seems to have foreseen the trap of superficiality into which so many analyses of theological thought stumble when theologians are reduced to the procedures of research, foundational priorities, or even the spiritual training and faith that have infused their most creative work.

In Rahner's case the sheer scope of his literary productivity and the variety of topics that became objects of his investigations make even more perplexing any attempt to distill from his writings a possible methodological key to reading him correctly. Even his 1969 essay in which he wrote about theological method for the first time provides only clues to how he would conceptualize his own approach to the theological enterprise.[80] He was aware that analyses of his theology often seemed to dead-end in neat reductionist formulas such as claims that his method is purely "transcendental," or solely "anthropological," or singularly built upon philosophical foundations in such a way that for a long time he emerged as merely an eminent theorist of Catholic orthodoxy.[81]

Such reductionisms, however, appear to detour around Rahner's own declarations on doing theology and the evidence that includes his stated intention to promote the convergence of both transcendental and historical perspectives in addressing theological issues or in undertaking any theological investigation. We note, for instance, that rather early in his theological career, Rahner admitted his reliance on an approach to the problem of theological discourse that combined a transcendental method with "reflection on the historical experience humanity has of itself."[82] Later, in an essay on "nature and grace," Rahner argued the point that metaphysical reflection "on the actual nature of humanity can be complete only 'when human experience is viewed in the light of the whole history of humanity, where alone its development is fully realized.'"[83] In 1969, in the lectures that became his "Reflections on Methodology in Theology," Rahner again emphasized the necessity for historical reflection that is prior to transcendental analysis.

From these statements, which are borne out in length in the vast corpus of his writings, one can only conclude that Rahner's way of doing theology embodies a dialectic of the transcendental with the historical. Rahner keeps each pole of this dialectic in reciprocal interdependence enabling him in his theological reflections to achieve a remarkable degree of consistency and experiential validation. Rahner correlates what is called the "essential" of God's presence as creator and sanctifier with the humanly historical. For him, "the human world God calls to share in God's life can only achieve that genuine fulfillment by living through *its own time* toward God's absolute future."[84]

Rahner's method, then, is to combine through theological analysis that which he claims has already been united in historical reality, God and the human person, the holy mystery itself and the symbols of that mystery, the transcendental and the experiential-anthropological. He does this with the avowed intention of retrieving the past truth of Christian faith in tandem with an openness to what he envisions as the absolute future of God's historical presence in creation. In exploring the dimensions of Rahner's mode of doing theology, therefore, the following discussion of his methodology shall begin where he does—that is, the first section will focus on the experiential-anthropological. In a second section, this aspect shall be expanded through reference to the Christology that both grounds and makes explicit the high point of the transcendent deity's becoming palpable in the concrete, experiential reality of Christ's incarnation. In a third section, the understanding of how Rahner's theology is a perennial search for the meaning of God and of human life taken together will be expanded through a study of how his writings are themselves refracted through his Ignatian, even mystical, spirituality. A final, brief section sketches some conclusions regarding Rahner's methodology.

THE EXPERIENTIAL-ANTHROPOLOGICAL DIMENSION

After he had retired from teaching, Rahner declared that his intention in doing theology had always been to alert people to the fact that, whether they are aware of it or not, whether they accept or repress it, they do "have an experience of grace from within." For Rahner, "this is the most original and most important root of all Christian piety and holiness."[85] Such an approach indicates the priority Rahner gives to the human person as subject and to the experiential. According to Rahner, the meaning attained through the process of analyzing one's personal history is intelligible only if the words are grounded in the human experience of transcendent meaning—that is, in God. Hence, he wrote in an early section of his *Foundations of Christian Faith* that the "meaning of all explicit knowledge of God in religion and in metaphysics is intelligible and can really be understood only when all the words we use there point to the unthematic experience of our orientation toward the ineffable mystery."[86] Rahner is convinced that this "unthematic experience" presupposes the possibility of attaining a knowledge of God through the prior signals of God's presence within one's personal existence. Rahner calls such a knowledge "unthematic" because for him it does not derive from or hinge on the "programation" of such knowledge by concepts, words, or sentences fed to the human mind from without.

Openness to the Absolute in the Search for Meaning

This primal orientation to God in creation leads the human subject into a seemingly endless search for meaning. When Rahner speaks of the questioning intrinsic to the process of becoming aware of oneself as a self addressed by God, he draws on his conviction that as humans we are essentially open to everything. Nothing ever completely satisfies or fulfills. It is the same restlessness of heart that Augustine described in his *Confessions* and that Rahner sees at the roots of the human search for meaning and fulfillment. People tend to pine for and to question every explanation that claims in an absolute way to unravel the riddle of existence. This palpable yearning provides an important context for Rahner's invocation of our transcendent nature in his effort to explain why we experience dissatisfaction with whatever purports to exhaust the complete and final answer to the question of existence. According to Rahner, it is in their nature as spirit that people continue to open themselves to the unlimited horizons of the human quest for meaning. The human person is drawn toward the holy mystery in which the "horizon of the human spirit as the infinite question is filled by this ineffable self-communication of God with the believing trust that this infinite question is answered by God with the infinite answer which God is."[87]

Such opening is, therefore, an essential dimension of Rahner's description of the power of self-transcendence that is, in effect, never ending. One's subjectivity is honed in the experience of radical questioning that moves people to evade the constricting definitions, smothering analyses, and glib reductionisms that pretend to explain who and why they are. This is why Rahner insists on acknowledging the transcendent and why his approach to theology is often said to be transcendental, even as his "method" is rooted in the anthropological and experiential. He claims that all things evoke a question for people within the limited scope of their understanding. However, as they continue to question their experiences and to enlarge the horizons of understanding, under the attractive force of God's Spirit and their restless search for satisfaction, they show themselves to be people of those "unlimited horizons" that catalyze the drive for and promise of absolute fulfillment. Such stretching of the boundaries of being human is the ground of Rahner's assertion that, by virtue of creation itself, people are transcendent beings or "spirit" in this world. All points of arrival at the end of paths leading to meaning and satisfaction become in turn the launching platform of new questioning and further explorations. In effect, the quest for the meaning of life that we set in motion has no limits.

35

Tacit Dimension of One's Knowledge of God

Rahner observes, further, that this is a transcendence set in a deeper consciousness of infinite reality that is unthematic, preconceptual, and prereflective, neither directly grasped nor adequately conceptualized. It is, for Rahner, the tacit dimension of one's knowledge present in the process of conceptualization, but which is, in itself, an anticipation of the fulfillment that is found in God alone, the prime but gentle mover behind the urge to know truth, to love goodness, and to live free. Such a "tacit dimension" is an "ultimate ground" of one's human transcendence and forms a horizon of infinite possibility in a person's preconception of life's ultimate and penultimate meaning. It is, as one perceptive student of Rahner's theological methodology has claimed, "an infinite reality which wills the limits and boundaries of the partial, fragile but positive beings of our existence."[88] This implies that in Rahner's description of the human, experiential fundament of theological reflection, people are, as questioning spirits, not in full control of their lives. They are, rather, disquieted by the way the possibilities of being remain open to something they find to be ineffable. In effect, they sense in themselves an openness to the holy mystery from whom they are to receive life as a grace. Such openness, Rahner points out, is itself a vital element in the experience of that transcendence that lies at the source of self-knowledge, of personal moral responsibility, and of the experience of infinite being. This experience unfolds, in turn, into God's word to and personal presence for people, and that process is at the heart of doing theology.

Rahner insists, therefore, that one does not begin to relate to or to theologize about God only when God has been explicitly named, or when the thematic, conceptual structures are in place. The secondary reflection in the process of conceptualizing and articulating religious experience is important. Indeed, it is Rahner's greatest achievement. But it remains secondary because it must be at all times "sustained by a previous, unthematic, transcendental relatedness of our whole intellectuality to the incomprehensible Infinite."[89] Rahner's aim in theology is, then, to deepen, enliven, and make explicit the primal, transcendental relationship with God in creation and incarnation that activates theological awareness and enriches one's dialogue with the source of all being and of all theological articulation of the significance of such a relationship. This deference to God's presence in the holy mystery as the absolute horizon of one's being hearer of God's word and searcher after spiritual meaning is so essential to Rahner's theological method

that he issues a very strong caution against stifling these "deeper realities of the spirit." Writing on the priesthood, for example, he asks that
we allow this "primitive awareness" of God to emerge:

> If we do not learn slowly in this way to enter more and more into
> the company of God and to be open to God, if we do not constantly
> attempt to reflect in life primitive experiences of this kind—not de-
> liberately intended or deliberately undertaken—and from that point
> onwards to realize them more explicitly in the religious act of med-
> itation and prayer, of solitude and the endurance of ourselves, if we
> do not develop such experiences, then our religious life is and re-
> mains really of a secondary character and its conceptual-thematic
> expression is false.[90]

Existential Search for Meaning and Fulfillment

Rahner wishes, therefore, to explain human existence as primarily a
process of being and becoming under the attractive force of the primal, creative offering of God's own self to people. Rahner insists that
God's personal manifestations in one's individual experience and in the
wider history of God's salvific overtures to people everywhere elicit the
only hope that could satisfy a person's insatiable desire for complete
fulfillment. God's presence among God's people confers on them an
inner core of meaning in their experiential knowledge of themselves
that springs from interaction with the world of people and things at
every level of their existence. Rahner depicts God as the foundational
impulse behind every attraction to know truth and to love goodness.
This may or may not reach the level of explicit knowledge and coherent
articulation; the experience may, in fact, remain at a tacit, albeit fulfilling level of awareness. When one's knowledge is expressed objectively
in concepts and words, it becomes what Rahner calls "thematic" or conceptual knowledge. Yet such thematization, the product of reflection
and objectification, is never adequate to the original reality or vision.
Rahner acknowledges that one can never do conceptual justice to the
enhancement of knowledge and love that people experience through
the presence of the holy mystery in their lives. The symbols of that experience are never the same as the experience itself. For this reason,
Rahner insists that people must always retrace the symbols of their faith
to their inspirational source. In short, they must continually vivify the
memory of their encounter with the divine and the modes of reflective expression that enable them to clarify what they have experienced
and communicate it to others. Such retracing becomes in turn a vital

stage of the search for God, who is the ultimate goal of all theological reflection.[91]

It is at the same time a quest for the ultimate significance of the self and of the destiny of human existence. For Rahner, all experience becomes in some way an experience of one's self. In every act of knowing people are as aware of the historical reality that contextualizes their existence as they are aware of and present to themselves. Out of this experience, according to Rahner, consciousness of the freedom to choose one's destiny and to become a determinate self is born. Rahner notes that the whole process of exercising personal responsibility and experiencing freedom stirs within people an alertness to the spiritual hunger that agitates the heart and attests to their nature as "spirit in the world." People of faith must become more than those whose satiety ends at the world of unreflected experience and the lure of the material. Consciousness of the spiritual heart of one's being, according to Rahner, bears with it the inevitable consequence of being freed from the false impression that human success and fulfillment require only possession of the totems of material success. Our restlessness and sense of being incomplete draw us, he contends, to the attractive force of ultimate meaning. In this, we are to actualize our freedom in those yearnings for spiritual satisfaction whose pursuit can alone satisfy the restless heart.

Rahner observes that every dynamic thrust toward such fulfillment and meaning points to the divine presence in God's world of grace, the source of the ultimate question of meaning posed to human existence. He links the moment of revelation with the impact of God's presence in creation at the heart of this human yearning for fulfillment: "The immediacy of God in God's self-communication is precisely the revelation of God as the absolute mystery which remains such. But the fact that this can happen, that the original horizon can become object, that the goal which human beings cannot reach can become the real point of departure for their fulfillment and self-realization, this is what is expressed in the Christian doctrine which says that God wants to give human beings an immediate vision of God's own self as the fulfillment of their spiritual existence."[92]

The search for the source of this fulfillment has its starting point with Rahner, then, in an anthropology open to the transcendent. Rahner's strength in doing theology in this manner is to be able to draw on his mastery of the Thomistic tradition that affirms the potential of one's knowing what is beyond the physical, finite world, namely, the graced potential to know and love God. In his first published book, *Spirit in the World*, for example, Rahner, following Aquinas, insisted that the human person is unthematically open to the transcendent in the act of knowing and loving. By seeding Kant with the insights of Aquinas, Heidegger, and Maréchal, Rahner hoped to avoid the dead-end of Kant's rejection of the possibility of theoretical knowledge of God on the assumption that all human knowledge is rooted in sensible intuition. Rahner admits that human knowing takes place in the world of experience and that the metaphysical is known in and at the world as the mind is constantly turned to sensory phenomena, or what Aquinas called the "conversion to the phantasm." However, as Francis Schüssler Fiorenza has so convincingly argued, Rahner answers the Kantian question and offers a new understanding of Aquinas by proposing "a transcendental understanding of God, who is not known by man as an object of reality, but as the principle of human knowledge and reality." Fiorenza adds that

> this fundamentally non-objective transcendental knowledge of God as the principle of knowledge and reality is central to Rahner's whole theology. It forms the background for his understanding of God's presence to man in grace and revelation, of the ontological and psychological unity of Christ. Rahner's discussions on the development of dogma, the anonymous Christian, the human knowledge of Christ, and on many other themes must be seen within this context. This transcendental orientation of man to God is the unifying principle of Rahner's theology.[93]

Rahner thus depicted the human subject as essentially open to the fulfillment that beckons beyond the sensate objects of this world but also as gifted with a capacity for transcending the sensate and experiencing the unattainable, incomprehensible holy mystery in the historical world of human personhood. Rahner claims that by their divinely graced nature people become endowed with the ability to listen for and to hear God's word in their nature, in their world. In Rahner's words: "For the rest of one's life one can preserve the revelation only in its form in human speech and in so doing must refer back to this special point in one's individual history as the humanly unique point in which God's revelation was originally given."[94] Human history thus becomes for Rahner not only the concrete locus of God's revelation but also the prime matter for theological reflection.

Anthropological Foundations of the Knowledge of God

As early as 1957 Rahner proposed an anthropology that could become the basis not only for demonstrating the unity of dogmatic statements about personhood but also for understanding the nature of theological reflection itself. For him,

> Theology is extrinsic to anthropology only in the sense that human beings' center is outside themselves; it is in God. Insofar as human beings accept this exteriority and are willing to see their center as outside themselves, they truly find themselves.... The attempt to leap beyond one's own self in an anti-anthropocentric manner, in whatever dimension of human existence that attempt is made, would be inhuman and thus against God—God to whom one cannot come close by diminishing oneself but only in the frank awareness and realization that God has created all things that they might be (Wis. 1:14).[95]

Rahner points to the incarnation as an illustration of his conviction that the historicity of human existence is a regulative factor in the possibility of God's presence becoming integrated into one's human personhood. In acknowledging and accepting Jesus Christ as the human representative of God's becoming one with God's people in their historical consciousness, believers are prompted to become more conscious of the inner dynamics of their faith and of their having been addressed by God in the free and freeing word spoken through God's own son.

In thus casting his theology into anthropocentric foundations, Rahner strove to give greater coherence to the process whereby one's personal subjectivity could be open in faith to recognize and to receive God's revelation. He wished also to overcome the traditional Roman Catholic dichotomy between nature and grace that was part of the heritage of "textbook theology." One's life, according to Rahner, is graced by God's own self-expression as God the creator enters into dialogue with creatures. This is a "unitive way" in which God has already been in relationship with human beings through a caring presence in creation and providence even before theologians and church leaders articulate the reality. Rahner was aware of the crudity that often prevailed in official teaching on grace, making it look as if God "poured" layers of supernatural grace onto a substratum of a weakened nature untreated by any meaningful contact with the divine.

To counteract this impression, which seemed so misleading to him, Rahner contended that it is at the level of one's existence as a conscious and free subject open to the pursuit of truth that there spontaneously wells up a special experiential knowledge of reality. Such knowledge is qualitatively different from a subsequent, secondary level made possible by the reflections and conceptualizations that relate one's ideas back to the original experience. In short, we are already in touch with this world before the exact nature of our relationship with earthly reality is grasped. In their search for meaning people must always grapple with the way their intelligent reflection sieves out the truth of things from their raw experience. The tension between what is happening to the conscious, searching subject and the objective identification of his or her encounter with both the human and the divine is so enthralling for Rahner because he sees in this process the way human subjects experience their self-transcendence. Rahner calls this a "transcendental experience" or "the subjective unthematic, necessary and unfailing consciousness of the knowing subject that is co-present in every spiritual act of knowledge and the subject's openness to the unlimited expanse of all possible reality."[96]

In this experience, according to Rahner, one is immersed in the silence of being and orientated to the holy mystery even before theological reflection can infuse verbal meaning into the reality or proclaim the spiritual dimension of human existence. Rahner insists that this experience of transcendence is not one of lofty metaphysical abstraction. Rather it is embedded in the historical matrix of human existence itself. It is an *original* knowledge of God and thus a vital a priori of theological affirmation. In Rahner's words: "Insofar as this subjective, nonobjective luminosity of the subject in its transcendence is always orientated toward the holy mystery, the knowledge of God is always present unthematically and without name and not just when we begin to speak of it."[97] Speaking about it, though, in the Rahnerian analysis, is a search for the meaning of that original existential encounter with the holy mystery that permeates every human experience. Doing theology presupposes, then, for Rahner, the thrust consciously to grasp the incomprehensible and to be grasped by that which is in itself beyond the clutches of human intellection. There is also trust involved here that, as one yields to the incomprehensible mystery of God, one's knowledge is fulfilled by becoming love.

Rahner holds that the movement itself from experience to subjective luminosity to theological reflection depends on both anthropology and transcendence. Theology must begin with the human person who has become a hearer of God's word in creation and in God's Christ even if that word has not yet been "thematized." One is addressed by God at the fundamental human level in everyday experience. When Rahner speaks of transcendental experience, therefore, he is referring to what has already existed prior to the passage from a nonconceptual, nonexplicit, and nonreflective form of knowledge to a conceptualized, explicit, and reflected, even systematized, form of knowledge. To give an example, one can already experience love, sorrow, and joy before being able to articulate the experience at the level of conscious reflection. These are experiences of human existence accessible to the process of intellectual analysis and understanding, although words can never adequately contain the experiential reality one may be attempting to analyze. The effort to grasp and to thematize this reality is what Rahner calls the function of theological anthropology. He would even claim that "there is no longer any theoretical or practical theology that would not itself be anthropology."[98] This will be further illustrated in the analysis of the christological dimension of Rahner's methodology in the next section.

Through his anthropological emphasis Rahner is able to achieve a remarkable congruence between philosophy and theology. This is especially noteworthy in the way he has theology take with him a dramatic "turn to the subject." To do this, Rahner develops the interconnection of a person's Christian faith with what to him is the essence of human life and being itself, the latter often being the grist of philosophical analysis. His theological anthropology ponders the human structures of existence in terms of God's creation and abiding care for God's creatures. This is a preamble to his analysis of the Christian life and the gospel that he claims infuse deeper meaning into one's humanity. Rahner notes that the contact edges lie in the moments of God's graced advent in history that confer both spirit and meaning to the natural, the secular, the historical, and the human. Rahner refuses to speak of the merely natural or the merely human as if these could exist somehow untouched by God's presence, love, and concern.

The signs of the deeper meaning that Christ and his gospel bring to human existence and to history lie too in the realization of one's essential limitedness in the face of the absolute openness to the future represented in the humanity of Christ and in the experience of not "grasping" but "being grasped" by God. According to Rahner, "the concept of 'God' is not a grasp of God by which a person masters the mystery, but it is letting oneself be grasped by the mystery which is present and yet ever distant."[99] It is a word he insists we can all hear if we are endowed with the good fortune of faith and the mettle of Christian decisiveness. In short, faith can only help us recognize within ourselves what Rahner has called our orientation to the holy, incomprehensible mystery of God, an orientation that exists in creation itself prior to any explicit awareness of it.

The Supernatural Existential

Rahner insists, moreover, that this primal transcendental relationship with God—which is so immanent to the process of one's becoming more human and, therefore, more open to the attractive lure of truth and goodness—emanates from a gratuitous gift of God. In this way, he intends to confront the theological paradox of affirming at the same time God's freedom to be or not to be in relationship with creatures and God's historically attested self-communication. While remaining wholly other, God's presence in grace becomes intertwined with the entire process of the creative transformation of the self. Rahner avoids having his theology caged into static categories of those clearly defined moments when people either accept or reject God's seemingly explicit offer of God's self as word or grace. In short, and in traditional terms, he evades framing his theology around distinctions that derive from speculation on whether a person remains in pure nature or fallen nature or whether he or she is elevated to the "supernatural." Rahner has argued that God is ever present in enhancing one's freedom, uplifting consciousness, and provoking the awe, unrest, questioning, and movements of love that lead to a deepening of one's experience of both God and self. Rahner neither levels out the peak events of God's grace with other experiences nor isolates God's graced presence from moments deemed less sacred or from people who lack the privilege of either Christian baptism or an explicit religious affiliation of some sort. To explain both God's freedom to give or not to give God's self and the reality of God's graced nearness to all people, Rahner has coined an expression—the "supernatural existential."

For Rahner, this is the basic structure modifying the whole of human existence and permeating every experience in which a person is impelled toward the divine. It is a constitutive factor in the divinely initiated response to the God who has, in Augustine's words, become more intimate to us than we are to ourselves. Each of the terms has meaning because of the modification effected in one's being by God's gift of God's self. It is "supernatural" because it is not something to which a person can lay claim merely by virtue of being human. God's self-communication is as clearly gratuitous as the inability of human nature to demand God's grace as a right or as something owed to human nature in its very essence. Hence Rahner argues the gratuity of the supernatural existential, describing it as a dynamic quality given to one's nature, a dimension of being human in which a person's whole being is brought into intimate contact with the God who, by virtue of a promised graciousness, eternally wills the beatitude of God's people. This supernatural existential affects the whole of human personhood, structuring into one's nature the gift of being open to, even pining for, the divine source of meaning and fulfillment.

Human nature is thus enhanced in Rahner's theology by his portrayal of the person being drawn by God beyond mere openness to being toward the attractive horizon of one's most intensified aspiration, God's own fulfilling of human existence in the free gift of God's self. Rahner uses his theological construct of the supernatural existential to indicate that human nature with its openness to being—or, to borrow a traditional scholastic term, "obediential potency" for fulfillment in being—is transformed through the advent of God's unending presence. In such a way, a person's concrete existence or the "existential" becomes ordered to God and touched irrevocably by God.[100]

Rahner claims, consequently, that a person's actual existence in God's grace is integrated into his or her de facto existing nature. This grace, in turn, is the catalyst in seeking the highest fulfillment possible for human nature—that is, union with God. Grace is not something wholly external to being human. Nor is "it" a superstructure built upon a logical construct of "pure nature," if there can be such a thing. Rather, grace, for Rahner, is primarily God's orientation of God's creatures to the divine self, an orientation that occurs in the supernatural existential of being human. According to Rahner, God has drawn so paradoxically near that

> persons who open themselves to their transcendental experience of the holy mystery at all have the experience that this mystery is not only an infinitely distant horizon, a remote judgment which judges from a distance their consciousness and their world of persons and things, it is not only something mysterious which frightens them away and back into the narrow confines of their everyday world. They experience rather that this holy mystery is also a hidden closeness, a forgiving intimacy, their real home, that it is a love which shares itself, something familiar which they can approach and turn to from the estrangement of their own perilous and empty lives.[101]

The Fundamental Option

To explicate how this nearness to God is a possibility even before an explicit confession of faith, Rahner correlates the supernatural existential with what he calls a theology of the "fundamental option." Rahner uses this rubric to describe the dynamism of the self's inner core through

which people are conditioned in full freedom by God's graced presence to make the choices in which they both find expression of who
they are and give meaning to their lives. Rahner's analyses of how the
fundamental option influences a person's sense of value and strength
of decision are, moreover, among his greatest contributions to the theology of freedom and Catholic moral theology today. Rahner refers to
this fundamental option as the outgrowth of God's impacting on people
in their growth toward and exercise of spiritual maturity. But he also acknowledges that this option can entail rejection of the overtures God's
love may be making to individuals in the variety of forms of God's presence and in the many possible directions of their future. Rahner wishes
to establish that what people do with their lives is itself governed in
some way by their experience of the holy mystery of God. Somehow
the attractiveness of divine love lures the human spirit into ultimately
orientating itself and its choices toward God.

This is why Rahner sets his concept of the fundamental option within
the context of God's gift of God's self in the conferring of grace and
freedom. For Rahner, one is free not only in the conscious choices that
are the exercise of one's responsibility to God, self, and others, but also
in the way one becomes a more mature self. In Christian theological
terms, this takes place in the process of growth to maturity in Christ.
Rahner's fundamental option is as much the self disposed to God or,
alternately, turned in on itself as it is the inner dynamism of the options
or decisions in which freedom is expressed.

This gift of freedom, according to Rahner in his most detailed probing into the nature of the fundamental option, cannot be reduced to a
mere choice between diverse objects.[102] While it is true that a detailed
analysis of one's development as a person must include the string of
self-creating options, that is not Rahner's point. Rahner contends that
God's once-for-all gift of freedom is interwoven in one's being human.
Hence his understanding of freedom begins in the radical encounter
with God in the world of creation and especially in the neighbor whom
God has given to be known and loved. In exploring the implications
of the fundamental option, therefore, Rahner prefers to speak of the
"transcendental horizon" of freedom that not only makes freedom possible but also constitutes its proper object. This horizon, the fullness of
being in God, moves people as the source from which the drive toward
truth and goodness begins and beckons them as the goal toward which
human experience, in the quest for meaning, aspires. The fundamental
option thus becomes animated by God's presence in the human subject
in the inner moment when a person's life becomes orientated to God

and one's self becomes enhanced in the process of saying yes or no to God. For Rahner, the transcendental horizon of being and its promise of perfection are never distant possibilities ever receding from the self's goal of fulfillment. They are, on the contrary, God's immediate offer of God's self in absolute nearness, an offer to become the whole project of human beings' lives and the sole source of transcendent meaning to them in their concrete human experiences.

Hence Rahner refuses to atomize either the human potential for a relationship with God or the choices one makes in individual acts of freedom. Rahner's idea of freedom is that of the created capacity for God in a movement of self-realization that only God can orchestrate, while allowing room ironically for the individual, wittingly or unwittingly, to turn away from the very source and goal of the fullness sought. There is a totality in this concept of freedom that Rahner attempts to incorporate into his elucidation of the fundamental option. It is only in the unraveling of the whole of human experience and of the entire skein of one's finite life that there can be revealed fully the horizon from which individual acts of freedom receive their proportionate value and ultimate meaning for salvation. One's intentionality or self-directed élan toward the absolute good, which is God in the concreteness of life's options, is shaped by the fundamental option in which one begins to attain selfhood or growth in God.

Rahner's fundamental option becomes, therefore, a central factor in assessing both a natural law ethic and the moral ideals that translate into norms of conduct. These are the secondary, concrete moments in the experience of being people drawn toward truth and goodness and touched by the presence of God in self and others. The free acts flowing from this more fundamental orientation of the self toward good or evil derive their moral significance from it. Rahner insists that these acts must be fitting expressions of the human person grasped by the holy mystery of God in whom love is experienced as being loved absolutely and unconditionally and being impelled to love others in turn.

In many ways Rahner's fundamental option correlates well with Paul Tillich's "Ground of Being," particularly at the level in which both claim human existence is itself intertwined with and grounded in the creative source of all being and freedom. In Rahner's perspective, God is the "ground" of true freedom. One's goodness or badness emanates from the fundamental option and the resulting stance for or against God in the ground of one's being. Rahner integrates this perspective into his theology of freedom in the following incisive declaration:

46

Freedom in its origin is freedom of saying yes or no to God and by this fact is freedom of the subject toward itself... in its finality and thus is freedom toward God, however unconscious this ground and most proper and original "object" of freedom may be in the individual act of freedom.... Freedom is first of all "freedom of being." It is not merely the quality of an act and capacity exercised at some time, but a transcendental mark of human existence itself. If human beings are to be really and finally able to be masters over themselves, if this "eternity" is to be the act of their freedom itself, if this act is to be really able to make them good or bad in the very ground of their being, and if this goodness or badness is not to be merely an external accidental event happening to them,... then freedom must first of all be thought of as freedom of being.[103]

For Rahner, the freedom that comes from God and that, in turn, conditions the orientation of the individual person toward God is shaped by the fundamental option in which one's destiny is bound up with God or with the self alone apart from God.

With his convictions about the supernatural existential and the fundamental option in place as cornerstones of his anthropology, Rahner's theology proceeds to recognize that, even before the advent of Christ, the human spirit's natural dynamism, impelling people to become seekers after truth and goodness, was transformed into an ontological orientation to and desire for the one who alone can promise and deliver spiritual fulfillment. Christian believers are thus predisposed to welcome God as Father, to recognize Christ as brother, and to accept their Spirit of love moving people to follow in word and action the one confessed to be the word and presence of God enfleshed. Because Christ embodies God's word of judgment on the meaning of human existence and is himself addressed as the way, the truth, and the life, Rahner sees in him the validation of his anthropological approach to theology. His Christology becomes, in fact, both the center of his spirituality and the principal point of reference in his doing theology.

THE CHRISTOLOGICAL DIMENSION

While Christology is at the inner core of Rahner's theological creativity, his uniqueness of approach lies in his interpreting the person and historical mission of Jesus in tandem with his reflections on the essential structures of human existence, such as we have seen above. Early in his teaching career, Rahner referred to Christ as the theological high point and, therefore, primary symbol of God's inner relationship with the world of God's creation. The idea that God should endow humans with a transcendental openness to being in the holy mystery and that God should exist absolutely in a creative, caring relationship with people is historically grounded for Rahner in the incarnation. It is in the uniqueness of Jesus Christ that Rahner establishes the point of reference for his contention that God's people are those orientated to the absolute source of meaning and gifted with transcendence impelling them to seek the highest good of being in God alone. One yearns not only for communion in God's being but also for the historical manifestation on God's part that the restlessness of one's soul can be satisfied only in God. The enfleshed epiphany of God's promise and the foundations of faith become concretely and historically validated for Rahner in Jesus the Christ.

Transcendental Christology

As in his anthropology, Rahner develops a "transcendental Christology" to explain not only the significance of Christ but also why the prior human structure of being open to the absolute mystery of God conditions a person at the same time to become a believer in the Christ of Christian dogmatics. In a way, Rahner's theology seems to say that the possibility of affirming belief in Christ can be "deduced" from a person's own self-understanding, although historically and theologically Christ himself does not in any way "depend" on such understanding. Rahner argues that people have reason for expecting God's historical promise and the inner yearning of their heart to be fulfilled in some concrete, somatic way in God. What people seek in their relatedness to God is, in turn, the transcendental experience of truth, goodness, beauty, freedom from suffering, and freedom for love—in a word all the transcendental possibilities that ignite the drive to be more humanly human and to be at peace.

These possibilities translate into the existential questions of meaning posed to people that in practice dangle before them the hope of fulfillment that can come only from God. Rahner sees the person of Christ as the tangible reminder that God alone "saves" and that we must look for peace and affirmation in the concrete history that is the locus of God's relationship with us in Christ. Christ, however, is not to be a mere "deduction" from the human drive for fulfillment. Rather, he is God's gratuitous expression of how the promise and the fulfillment can be conjoined in a human lifetime in which the person of faith accepts the transcendental possibilities already given in the life, death, and resurrection of Jesus Christ. In Rahner's opinion, "one would be blind with regard to this actual history if one did not approach it with that reflexive and articulated hope for salvation which is reflected upon in a transcendental Christology. Transcendental Christology allows one to search for, and in this search to understand, what one has already found in Jesus of Nazareth."[104]

Rahner's point of departure for Christology is always faith. In explaining one's relationship with Christ he depicts the orientation of people toward God as also an orientation by and toward Christ. According to Rahner, in Christ one finds the satisfaction that one has always been seeking. This is why Rahner calls Christ the "absolute bringer of salvation." He contends that human beings' salvific relationship with God in Christ is essential to all Christologies because God's word in Christ pulsates at the center of the mystery that is alternately hidden and made known in God's intercommunion with people. His foundational conviction on this point moves Rahner to insist strongly, in explaining why he calls Jesus the "absolute savior," that

> this question has to take into account the salvific nature of all history and of the activity for which all people are responsible in a common history of salvation which is still going on. We are calling this relationship absolute because we are dealing with the definitive salvation of the whole person and of the human race, and not with a particular human situation.... But wherever it is, there is Christianity. Wherever it is interpreted adequately and legitimately in a profession of faith and hence unites people in this profession, there is ecclesial Christianity. Wherever this relationship is not actualized in history and interpreted as absolute, real explicit Christianity ceases to exist.[105]

Rahner's transcendental Christology would thus conjoin both the ontological concretization of God's revelation that is at the core of Christology and the functional mission of the incarnate Word that structures accordingly how Jesus brings salvation.

Christology from Below and from Chalcedon

With that connection in view, Rahner's mode of doing theology ultimately came to favor a Christology "from below" that begins with an emphasis on Jesus' humanity and historical existence, a move Rahner believes to be at the same time in line with the church's traditional dogmatics. Christ becomes illustrative of the transcendental openness to God's self-communication that is also characteristic of the human

49

person in Rahner's theology. Rahner declares that Christ is the ultimate concretization of this self-communication, thus offering validation of the essential relationship God has initiated with God's people at creation. This approach also permits Rahner to show the continuity between a Christology that begins from a scriptural, experiential level and the ecclesially formulated dogmatic culmination of reflection on one's faith in and experience of God in Christ. But Rahner insists that this is likewise a history that must include the contemporary moment. If the dogma of Chalcedon is the foundational framework of his Christology, Rahner focuses on the historical figure of the incarnate one to complete his hermeneutical circle in which each aspect offers ballast to the other. But it is the historical experiential that provides the openings for his reinterpretation of Chalcedonian Christology.

To do this he adopts an evolutionary perspective on Christ while affirming all the while the continuity of christological doctrine with both the historical Jesus and the Christ known in the light of current theological investigations. Rahner's method of dealing with the traditional teachings on Christ achieves a remarkable melding of unity and diversity even as Rahner completely rethinks Chalcedon's conclusions on the unity of the two natures in the one person of Christ. This has been noted by Rahnerian scholar Anne Carr, who links Rahner's approach to a major theme in his writings, "the unity and diversity of the doctrines of creation and Christology." She adds that "this unity . . . is the foundation for the unity in diversity he describes between the orders of creation and redemption, secular and salvation history, nature and grace, symbol and reality."[106] For Rahner, the church's defined dogma is both an a priori starting point and, through a process of intelligent, hermeneutical retrieval, the provisional terminal point of the contemporary search for the theological and pastoral meaning of one's relationship with God. Rahner analyzes the dogma to expose the ontological, anthropological presuppositions that led to the original formulation. Then he adroitly circles back to the dogma itself through a process of questioning the presuppositions, offering alternative ways of interpreting the scriptural or dogmatic data through the innovative suggestions of modern exegesis, or the new possibilities opened up by scientific discovery, or by creative thinking in the fields of psychology, philosophy, and theology, or by human experience itself. In essence, he likes to put the a priori of dogma in confrontation with the a posteriori of the historical, the anthropological, the experiential, and the existential. In this, every point of arrival must become a new plateau in the endless pursuit of meaning if church teaching is to retain its credibility, fresh appeal, and impact.

Christ's Historicity and the Relativity of Dogma

Through his seemingly endless probing into the meaning of the traditional christological doctrines, Rahner became a thorny reminder to his church that, despite its claims to possess the so-called fullness of truth in a "deposit of unchanging teachings" duly preserved from error, it too is historical and limited in its ability to express truth. All its sacred formulations can never be viewed as perfect expressions of the faith. They too are conditioned by the same historicity that demands for the sake of life that statements of truth be continually questioned and allowed to grow into contemporaneity through clearer formulation, more insightful interpretation, and more critical assessment of meaning. This is the process he traces in his essay entitled "Current Problems in Christology," where he cautions the church to take seriously Christ's own historicity when it formulates truth:

The clearest formulations, the most sanctified formulas, the classic condensations of the centuries-long work of the church in prayer, reflection, and struggle concerning God's mysteries: all these derive their life from the fact that they are not end but beginning, not goal but means, truths which open the way to the—ever greater—truth. . . . Anyone who takes seriously the "historicity" of human truth (in which God's truth too has become incarnate in revelation) must see that neither the abandonment of a formula nor its preservation in a petrified form does justice to human understanding.[107]

Although his critics have sometimes considered this process of dogmatic retrieval a departure from orthodoxy, Rahner defends it in the case of Christology as a "most modest attempt, undertaken with the most inadequate means, to depart from the Chalcedonian formula in order to find the way back to it in truth."[108]

It seems clear from this that Rahner's aim in his theology is not to beef up the traditional teachings with fresh insights but to search out again the ancient questions that converged in the dogmatic answers now part of the church's credal legacy. He calls, therefore, for a reinvigoration of historical memory in order to offset the "history of forgetting" that would detach current theology and official church teaching from their rootedness in a historical past.[109] Rahner does more than retrieve the past; he confronts it with the present. In particular, as Rahner examines the traditional christological teachings, he notes the unanswered questions and the limitations of formulation. Merely to engage in an uncritical repetition of the original phrases, however settling in a fifth-century church, would, in Rahner's opinion, deprive the church of what

51

is needed to revivify its doctrine with the new life of transcendental reflection and the contemporary search for meaning.

For Rahner, Christology is the foundation and pivot for theological creativity. This explains why his anthropology, ecclesiology, and spirituality—in a word, his entire theological legacy—seem in some way to converge around the uniqueness of the person of Christ rescued through Rahner's searching transcendental reflection from the frigidity of an unchanging and unbending ecclesial orthodoxy. While not all of Rahner's theological investigations begin with his christological probings, nonetheless, he uses Christology retrospectively in order to ground and elucidate his anthropology and, indeed, all the categories of how God communes with people in all the historical epochs of God's continuing creation and care. Nowhere does he state this more forcefully than in a passionate assertion in his essay "Current Problems in Christology." There Rahner argues that Christ must be integrated into the total reality of God's creation, investing people with the potential to accept this God who in Christ has become the fulfillment promised to creation.

> The incarnation of the Logos (however much we must insist on the fact that it is itself a historical, unique event in an essentially historical world) appears as the ontologically... unambiguous goal of the movement of creation as a whole, in relation to which everything prior is merely a preparation of the scene. It appears as orientated from the very first to this point in which God achieves once and for all both the greatest proximity to and distance from what is other than God (while at the same time giving it being); in that one way God objectifies God's self in an image of that self as radically as possible, and is thereby precisely given with the utmost truth; in that God makes most radically God's own what God has created, no longer the mere ahistorical founder of an alien history but someone whose very own history is in question.[110]

In exploring Rahner's extensive writings in regard to this declaration that Christ's history is congruent with God's own historical relationship with creation, it becomes clear that his Christology establishes a methodological continuity with his earliest attempts to enunciate a foundational theology. This Christology provides the structural bridges to a metaphysics of knowledge, a philosophy of the human person, and an anthropology respectful of God's graced presence in creation itself as well as throughout the history of God's relationship with God's people. Here, too, is set the basis for his theology of revelation, his doctrine of the Trinity, his treatises on grace and the sacraments, and his analysis of all aspects of church life. Here, too, lies the point of reference in his attempt to make acceptable the historical-critical approach in the reformulation of Catholic dogma and in the continuing theological enterprise that is such an essential factor in magisterial pronouncements. Christology is, in fact, the nexus between Rahner's theological anthropology and his understanding of the church's mission to teach religious truth. Rahner's theology attempts to rethink critically the sources of that mission and the mode in which the church leads people to become themselves hearers of God's word.

This christological emphasis enables Rahner to shift "the weight of divine authority to the christological source," thus reflecting "the relativizing of credal and dogmatic propositions that comes with historical consciousness."[111] Christ is the ultimate source of meaning as Rahner retrieves from the past history of dogmatic statements the dynamic spirit that allows for the development of dogma and the validation of traditional theological statements that are not only part of Christian history but also valuable sources for the church's mission as teacher and herald of God's word. For Rahner, Christ is the symbol of God and the unique expression of utmost significance of the human person. Not only does Christ become the privileged moment of God's revelation in history; in Rahner's theology, he encapsulates in his own person what God has made known of the trinitarian outreach to creation and of the providential care of that creation; God makes these things known through a graced call to God's people to find in God their ultimate happiness.

Christ in the Evolutionary Worldview of Theology

The process of reaching that destiny and the manner in which Christ stands as the Alpha and Omega, the beginning Wisdom of creation and the high point and end of history—these are linked in Rahner's theology by his integration of faith with an evolutionary worldview. Rahner was convinced that the faith to affirm Christ's role in the evolution of creation and in God's inspiriting of historical processes can exist only within a person concretely attuned to the significance of history. For him, faith is always embedded in people's secularity and can never be severed from its essentially historical, temporal moorings; if such a severing occurs, faith dies the death of disembodied abstraction. Rahner's essay "Christology within an Evolutionary View of the World" is a case in point. Here he refuses to conceive of matter and spirit existing apart, unrelated to each other. To offset such a false dichotomy, he constructs his theological anthropology in a way fully congruent with his evolution-ist understanding of the world and of all the energetic growth processes at work in the world, including the dynamics of faith. He sees all of hu-manity, through the giftedness of individuals and communities of faith, having to reach out to the God of compassion and justice while remain-ing rooted in this earth. Like Christ himself, people are kindred to the various forms of life inspired by the same God of material and spiritual reality.

What Rahner has proclaimed of the self-transcendence of the human person includes the world of nature. There is more than a convivial bond between the two. The human person, according to Rah-ner, is not only a "spiritual *observer* of nature," that person is "part of it and, in particular, must continue its history too." Hence Rah-ner joins the two in a common goal they can reach "only by activity which is spiritual and by spirituality which is activity." This goal, like the evolutionary worldview of which it is a part, "remains hidden and unattainable" for one's natural powers because it "corresponds to the transcendence of the human into the absolute reality of God who is the infinite mystery."[112]

In his transcendental approach to the divinely energized unfold-ing of historical reality, moreover, Rahner relates God's transcendent causality to the process whereby the human spirit, drawn to the divine Spirit, reaches toward and actually becomes itself the goal of historical development. This goal, he insists, is none other than that fulfilled in essence in the humanity of Jesus living in radical solidarity as well as confrontation with people in whatever their historical condition. It is through Jesus that humans are not only promised but actually drawn into communion with God. This one history highlighted by Christ's inner oneness with his Father leads Christ to that transcendent ful-fillment that vindicates his sacrificial death and gives him the glory in resurrection that was always his. For Rahner, all the transformative events in Christ's life, as in that of God's people, are made historically possible by God's creative Spirit animating the process of an active self-transcendence within our humanity. This is what Leo O'Donovan, in his perceptive comments on Rahner's evolutionary theory, has called "the created possibility for final fulfillment through communion with God's own reality. It is then that ground and goal may be conceived as one."[113] Rahner's theory depends on the affirmation of that radical openness to the divine presence exemplified in Christ. As with Christ, so God's graced power attracts and impels creation to fulfillment in communion with God.

Much of Rahner's mode of doing theology is, therefore, grounded in his conviction that all the dynamics of human life exist in unity within the cosmos and that individual history takes place in the history of Christ and in that of humanity as a whole. For him, the final result of the evolutionary, historical process is still a person's life in God—the very God with whom the people can enjoy a unique relationship in the mystery of God's oneness with them. The spiritual person can thus be set apart by God's self-communication. God is the ultimate ground of the historical process viewed in terms of how grace and glory converge in the story of Christ and at the consummation of history. Christ is an anticipation of God's reign at the end of history. This is a vital part of the meaning of Christ's resurrection in Rahner's theology. This, too, is part of Rahner's explanation of why God must be confessed as the innermost life of the universe and why he can declare of the evolutionary process: "Before and behind every individual being which has to be incorporated into an overall order and in view of which the sciences engage in their search, there always stands, and is already presupposed the infinite mystery—and it states that in this abyss, the origin and the end are the beatifying end."[114]

This attitude toward the historical process, like all of Rahner's theology, is primed by his compelling portrayal of Christ as the subjective expression of God's self-communication. To this end, Rahner declares that in the special event of Christ, "this self-communication realizes its proper nature and . . . breaks through." He also notes "that this moment in which the irreversible character of this historical self-communication of God becomes manifest refers equally to the communication itself and to its acceptance."[115] It is here that Rahner links his affirmation of Christ as savior to the fact that in him God's giving of God's self in word and deed becomes irrevocable. Indeed, Rahner bases his analysis of the entirety of God's self-communication to God's people in the historical context of this event, stating that Christ is the climax of God's self-communication and the absolute pledge of God's self to people. For Rahner, "The whole movement of this history lives only for the moment of arrival at the goal and climax—it lives only for its entry into the event which makes it irreversible—in short, it lives for the one whom we call savior."[116] Christ is the point at which the history of the world, viewed salvifically, the history of the church and its correlative, the history of dogma, and the evolutionary perspective all seem to come together. One makes sense of the other. Together they create a coherence in Rahner's theological reflections.

THE MYSTICAL ELEMENT IN RAHNER'S METHODOLOGY

That coherence is enhanced by Rahner's desire to integrate a mystical perspective into his religious thought. In fact, as Harvey Egan has remarked, commentators miss the real key to Rahner's theology if they ignore the mystical element.[117] Rahner himself, in his book *Opportunities for Faith*, had remarked that Teresa of Avila "does theology because she teaches something about mysticism."[118] He signals out Teresa of Avila and John of the Cross for satisfying a fundamental need in theology, namely, "initiation into the experience of our basic orientation to God."[119] His own theology exhibits what he once acknowledged as a conviction that "an immediacy between God and the human person (we need not say creator and creature) is of greater significance today than ever before. All the societal supports of religion are collapsing and dying out in this secularized and pluralistic society. If, nonetheless, there is to be really Christian spirituality, it cannot be kept alive and healthy by external helps, not even those which the church offers, even of a sacramental kind, . . . but only through an ultimate immediate encounter of the individual with God."[120] He has even called Ignatius's *Spiritual Exercises,* which so strikingly shaped his spirituality, a "literature of piety which forestalls theological reflection."[121] These assertions are not surprising, given Rahner's insistence that one's entire life is orientated to the holy mystery of God who in Christ makes possible the intimate communion with God's creatures, a communion that occurs through the Father and Son's Spirit of love. Indeed, Rahner's theology of Trinity and revelation seems to hinge on his prior affirmation that God is the absolute mystery who in historical self-communication in creation and in incarnation has insinuated God's own selfhood into the most interior core of one's humanity. God has become not only a God with us in the force and concern of creation but also a God in and for us in the son, Christ, and in their Spirit.

Finding God in All Things

This is the God whose communication to people in silent, caring presence and explicit word stirs up in them the "deepest, fundamental experience, what haunts the very roots of our being, . . . a God who remains mystery, [who] is the word of revelation to our spirits and the love which embraces us in utter intimacy."[122] It should be clear from this affirmation of God's intercommunion with people that the lifeblood of Rahner's way of doing theology, as of his religious commitment itself, is driven by the very heartbeat of Ignatian spirituality: "finding God in all things." It would appear from Rahner's own analysis of his theological mission that his point of departure and the a priori for his theological reflections are his personal experience of God and the faith that is catalyst for his endless probing into the meaning of the holy mystery at the center of one's personal life. Harvey Egan is correct in his observation that Rahner's philosophical and theological writings have been radically influenced by his own Ignatian religious experiences. His "spiritual" writings are not merely the "overflow" or practical application of his more theological or philosophical investigations. Indeed, a "mystical eros" is detectable at the roots of Rahner's theological enterprise, such that what Rahner once said of Aquinas could also be said of him: "Thomas's theology is his spiritual life and his spiritual life is his theology."[123] Egan thus agrees with Johann Metz's observation that Rahner's theology is "a mystical biography of religious experience."[124]

Rahner's way of doing theology is grounded, therefore, in the affirmation of transcendence in which people, although perhaps only tacitly aware of God's presence, become in creation personal subjects open to transcendent meaning. Rahner views people as grasped by God's graced revelation of God's self in the hiddenness of their being human; they are empowered to acknowledge who they are in Christ. Rahner asserts, further, that in the giftedness of God's creative, incarnational presence and care, people are immersed in the fullness of God's own being. Commenting on this aspect of Rahner's anthropology in her essay on Rahner entitled "Starting with the Human," Anne Carr observes that one can, indeed, find here a coherent articulation on his part of the theological meaning of human personhood. Extrapolating from Rahner's description of the self drawn into communion with God, she concludes with Rahner: "It is only in the horizon of transcendence that we are really able to know ourselves, and thus assume responsibility for ourselves as persons. Only in this horizon do we recognize what Pascal so vividly described: our greatness as transcendent spirit and our smallness as finite, limited, receptive beings. The paradoxical union of both elements is the meaning of human personhood."[125] If this be true, then the experience of transcendence, as depicted by Rahner, is not one moment among many in a human lifetime. It is, in fact, present in some way in every other experience. As spiritual persons in whom our creatureliness is a relationship that we discover only in transcendental experience, we are, according to Rahner, orientated to the holy mystery of God's absolute being as the ground of all our knowledge of truth and of our responsible doing of good.

This orientation constitutes for Rahner an ontologically silent impulse in one's spiritual encounter with reality. The human person is other than God, to be sure. But in the Rahnerian perspective, people are nonetheless related in radical dependence on God as the ground of their autonomy, freedom, and ultimate fulfillment. Such dependence-in-freedom, which both demythologizes and denumenizes the world and its claims upon people, is Rahner's a priori condition for theology's most energetic quest, finding God in this world. Rahner wishes to avoid the trap of unqualifiedly identifying God with any one categorically mediated religious presence, such as one finds in an inspired book, in miracle and divine intervention stories, in prayers of petition, in covenants and sacramental signs, in an authoritative leader's pronouncements on the will of God, and in other human claims to somehow know the "mind" of God.

For Rahner, all these have only the potential to be "concrete historical actualizations of God's transcendental self-communication" that "is already intrinsic to the concrete world." He asks, however, that when we hear these claims that God is "here" or "there" or in a particular individual, we should recognize that "every real intervention of God in God's world, although it is frcc and cannot be deduced, is always only the becoming historical and becoming concrete of that 'intervention' in which God as the transcendental ground of the world has from the outset embedded God's self in this world as its self-communicating ground."[126] Rahner clearly wishes in every theological endeavor to let God be God and "not simply an element of the world."[127] At the same time, he affirms the paradoxical conjoining of God's transcendental otherness or beyondness and God's categorical, thematic accessibility. This is a relationship in tension that his theology addresses. The objective representations of God's interventions in history play a valuable role for Rahner in one's transcendental experience of God but only if they remain within the subjective, transcendental religious experience as their source and sustaining power.

The "Mystical Moment"

In terms of theological methodology this implies that Rahner's religious thought begins in what can be called the "mystical moment" that springs from God's having touched the human person before the onset of reflective awareness. Rahner is convinced that at the core of every person's inner being is the experience of God's self-communication generating an inquiry into and a deepening reflection upon the meaning of life in communion with absolute truth, goodness, and love. This "moment" unfolds during a lifetime, highlighted by intensified awareness of and peak episodes of insight into what it means to have been addressed and nurtured by the word of God and by the concrete forms in which that word lives. Theology itself becomes, then, for Rahner, "the experience that human beings continually lose track of themselves in the uncomprehended and intractable mystery."[128]

Rahner's opening gambit in the search for theological understanding is, accordingly, to reflect on the human person brought in a concrete way into an intercommunion with the holy mystery of God. In doing theology Rahner makes explicit, through transcendental reflection, the continuing encounter with God in the various forms of a person's historical return to the one in whom people live and believe. Thus he aims in his theology to enable the contemporary person to appreciate his or her faith in conjunction with those concrete graced experiences in which a person comes to understand the transcendent meaning of life. The mystical element in the experience of grace becomes the grist of Rahner's theological reflections as he explicates faith in its original unreflected mode prior to the conceptualizing and thematizing structuration of what God has accomplished. Rahner argues that theology "should be a 'living and courageous mystagogy' into the core experience of grace, a theology which can heal the breach between a living piety and abstract theology. Theology must plunge into its deepest source, its slender root, its origins before it burgeons into the various branches of knowledge. It must explore the fine point of the person's spirit which has been lovingly drawn, illuminated, and embraced by mystery. It must center upon the boundary between the human person and loving mystery."[129]

Put simply, Rahner would anchor all the truths of faith to a mystical anthropology looking at the human person against the horizon of God's transcendent word spoken in paradoxical nearness to God's people. He contends that the holy mystery has entered human history, making it the theater of God's unparalleled intimacy with the human person. In Rahner's opinion, God resonates with the drive for truth and goodness intrinsic to the personal quest for self-fulfillment. This approach makes the revelation of God in history more intelligible to Rahner as he draws the so-called truths people learn about God through the prism of their divinely driven, transcendental search for ultimate meaning.

It is, moreover, because of this mystical foundation of Rahner's theology that Leo O'Donovan has cautioned against interpreting Rahner's method in theology in a one-sided, transcendental, and anthropological direction. Rather, he notes, the dialectic in Rahner seems to parallel the movement in Vatican II's documents from liturgy to social responsibility, from worship of God to being church in the world, then only to return to God in worship. In Rahner's case, the movement begins with recognizing God's graced presence, proceeds to the experience of community in the freedom of Christ, and then leads toward "a worship without words."[130]

The original inspiration for Rahner's theology, then, is not its philosophical search for foundational truth on which to build a system, although such could be the superficial impression given in his dissertation, *Spirit in the World*, and in his lectures on the philosophy of religion, *Hearers of the Word*. Rather, even these works reveal a theological viewpoint inspirited by a faith seeking to understand more fully and, thereby, to pray more lovingly in a movement that seems to generate its own foundational setting from within. Doing theology is, for Rahner, a reflecting on faith aided by a coherent, compelling understanding of the meaning of one's being human in a multidimensioned world imbued with God's Christic presence and Spirit. Rahner has argued that this world has already been touched by God's loving presence. That is why he speaks of one's "natural ordination ... to the supernatural," in a world in which "everything else exists so that this one thing might be: the eternal miracle of infinite love. And so God makes creatures whom God can love: God creates human beings. God creates them in such a way that God *can* receive this love which is God, and that God can and must at the same time accept it for what it is, the ever-astounding wonder, the unexpected, unexacted gift."[131]

We see in this affirmation of God's creative benevolence that the mystical element in Rahner's theology seems to preclude the parceling out of grace into clearly identifiable moments of God's direct, sacramental interventions. People are continually orientated through creation itself to accept the God of love even before the explicit instance of a baptismal commitment or penitential turn to God in repentance. In short, a person is conditioned in God's graced creation to be a hearer of God's word. Rahner insists strongly that it is the Holy Spirit who moves us to trust God with utter abandonment. Commenting on that insistence, O'Donovan sees in it an understanding of nature as "a moment within a larger dialectic of the history of grace which bears our world toward God's own life, there to constitute a new heaven and a new earth."[132]

Rahner's theology begins, therefore, in the faith that affirms the experience of God in the world. In an interview toward the end of his life, Rahner remarked that his "life was characterized ... by a certain monotony, a regularity, a homogeneity that comes from a person's turn-ing toward the final theme of theology, of religious life, and also of human life in general which comes from the one, silent, absolute but always present reality of God."[133] In that same interview he admitted that the new important tasks he envisaged for a systematic, speculative theology were born not of his jousting for truth in the university, but of his spirituality and his experience "of pastoral or ministerial work." He acknowledged this because of his lifelong conviction that God is the only absolute future bestowing and sustaining meaning in one's personal life and in the world's historical meanderings.[134]

CONCLUSION: RAHNER'S WAY OF DOING OF THEOLOGY

In summing up the main points in this analysis of how Rahner does theology, one can say that his questions are the question of faith, the question of salvation, the question of the church's mission, the ques-tion of one's basic social needs and prayer—in essence, he addresses the most urgent needs of the individual Christian and of the Chris-tian community. Rather than focus on developing a coherent system, he preferred, with his vision of church as sacrament proclaiming God's all-pervasive love, to move directly to the issues of truth and meaning. These were issues faced by people and Christian communities in the ex-periential pondering of their destiny and in their yearning for personal fulfillment. He refused to ignore the controversial questions raised by the current exigencies and problems of people seeking to understand in a church claiming "to sanctify" as well as "to teach and to govern." In this he was unflinchingly one with Ignatius of Loyola, founder of the Jesuits, who wanted his religious followers to serve people in the freedom that was Christ's own, seeking to help people in need every-where and anywhere. Only this fidelity to the gospel call can explain in large part the wide range of Rahner's theological and pastoral con-cerns. To the end, Rahner's theology remained rooted in the spiritual traditions of his church and exhibited the prayerful, mystical inspiration that characterized many of the fathers of the church.

It is not easy to characterize Rahner's religious thought in a few words or even in an entire volume. Rahner's theological genius was expressed in the context of his mission as a Jesuit to a church and to a people he believed to be inspirited by God in a world graced by God's loving presence. Rahner had reverence for the truths taught by his church, but always with a sense that historical experience, cul-ture, language—indeed, all the dynamics of human development—were important factors in any honest assessment of these truths for their contemporary relevance. He was able to integrate the wisdom of a church's past with the novel possibilities of the present and the future search for meaning. Labels attached to his theology seem wide of accuracy to those who have learned much from him about God's incomprehensible mystery and the depths of what it means to be called by God into a communion of love with God and with those God has placed in brotherly and sisterly solidarity through the humanity of God's son, Jesus. The selections from Rahner's writings that follow in the next section of this book are, it is hoped, an illustration of how Rahner himself spoke of that communion and solidarity as he led people into a deeper appreciation of the holy mystery at the center of their lives.

SELECTED TEXTS

1

ON PRAYER AND THE SPIRITUAL LIFE

It would be a misunderstanding of Rahner to view his role in the making of modern theology as solely that of an academic and professional theologian; it would not be enough to see him as a very creative professor of dogmatics and theological anthropology whose speculative, philosophical strengths enabled him to open up Catholic theology to entirely new vistas in a postconciliar era that he helped make possible. It would not be inaccurate to call him, as many have done, the greatest Catholic theologian of the twentieth century, but such would still describe only part of the man and part of his work. Rahner's pastoral concerns as a Jesuit, reflected in the prolixity of his so-called less-than-scholarly writings, were, in point of fact, much more important for him in his personal assessment of his work than his critically acclaimed scholarly books and essays on nearly every aspect of theology. Rahner was a prolific author of books of prayer, collections of sermons, books of devotion, and works on pastoral care, despite his heavy commitment to the academic load of German university life and the demands on his talent as a professional theologian and lecturer. Rahner, the Jesuit priest, confessor, retreat master, and mystic, is also one in whom people have discovered new inspiration in their Christian life and in whom priests, religious, and laity alike have found spiritual nurture.

Rahner's collected essays on pastoral theology constitute a bold challenge to churches to cease being defensive in their ecclesiastical ghettos. He urges Christians and their leaders to be renewed in a humble, inner commitment to Jesus Christ and to become more courageously and compassionately involved in the pastoral care of people. Rahner succeeds, unlike any other theologian, in bringing together creative theological insights and intelligent reflection on the practical, everyday concerns of Christian life. For him, no barbed frontiers exist between the doing of theology in the context of church and the life of prayer, meditation, and commitment to people that, he insists, is also part of faith's seeking to understand the meaning of God's love. The selections in this section are from among Rahner's earliest published writings. They are also an illustration of how Rahner's ministry in the church accentuates the caring, pastoral aspect of Christian life. Included here are a sermon, a meditation, and an es-

say on Ignatian mysticism that appears to reveal, at least in part, how Rahner understood his own calling as a Jesuit priest.

ON THE NEED AND BLESSING OF PRAYER

The first selection from Rahner's writings in this volume is a sermon that was part of his Lenten series in St. Michael's Church, Munich, in 1946. These sermons were published as Von der Not und dem Segen des Gebetes *(On the need and blessing of prayer) in 1948. The English translation, published in 1958, was alternately entitled* Happiness through Prayer *(British edition) and* On Prayer *(American edition). These sermons were delivered in the somber ambiance of a city still digging out of the rubble and ruin caused by Allied bombing, the aftermath of the conquest of Germany, and of a citizenry still grieving for their loved ones. In his preaching Rahner found a way to fill the hearts of the parishioners with hope in the midst of their suffering. His chosen topic, prayer, allows him to address the survivors of an oppressor nation, themselves victimized by a criminal government, with a challenge not only to rediscover the wellsprings of their faith and the sources of their strength in Christian community and prayer but also to try to fathom with him the lessons to be learned from those years of spiritual crises within the Third Reich. They were, he said, seduced by the promises of evil leaders. "But men and women were so busy crying 'freedom' up and down the highways of life, that they had not perception to see that they were forging for themselves a new slavery. This was not an external slavery, as symbolized in the figure of the dictator with his iron heel on the necks of a whole nation, and the smoking crematoria of his concentration camps as the sign of his power; nor was it even the slavery of poverty and hunger in the aftermath of war. It was an internal slavery, a chaining of the minds of men and women with fetters forged by themselves" (p. 22).*

In the text that follows, the sermon entitled "Prayer in Our Needs" (pp. 56–68 of the original), we see Rahner leading his listeners to turn toward God in their anguish and fears. He analyzes what it means to speak to the God who in Christ shared the human condition and experienced human need in the pathos of Christ's own destiny and in his determination to be faithful to his Father. In Rahner's moving sermon he urges people to learn from Christ how to pray: "We have learned from him to plead with the Father, but to find our peace of soul in the answer the Father mercifully gives." Herbert Vorgrimler, a former student and colleague of Rahner's, was so impressed with this collection of sermons that he described the book, together with Rahner's prayerbook, Encounters with Silence, *"as the best and most influential part of his work; for in the last resort, what is learning by comparison with the realization of God in the heart of the individual and solitary human being?" (Herbert Vorgrimler,* Karl Rahner: His Life, Thought and Works *[London: Burns and Oates, 1965], 43).*

Of all types of prayer, the one which is most often arraigned before the bar of human judgment is the prayer of petition. "I have prayed," cries the anguished, embittered human voice from the wilderness of its pain, "and God has been deaf to my pleadings." In human affairs, accusations and denunciations may be justified in certain cases; and we must remember that however clearly the innocence of the accused may be established, the very necessity for such defense is regarded as in some sense a tacit admission of guilt. From this point of view, it becomes immediately evident how difficult it is to defend the worth of the prayer of petition against those who denounce it as vain and useless. We must listen seriously and with great human sympathy to such denunciations, for they came from those on whom the burden of life has pressed most heavily and who think that God has failed them. Despite all this, however, we must renew our faith in such prayer, and uphold its vital necessity.

Life itself is the accused, and embittered hearts are the self-appointed judges. The witnesses for the prosecution are the great weary mass of those whose lives are shadowed with unhappiness, misery, and pain. Their name is legion; for a vivid sense of one's own unhappiness is fostered in nearly all of us by brooding and self-pity. We may sift the evidence for the prosecution, and dismiss from the case those witnesses who are motivated by sheer insolence and petty grumbling, as well as those whose grounds for complaint are frivolous and unworthy of notice. Yet, when all this has been done, the poverty and misfortune of the vast majority of humankind qualify them to enter the witness stand in the case against the worth of prayers of petition. These witnesses come from everywhere, from all nations, age groups, and social classes; and they all voice the same denunciation, born of despair or disappointment, of incensed or weary skepticism about the prayer of petition. It is a monotonous cry that goes on and on.

"We have prayed," sobs the weary chorus, "but God has not answered. We have cried, but there has been no response. Our cheeks have been wet with burning tears, but in vain. Too well indeed could we have proved to God that our little requests demanded no great concessions from one who is almighty. Nay more, we could have shown how the granting of our requests would have been but the manifestation of God's glory on earth, the furthering of God's kingdom among human beings. We could even have held out the cold threat that God's lack of response was the annihilation of our belief in God as a Father of mercy and compassion—or indeed our belief in God's very existence. And we are justified in being embittered by this silence. File after file we lay before God: the unheard prayers of children dying from starvation and of infants frozen by paralysis; the cries of children beaten to death, of exploited slaves and betrayed women, of those crushed by injustice, liquidated in concentration camps, mutilated and dishonored. Only the silence of God meets those bewildered questions raised to heaven by perplexed minds in every age: Why do the wicked prosper, and the good fail? Why does the lightning strike both the good and the wicked? Why must children suffer for the sins of their parents? Why can truth be abused in such a brazen fashion? Why is world history a swirl of stupidity, meanness and brutality?

"We could continue by appealing to God's honor and glory, and above all to God's name that God wills should be honored among human beings. God must take care that God's guiding hand can be clearly seen in the world of men and women; otherwise, this world becomes a meaningless chaos wherein there is no evidence of God's wisdom, justice, and goodness. Surely this demands that God's help should come to us so clearly marked as divine that our enemies cannot dismiss it as due to natural causes and therefore proving nothing. May we not demand a greater warrant of success from God than that given us by the laws of chance? Otherwise, life becomes a mere lottery, and it makes no difference whether we pray before or after a purely accidental stroke of luck. It would be quite unscientific to ascribe to God what is simply the outcome of mere chance.

"We could have spoken to God of God's son, who knows how we think and feel, since he has shared our human life. All this we could have done—and, indeed, all this we have done. Did we pray? Of course we did. Did we follow his own counsel, by subjecting the kingdom of heaven to the 'violence' of our impetration? Our eager words have burst into flame before the very throne of God—and all in vain. We have cried like lost children seeking the kind and guiding hand, but no one came to wipe away our tears and speak words of comfort. We have prayed, but we have not been heard. We have cried to God, but God did not answer. We were speaking only into a gulf of silence. Indeed, our pleadings were saved from becoming ridiculous and absurd merely by the fact that they were voices from the depths of suffering and despair."

The case for the prosecution is complete: the accusations against the prayer of petition have been pleaded from every angle. But what is the verdict of the jury? There is a division into a convinced majority and an equally convinced minority, both sections, however, reaching the conclusion by different roads that prayer is useless against human misery. For the majority, there is no God who hears our petitions. Either God does not exist at all, or God dwells in a remote glory far beyond the reach of our prayers, allowing creation to work God's glory, through its blood and its pain. God's calm unconcern is like that of the gods "careless of mankind," who, as the poet says,

> smile in secret, looking over wasted lands,
> Blight and famine, plague and earthquake, roaring deeps and fiery sands
> Clanging fights, and flaming towns, and sinking ships, *and praying hands*.

In moments of respite from pain, humankind may even indulge in some philosophizing about the remoteness of God. Why should God stoop to an undignified meddling with the petty affairs of a petty world that God has indeed created? At the outset, God must have set this clock-work world spinning with the utmost accuracy, to last as long as God willed. God must be now unaware even of its humming. The world was designed by God to have its own complete meaning; it was not intended that God should perpetually stoop to it, to adjust and rearrange what God had already created adequate in itself. It is childish, therefore, to address petitions to God, for they are an insult to the omnipotence of God and a presumptuous overrating of our own importance. This is the line of reasoning taken by persons whose lives are, for the moment, reasonably comfortable. Our salaries, our doctors, our police have their uses; but there is no need for the prayer of petition. But let things take a turn for the worse, and these same persons are vehemently protesting that the prayer of petition is useless, because God has not rushed to anticipate their petition even before they had voiced it. Thus the mentality of the majority of the jury.

The minority hold a different opinion. They indeed tolerate prayers of petition, but only when such petition concerns the lofty needs of the soul. Our prayer to God must not degrade itself by becoming a concern for our daily bread, for bodily health, for long life, for protection from lightning and from catastrophes; nor should we pray to be shielded from pestilence, famine, or other tribulations. We must pray only for purity of heart, for patience, for willingness to endure such sufferings as God may will to send us. Our prayers of petition are regarded as childish when they concern such protection and shielding from suffering, since they imply a lack of readiness to accept unconditionally the designs of God toward us. Rather than seek to have sufferings deflected from us, we should ask God for strength to bear the crosses God wills to send us. Apart from a few alleged miracles in answer to prayer—miracles of doubtful authenticity—the benefits reaped from the prayer of petition are of a spiritual kind, for this is the only type of largesse dispensed by God. The world pursues its inexorable course, the law of cause and effect functions ruthlessly in every age, and it is in vain that we hope to alter this by our tears or by our prayers.

Thus, then, the majority verdict and the minority verdict. According to the first, we are coldly alone on this earth, and cannot hope for any heavenly assistance; according to the second, we may indeed look to heaven for spiritual strength, but it is presumptuous of us to seek protection and material aid, since God does not listen to such pleas.

It is against God that this manifold indictment is drawn up. But God has preserved unbroken silence through age after age. Through divine messengers, God has told humankind that God will not speak until the day of judgment; and meantime the accusations will pile up continually—accusations wrung from sorrow, accusations from those who "search into high matters," accusations on the lips of the cynical, accusations from those whose hearts lead their heads, accusations which reveal a spirit of infidelity.

Yet, despite this urgent plea against it, we feel a deep need to turn to God and lift pleading hands of prayer to God. All these accusations are a source of distress to us, because we cherish a profound faith which cannot be shaken, despite what seem endless disappointments. We have been told: "When ye pray, ye shall say: Our Father . . . give us this day our daily bread." We have no wish to argue with God, to convince God that our will is God's glory; we are content to call humbly upon God's mercy. Nor have we any desire to search into the secrets of life, to anatomize prayer, to question its *why* and its *wherefore;* we simply want to learn how to pray. It is not our aim to meet this case for the prosecution with a defense shattering in its greater logic and cogency. Suffice that we know we are suspended over the abyss of our nothingness by a thread of the mercy of God, and that we cling to that mercy. We seek only such light and strength as will enable us to persevere in prayer, lest our courage should fail us and our prayer turn to ashes in our mouth. We desire only the strength to persevere in the face of disappointment, while we await that day wherein will be justified "the ways of God to humans." In that day, we shall be comforted and we shall understand all.

However, when we set aside for a moment our obsessive preoccupation with the pursuit of happiness on earth—which, after all, is not our purpose in life—we can listen to divine promptings which suggest a number of answers to those who would dismiss the prayer of petition as vain and useless. Why, our conscience whispers, do we suddenly demand God's assistance in disasters brought on us by our own sins? We cry out only when such disaster hits *us,* whereas we were perfectly contented and unmoved in face of the misfortunes of others. There is a certain hypocrisy in our attitude: while we thought we could get along quite nicely on our own, we ignored God; and now, when we find things getting too much for us, we call upon God, who had no part in us when life smiled on us. But now our little nest of content is shaken by rough winds, and we expect the kingdom of heaven, so blissfully ignored, to be immediately concerned with setting things right again for us, in order that we may again be in the "happy" state of having no need of God. We have never really grasped that the glory of God in this world is the cross of God's son.

We profess our belief in the everlasting happiness of heaven, but we want from this life as much comfort as is demanded by those whose thoughts do not reach beyond it. With a worldly shrewdness which is the very negation of the Christian spirit, we want our "bird in the hand" as well as our "birds in the bush"—happiness here as well as hereafter—in fact, the best of both worlds. We complacently regard our successes as the well-earned blessing and approval given by God to our work; and when God fails thus to bless with success our self-centered undertakings, we sternly ask what we have done to deserve such treatment. Childishly impatient, we are incapable of waiting for that day wherein God will end God's long silence by calling to the great reckoning the teeming generations of humankind. God has eternity wherein to set right what appears to have gone astray in the course of time. Do we really understand who God is, and who we are? Do we realize that, since God is omniscient, God's ways and judgments are beyond our powers of understanding? Do we understand that a creature cannot claim to be judge of the creator? "Whom the Lord loveth, he chastiseth" seems blatant paradox to worldly wisdom, which cannot understand that the ways of God are so inscrutable that even God's love and mercy must needs appear to us to be wrath and vengeance.

Let us repeat: all our suffering stems from our sins. We have refused to relinquish the cause, and now demand that God should deliver us from its effects, but leave us the cause. Which of us can honestly claim that she or he has not deserved this or that suffering? We are all sinners, and therefore we deserve greater suffering than any we are called upon to endure. Of course, a thousand excuses for sin are ready to hand: heredity, the pull of circumstances, the absence of the real malice of a desire to rebel against God. Surely God must understand that we are weak, that we want a bit of happiness in a grim world, that the fruit of the forbidden tree is sweet to the senses, that the tree of goodness has a somewhat ascetic taste. Besides, the fruit of that forbidden tree hangs down temptingly, while one is forced to reach up painfully for the fruit of the tree of good. Yes, surely God must make allowances.

Such are the sophistries with which we try to evade our guilt. Yet, sin is a crime against the Most Holy, and sin is our doing. Why do we not endeavor to minimize our sufferings by similar sophistries? In our own time we have heard the theory propounded that it is good for the race that a certain section of humankind should go under periodically in the struggle for survival. Most of us have listened unmoved to eugenic theories and theories about racial purity, about the elimination of the "inferior" stock. On what grounds should we complain, if we happen to belong to a group marked for elimination? If the honor of God and the will of God are regarded as so unimportant, by what criterion do we set a value on our own wishes? God says to us, "When you are angry and embittered, do not forget who *you* are and who *I* am." Why, indeed, should we complain because God does not give to our prayers the answer demanded by our persistent selfishness?

It is not God who must prove to us that God is good and holy: it is we who are called upon to show that we do not need the bait of constant reward to keep us faithful in our love. Sometimes the clouds gather and all seems impenetrably dark. It is then that we are called upon to love in faith—to nurse our firm belief in the stars of sweet reasonableness that continue to shine behind the darkness of events which seem to us sour and grim and beyond our understanding. That our limited sense-bound minds cannot fathom the ways of God, does not mean that God no longer exists. "O man, who are thou that repliest against God?" (Rom. 9:20).

Let us now consider the evils from which we pray to be delivered. Are we so sure that, measured by the standards of God, they are really evils? They may indeed be so, and therefore God would have us ask God to deliver us from them. But it is for God to judge, and we must not anticipate God's decision. We must realize how often the true meaning of our petition is: "Give us abundance, health, security, and peace, and *then* we will love and serve you sincerely and faithfully." Yet, when we have all these, we are quick to forget our promise of love and service, with the result that these very blessings do us harm. The misfortunes sent to us may then be called "shades of God's hand outstretched caressingly" to awaken us from our complacent torpor; the lash of stern compassion mercifully given. Our prayer was not a genuine lifting up of our real or imagined sorrows to God, but just a selfish whine to have things adjusted our way. We did not leave it to the inscrutable wisdom

70

and infinite goodness of God to decide whether distress or prosperity, success or failure, life or death, was best in the interests of our eternal salvation. If, when we make our request, our intention is rather to force our own wishes on God than to abandon ourselves to God's omniscient and merciful wisdom, then our petition is not a prayer but an act of arrogance and rebellion. We owe submission and adoration to God at all times; and most of all when we kneel to God in our distress.

When we listen to the voice of conscience, we hear all these answers to our complaints about the inefficacy of the prayer of petition. But the essential reply to such complaints has been given us by God, when God "emptied God's self, taking the form of a servant." Hanging on the cross, Jesus Christ too knew that moment of desolation when the eternal Father seems to have left his human soul in desolation: "My God, my God, why hast thou forsaken me?" His coming among human beings, "like unto them in all things, but without sin," was the answer to those ages of expectation wherein humankind had longed for Emmanuel, for God walking our ways. We have not, therefore, been harshly commanded to continue our prayer, with only the assurance that all will be righted on the day of judgment. Christ has come among us, to teach us how to pray, and to teach us the meaning of suffering. Through the incarnation, the ecstatic prayer of the son of God in the bosom of his Father has become a human prayer on the lips of Christ, a prayer from the depths of the human misery and suffering of God made a human being. In Christ, we find the true answer to the alleged inefficacy of prayer. He does not teach us the philosophy of prayer, nor does he discuss the conditions for prayer. We do not look to him for the solution of those problems inherent in prayer: the readiness, for instance, we must show to accept God's answer to our petition, despite our longing that this answer should be the one we ourselves desire; the seeming paradox that, while prayer is efficacious, we cannot control the free decision of God in our regard; or, finally, the fact that, although we have been promised that prayers offered in the name of Jesus will be heard, we find that so many of our prayers so offered go apparently unanswered. The great significant fact for us is that Christ taught us *how to ask* in prayer. Therefore, while we await in faith that day of judgment which will reveal all, we have Christ as our answer to all accusations against prayer. Our answer is that Christ of whom the Scripture says: "In the day of his flesh, offering up prayers and supplications with a strong cry and tears to him that was able to save him from death, was heard for his reverence" (Heb. 5:7).

Christ has answered our questions by teaching us how to pray. He has taught us to pray in words of direct supplication, of holy confidence, of complete submission. His supplication was direct: "Remove this chalice from me." During his agony in the garden, he prayed with all the fervor of a person encompassed by terror and anguish. So earnest was his appeal that his sweat became as drops of blood. It pleased his infinite goodness to let us hear in his words the anguished cry of a *human being;* for he did not ask for something sublime or heavenly, but for that mortal life to which we all cling so tenaciously. He shrank from the torture and disgrace he saw before him, and asked his heavenly Father to deliver him from it. However, we know that he also spoke words which manifested complete confidence in his Father: "I know that thou hearest me always" (John 11:42); and in the prayer of his agony, we are shown that complete submission which must animate all prayer: "Not my will but thine be done" (Luke 22:42). Apparently forsaken by his Father, tortured and crucified, he commended his soul into the hands of his Father.

Let us consider how all this points to the great inner harmony in the heart of Jesus. He wrestles with the will of his heavenly Father, and yet has entirely submitted to that divine will; he cries out in anguish, and yet is certain that he will be heard; he knows that he is heard always and in everything, and yet wishes to do nothing but the inscrutable will of his Father; he begs for his life with the utmost urgency, and yet this prayer is an offering of his life to the Father. All these contrasts are harmonized in the prayer of Jesus, in a mysterious harmony wherein lies the secret of truly Christian prayer, because the prayer of Jesus is the model of Christian prayer. For as in Christ the divinity and humanity of Christ were united in one person, so human prayer and divine prayer were united in the prayer of Christ.

A truly Christian prayer of petition is a prayer which is essentially human. We turn to God for assistance in our fear of earthly distress, in our desire for protection, in our sorrows and sufferings. Such prayer is the cry of elementary self-preservation, a naked expression of our instinctive clinging to life, arising from the very depths of human life and human anguish. Yet, such prayer is also essentially divine. In the very act of, as it were, defending our earthly life against God, we adopt an attitude of complete submission to God and to God's inscrutable designs for us. We subordinate our instinctive self-preservation, wholly and unconditionally, to the will of God, and we regard this divine will as the source from which the final decision is to come. Thus, our prayer of petition is, in the ultimate analysis, not a plea for life and the things of this life, but a submission to the will of God even when that will points to deprivation and perhaps to death.

Such prayer is both human and divine. It is human inasmuch as it is a cry from the human heart in its misery and pain: it is divine insofar as it is an act of submission to the divine will. The more like our prayer is to that of Christ, the more vigorous, vital, and truly human it becomes. Thus transfused with the light and love of God, the earthly tribulations and desires which are the matter of our prayer are lifted to a higher plane, wherein they take on a higher significance as offerings of our submission to the will of God. Such submission is a kind of divine alchemy by which both our failures and successes are transmuted to the pure currency that wins an eternal reward. By means of it, there is a mysterious fusion between the human will and the will of God—a fusion through which human beings are lifted to the heights of their true greatness. Christ has promised that all true prayer will be heard. He implements that promise always in the most exalted manner possible, by answering every prayer in accordance with the will of God. The divine will of Christ is always at one with the will of his heavenly Father, and therefore the Father always hears him. As children of the Father and as brothers and sisters of Christ, we have been promised that our prayers too will be heard to the extent to which we identify our will with that of the Father. In other words, whatever our request, our ultimate wish must be that God may answer in such a way as to promote God's own glory and increase God's life in our souls. Such singlemindedness—"if thy eye be single," said Christ, "thy whole body will be lightsome"—casts out from our prayer of petition any shadow of selfish desire to make God's will conform to ours, rather than ours to God's; and thereby we become perfect children of God. While maintaining that freedom and autonomy of will which is our human prerogative, we yet establish with God a pure relationship of sympathy, a perfect harmony wherein we freely choose to submit our will to that of God. Thus, true to our nature, we may desire and pray for what we regard as conducive to our happiness; and yet know that we shall certainly receive the answer we desire, even in an apparent refusal of our request, because we desire only that the will of God may be done.

We do not put all this forward as an explanation of the mystery of prayer, since it is simply a restatement of the mystery of the Christian life in general. We explain the mystery of prayer by referring to the mystery of the whole Christian life; and though this may be to explain one mystery by another, nevertheless it is sufficient for one who has faith. Heaven and earth are realities. On the one hand, there is the living, free, and almighty God; on the other, there is the truly free nature of human beings, God's creatures. These two freedoms meet in prayer, wherein we find a cry of distress, a pleading for some good, coexisting with an attitude of complete submission to the inscrutable judgments of God. These two aspects—human beings' freedom to plead: and their submission to the free decision of God—are always found together in true prayer. "Unless you become as little children," said Christ—thereby pointing to the sublime virtue of simplicity which is the essence of Christian perfection. To lead a truly Christian life is to place one's whole being into the hands of God as confidently as a child takes the guiding hand of its father. The child's confidence is complete and without the slightest trace of reservation: the hand it grasps is of one who knows best, who loves, who will not lead it into any danger, who will shelter it from evil—but who certainly will not reach down that sharp knife or that poisonous liquid, however much the child, fascinated by the glitter or the color, may clamor to have it. The profoundest secret of the Christian life and of Christian prayer is to become a child in our relations with God—a child whose quiet confidence and silent submission do not fail in moments of trial when God appears to have turned from us. Christ has given us the perfect example of this: "He went down to Nazareth and was subject" to Mary and Joseph, because it was the will of his Father; he summed up his public life with the words—"I do not my own will, but the will of him that has sent me"; and he ended his earthly life as one "obedient unto death, even unto the death of the cross." We have learnt from him to plead with the Father, but to find our peace of soul in the answer the Father mercifully gives.

This apology for prayer will be understood only by one who prays, for it is an understanding that can be reached only in the act itself of praying. We may indeed pray for material good—for necessities, for health; but always in such a way that our manner of asking redounds to our eternal glory, whatever the answer we receive. In asking, we must make an oblation of our will to that of God. We must pray with a constancy and perseverance which is a living proof of our trust in God's guidance of human affairs; of our hope in a world full of the shadows of death; of a true love for God which is not simply pious self-seeking and does not depend on incessant rewards. Since we are on this earth as "strangers and pilgrims" on a journey to eternity, we must not pray as though we had here "a lasting city." We know that it is through sickness and death that we shall enter into that life which is the final object of all our prayer. As long as we keep our minds raised to God in prayer, even when disappointments and misery crowd about us, we are sustained by the invisible

and mysterious, yet true and real, power of God's grace and of participation in the life of God; and, when "this mind is in us," death loses its
terrors and becomes a swallowing up in the abyss of God's everlasting
love.

*

GOD WHO IS TO COME

This selection is the last chapter (pp. 79–87) from Rahner's spiritual classic,
Encounters with Silence. *Originally written as a series of meditations for the
Jesuits in 1937, the German text,* Worte im Schweigen, *was published by Fe-
lizian Rauch Verlag of Innsbruck in 1938 and has been one of the most popular
of all Rahner's works on the spiritual life. Each of the meditations describes an
aspect of God, who can only be encountered in the silent, prayerful reflection
that leaps beyond the more erudite words of the professional theologian. In successive meditations Rahner speaks directly to the one who is God of his life, of
his Lord Jesus, of his prayer, of his knowledge, of law, of his daily routine, of
those who are living, of his brothers and sisters, and of his vocation. Finally, in
this chapter, Rahner addresses the God of his future, a God of eternal advent
and promise. This is a God whom Rahner portrays as able in the gift of hope
to make every hour of a human lifetime the hour of a new advent.*

Every year your church celebrates the holy season of Advent, my God.
Every year we pray those beautiful prayers of longing and waiting, and
sing those lovely songs of hope and promise. Every year we roll up all our
needs and yearnings and faithful expectation into one word: "Come!"

And yet, what a strange prayer this is! After all, you have already
come and pitched your tent among us. You have already shared our life
with its little joys, its long days of tedious routine, its bitter end. Could
we invite you to anything more than this with our "Come"? Could you
approach any nearer to us than you did when you became the "Son of
man," when you adopted our ordinary little ways so thoroughly that it's
almost hard for us to distinguish you from the rest of our fellow human
beings?

In spite of all this we still pray: "Come." And this word issues as
much from the depth of our hearts as it did long ago from the hearts of
our forebears, the kings and prophets who saw your day still far off in
the distance, and fervently blessed its coming. Is it true, then, that we
only "celebrate" this season, or is it still really Advent?

Have you really already come? Was it really you, the God we were expecting when we poured forth our longing for "him who was to come," for the mighty God, Father of the future, prince of peace, the God of light and truth and eternal happiness? Indeed, your coming is promised in the very first pages of Holy Scripture, and yet on the last page, to which no more will ever be added, there still stands the prayer: "Come, Lord Jesus!"

Are you the eternal Advent? Are you the one who is always still to come, but never arrives in such a way as to fulfill our expectations? Are you the infinitely distant one, who can never be reached? Are you the one whom all races and all ages, all the longings of all people's hearts must plod toward eternally over never ending highways?

Are you only the distant horizon surrounding the world of our deeds and sufferings, the horizon which, no matter where we roam, is always just as far away? Are you only the eternal today, containing within itself all time and all change, equally near to everything, and thus also equally distant?

Is it that you don't want to come, because you still possess what we were yesterday and today we are no more, and because you have already gone infinitely beyond what we shall be in the farthest future? When our bleeding feet have apparently covered a part of the distance to your eternity, don't you always retreat twice as far away from us, into the immense reaches filled only by your infinite being? Has humankind drawn the least bit closer to you in the thousands and thousands of years that have elapsed since it boldly began its most exciting and fearsome adventure, the search for you?

Have I come any nearer to you in the course of my life, or doesn't all the ground I have won only make my cup all the more bitter, because the distance to you is still infinite? Must we remain ever far from you, O God of immensity, because you are ever near to us, and therefore have no need of "coming" to us? Is it because there is no place in your world to which you must first "find your way"?

You tell me that you have really already come, that your name is Jesus, son of Mary, and that I know in what place and at what time I can find you. That's all true, of course, Lord—but forgive me if I say that this coming of yours seems to me more like a going, more like a departure than an arrival.

You have clothed yourself in the form of a slave. You, the hidden God, have been found as one of us. You have quietly and inconspicuously taken your place in our ranks and marched along with us. You have walked with us, even though we are beings who are never coming, but rather always going, since any goal we reach has only one purpose: to point beyond itself and lead us to the last goal, our end.

And thus we still cry: "Come! Come to us, you who never pass away, you whose day has no evening, whose reality knows no end! Come to us, because our march is only a procession to the grave." Despairing of ourselves, we call upon you—then most of all, when, in composure and quiet resignation, we bring ourselves to accept our finiteness.

We have called out to your infinity—its coming is the sole hope we have of attaining unending life. For we have learned—at least those of us to whom you have granted the gift of knowing the final meaning of this life—that our search was in vain, that we were seeking the impossible. We had thought to escape by our own power from the strangling anxiety of being frail and transitory. We had hoped by a thousand different methods of our own clever devising to run away from our own being, and thus become masters of an eternal existence.

But bitter experience has taught us that we cannot help ourselves, that we are powerless to redeem ourselves from ourselves. And so we have called upon your reality and your truth; we have called down upon ourselves the plenitude of your life. We have made appeal to your wisdom and your justice, your goodness and your mercy. We have summoned you, so that you yourself might come and tear down the barriers of our finiteness, and turn our poverty into riches, our temporality into eternity.

You promised that you would come, and actually made good your promise. But how, O Lord, how did you come? You did it by taking a human life as your own. You became like us in everything: born of a woman, you suffered under Pontius Pilate, were crucified, died, and were buried. And thus you took up again the very thing we wanted to discard. You began what we thought would end with your coming: our poor human kind of life, which is sheer frailty, finiteness, and death.

Contrary to all our fond hopes, you seized upon precisely this kind of human life and made it your own. And you did this not in order to change or abolish it, not so that you could visibly and tangibly transform it, not to divinize it. You didn't even fill it to overflowing with the kind of goods that human beings are able to wrest from the small, rocky acre of their temporal life, and which they laboriously store away as their meager provision for eternity.

No, you took upon yourself our kind of life, just as it is. You let it slip away from you, just as ours vanishes from us. You held on to it carefully, so that not a single drop of its torments would be spilled. You hoarded its every fleeting moment, so you could suffer through it all, right to the bitter end.

You too felt the inexorable wheel of blind, brute nature rolling over your life, while the clear-seeing eye of human malice looked on in cruel satisfaction. And when your humanity glanced upwards to the one who, in purest truth and deepest love, it called "Father," it too caught sight of the God whose ways are unfathomable and whose judgments are incomprehensible, who hands us the chalice or lets it pass, all according to God's own holy will. You too learned in the hard school of suffering that no "why" will ever ferret out the secret of that will, which could have done otherwise, and yet chose to do something we would never understand.

You were supposed to come to redeem us from ourselves, and yet you, who alone are absolutely free and unbounded, were "made," even as we are. Of course, I know that you remained what you always were, but still, didn't our mortality make you shudder, you the immortal God? Didn't you, the broad and limitless being, shrink back in horror from our narrowness? Weren't you, absolute truth, revolted at our pretense?

Didn't you nail yourself to the cross of creation, when you took as your own life something which you had drawn out of nothing, when you assumed as your very own the darkness that you had previously spread out in the eternal distance as the background to your own inaccessible light? Isn't the cross of Golgotha only the visible form of the cross you have prepared for yourself, which towers throughout the spaces of eternity?

Is that your real coming? Is that what humankind has been waiting for? Is that why men and women have made the whole of human history a single great advent-choir, in which even the blasphemers take part—a single chant crying out for you and your coming? Is your humble human existence from Bethlehem to Calvary really the coming which was to redeem wretched humankind from its misery?

Is our grief taken from us, simply because you wept too? Is our surrender to finiteness no longer a terrible act of despair, simply because you also capitulated? Does our road, which doesn't want to end, have a happy ending despite itself, just because you are traveling it with us?

But how can this be? And why should it be? How can our life be the redemption of itself, simply because it has also become your life? How can you buy us back from the Law, simply by having fallen under the Law yourself (Gal. 4:5)?

Or is it this way: Is my surrender to the crushing narrowness of earthly existence the beginning of my liberation from it, precisely because this surrender is my "Amen" to your human life, my way of saying "yes" to your human coming, which happens in a manner so contrary to my expectations?

But of what value is it to me that my destiny is now a participation in yours, if you have merely made mine your own? Or have you made my life only the *beginning* of your coming, only the starting point of your life?

Slowly a light is beginning to dawn. I'm beginning to understand something I have known for a long time: you are still in the process of your coming. Your appearance in the form of a slave was only the beginning of your coming, a beginning in which you chose to redeem human beings by embracing the very slavery from which you were freeing them. And *you* can really achieve your purpose in this paradoxical way, because the paths that *you* tread have a real ending, the narrow passes which *you* enter soon open out into broad liberty, the cross that *you* carry inevitably becomes a brilliant banner of triumph.

Actually you haven't come—you're still coming. From your incarnation to the end of this era is only an instant, even though millennia may elapse and, being blessed by you, pass on to become a small part of this instant. It is all only the one, single moment of your single act, which catches up our destiny into your own human life, and sweeps us along to our eternal home in the broad expanses of your divine life.

Since you have already begun this definitive deed, your final action in this creation, nothing new can really happen any more. Our present era is the last: in the deepest roots of all things, time is already standing still. "The final age of the world has come upon us" (1 Cor. 10:11). There is only a single period left in this world: your Advent. And when this last day comes to a close, then there will be no more time, but only you in your eternity.

If deeds measure time, and not time deeds—if one new event ushers in a new age, then a new age, and indeed the last, has dawned with your incarnation. For what could still happen, that this age does not already carry in its womb? That we should become partakers of your being? But that has already happened, the moment you deigned to become partaker of our humanity.

It is said that you will come again, and this is true. But the word *again* is misleading. It won't really be "another" coming, because you have never really gone away. In the human existence which you made your own for all eternity, you have never left us.

But still you will come again, because the fact that you have already come must continue to be revealed ever more clearly. It will become progressively more manifest to the world that the heart of all things is already transformed, because you have taken them all to your heart.

You must continue to come more and more. What has already taken place in the roots of all reality must be made more and more apparent. The false appearance of our world, the shabby pretense that it has not been liberated from finiteness through your assuming finiteness into your own life, must be more and more thoroughly rooted out and destroyed.

Behold, you come. And your coming is neither past nor future, but the present, which has only to reach its fulfillment. Now it is still the one single hour of your Advent, at the end of which we too shall have found out that you have really come.

O God who is to come, grant me the grace to live now, in the hour of your advent, in such a way that I may merit to live in you forever, in the blissful hour of your eternity.

*

IGNATIAN MYSTICISM OF JOY IN THE WORLD

This selection first appeared in 1937 in the Zeitschrift fur Aszese und Mystik *(Journal of asceticism and mysticism), which from 1947 on has been called* Geist und Leben *(Spirit and life). In English translation it appeared in volume 3 of the* Theological Investigations *in 1967 (pp. 277–93). The essay is one of the most revealing sources for appreciating the manner in which Rahner's vocation as a Jesuit intersects with his mission as a theologian in the church. Here Rahner offers not only an analysis of the mysticism of Ignatius but also a statement of how he conceives his own religious calling as a follower of Ignatius. Rahner the Jesuit sees in Ignatian piety a relentless search for God in which the paradox of fleeing the world in order to find God in the world is reconciled. The point of reconciliation for him is the "foolishness" of the cross of Christ through which God is made known as the inner center of all Christian existence and as one able to invest this world with the joy of God's presence and the thrill of discovering God anew in the countless forms of Christian living, even in the pathos of suffering.*

Hence Christians are those both called from and sent to the world and told that they can find God in all things. As a consequence, following the Ignatian model, one must be "indifferent" to the glamor or to the "whither" of God's call. The one law is to seek God in all things and to surrender to the God who has already found the believer even before the search has begun. Much of the Ignatian spirituality, so evident in Rahner's sermons, meditations, and prayers, inspirits Rahner's theological search for "the God of supramundane grace who deals with human beings freely and personally, and 'historically.'" The follow-ing text illustrates the joy Rahner himself found in harnessing theology to the faith that seeks God in contemplation only to find God ironically within the world and at the center of the personal longing for fulfillment as one gradu-ally learns to conform to God's son, Jesus. This is a search that is carried out paradoxically both in one's seclusion from the world as well as in one's life-long commitment as a Christian to be the extension of God's care in the wider sphere of God's creation.

What is mysticism, and what is joy in the world (*Weltfreudigkeit*), and how far do these two human attitudes have something in common in the case of Ignatius of Loyola, so that one can speak of an Ignatian mysticism of joy in the world? These are clearly the questions brought to mind by the title of these considerations, and it may almost seem that the question thus posed concerns something not merely obscure but also in itself contradictory.

For what have delight in the world and mysticism in common? Does mysticism not mean God, and does joy in the world not mean world? And what do God and world have to do with one another in Christian mysticism, since for Christians the world is in a bad way and they have heard the divine voice of free, supernatural revelation calling them out of this world into the life of God beyond the world? Surely for Ignatius, as for every mystic, those words of the first Ignatius are valid: "Of no use to me are the frontiers of the world or the kingdoms of this present time. It is better for me to die into Christ Jesus, than to reign unto the uttermost ends of the earth." Is not every mysticism an abandonment of the house of this life and this world and a stepping out into the night of the senses and of the spirit, in order, as all things fall silent and every star in the world is extinguished, in the dissolution of everything created with Christ crucified and abandoned, precisely in that way to become aware of uncreated being? Once more, what have mysticism and joy in the world in common? This is asked not in the sense of a harmless rhetorical question, where the question disappears as soon as it receives an answer and that answer is explained. We are concerned here much more with a question which will be fully answered only when in the an-swer the question itself is transformed and given its correct meaning. For the question we contemplated above seems to assume at first sight that we know what joy in the world is. In truth, however, only the an-swer to the question can really tell us what we meant when we asked about the joy in the world in Ignatian mysticism. Certainly, this title will evoke this or that concept in our mind, perhaps something great and important. But how do we know that what we are understanding by it is that joy in the world which is that of the mystic? It is surely evident from the start that not every thinkable form of orientation to the world, acceptance of the world, delight in the world, or whatever one may call an attitude of readiness to enter into the world, into its beauty and its mission, in a loving and effective way—that not every thinkable form of such an approving reference to the world can be that of the mystic. What then is the joy in the world of the mystic, in particular of Ignatius? This much can surely be taken as evident through this simple consideration: our question can not be tackled by presupposing some particular conception of joy in the world which *we* import into it, and then seeing whether we can discover this joy in the world which is ours also in Ignatius. But whether we will by this means find the inner law of that life and the original spirit of his doctrine seems to be more than questionable. I fear that in the end we would merely have discovered our own spirit and its doubtfulness. This, then, is the only way which is open to us: to investigate the mysticism of Ignatius and to advance from it to an understanding of what at all can be meant by Ignatian and therefore Jesuit joy in the world.

THE MYSTICISM OF IGNATIUS

There are some words in which the knowledge, the hope and the love, the ideals of whole generations and centuries are gathered, words which attempt to say at once all that moves humankind, and which, because they attempt to say everything, are in constant danger of signifying everything and therefore nothing. Such words were, for example, in the history of the West: Logos, illumination, spirit, nation (*Volk*), and others. And among them also belongs the word "mysticism." This too is one of those words in which humankind seeks to comprise everything that it believes and wants to be. It has a meaning for the composer of the Upanishads and for Lao-Tse, for Plotinus and the devout adherent of the Sufis, for a Gregory of Nyssa, a Paracelsus, and a Goethe. But what meaning remains to this word, if it has something to say to all of these? ...

We do after all possess a vague empirical concept of Christian mysticism: the religious experiences of the saints, all that they experienced of closeness to God, of higher impulses, of visions, inspirations, of the consciousness of being under the special and personal guidance of the Holy Spirit, of ecstasies, etc., all this is comprised in our understanding of the word "mysticism," without our having to stop here to ask what exactly it is that is of ultimate importance in all this, and in what more precisely this proper element consists. In this sense we may now state that Ignatius was really a mystic.

There can be no doubt about that. With this bare statement we must here be satisfied. Not as though we had no historical information about his mysticism: we cannot of course use as a term of comparison our knowledge of the interior life of the great Spanish mystics Teresa and John of the Cross; nevertheless we are very well informed about the mystical grace-life of St. Ignatius as well. A careful analysis of his *Spiritual Exercises,* of his autobiographical notes, of the fragments of his diary, of the information given by his trusted companions—by a Laynez, Nadal, and Polanco—gives us indeed a quite clear picture of his mysticism....

We have to treat of his mysticism here only insofar as it renders comprehensible the fact and the nature of that which we commonly call Ignatian joy in the world. When we seek to comprehend his mysticism under this aspect, then it is obviously no longer of importance to isolate that characteristic of mystic piety by which it is distinguished from a "normal" piety and way of prayer, one which does not possess the characteristic of immediate contact with God in the same way and to the same degree as is met with in the experience of the mystic. Therefore as long as we keep in mind that the characteristic piety of mystics is given a special depth and power by the specifically mystic element of their piety, we may simply proceed to discuss the character of Ignatian *piety,* from which the fact and the meaning of its acceptance of the world will become understandable.

When we try to explain Ignatian piety under this aspect, then—so it appears to us—we have to lay down two propositions about it:

1. Ignatian piety is a piety of the cross, and therein is revealed its inner continuity with the universal stream of Christian piety before it and so its Christian character.

2. Ignatian piety, because it is Christian, is directed to the God *beyond* the whole world, and it is precisely in the emphasis of this attitude that its peculiar character is to be found, as well as the foundation for the fact and the meaning of its joy in the world. We shall proceed in what follows to discuss these two propositions.

a. Ignatian piety is a piety of the cross, like all Christian mystic piety before it. One would lay oneself open to the danger of completely misconstruing Ignatian piety, were one to overlook this first fundamental characteristic. We must take note of the fact that Ignatian piety is and intends to be primarily "monastic" piety; "monastic" not in a juridical sense, nor monastic in the external arrangement of the community life of his disciples, but "monastic" in the theologico-metaphysical sense which constitutes the first and last meaning of this word. What we mean to say by that is that Ignatius in his life, in his piety, and in the spirit which he impresses upon his foundation is consciously and clearly taking over and continuing that ultimate direction of life by which the life of the Catholic orders...was created and kept alive. Proof of this is the simple fact that he and his disciples take the vows of poverty, chastity, and obedience. And with them they necessarily take over the attitude of the *monachos*, of one alone in God far from the world. Ignatius stands in the line of those who existentially flee into the desert in a violent *fuga saeculi*, even though it may be the God-forsaken stony desert of a city, in order to seek God far from the world. It is nothing but superficiality if one allows the difference in external mode of life between Jesuit and monk to mask the deep and ultimate common character which dominates the ideal of every Catholic order.

What, however, is the monk? He is the man who has put on the pattern of Christ; the man in whose ascesis—poverty and virginity are the paradigms of this renunciation—the attempt is made, and should be constantly made anew, to allow that dying with Christ, which was in essence and in principle brought about in baptism, to become a reality throughout a whole life and in its complete significance. For the primitive church, Christian perfection and martyrdom were practically identical terms, so that the martyr represents the first class of saints, holy men are officially called even today "confessors," and the only other official ecclesiastical category for saints besides these is the "virgin"—virgin because her being is in fact nothing else than the martyrdom of the invisible silent struggle and dying in herself. It is this spirit of the primitive church which the monk seeks to carry further, and here the discussion about the empirical connection between persecution and monasticism can be left aside as irrelevant. Thus the monk is the man who dies into Christ. He takes upon himself the Lord's renunciation, he is clothed in his garment, a fool for Christ's sake, the man for whom the enjoyment of the world has been submerged by poverty, earthly love by virginity, the secret blessedness of self-assertion by the denial of his will in the will of another; the man who still prays in the words of the primitive Christian prayer: "May grace come and may this world pass away" (*Didache* 10). The monk flees out of the light of this world into the night of the senses and the spirit, if we may apply these mystical words in this way, in order that grace and the mercy of the eternal God should come to him.

Did Ignatius perhaps intend and choose another life? He wants to follow the poor Jesus, the despised and ridiculed, the crucified. The height to which he wants to lead in the *Exercises* is the foolishness of the cross.

Lovingly let us direct our minds to this fact—for it is this which has great, even decisive weight before our creator and our Lord—how much does all growth in the spiritual life depend upon our rejecting utterly and not merely half-heartedly all that is an object of the world's love and longing, and upon our accepting, nay, demanding, with the whole power of our soul that which Christ our Lord loved and took upon himself.... Those, namely, who walk thus in the spirit and the true imitation of Christ have only one love and only one burning desire: to wear the robe and the sign of Christ out of love and reverence for him. If it were possible without offending the divine majesty and without sin on the part of another, they would wish of themselves to bear the suffering of insult and calumny and injustice, the treatment and the consideration which is shown toward fools. All this because they have only one desire: following and being conformed to Jesus Christ, their Creator and Lord, wearing his robe and his mark, which he wore as an example to us for the sake of our salvation, in order that we might imitate and follow him in everything that our strength in his grace allows, him who is the true way leading human beings to life. (*Constitutiones*, Examen Generale 4.44)

Is such a spirit joy in the world, acceptance of the world? Howsoever this question may be answered ultimately, this much is in any case clear: Ignatius does not admit for himself or his disciples any joy in the world in which the world and God, time and eternity, are from the beginning reconciled in amicable harmony. In the case of Ignatius, then, there can be no question of an acceptance of the world by which human beings are in the first place and as a matter of course in the world, that is by which they take their first stand in the world, in its goodness and its tasks, strive for the fulfillment of humanity within this world and then finally— and as late as possible after this—also await happiness with God, to guarantee which, over and above their obvious task in the world and a moral life, they have to fulfill a few other conditions of a rather juridical and ceremonial kind.

By saying that, have we not come to the opposite of the position we wanted to reach, to the *fuga saeculi* instead of joy in the world? And more important: What is the ultimate meaning, the metaphysical basis of such a flight from the world?

The answering of this question will be at the same time the way leading us to the fact and meaning of Ignatian joy in the world. The basis of flight from the world constitutes the intrinsic possibility of Ignatian acceptance of the world. And both are based on what we called the second fundamental assertion about Ignatian piety:

b. Ignatian piety is piety toward the God who is beyond the whole world and who freely reveals the divine self. In this—to repeat once more—is to be found at once the reason for flight from the world and the possibility of an acceptance of the world.

In order to achieve an insight into this characteristic of Ignatian piety, let us begin by grasping it from that angle from which our considerations up to this point have proceeded. And so we ask: What is the ultimate reason for Christian flight from the world, which has achieved expression in monasticism and also in Ignatian piety as a piety of the cross?

The living personal God has spoken to humankind in Christianity, that is in Jesus Christ. With that a frightening reality has entered into the life of human beings, which renders impossible any attempt on the part of a human existence attuned to a world closed in upon itself to enter into God. Certainly it is possible to come to a knowledge of God from God's creation, from the world. But this knowledge has a peculiarly double character. On the one hand, we acknowledge God as the ground of the world, as the guarantor of its being, as the ultimate background of everything we meet as human and world in its own reality. Thus we have knowledge of God insofar as God is able to appear to us in the mirror of the world, so that it almost seems as though the world were the raison d'être of God, at least of the God who shows God's self and insofar as God can be revealed in the world, of the God, that is to say, whom alone we meet as philosophers. On the other hand, in our seeking for God in metaphysics, at the same time as the fact that God appears to us as the ground of the world and the world as the meaning of God, we come to know God as the free, personal, and eternal being and thereby as the God beyond the whole world and all finitude, so that the world does not properly express what God is and may be as the personal and free and eternal being. The world does not reveal to us the raison d'être of God. But with that the human metaphysical question of God has already terminated in an essential failure: it is faced with a free Person closed in itself, the God who covers the divine self in silence. And what this infinite God is in God's self, and how this free personal God wants perhaps, as is possible, to deal with us, this question which for all its obscurity is yet decisive for our existence cannot be illuminated by the natural light of reason. Whether God wants to meet us immediately and personally, whether God wants to remain silent, what God will say to us if God does want to speak—all this is an essential mystery for all metaphysics, for every impetus of human beings' passionate desire to know which originates in the world. So in itself all metaphysics would have to conclude in an eternally watchful readiness of human beings to keep their ears cocked in case this distant, silent God should will to speak, in a readiness for the perhaps possible possibility of a revelation. But will human beings be able to endure this ecstasy of their being, this remaining on the lookout, to see whether perhaps God will come? Will they not rather succumb to the ever-present temptation of making the world the finally valid revelation of God, of so making God the raison d'être of the world that the world becomes the raison d'être of God? Was there ever a philosophy in all history outside Christianity which did not yield to that temptation, beginning with the Greeks right up to Hegel? For all of this philosophy was God not always ultimately the *anima mundi* [soul of the world], the God who can live only in the world itself as its inner radiance, as its secret luster of absoluteness? And is not this original sin in the history of philosophy in the field of knowledge only an expression of that which happens constantly over and over again existentially in the life of humankind unredeemed: to allow God to be only what the world is, to make God in the image of the human, to conceive piety as consideration for the world? All idolatry is nothing else than the concrete expression of that existential stand-point of human beings based on the belief that God is nothing other than the primeval unity of those powers which hold sway throughout this world and govern its fate. And even the most spiritual of philosophies in a Hegel still worships—so it would seem—an idol: absolute Spirit, finding itself in humankind and in the development of humankind's being. The God according to our desires, according to our image and likeness, would be a God who had nothing else to do but let human beings increase and multiply, to bless them when they make the earth subject to them, who would be nothing but what we could know of God by natural means, who would therefore be nothing but the horizon remaining always in the distance, in which is unfolded the finite infinitude of humankind in accordance with its own proper law; God would be nothing but the divinity of the world. And it is then a matter of no consequence whether this God in our image bears the features of Apollo or of Dionysius.

But God is more than that. And as this more-than-the-world God has broken in upon human existence and has shattered the world, that which theology calls "nature." God has revealed God's self in Jesus Christ. This revelation has taken place in the dual unity of a communication of supernatural being and of the word. And the ultimate meaning of this revelation is a calling of human beings out of this world into the life of God, who leads a personal life as the being exalted above the whole world, as the tripersonal God, in inaccessible light. God is thereby bringing the divine self immediately face to face with humankind with a demand and a call which flings human beings out of the course preestablished by nature, which they would have followed within the horizons of the world. This gives rise to a transcendence of human beings' mission and destination, which must necessarily be felt as somehow constantly standing in opposition to nature and the world in which the temptation to round themselves off in themselves is essentially inherent, the temptation to seek completion, before God, it is true, as the ultimate ground and background, but yet essentially in themselves. "Nature," that is everything finite which does not arise from, and in, immediate encounter with God as free and self-revealing in word, has ever as something rounded and completed in itself in a true sense the tendency to rest in itself, to defend and perfect the closed harmony of its immanent system. If God as self-revealing comes face to face with such a nature, then there arises the most immediate possibility that God might issue commands to humankind which are not at the same time the voice of nature, are not *lex naturae* [natural law]. And if God calls human beings in this command of God's revealing word to a supernatural, supramundane life, as has in fact happened in the revelation of Christ, then this command must always necessarily be a breaking-up of the roundedness in which the world seeks to rest in itself, and so it becomes a degradation, by which the world—even the good world, the world insofar as it is the will and law of God—is condemned to a provisional status, a thing of second rank, subject to a criterion which is no longer intrinsic or proper to it.

In this way, however, a sacrifice of the world, a renunciation, a flight from the world, an abandonment of its goods and values becomes possible, which goes essentially farther than one that would be thinkable in any meaningful way if these goods and values in a merely natural order constituted the highest fulfillment of the existential task demanded of human beings. Indeed, such flight from the world is in this case not only meaningful, but also, at least to a certain degree, necessary. The obscurity of Christian faith is the essential and decisive beginning of it. A flight from the world of this kind becomes necessary because the need to take into account the possibility of a free act of revelation on the part of the personal God, which is a fundamental constitutive character of a finite spirit in any hypothesis, is transformed by the actual fact of such a revelation into the duty of living existentially the need of obedience vis-à-vis the God of revelation. But if we leave aside the acceptance without contradiction of the communication of supernatural life which takes place in revelation, the only thinkable response of human beings coming as it were from below to the God of revelation calling from far beyond the world is a sacrifice of the world to a degree which goes beyond any which is meaningful in an intramundane even though theonomous ethic. For human beings can only confess existentially that God has moved the center of their human existence out of the world, if they negate their intramundane existence in its immanent signification by a *fuga saeculi* [flight from the world]. Thus all Christian mortification has from the beginning progressed beyond the struggling self-mastery of pure ethics—of course not by excluding it—it is already, as the primitive Christian *Didache* prays, *allowing the world to pass by* in order that grace may enter. Christianity is consequently in essence *fuga saeculi*, because it is the commitment to the personal God who freely reveals God's self in Christ, the God of grace which is not the fulfillment of the immanent craving of the world for its completion, even though it brings this completion of the world about eschatologically in a supereminent way. All adherence to the cross, which is proper to both monastic and Ignatian piety, is only a realistic putting into practice of such an essentially Christian flight from the world.

In these considerations we may appear to have digressed considerably from our topic. But it is not so. For we have already prepared ourselves, in this theological metaphysics which explains the first fundamental characteristic of Ignatian piety, the commitment to the cross, for an appreciation of the significance of its second fundamental characteristic.

The God of Ignatian piety is the God of supramundane grace who deals with human beings freely and personally, and "historically."

There can be no doubting the proposition itself. For Ignatian piety God is the *Divina Maiestas*, the Lord on whose sovereign will everything depends, in face of whom it is not human beings and their longings and desires that come into consideration, but only what may please the Divine Majesty. Because this Divine Majesty is the free being above the whole world, for Ignatius everything depends on how this Lord has dealt with human beings historically, for only the Divine Majesty's free action in history can reveal to us what this Lord is in himself and how he wills to be related to human beings. The meditation on the fall of the angels, on original sin, and on the life of Jesus in the *Exercises* is ultimately based on such a picture of God. If the *Exercises* are one great inquiry after the most holy will of the Divine Majesty, then this will is not intended inasmuch as it manifests itself in the desires and the longing of one's heart, but it is that free will of God which is sought, by means of which alone God still disposes freely of human beings' judgment, their will and their heart. All the discernment of spirits—that most important part of the *Exercises*—is ultimately based upon it: in the last analysis it is not a discernment of the impulses of one's own heart on the basis of general moral criteria, but a listening to the word of command from God, the seeking and finding of the free decree of the will of the personal God for human beings in their concrete situation. And because Ignatius encounters this God in Jesus Christ, he commits himself to the cross and to the foolishness of Christ. For all this foolishness of the cross is for him only an expression and putting into practice of the readiness to follow that free God even when that God calls us out of the world, out of its inner meaning and its light into God's own light, in which it seems to us as though we were entering into the night.

However, it is precisely from this attitude, from such a picture of God and such a response of readiness for the cross, that there springs that which is in reality Ignatian affirmation of the world and joy in it. And now we are in a position to grasp the fact and essence of it, now that we have brought to mind, at least in its most general outlines, the basic characteristics of Ignatian piety and mysticism.

THE JOY IN THE WORLD OF IGNATIUS

In order to penetrate the meaning of this joy in the world, let us begin once more with what we have said about the theological signification of Christian flight from the world in general. The *fuga saeculi* which belongs essentially to Christian existence appeared to us as the commitment to God, insofar as God is, as the being beyond the world, the inner center and goal of our Christian existence; as the existential reaccomplishment of the shifting of the center of our being into the triune God, a shifting already accomplished by the self-revelation of the God of grace. But this existential commitment can only be itself if it really acknowledges the God of *free* grace. And this means that it must, at the same time as it asserts the center of our lives to be beyond the world, also acknowledge that this new center of our existence is bestowed upon us exclusively by the free grace of God, and therefore not by the sacrificing flight from the world itself.

In this way, however, it becomes evident that Christian flight from the world is to be distinguished not merely from an ethic which is immanent to the world, even though guaranteed by its theonomy, and its demands for renunciation, insofar as it is a flight from the world in opposition to a mere domination of the world and of oneself; the Christian *fuga saeculi* is distinct also from every extra-Christian denial of the world which may perhaps be found in Orphic, neoplatonist, or Buddhist asceticism and mysticism. For all these forms of flight from the world do ultimately regard the renunciation and annihilation which is begun by human beings, as it were from below, as being *the* means which of itself and with nothing further compels the awareness of the absolute. All such annihilation is consequently only a way fundamentally parallel to, though leading in the opposite direction from, the way to an immanent divinization of the world. Renunciation, flight from the world, is for such non-Christian mysticism of annihilation in itself already the conquest of God. But Christianity acknowledges the free grace of God, that is a divine life in human beings which is first and last dependent upon the free, personal decision of God's love. Accordingly, Christianity is aware of the fact that not simply dying, renunciation, flight from the world of themselves can achieve possession of the absolute, knows that asceticism of this kind is not the way in which admittance could be *forced* by *human beings* into the inner life of God. Christians know that their flight from the world is only an answering gesture, though a necessary one, when faced with the God who freely reveals and opens God's self, who gives that self to us out of a voluntary love.

Since, however, the grace of God is in this sense free, the Christian knows, even in loving the foolishness of the cross above everything, that the free God can bless and allow to become a step forward into God's presence even those actions of human beings which do not of themselves already bear such a significance, as does the dying flight from the world, which is meaningful only where it is a dying into the new life of God. Provided that human beings have once submitted themselves in faith to the claim of God's self-revelation, God can accept in grace also their service of the world, which is, after all, God's creation, as a way to that divine self who is beyond the world, so that human beings encounter the absolute God not only in a radical opposition to the world, but also *in* the world. Once human beings have placed themselves under the cross and have died with Christ, once they have entered into the obscurity of faith and the ecstasy of love for the distant God, then, to express it in the technical language of theology, every act which is good in itself, therefore also one which is already meaningful within the world, can be supernaturally elevated by grace in such a way that its aim and its meaning extend beyond the significance it has within the world, beyond the *ordo legis naturae* and into the life of God itself. This fact removes from Christian flight from the world that *hybris* which would otherwise be inherent in it as the exclusive way to God: in their flight from the world Christians must acknowledge that one can also reach through the world this same God who is beyond it, to find whom the Christian abandoned the world to go its own way. Whoever remains a virgin for God's sake must recognize that marriage is a sacrament; whoever lives the *vita contemplativa* [contemplative life] of flight from the world will only do this in a Christian way if he or she is vitally aware that God has also blessed the *vita activa* [active life] of work within the world and has raised it to the level of divine life.

It is only upon these deep foundations that there is built the Ignatian affirmation of the world.

That there is such a thing which can be designated by this title has always been seen, even though it has seldom been grasped in its true essence. Adaptation, the acceptance of the demand upon time, the fostering of culture, love for the sciences, acceptance of the humanism and individualism of the Renaissance, the cheerful brightness of baroque, the avoidance of the external forms of monasticism, all this and much besides has been regarded—and rightly—as a sign of Jesuit affirmation of the world. But one has really grasped this phenomenon only when one is able to explain it as arising from *one* spirit: how this one spirit inspired those possessed of it in the seventeenth and eighteenth centuries both to build baroque churches with their joyous exuberance of a shining transfiguration of the world *and* at the same time to offer themselves for the distant missions in order to die agonizingly for Christ in the boiling fountains of Japan or the bamboo cages of Tonkin.

Ignatius approaches the world from God. Not the other way about. Because he has delivered himself in the lowliness of an adoring self-surrender to the God beyond the whole world and to God's will, for this reason and for this reason alone he is prepared to obey God's word even when, out of the silent desert of his daring flight into God, he is, as it were, sent back into the world, which he had found the courage to abandon in the foolishness of the cross.

From this results the double characteristic which is proper to Ignatian joy in the world: the maxims of *indiferençia* [literally: "indifference"; see below for further explanation] and of "finding God in all things." The first is the presupposition of the second.

Indiferençia: the calm readiness for every command of God, the equanimity which, out of the realization that God is always greater than anything we can experience of God or wherein we can find God, continually detaches itself from every determinate thing which human beings are tempted to regard as *the* point in which alone God meets them. Hence the characteristic of Ignatian piety is not so much situated in a material element, in the promotion of a particular thought or a particular practice, is not one of the special ways to God, but it is something formal, an ultimate attitude toward all thoughts, practices, and ways: an ultimate reserve and coolness toward all particular ways, because all possession of God must leave God as greater beyond all possession of God. Out of such an attitude of *indiferençia* there springs of itself the perpetual readiness to hear a new call from God to tasks other than those previously engaged in, continually to decamp from those fields where one wanted to find and serve God; there springs the will to be at hand like a servant always ready for new assignments; the courage to accept the duty of changing oneself and of having nowhere a permanent resting-place as in a restless wandering toward the restful God; the courage to regard no way to God as being *the* way, but rather to seek God on all ways. Moved by such a spirit, even the passionate love of the cross and of sharing in the ignominy of the death of Christ is still ruled by *indiferençia:* the cross, yes, *if* it should please his Divine Majesty to call to such a death in life. *Indiferençia* is possible only where the will to a *fuga saeculi* is alive, and yet this *indiferençia* in its turn disguises that love for the foolishness of the cross into the daily *moderation* of a *normal style of life* marked by *good sense*. Filled with such *indiferençia*, Ignatius can even forgo manifestations of mystical graces—after all God is beyond even the world of experience of the mystic—he can forgo the mystical gift of tears because the physician wanted it—St. Francis had angrily rejected precisely the same remonstrances of the physician.

In brief: such *indiferençia* becomes a seeking of God in *all* things. Because God is greater than everything, God can be found if one flees away from the world, but God can come to meet one on the streets in the midst of the world. For this reason Ignatius acknowledges only one law in his restless search for God: to seek God in all things; and this means: to seek God in that spot where at any particular time God wants to be found, and it means, too, to seek God in the world if God wants to show God's self in it. In this seeking-God-in-all-things we have the Ignatian formula for a higher synthesis of that division of piety into a mystical one of flight from the world and a prophetic one of divinely commissioned work in the world, which is customary in the history of religion. In that formula these contradictions are in the Hegelian sense "resolved" (*aufgehoben*). Ignatius is concerned only with the God above the whole world, but he knows that this God, precisely by being really above the whole world and not merely the dialectical antithesis to the whole world, is also to be found *in the world*, when God's sovereign will bids us enter upon the way of the world.

If we leave aside the somewhat excessively Greek coloring of the concepts, we can find the problem of the dialectic between flight from the world and acceptance of the world repeated in the dialectic between the two medieval Christian concepts of *contemplatio* [contemplation] and *actio* [action], of *vita contemplativa* and *vita activa*. *Contemplatio* is adherence to the God who is the goal of Christian existence, therefore to the God of a supramundane life. *Actio* is the fulfillment of one's duty within the world, including that of natural morality. This indication of the designation of these concepts allows us to understand the formula of Ignatian acceptance of the world which originated in the first circle of his followers: *in actione contemplativus* [in contemplative action]. Ignatius seeks only the God of Jesus Christ, the free, personal absolute: *contemplativus*. He knows that he can seek and find God also in the world, if this should please God: *in actione*. And so he is prepared in *indiferençia* to seek God and God alone, always God alone but also God everywhere, also in the world: *in actione contemplativus*.

Here we must break off. We were unable even to touch on many questions which would have to be inserted in any closer investigation into what has been said, or which could follow as new questions as a consequence of what we have said. Thus we have not touched, for example, upon the question of the specific formation which the Ignatian basic attitude receives by its dedication to the apostolate in the service of the church and its mission. We were likewise unable to discuss how this Ignatian outlook, which is after all primarily that of the monk, of the member of a religious order, would present itself, if it were transferred to the level of a properly lay piety....

Ignatian affirmation of the world is not a naive optimism, not an installing ourselves in the world as though we had in it the center of our lives. Ignatian joy in the world springs from the mysticism of conformity with him whom we have joined in the flight from the world contained in the foolishness of the cross. But once we have found the God of the life beyond, then such an attitude will break out of deep seclusion in God into the world, and work as long as day lasts, immerse itself in the work of the time in the world and yet await with deep longing the coming of the Lord.

2

ON GRACE AND FREEDOM

Rahner's analyses of the reality of grace are among the best known of his writings. Nearly all his theology is somehow rooted in human religious experience where the question of who God is intersects with the question of what being human and being spiritual mean in a world graced by God's presence. For Rahner, God and humanity, grace and nature, must be seen together because through creation they are together. His theology addresses the problem of how grace is related to nature in a manner that enhances one's freedom and establishes the goodness of one's humanity. In this Rahner seeks to restore what he perceives to be the original unity between God's grace and human existence. He refuses to separate the world of a supernatural "beyond" from the "lower" world of nature immersed in the here and now and portrayed in textbook theology as uprooted from its divinely graced source of life and meaning. In Rahner's opinion, the manual or neo-scholastic theology of grace had made God's grace so extrinsic to human existence that there emerged a distorted impression that God was remote from God's creation, supremely indifferent to God's people, keeping them at bay from any real intimacy. This attitude had unfortunately been reinforced by catechisms that made grace something "material" to be "poured into" receptive souls and by church services in which God's distance and aloofness were emphasized, despite the biblical portrait of God who had drawn near to people in his son, Jesus. Rahner's theology of grace counteracts these impressions by affirming the intimate communion of God and humanity. In Rahner's theology God's nearness makes possible a graced transformation of human consciousness as God presents to God's creatures an attractive horizon of meaning to which people aspire in their conscious and unconscious search for meaning. As a consequence, people become gradually aware of their belongingness to the one in whom they "live and grow and have their being." The selections that follow bring out aspects of Rahner's theology of grace: the relationship of nature to grace, the "supernatural existential," and the freedom that that God makes possible in the gift of God's immanent presence to human experience.

NATURE AND GRACE

The text that follows shows Rahner's manner of criticizing the standard neo-scholastic explanation of the relationship between nature and grace. Rahner points out how the extrinsicity of this approach renders it difficult for people to get excited about what is presented as a mysterious superstructure of their existence. Rahner approaches this question from a more Scotist insistence that the incarnation is indeed God's self-offering to God's creatures. God, then, is immanent to God's people, enabling them to experience themselves as included in the inner life of God. According to Rahner, through the gift of grace, people are immersed in God's presence, inspirited by God's love, and filled with a sense of their common destiny, in union with Christ, to be fulfilled by God alone.

Rahner first composed this essay as the chapter "Natur und Gnade" for the dogmatics section of the book Fragen der Theologie heute *(Questions of theology for today), edited by Johannes Feiner, Josef Trutsch, and Franz Böckle, and published by Benziger Verlag in Einsiedeln in 1957. In its English translation by Dinah Wharton this became chapter 5 of the book* Nature and Grace: Dilemmas in the Modern Church, *published in 1964 (pp. 114–43).*

By and large nowadays only "specialist circles" concern themselves with the subject "nature and grace." But at least it *is* again being talked about, and not disregarded except when mention of it cannot be avoided. It is a subject which arouses passionate discussion. Views differ over it and the controversy is not merely academic. This is splendid. For since the controversy between Catholic and Protestant theology died down and became sterile in the eighteenth century, and the traditional scholastic theology was won back in victory over the thin-blooded theology of the Enlightenment in the nineteenth century, for a short time it was generally thought that the subject "nature and grace" was closed, that everyone was agreed about it and more or less everything worth knowing was now known.

If we are going to try and describe this standard view of nature and grace in post-Tridentine and neo-scholastic theology, we must emphasize that we really do mean *standard*. Of course the theology of today possesses all the riches of yesterday and all past ages. In the church nothing is ever completely forgotten. And the truth expressly stated contains within it, unexpressed, depth upon depth of implications. And so it is easy to make mistakes in a description of the standard view of a subject in current theology. And yet this standard view does exist. And it is often more important in the church's life than the sublimer insights of the few.

What was neo-scholasticism's standard view of the relationship between grace and nature? In order to see it as it really was (although it did not fully realize this itself), we must start from a problem in the doctrine of grace which is apparently only a peripheral problem. The supernatural grace through which human beings are justified and can do just works was regarded as something in itself beyond consciousness. This is a theological opinion which has always been in dispute. But it is the prevalent one and has determined the standard view of the subject: Supernatural grace is a reality which we know about from the teaching of the faith, but which is completely outside our experience and can never make its presence felt in our conscious personal life. We must strive for it, knowing as we do through faith that it exists, take care (through good moral acts and reception of the sacraments) that we possess it, and treasure it as our share in the divine life and the pledge and necessary condition for life in heaven. But the conscious sphere in which we experience ourselves is not itself filled by this grace. We cannot experience what difference being supernaturally "elevated" has made to our spiritual and moral acts (the acts themselves as opposed to the objects, distinct from the acts, which they are intentionally directed toward). Thus, in this most widespread view of it, grace is a superstructure above human beings' conscious spiritual and moral life, although it is, of course, also an acknowledged object of their faith and recognized as the highest, the divine, life in them which alone has power to bring them salvation. It looks as if this conception must be the right one; we can know nothing about our supernatural state (or only conclude something about it with some degree of probability from certain indications); we cannot "see" anything of the action of grace (or at most only those helps of "healing grace," which are in themselves natural, to fulfill the natural law)....

Once one has this view, then of course the sphere of our spiritual and moral actions, within which we are present to ourselves, seems to be identical with "nature" in the theological sense. And this sphere is even made a definition of what we mean by nature; nature is what we experience of ourselves without revelation, for this is nature and nature *only*. And vice versa, only nature and its acts constitute that life which we experience as ours. We make up from the elements of our natural powers, habits, and so on, those acts in which we intentionally direct ourselves toward God's revealed mysteries and which we know to be "essentially" (but only "essentially") supernaturally raised. Supernatural "enlightenment," moral "impulsion" and "inspiration" to do good, the "light" of faith, the working of the Holy Spirit—scriptural and traditional terms like these are reduced to this purely entitative elevation of our natural moral acts, or to natural psychological influences (which are, however,

97

regarded as being, under God's providence, directed toward our supernatural salvation). In short, the relationship between nature and grace is thought of as two layers laid very carefully one on top of the other so that they interpenetrate as little as possible. And accordingly, nature's orientation toward grace is thought of as negatively as possible. Indeed, grace is in fact the most perfect fulfillment of nature; indeed, God the Lord of this nature can require human beings to submit themselves to God's will that they should have a supernatural life and destiny, and to open themselves to grace; but nature in itself has only a *potentia obedientialis* [obediential potency; for further explanation see the section on "The Supernatural Existential" in the Introduction] to do this, thought of as negatively as possible; the mere absence of a contradiction in such an elevation of nature. Nature itself can be fulfilled in a purely natural destiny, content and harmonious in its own sphere, without direct contact with God in the beatific vision; when it turns in on itself in its immediate self-awareness (as it is in the nature of spirit to do ...) it is aware of itself as if it were a "pure nature." In its present fallen state it differs from "pure nature" only ... as the person who has lost his or her clothes differs from the person who has never had any. The lack of grace is only thought of as a deprivation because of a decree of God (which "demands the possession of grace") and an event in the past (Adam's sin); it is not as if the lack itself were any different in the two cases.

This standard view cannot be acquitted of a certain "extrinsicity," as it has been called—granted, of course, that when formulated with proper precision it can be shown not to go against any teaching of the magisterium on the relationship between nature and grace. Neither can we deny (although we sometimes may not like hearing this said) that in practice it is not without danger. For if it is the true view, then all that human beings can experience of their spiritual life takes place within the bounds of nature alone, and this nature is divided into two sectors: the "purely natural," which (with its supernatural elevation considered as completely above consciousness) is the life of nature alone, and then those acts (e.g., faith or the desire to serve God) which are (subjectively) constituted of purely natural elements and are only directed toward the supernatural as their object. If this is so, then it is not surprising (although of course not always justified) when a human beings take very little interest in this mysterious superstructure of their being; this grace is not present where they are present to themselves, in their immediate self-awareness. One can get the impression (although it may not be objectively justified) that during the course of the theological development in the Middle Ages, what had originally been called grace came to be thought of as the act of nature performed with natural powers (e.g., the power to love God above all things), and in order to get round this, what was basically the same thing was superimposed upon nature and called "supernature," and then, of course, it was pushed away into the region above the consciousness and became an unconscious modality of the spiritual and moral in nature, and it was hard to see what further use it could be. Think, for example, of the distinction—right, of course, in a certain sense—between natural and supernatural "love of God above all things"; how can these two loves differ *as love*, i.e., spiritual, when the supernaturalness of the supernatural love only rests in an entitative "elevation"? Would one be completely mistaken in seeing a connection with modern naturalism of this theory too? If it is true that the modern lack of interest in the supernatural could only have developed on the basis of this conception of grace (which is of course in some measure nominalistic)? . . .

In the field of history of theology the main concern was with the history of theological reflex knowledge of the supernatural, and how it differs from the natural. It was realized that the modern theological concept of the supernatural (and the natural as its counterpart) only developed slowly and the application of these terms to the many individual theological problems was only slowly worked out (problems, for example, like the necessity of strictly supernatural and internal grace for every act profitable to salvation; the possibility of distinguishing between natural and supernatural morality and defining the boundaries between them; the difference between supernatural actual and habitual grace; the impossibility of positive preparation for justification through moral acts performed without saving grace; whether a purely natural destiny for human beings after death is conceivable). On the whole it is true to say that the development has been legitimate and a true unfolding of the facts given in revelation; it has not been a false development. It is also true that with St. Thomas it had already progressed far enough to make what comes later clearly visible in him (which is not to say that he reached the point reached by Cajetan and post-Tridentine theology). But now we are getting a picture of the process of development itself. We see more clearly that we cannot read all the later insights and distinctions into the earlier theology. And because we can see this we are in a better position to inquire whether during the process of development earlier valuable knowledge has not been lost, whether the gain has not been at the cost of the loss of other knowledge, and that there is, therefore, much to be regained which theology once possessed. . . .

A[n] . . . incentive to reapproach the question of the relationship between nature and grace has come from the revival of the dialogue between Catholic and Protestant theology. In the nature of the case Protestant theologians are bound to be concerned with this problem too (although, of course, from different points of view). And they have recently reexamined it, taking as their starting point the Bible, Luther, and controversy with modern humanism and Anglo-Saxon-American optimism. They were bound to ask what else are human beings besides sinners, how far do they remain sinners when they have been justified. We find in early Protestant doctrine that in the human being without grace there is absolutely nothing good (which serves toward *salvation*). But this teaching (which, rightly understood, is held also by Catholics) is only the beginning of the investigation; and this is where there are new possibilities of discussion with Catholic theologians. And these opportunities have already been partially made use of. And, vice versa, Catholic theology has been driven to examine afresh (even though only a few Catholic theologians may actually be doing so) what is right in the Protestant doctrine and how it can be made more clearly valid for us; we must see Christ as the center of the whole existing world and economy of salvation; we must show that the supernaturalness of grace does not mean that the human being in its "natural" being is a closed system complete in itself with grace as a pure superstructure which leaves what is beneath unchanged; we must investigate whether and in what sense a Catholic can hold the axiom *simul justus et peccator* [at the same time, a just person and a sinner]; we must make our own the idea of existential, personal "moments of grace," which is also implicit in and proper to the Catholic doctrine of grace, and we must clear up the misunderstanding which leads people to think that the idea of a "state" of grace, when grace is "present" but not necessarily "active," is an aberration from the true biblical doctrine of grace. We need not waste much time in saying that the "modern mentality" has stimulated theological thought in this direction. We want a single complete picture of human beings, we want a synthesis of all the different things we know about them. We think "existentially." And so we want as far as possible to "experience" the reality of grace in our own existence where we experience ourselves; we want to see and feel its power at work in us. And in accordance with other modern tendencies, we shall not only want to see grace as it concerns the individual, but also consider more explicitly its ecclesiological aspects, grace in the history of salvation not only within the church, the possibility of grace and its highest manifestations in the world of non-Christian religions. When in what follows we give the "findings" of these theological investigations, of course this does not mean that they have already been officially accepted or already become *sententia communis* [commonly held opinion]. The development of the church's teaching does not progress so quickly. Especially when, as at the moment, immediate problems of the day (particularly moral problems) and Mariology demand even more attention than these more complex problems, which inevitably need a long time to ripen. And so here we can do no more than tentatively outline the main line of development of these investigations. We may hold that the problem of "uncreated grace" can be carried further. Pius XII said in his encyclical *Mystici Corporis* that there are questions here still open and purposely left open by the church's magisterium. If (as Pius XII says) grace and glory are two stages of the one process of divinization, and, as classical theology has always held, in glory God communicates God's self to the supernaturally elevated created spirit in a communication which is not the *efficient* causal creation of a creaturely quality or entity distinct from God, but the quasi-formal causal communication of God, then this can also be applied to *grace* much more explicitly than it commonly has been in theology up till now. "Uncreated grace" will then no longer be regarded as merely the consequence of the creation of "infused" grace, constituting the state of grace, as a "physical accident"; but rather as the very essence of grace (which also explains much better how grace can strictly be a mystery, for a purely created entity as such can never be an absolute mystery). God communicates God's self to human beings in their own reality. That is the mystery and the fullness of grace. From this the bridge to the mystery of the incarnation and the Trinity is easier to find....

Perhaps we should go even further. The connection between the incarnation and the order of grace is usually regarded as purely factual. In fact God willed that the order of grace should be dependent on the incarnate word. It is tacitly presupposed that it could have been otherwise. Is this presupposition clearly and certainly right? The order of grace and the incarnation both depend on a free gift of God. But does it follow that these two objects of God's free gift, in both of which God communicates God's very self to human beings (although of course in different ways), are *two* acts of God's loving freedom? Isn't it possible (on Catholic principles) to hold with the Scotists that the original act of God (which settles everything else) is God's self-emptying, Love giving up itself, in the incarnation, so that with the incarnation the order of grace is already *there* and without this decision of God to give up God's self it would be quite inconceivable? And who can produce fully convincing arguments to refute the person who holds that the *possibility* of the creation depends on the possibility of the incarnation, which is not to say that the reality of the creation (as nature) necessarily involves that the incarnation should happen. If this is accepted (its very simplicity recommends it even apart from other more positive indications, e.g., pre-Nicene and pre-Augustinian Logos-theology), then grace takes on a much more radically christological character; the incarnate Word come into the world is not only the actual mediator of grace through his merit (which is only necessary because Adam lost this grace), but by his free coming into the world he makes the world's order of nature his nature, which presupposes him, and the world's order of grace his grace and his milieu. And from this point, as we said, it would be possible to reach a much deeper understanding of the inner life of the Trinity. The Word would not then be only one of the divine persons any of whom could become human if that person wanted to, but *the* person in whom God communicates God's self hypostatically to the world; the incarnation mirrors the unique personal character of the second divine person, the Word. From the Trinity's external work we can get a glimpse into their inner life. This cannot be impossible because the axiom that the efficient causality of God in God's external acts is a causality of the three persons acting together as the one God cannot be applied to quasi-formal causality. At this point the speculation of pre-Nicene and Greek theology needs to be reexamined. It will appear that in this Augustine understood too little of the earlier theology, that precisely the Logos is the one who appears and must appear if God wants to show God's self personally to the world.

From a more precise understanding of "uncreated grace" we can also see more clearly that because of the very thing which distinguishes the Catholic theology of grace (that grace is not only pardon for the poor sinner but "sharing in the divine nature"), the idea that it holds grace to be merely a created state in the order of being, and so merely "ontic" and unexistential—a "physical accident"—cannot be maintained. Grace *is* God, God's communication, in which the divine self-gift to us is the divinizing loving kindness which is God. Here God's work is really *God's self*, as the one communicated. From the very first this grace cannot be conceived as separable from God's personal love and human beings' answer to it. This grace must not be thought of "materialistically"; it is only put "at human beings' disposal" by letting itself be used as is the way with the freest grace of all, the miracle of love. We only think here in ontic categories (also Catholic) because a Catholic theology has got to think of the real (and what more real and more powerful than the love of God?) as "real" and "existing," has got to express the highest things in the most abstract words, and so God's act of love to us, precisely because it is God's and not our act (although of course it frees us not only to have things done to us but to do things), must be thought of as coming before our act of love and faith and making this act possible, and thus, inevitably, it must be thought of in categories of being—state, accident, habit, infusion, and so on. These expressions do not lead anyone astray who understands them and never forgets that grace is always the free act of God's love which human beings can "dispose" of *only* in the measure in which they themselves are at this love's disposal. We must of course always remember that God does not thereby become smaller but the human being greater. And finally we must realize that Christianity is not a religion based only on the feelings; our praise of the greatness to which God has raised us, and thus our praise of God, must come from our minds too, and not only our grateful hearts. This is true of Mariology and it is true of the doctrine of grace, of which Mariology is only the most beautiful part.

Grace also penetrates our conscious life, not only our essence but our existence too. The teaching of St. Thomas on the specific object of the entitatively supernaturally elevated act, an object which (*qua* formal) cannot be reached by any natural act, must be rethought and made prevalent again. Here "object" does not mean "objectively given, distinguishable from others through reflection and seen together *with* others." A formal object is neither an object of knowledge nor just the bringing together of what is common to many individual objects by abstracting it afterwards; it is the a priori "mental horizon," which we are conscious of in being conscious of ourselves, which is the context for all our knowing and recognizing of a posteriori individual objects. If we take the ancient scholastic teaching of the formal object as the "light" by which and in which all other objects are seen, then we cannot object to the Thomist doctrine of the supernatural formal object on the grounds that it cannot be "experienced." We must, moreover, remember that the a priori formal object of an act is conceptually different from another formal object clearly distinguishable from it on reflection afterwards. There is no particular difficulty for a metaphysic of knowledge in seeing that transcendence to being at all, the natural openness to being as a whole, is not clearly distinguishable in reflection afterwards from the supernatural transcendence, by grace, of the Spirit, in every one of its supernaturally elevated acts, to the God of eternal life and to the immediate experience of (threefold) being, although both kinds of transcendence (formal object of the natural spirit and formal object of the supernaturally elevated spirit) are conscious....

At this point we can note, and should be able to see more clearly than usual, that not only the justified perform supernatural acts. There are impulsions by grace which precede the acceptance of justification in free faith and love. And there is grace outside the church and its sacraments. If we think of God's invitation by grace to human beings compelled toward the possibility of making an existential decision in their immediate spiritual development not as intermittent grace, "actual" in the sense that it is temporary and is only given in special circumstances (and there is no theological reason which forces us to do so), but mean by "actual" only that the grace is specially given for an existential decision, as an "invitation" and as a "possibility" (to act freely for salvation), if we consider that in this sense human beings' moral freedom is not curtailed but continues to be at their disposal even when they have been given by grace the possibility of performing supernatural acts, then we can say that this supernatural transcendence exists in every human being who has reached the use of reason. They are not necessarily thereby justified; they can be sinners and unbelievers; but insofar as they have the concrete possibility of doing morally good actions they are open to transcendence to the God of supernatural life, whether their free action accords with or contradicts this potentiality of their supernaturally elevated spiritual existence. *If* in each moral act they take up a positive or negative position toward the *totality* of their actual existence (and this we do not need to go into here), then we should have to say that every morally good act done by a human being is in the order of salvation also a supernatural act of salvation. . . .

We have shown this by the line of argument which we have outlined; it is perfectly acceptable to hold that human beings' whole spiritual life is permanently penetrated by grace. Just because grace is *free and unmerited* this does not mean that it is rare (theology has been led astray for too long already by the tacit assumption that grace would no longer be grace if God became too free with it). Our whole spiritual life takes place within God's will for our salvation, God's prevenient grace, God's call making itself heard; all this is going on, perhaps unrecognized (if it is not recognized from the message of faith coming from outside), in our conscious sphere of existence. Human beings live consciously even when they do not "know" it and do not believe it, that is, cannot make it an individual object of their knowledge merely by introspection. This is the inexpressible but existing ground of the dynamic power of all spiritual and moral life in the actual sphere of spiritual existence founded by God, that is, supernaturally elevated, a "merely a priori" existing ground, but still existing, something which we are conscious of in being conscious of ourselves, not as an object, but nevertheless existing.

We do not need to explain that this supernatural a priori in our spiritual existence, even though it can only be clearly brought to light and turned into objective knowledge through interpretation by revelation coming from without, nevertheless manifests itself in a thousand ways as a secret entelechy of individual and collective life, which would not happen if it were not at work. It follows from this that the history of religion, even outside the official history of revelation, is not just the result of natural reason and sin but the result of natural spirit, grace, and sin (also in its *conscious* history, in its objective spirit). When human beings are called by the message of faith of the visible church, this call does not come to those who are brought by it (and by their conceptual knowledge) for the first time into contact with the reality proclaimed; but it is a call which makes them reflect on and realize (and of course makes them take up a position toward) what was before the unrealized but truly existing grace present in them as an element of their spiritual existence. Preaching is the awakening and making explicit of what is already there in the depths of human beings, not by nature but by grace. Grace which enfolds human beings, sinners and unbelievers too, as their very sphere of existence which they can never escape from.

At this point we have now at last reached and can properly formulate the actual problem "nature and grace" in the narrower sense. It is clear that in the living of their mental and spiritual lives human beings are aware of their "nature," even in the theological sense in which it is the opposite to grace and the supernatural. For when they reflect on themselves, they experience themselves in every judgment of themselves in which they look at themselves as an object and sees themselves in their transcendence toward the infinite as something which they are necessarily, a unity and a whole, which cannot be dissolved into unknown quantities, and which exists as a whole or not at all; they grasp their metaphysical essence, spirit in transcendence and freedom. And from this transcendental analysis of what is said implicitly about human beings in every human act, they must then go on to see many other things as "essential" to them; their being in the world, their bodiliness, their belonging to a community of fellow human beings. In short, there is a metaphysical knowledge of human beings' essence, primarily here, of their nature, by the light of their reason, meaning independent of revelation; but also through a means (their reason) which is itself a part of the essence thus grasped. But for the theological reasons already given, it is also true that the actual human nature which is here experiencing itself need not, and cannot, regard all that it thus experiences as "pure" nature, as distinct from supernatural (particularly if this self-experience of human beings is seen in the context of the whole of human history, without which it cannot reach full awareness). Actual human nature is *never* "pure" nature, but nature in a supernatural order, which human beings (even the unbeliever and the sinner) can never escape from; nature superformed (which does not mean justified) by the supernatural saving grace offered to it. And these "existential facts" of human beings' concrete (their "historical") nature are not just accidents of persons' being beyond their consciousness but make themselves apparent in human beings' experience of themselves. They cannot clearly distinguish these "facts" by simple reflection (by the light of natural reason) from the natural spirituality of their nature. But when once they know through revelation that this order of grace exists, which is given to them unmerited and does not belong to their nature itself, then they will be more careful; they must take into account that perhaps many things which they concretely experience in themselves and ascribe almost involuntarily to their "nature" are in fact due to the working in them of what they know from theology to be unmerited grace. Not as if they now no longer knew what was nature in them. The nature of a spiritual being and its supernatural elevation are not like two things laid one beside the other, or one against the other, which must either be kept separate or the one exchanged for the other. The supernatural elevation of a human being is the absolute (although unmerited) fulfillment of a being which, because of its spirituality and transcendence toward infinite being, cannot be "defined," that is, "confined," like subhuman beings. These are "defined" through its being of their very essence to be limited to a particular sphere of reality. (It would therefore be impossible, for example, for them to be "elevated" to a supernatural fulfillment; this elevation would take away their essence which essentially "confines" them.) The "definition" of the created spirit is its openness to infinite being; it is a creature because of its openness to the fullness of reality; it is a spirit because it is open to reality *as such*, infinite reality. So it is not surprising that the greatness of the fulfillment—the openness does not of itself *require* this absolute and unsurpassable fulfillment and has a meaning without it— cannot be immediately recognized as either "owing" or "unmerited." Nevertheless, in spite of the difficulty in distinguishing what is "nature" and what is not, nature is not thereby overthrown. The beginnings of this fulfillment already exist—the experience of infinite longing, radical optimism, discontent which cannot find rest, anguish at the insufficiency of material things, protest against death, the experience of being the object of a love whose absoluteness and whose silence our mortality cannot bear, the experience of fundamental guilt with hope nevertheless remaining, and so on. Because these beginnings are brought to absolute fulfillment by the power of God's grace, this means that in them we experience *both* grace *and* nature. For we experience our nature where we experience grace; grace is only experienced where by nature there is spirit. And vice versa, in fact, as things are, when spirit is experienced it is a supernaturally elevated spirit.

As long as we keep these remarks about the relationship between nature and grace to the general and formal, no particular difficulty arises, although we are saying that we can only encounter nature as spirit in the supernatural order and never the spirit as "pure nature." But it becomes more difficult when we try and make precise statements on the concrete and individual level. What, precisely, in this nature is nature, and what would not be there but for its elevation to the supernatural order? For example, is the resurrection of the body part of human beings' natural destiny as spiritual persons, or does it only happen through grace? Or what would the final destiny of a pure nature be like in the *concrete?* These are questions which could only be answered if we could experiment with pure nature, and use our results as the basis of a theory of its final destiny. But as things are we cannot go beyond an essentially formal doctrine of a "natural" final destiny which—as from what has been said is naturally to be expected—is merely an abstract formalization of the concrete doctrine of a supernatural final destiny. This goes to show that medieval theology did well not to bother too much about a natural beatitude. Not only because there is in fact no such thing, but also because it is basically only the abstract formalization of the actual supernatural final destiny taught by theology (and not so very helpful), and because if an attempt is made to make it concrete, it is bound to borrow unjustifiably from theology.

In fact this "pure" philosophy of human beings' natural essence is not even necessary. If we are talking to non-Catholics we have only to remember not to base our argument on revealed facts which they do not accept. If in this conversation we refer to human beings' experience of themselves, we must note at once what non-Christians do not accept in this experience. If they will not accept it on a certain point then it may be that they themselves are not capable of a legitimately "natural" experience, either because they have been badly instructed or because in spite of good instruction they cannot grasp it by reflection (although they have it), or it may be that *we* are speaking of an experience which was in fact through grace, and the non-Christians' experience is not as clear as ours (they have it, though, in some measure, as we said above) and so they cannot understand our argument. Because both cases are possible, because it is not easy even for a Christian to distinguish clearly between them, and because a supernatural argument can be meaningful and successful even with a non-Christian (when an argument from revelation is not possible), the question whether a metaphysical (i.e., pretheological) argument has as its real starting point "pure" nature or historical nature is in the concrete case of no great importance.

The concept of pure nature is a legitimate one. If someone says: I experience myself as a being which is unconditionally directed toward the immediate possession of God, he or she has not necessarily said anything untrue. The statement is only untrue if she or he says that this unconditional longing belongs to "pure" nature or if he or she says that this pure nature (which does not exist) *cannot* exist. When human beings know through revelation that the beatific vision is through grace, and experience it in their longing for it as a miracle of God's gratuitous love, they have to say that it is a free gift, not due to them by nature, not pledged to them by their having been created (so that our creation, which was a free act of God, not due to us, and the free gift of grace to the already existing creature, are not one and the same gift of God's freedom). The concept of "pure nature" is implicit in this statement. It is not just a meaningless extravagance of idle theological speculation, but it is the necessary background against which to see the beatific vision as free grace, not due to us; not due to us either as sinners or as creatures.

The attempt to work out more clearly the way in which nature is ordered to grace . . . is still meaningful when we realize that grace is not due to nature, whether sinful or not. This does not make it necessary to think of this *potentia obedientialis* for grace more or less as the mere lack of contradiction to it, with the resulting "extrinsicity" already spoken of. Being ordered to grace and being directed to grace in such a way that without the actual gift of this grace it would all be meaningless, are not the same thing. Even though a spirit (i.e., openness to God, freedom and conscious and free self-possession) is essentially impossible without this transcendence, whose *absolute* fulfillment is grace, yet *this* fulfillment does not thereby become due; supposing, of course, that the conscious self-possession in freedom is itself meaningful in God's sight (and not just a means, a mere phase on the way, toward possessing the beatific vision). This supposition is perfectly legitimate. For the absolute (not infinite) worth and validity in itself of every personal act makes this supposition. If it is legitimate, then this is how things stand: Without transcendence open to the supernatural there is no spirit; but spirit itself is already meaningful without supernatural grace. Its fulfillment through grace is not, therefore, an exigency of its nature, although it is open to this supernatural fulfillment. And when this is clear we are no longer in danger of forgetting the supernaturalness of grace, and can proceed without further hindrance to work out with all due precision the exact meaning of this transcendence of the spirit toward the supernatural. We can only fully understand human beings in their "undefinable" essence if we see them as *potentia obedientialis* for the divine life; this is their *nature....*

In Scripture God is love ...; we can therefore only fully understand human beings and their absolute fulfillment (through grace) if we see them as freedom and love—and this not only as the complement and emotional accompaniment of knowledge. For reasons already given it is not at all a bad thing that in this analysis of the human being as *potentia obedientialis* there has been no "chemically pure" description of pure nature, but mixed in with it there are traces of elements of historical nature, that is, nature possessing grace. Who is to say that the voice heard in earthly philosophy, even non-Christian and pre-Christian philosophy, is the voice of nature alone (and perhaps of nature's guilt) and not also the groaning of the creature, who is already moved in secret by the Holy Spirit of grace, and longs without realizing it for the glory of the children of God?

There is still much more to be said on the subject of the present state of the theology of grace, what it is and what it should be. We should discuss grace in its relationship to the church, what it means and how it is ordered to society; the current textbooks tend to treat it with a curiously individualistic narrowness. And we should mention the renewed interest in the relationship between grace and human beings' personal action. But there is no more room for this here.

Little advances and shifts in the field of the theory of any science are often not of immediately evident importance. At first these changes may look like mere passing fashions or scholarly quibbling. But if we realize that these new insights enter the common consciousness and become the unquestioned suppositions which are the basis for our action, then we may begin to see that a great deal, sometimes everything, depends on them. It is a strange thing that we Christians are often convinced enough of the power of "theory" to produce very practical results; but by "theory" we are not so likely to mean theology as church politics, social questions, propaganda methods, and suchlike. Living theology itself is not very highly thought of. Many people in the church often have the impression that it goes on fussing superfluously with questions which were settled long ago, causes disturbances, and keeps people from attending to more important things. These people do not realize that a lively and inquiring theology of today is working to make tomorrow's preaching reach mind and heart. This work of theology's may often look inconsequential and fruitless. But it is necessary. Even though heart and grace are the only things which we cannot do without.

*

THE SUPERNATURAL EXISTENTIAL

The phrase "supernatural existential," which forms the title of this selection, was coined by Rahner in an article on the relationship between nature and grace ("Über das Verhältnis von Natur und Gnade") that appeared in the journal Orientierung *in 1950. The article was later incorporated into volume 1 of his* Schriften, *published in 1954. The English translation, from volume 1 of* Theological Investigations *(pp. 309–17), followed in 1961. Rahner uses the expression as a short rubric for affirming that all persons are created into a relationship with God by virtue of their human existence and not, as in textbook theology, by virtue solely of a superstructure of divine power flowing into a person through ritualized action. For Rahner, this is the necessary conditioning of the human spirit whereby God not only ordains people to the "supernatural level" but, in the gift of God's caring presence to the human spirit, creating a restless drive for union with God, makes them capable of accepting that which will modify their very existence.*

Although Rahner insists that this "supernatural existential" is not grace itself, it seems clear that he looks on this aspect of God's impacting on one's being human as a necessary preamble to the actual moment of the graced relationship between God and God's people. Hence, the term "existential," borrowed from Heidegger, indicates that what God effects in the human soul is intrinsic to the whole structuration of one's humanity. It is intrinsic to human nature that people be drawn to the God who creates and who calls God's creatures to a graced life transforming human existence to the extent that a person may be said to have been "raised" to a "supernatural" level. God's own life is thus shared with God's people in a way that can only be called mysterious. Rahner's insights into this supernatural existential mode of God's being related to God's creatures are, in turn, at the root of his openness to and optimistic attitude toward non-Christian religions. As Rahner hints toward the end of the text that follows, theology must move away from the more formal, ontological categories of a neo-scholastic approach to grace toward the personal categories of love, intimacy, and self-communication that more aptly describe God's giftedness to God's people.

The paradox of a natural desire for the supernatural as a link between nature and grace is conceivable and necessary if by "desire" is understood an "openness" to the supernatural, and it is taught in every type of Catholic theology, even if this often interprets the *potentia obedientialis* in too purely formal and negative a way as a mere nonrepugnance. But a "desire" which is natural and at the same time, even if only objectively, inevitably attracts grace to itself (the desire itself, not just God's wisdom and God's promise but the latter through the former!), is a desire which "demands" grace, demands precisely because it would otherwise be meaningless. But this is incompatible with the unexactedness of grace.

After this critique of an unconditional and yet natural ordination of human beings' to the supernatural, we should like to try to suggest in a few brief words how we ourselves conceive of the relationship between human beings and grace. God wishes to engage in self-communication, to pour forth the love which God is. That is the first and the last of God's real plans and hence of God's real world too. Everything else exists so that this one thing might be: the eternal miracle of infinite love. And so God makes a creature whom God can love: God creates human beings. God creates them in such a way that they *can* receive this love which is God, and that they can and must at the same time accept it for what it is: the ever-astounding wonder, the unexpected, unexacted gift. And let us not forget here that ultimately we only know what "unexacted" means when we know what personal love is, not vice versa: we do not understand what love is by knowing the meaning of "unexacted." Thus in this second respect God must so create human beings that love does not only pour forth free and unexacted, but also so that human beings as real partners, as ones who can accept or reject it, can experience and accept it *as* the unexacted event and wonder not owed to them, the real men and women. As unexacted, not only because they do not deserve it as *sinners*, but further because they can also embrace it as unexacted when, already blessed in this love, they are allowed to forget that they were sinners once. That is all we have to say on this matter "kerygmatically." It will appear that one need not discourse at such great length about nature and the supernatural in one's proclamation of the gospel as one has been accustomed to do in this connection.

Now if one quite rightly sets about transposing these simple propositions, which all Christians can in a true sense make their own, into "theology," because this transposition is necessary for theologians and preachers if they are to be preserved from the danger of misinterpreting them or rendering them innocuous, the following points may be made.

1. Human beings should be *able* to receive this love which is God; they must have a congeniality for it. They must be able to accept it (and hence grace, the beatific vision) as people who have room and scope, understanding and desire for it. Thus they must have a real "potency" for it. They must have it *always*. They are indeed always addressed and claimed by this love. For, as they now in fact are, they are created for it; they are thought and called into being so that love might bestow itself. To this extent this "potency" is what is inmost and most authentic in them, the center and root of what they are absolutely. They must have it *always:* for even the damned, who have turned away from this love and made themselves incapable of receiving this love, must still be really able to experience this love (which being scorned now burns like fire) as that to which they are ordained in the ground of their concrete being; they must consequently always remain what they were created as: the burning longing for God in the immediacy of God's own threefold life. The capacity for the God of self-bestowing personal love is the central and abiding existential of human beings as they really are.

2. The real man or woman as God's real partner should be able to receive this love as what it necessarily is: as free gift. But that means that this central, abiding existential, consisting in the ordination to the threefold God of grace and eternal life, is itself to be characterized as unexacted, as "supernatural." Not because human beings first of all—"obviously"—have a fixed, circumscribed nature in the sense that measured by it (as a fixed quantity known beforehand) grace, which is to say ultimately God, appears to be out of proportion and must therefore be called supernatural. But because the longing for, the ordination to, God's love, this existential for supernatural grace, only allows grace to be unexacted grace when it is itself unexacted, and at the moment when, fulfilled by grace, it becomes conscious of itself *as* supernatural, that is, shines forth as unexacted by the real man or woman, not owed to him or her. Human beings are not to recognize themselves merely as part of God's free creation; because they exist and although they exist already, they are to accept God's love as gift and unexpected wonder. But if they were in a certain sense nothing but this existential, and were *this*—here there arises the *theological* word "nature" for the first time—simply their nature, that is, were it in absolutely no way capable of being dissociated from what they are otherwise and from what they could understand themselves to be, then they could certainly as free

agents always continue to behave contrary to this nature in the despite of love; but they could not accept this love as bestowed gratuitously and without exaction upon them, God's really existent partner. Were they simply this existential, and were this their nature, then it would be unconditional in its essence, that is, once it has been given, the love which is God would "have to" be offered by God.

3. Thus those who receive this love (in the Holy Spirit and thanks to the word of the gospel) will know this very existential for this love as not owed to them, unexacted by them the real human beings. *This* knowledge is what allows them to distinguish and delimit what they always are (their concrete, indissoluble "quiddity") into what is this unexacted real receptivity, the supernatural existential, and what is left over as remainder when this inmost center is subtracted from the substance of their concrete quiddity, their "nature." "Nature" in the theological sense (as opposed to nature as the substantial content of an entity always to be encountered in contingent fact), that is, as the concept contraposed to the supernatural, is consequently a remainder concept (*Restbegriff*). By that is meant that starting as we have done, a reality must be postulated in human beings which remains over when the supernatural existential as unexacted is subtracted, and must have a meaning and a possibility of existence even when the supernatural existential is thought of as lacking (for otherwise this existential would necessarily be demanded precisely by the postulated reality, and it could only be unexacted with respect to a purely possible human being, as an element in creation in general). But this "pure" nature is not for that reason an unambiguously delimitable, definable quantity; no neat horizontal (to use Philipp Dessauer's way of putting it) allows of being drawn between this nature and the supernatural (both existential and grace). We never have this postulated pure nature for itself alone, so as in all cases to be able to say *exactly* what in our existential experience is to be reckoned to its account, what to the account of the supernatural. Where life is a matter of concrete yearning for eternal truth and pure and infinite love, of the inescapability of a free decision before God, of the pangs of birth, of concupiscence, labor, toil, and death (hence of human beings' real essence and its achievement), all this is unquestionably experienced by persons who (consciously or unconsciously) are subject to the influence of the supernatural existential (if not of grace). Thus there is no way of telling *exactly* how their nature for itself alone would react, what precisely it would be for itself alone. This is not to deny that in the light of experience and still more of revelation it might not be possible in some determinate respect to use a transcendental method to delimit what this

human nature contains. "Animal rationale" may still in this respect be an apt description. Certainly philosophers have their own well-grounded concept of the nature of the human person: the irreducible substance of human being, established by recourse to human experience independently of verbal revelation. This concept may largely coincide with the theological concept of human beings' nature, insofar as without revelation the greater part of what goes beyond this theological "nature" is not experienced, and at any rate is not recognized *as* supernatural without the help of revelation to interpret it. But in principle the content of this philosophical concept of human beings need not simply coincide with the content of the theological concept of their "pure nature." It can in concrete fact contain more (i.e., something already supernatural, though not as such). When therefore one undertakes to state with precision what exact content is intended by such a concept of a pure nature, in particular as regards God and God's moral law, the difficulties, indeed the impossibility, of a neat horizontal once again become apparent for us, as the history of theology shows only too clearly. But these difficulties lie precisely in the nature of things: human beings can experiment with themselves only in the region of God's supernatural loving will, they can never find the nature they want in a "chemically pure" state, separated from its supernatural existential. Nature in this sense continues to be a remainder concept, but a necessary and objectively justified one, if one wishes to achieve reflexive consciousness of that unexactedness of grace which goes together with human beings' inner, unconditional ordination to it. Then in fact this unconditional ordination must itself be grasped as unexacted and supernatural; human beings' concretely experienced quiddity differentiates itself into the supernatural existential as such and the "remainder"—the pure nature.

4. Hence there is no longer any reason why speculative theology should avoid considering the relationship between the supernatural (including the supernatural existential) and nature in itself. It will be permissible to take hold with an easy conscience of the concept of *potentia obedientialis* scorned by de Lubac. The spiritual nature will have to be such that it has an openness for this supernatural existential without thereby of itself demanding it unconditionally. This openness is not to be thought of merely as a nonrepugnance, but as an inner ordination, provided only that it is not unconditional. It will be permissible at this point to point unhesitatingly at the unlimited dynamism of the spirit, which for de Lubac is the natural existential immediately ordered to grace itself. All one must guard against is identifying this unlimited dynamism of the *spiritual nature* in a simply apodeictic way with that

dynamism which we experience (or believe we experience) in the adventure of our concrete spiritual existence, because here the supernatural existential may already be at work—as subsequently emerges in the light of revelation. And one will guard against asserting that this natural dynamism is an unconditional demand for grace. How should we know this, if we never experience it "pure"? There is no reason why it could not retain its meaning and necessity even without grace, if on the one hand one can learn to see it as the indispensable transcendental condition of the possibility of a spiritual life at all; and on the other hand if this spiritual life, although in comparison with the beatific vision it remains eternally *in umbris et imaginibus* [in shadows and images], can at any rate be shown to be neither meaningless nor harsh but can always be seen as a positive, though finite, good which God could bestow even when God has not called human beings immediately before God's face. Even according to de Lubac the pure philosophy of human beings' nature (even their concrete nature) is not capable of discerning the possibility of a *visio beatifica*. Then de Lubac too must hold that a spiritual life toward God as an end approached merely asymptotically is not to be dismissed as meaningless from the start. But as has already been said, we have no pure experience of this purely natural dynamism (or at any rate the contrary is not proved). Thus one who believes that he or she or humanity in the concrete is driven on the most sublime ways of its history, even apart from verbal revelation, by an impulse which would be meaningless if it did not lead to the immediate vision of God, need not on that account go on to assert anything which would be opposed to this view. All that person would be bound not to assert (and this person's experience gives him or her no occasion for this either) is that this existentially (*existentiell*) real dynamism belongs to the substance of the nature of human beings in the theological sense.

Of course what has been said is far from providing an answer to all the questions which could be put concerning the relationship of nature and grace. It would be proper to speak with more precision of the *potentia obedientialis* of nature as such. It would be necessary to examine more closely how the supernatural existential is related to grace itself, and in what sense it is distinct from it. All the questions and theses concerning the relationship of nature and grace would need to be wholly rethought in terms of an explicit recognition of the fact that grace is not just a "neutral state" (however sublime), that it cannot be sufficiently described by purely formal ontological categories alone (created "quality," accident, *habitus*, etc.), but that personal categories (love, personal intimacy, self-communication) can neither be avoided in the description of what grace is, nor, because they do not belong to the realm of formal ontology, are on that account inaccessible to a more precise philosophical or theological reflection or stand in no need of it. In regard to the question of the nature-grace relationship it would be necessary to consider in more precise detail how a philosophical knowledge of a "nature" really comes about. Scholastic philosophy and theology do indeed rightly insist (as *Humani Generis* recently impressed upon us again too) that immutable "essences" and concepts of essences are to be found. But too little thought is given to how in fact one arrives at such an individual concept of an essence and in particular that of the essence of the human being, meaning by that something more than the most general metaphysical propositions (about entities in general, the transcendentals, and the most general metaphysical principles of identity, causality, finality, etc.). Even the distinction made above between a transcendental and an a posteriori empirical method in the investigation of the essence of the human being is not generally familiar. The view is too lightly taken as a starting point that whatever has been empirically observed in human beings "always and in all cases" also belongs *eo ipso* to the immutable substance of their "nature," which then supplies the foundation of the "lex naturae." But the question is not so simple. Can pure natures be produced? In atomic physics perhaps? Can and may human beings change their nature? Is the variable *eo ipso* something which lies outside the concept of nature as such? Even when this quantity once achieved (produced) was general and (relatively) stable? It might be asked whether the scholastic concept of "nature" as applied to the "nature" of the human being does not still owe too much to the model of what is less than human (in the train of archaic philosophy with its orientation toward "physics"). What is signified by the "definition," and hence the circumscription, of human beings' "nature," if they are the essence of transcendence, and hence of the surpassing of limitation? Is it meaningful at all in such a perspective simply to assign to this "nature" an end perfectly defined materially? Not as though the remotest doubt were being thrown here on the fact that the human being has a nature and that this in itself has an end assigned to it. But these must not and cannot be conceived in such simple terms as the mutual order of a pot and its lid or of a biological organism and its fixed environment. One has only to ask why a supernatural end can be set for human beings without annulling their nature, and why God cannot do this with the nature of something below the human. Then it becomes apparent at once that however universally the formal ontology of nature and end, and so forth, may extend, these concepts can only be used in the particular matter of each individual grade of being in a highly analogical way. There are many more such questions, and they are not idle subtleties. For that nature should remain nature for the sake of grace and yet always be grasped by Christians as an intrinsic element in the single object willed by God when God willed human beings as God's beloved in God's son—to bring this about is a task of the Christian life, and so a serious question for theology.

*

ON THE ORIGINS OF FREEDOM

Originally a lecture to the Evangelischer Kirchentag (Evangelical church day) in Cologne, July 29, 1965, this essay was first published in the same year as "Über die Freiheit" (On freedom), a chapter in the book Ursprünge der Freiheit vom christlichen Freiheitsverstandnis *(Origins of freedom from the Christian understanding of freedom), edited by M. Horkheimer, C. F. von Weizsäcker, and Rahner. It was reprinted in Rahner's* Gnade als Freiheit: Kleine theologische Beiträge *(Grace as freedom: Short theological essays), published by Herder in Freiburg in 1968. This latter German text was translated into English by Hilda Graef as* Grace in Freedom, *and published in 1969 (pp. 226–47).*

"Origins of Freedom" is one of Rahner's most explicit and detailed explanations of how he understands freedom theologically. For Rahner, freedom, like the grace from which it springs, must be construed in connection with the phenomenon of human transcendence. True freedom is always freedom in the presence of and in relationship with God. In effect, freedom is more than a mere choice of one course of action over another. It is rather the experience of God, not as one of many realities become the object of a decision for or against something, but as the "infinite horizon" from which every free choice derives its rationale and strength. Freedom is rooted in the graced encounter with God in which Christians choose themselves in tandem with the holy mystery at the center of life's meaning and allow themselves to be drawn into that mystery. For Rahner, this process is subsumed under what he has called one's "fundamental option." He thus constructs his theology of freedom as an expression of one's fundamental orientation toward (or against) and acceptance (or rejection) of the graced presence of God liberating people from the dead-ends of self-reification in narrow-minded pursuits and heartless decisions that rob them of the potential to be more human and, therefore, more Godlike. God's gift of freedom goads one to move beyond the closed systems of society and away from the dark choices of a heart turned in on itself. Freedom is, then, as

117

Rahner claims in this essay, that graced catalyst of being whereby God makes possible one's "fundamental option" and future fulfillment in God. This is because, for Rahner, freedom engenders a yearning to commit oneself once and for all to the God who is the absolute possibility and one's deepest attraction in every human search for meaning. Before and beyond freedom is the God who, in freedom, endows God's people with the dignity that is the core of their being free for themselves, for others in Christlike service, and, ultimately, for God.

It must first of all be clarified what freedom means theologically, and especially why it must always be conquered anew. We shall thus gain a proper understanding of the question why freedom must be conquered, and a deeper insight into the life of freedom.

FORMAL CHARACTERISTICS OF CHRISTIAN FREEDOM

In Christian theology freedom is not simply a freedom of choosing between individual realities and objects encountered in our life, it is not merely the freedom to decide upon one course of action among others. Whether we know it or not, true freedom is born from the transcendence of the human being, hence it is freedom before and toward God. Even if God is not known or not expressly visualized in the free act: wherever freedom is really exercised, this happens in silently stretching beyond all individual data into the ineffable, quiet, incomprehensible infinity of the primeval unity of all thinkable reality, in an anticipation of God. Thus we experience precisely in freedom what is meant by God, even if we do not name or consider this ineffable, incomprehensible, infinite goal of freedom, which makes possible the distance to the object of our choice, the actual space of freedom. God is not one of the many realities with which we are concerned in the freedom of our affirmation or rejection, but originally God is the infinite horizon which alone makes the free choice of individual things possible. As such a horizon God is always encountered in the free act and is present in it. Thus freedom is necessarily freedom before God; even if God is not named, it is a yes or no to God. Certainly, the free act is always also concerned with a finite object which one considers, which one desires, realizes, loves or rejects, destroys, hates, and so forth. And in explicitly notional religious knowledge, in explicit religious action God, too, can, indeed must become one of the explicitly conceived individual objects of the freedom of choice, because in finite notional knowledge God is expressly conceived and thus, in a strange duplication, the horizon and condition of all knowledge is itself once more conceived within this horizon. But our freedom is not concerned with God only in this case. It is always concerned with God in yes or no, wherever it is truly itself. For real freedom with respect to an individual object is possible only where transcendence in knowledge and deed is directed to that infinite and never attained goal which is the sphere of God. Wherever in absolute engagement—which no adult can avoid indefinitely—freedom takes up a position toward a definite finite truth, regardless of whether this position is correct or not, there the ineffable Whither of transcendence which we call God is affirmed or denied in the yes or no to the ultimate possibility of freedom. Hence moral freedom is necessarily always also religious freedom; even if this is not expressly known, it is at least silently experienced in the fact that this freedom cannot be transmitted, in the responsibility and infinity of freedom. For the experience of freedom is inseparable from the experience of God; the exercise of freedom is always at least implicitly the decision between existential theism and atheism.

In this act of freedom we decide our own destiny. Of course, the one free act in which we realize ourselves once and for all is dispersed in space and time in our many free actions, in which the one fundamental decision of the one man or woman is enacted. As regards its content, the one free act in which we commit ourselves is either an act of loving communication with another "I," and thus with God, or the act of absolute egoism, which refuses the risk of lovingly entrusting ourselves to another. The essence of freedom consists in this absolute commitment of the subject. We do not everlastingly do this or that, we do not constantly react to ever-new objects and situations, but by doing what we do we make ourselves, once and for all, despite the temporal sequence. Freedom is not the capacity for indefinite revision, for always doing something different, but the one capacity that creates something final, something irrevocable and eternal, the capacity of what by itself is everlasting. Freedom alone creates that which is final. Certainly, this depends on the possibilities God has given to freedom, not only on the formal structure of freedom itself. But we know through Christian revelation that God has given God's self as the absolute possibility and the absolute future in what we call grace, Holy Spirit, and justification. Hence the innermost essence of freedom is the possibility of absolute self-commitment to radical finality through the final acceptance or rejection of the self-communication of God, who thus becomes the horizon, object, and subject of our freedom. The one drama of God and human beings is enacted in our daily, free, and personal life, and only because this drama takes place does freedom in a radical theological sense exist at all.

GRACE AND FREEDOM

This formal characterization of freedom does not prejudge and antici-pate the Christian message of freedom. First of all, I do not think that today there is or should still be a controversy between the Christian churches and denominations as to whether freedom exists in salvation and justification and whether the theology of human beings should or should not describe them as free beings. In my view there is at least to-day a distinct experience and teaching in Catholic theology according to which God must be understood as the all-efficient giver who gives to God's self both the potency of freedom and its good act accord-ing to God's grace that is neither derived nor compelled, and which nothing in human beings precedes. Hence all specious sharing out of divine and human causality in this matter is false and a heretical at-tack on the absolute sovereignty of God. Even in the Catholic, and not only in the Protestant view of the relation between God and human be-ings the freedom of the latter as derived only from themselves is guilty and imprisoned egoism; hence as far as they are concerned, this free-dom refuses to accept God's self-communication and to let God be God. Hence God's grace, which ultimately means God's sclf, must set freedom free for God. It can therefore perform its very own deed to which it is called, namely to receive God from God through God, only in this way, and thus all truth of human beings as free beings proclaims either this liberation of freedom by God or the freedom by which human beings become guilty before God. Thus the theological doctrine of free-dom proclaims the grace of God, while the "natural" freedom of human beings in potency and act is only the presupposition, created by God, to make it possible for God to give God's self to human beings in love. Thus understood, the doctrine of freedom need not be a point of con-troversy between the denominations. This doctrine of freedom can pass over the question whether it is described as a property of the "natural" essence of the human being or emerges only through the call of God, who reveals and communicates God's self as love. For, on the one hand, this interpretation of freedom is historically possible only in the specifi-cally Christian view of the human person as it has developed through the gospel message. On the other hand, it says of human beings what they always are, because they are always called by God and, through the offer of grace, are confronted with the absolute question even when they have not yet received the historical word of the gospel. If we finally say that human beings experience what is meant by God precisely while exercis-ing their responsible freedom we do not mean that the *Deus absconditus* [hidden God] has thus already become the *Deus revelatus* [revealed God]. Under the secret call of grace in which God offers God's self, this freedom is always meant either for judgment or salvation, and only the gospel says reliably where this leap of freedom leads: it encounters the God of forgiving grace, indeed it is made possible only by that God.

FREEDOM AS DEMAND AND POSSIBILITY

There are thus three aspects of freedom: freedom as deciding the relation to God, freedom as finality, and freedom as final self-commitment, and these imply that freedom has to be realized. This sounds like a commonplace, but it is not. For human beings regard freedom mostly as an existing fact and thus fail to consider the question that freedom is something that has to be realized, and as such is not a fact, but a demand. Hence human beings are inclined to regard freedom as indeed the cause of certain things, but which has a meaning only with regard to the deed it performs. They are greatly tempted to value only the objective results of human action and the objective human states, regardless of whether they have come into being with or without freedom. Only too easily will the free act appear to them as the origin indifferent in itself of an objective state which might have originated in principle just as well without freedom and must be valued only for what it is. But if freedom is the final self-realization of the subject before God and if this self-realization, this eternity of human beings, can happen only in freedom, if the eternity of the creature is but the fruit of freedom and its own finality, then freedom is that which has to be realized. Then there are objective finalities which have to be realized but cannot except in freedom; then the final act of freedom, which also translates time into eternity, is the only thing that is radically subjective, because it is irreversible and irrevocable. Then the eternally valid can be realized only through freedom. And this makes freedom as possibility and as deed the only ultimate objectivity which has to be realized. God's eternity which God bestows becomes really my own when it is accepted by freedom and thus becomes human-made eternity. True, the free act by which God's self-communication is accepted is itself the gift of God and can only be realized as grace. Nevertheless, God gives and can give God's self only by giving us the act of our own freedom which accepts God. Hence grace happens essentially and can exist only as the deliverance of freedom toward God. This is not the place to show that this concept of freedom either exists explicitly in the creed of the church or is implied by the teaching of Christianity, that free faith justifies, that salvation must be

121

received from God in freedom, and that the eternity of salvation is not an indefinite continuation of time but must be understood as the final result of history itself which is produced by freedom.

THE CORPOREAL NATURE OF FREEDOM AND ITS SPHERE

Before speaking of the existence of freedom and in freedom something will have to be said about the specifically human creatureliness of freedom which will clarify the dialectical character of our relation to our own and other people's freedom.

Every human action is connected with some materiality. Space and time constitute the external atmosphere in which the free human act is accomplished. For the body and soul of each person are not two realities which have subsequently been united, but two constituents of one and the same human being which cannot be reduced to each other. They are not two separate beings, but two metaphysically different constituents of the one human being. The body is the exterior of the so-called soul and thus the act of the soul translated into the exterior.

Hence our freedom is bodily freedom, and this means it is realized as the original self-determination of a personal subject in space and time. It must be furnished with such material in which it must express and embody itself. Subjective freedom can only be realized in objects that are not identical with it. It aims at foreign objects; when the subject realizes itself it changes that which is different from itself; when the free subject returns to itself it enters the sphere of the other in order to find itself. Even the innermost act is still external, because it belongs also to the physiological sphere which is open to external influences. Hence a perfect interiority of freedom is impossible. The external element is necessarily part of the self-realization of freedom. This sphere of foreign bodies is at the same time the one open space in which subjects communicate with other subjects and with the world. Despite its original subjectivity freedom is realized in the common sphere of the unity of historical subjects. By realizing my own freedom I also partly determine the sphere of the freedom of others. True, I do not change their freedom, but the sphere in which their freedom is realized, hence this affects the possibilities of their subjective freedom. Freedom is always realized in a concrete sphere. Persons who realize their freedom are not the untouchable Monads envisaged by Leibniz. Every free act of one person changes the objective possibilities of the free act of his or her neighbor, it enlarges, changes, or limits the sphere of the other's freedom before this latter can freely intervene. Hence the realization of freedom is a concrete problem of human relations. True, there is an absolute freedom, but no absolute sphere of freedom, for this would amount to the solipsistic denial of other free subjects. But this freedom which is realized in the social sphere must contain a moral demand to be respected by others. Hence the relation of many freedoms within a common sphere is, both individually and collectively, historically variable. Because of its objective embodiment every free act produces a change in the sphere of freedom shared by all, hence this sphere is in constant historical motion, it is, as it were, always distributed anew. Therefore the distribution of this sphere will always give rise to controversy. The question whether revolution can be justified would have to be discussed in this context. True, every man or woman will have his or her own personal section of freedom within its one whole sphere, but the size and character of this personal section are in constant flux and cannot be defined once and for all. Hence we cannot decide a priori the question of how this common sphere of freedom can best be divided so that the freedom of each individual as well as of the whole community is preserved. What once did not belong to the material of freedom might well be part of it today as well as the other way round. There is no authority in the whole world which could plan the division of this sphere autonomously and for ever. This is so because the acting subjects are necessarily many, if for no other reason than because even in the most totalitarian system there would have to be at least one subject which does the planning and cannot be planned himself or herself. Hence the unplanned change in the sphere of freedom always takes place in the factual decision and contains the elements of unreflected spontaneity.

For this reason the Christian's historical action in society, state, and church bears inevitably the character of the risk, of uncertainty, of walking in the dark. For we know not what to ask, we must beg for gracious guidance from above, beyond what can be calculated and foreseen. If, because of this risk, Christians think themselves dispensed of taking individual decisions they sin against the historicity of their existence and become all the more guilty. For they must not only proclaim the ever-valid principles but also risk the concrete future, trusting to God. As Christians, too, they must not only suffer but act, without the correctness and success of their action being guaranteed by the correctness of their principles. This is generally valid, but especially as regards freedom and compulsion and their concrete adjustment. Christians must not only have the courage to represent a balanced eternal doctrine, but also to enunciate a contemporary slogan which they may, in certain circumstances, do in the name of Christianity, even though it cannot be pronounced by the official church.

Thus it can be understood what the existence of (and in) freedom ultimately means. The theologian cannot analyze concrete dangers and duties connected with the handling of this one sphere of freedom by individuals and groups of women and men. Some theoretical considerations must suffice; but it is to be hoped that these, too, will be practically useful.

THE CHANGE IN THE SPHERE OF FREEDOM

In the history of the last centuries the sphere of freedom of the individual has both been enlarged and also become more threatened, because human beings themselves can actively change it. It has been enlarged especially by the technological achievement of the present civilization and by the immensely enlarged possibilities at our disposal. It has also been enlarged by the emancipation of the sexes, by religious and civic tolerance and freedom, by the increasing abolition of rigid social structures and taboos, in short, by what we call a pluralist social order. At the same time this sphere of freedom exists often only in appearance, because all these achievements and social conditions inevitably define this sphere of freedom in a very special way. They do this without the free decision of the individual, and thus this sphere of freedom does not remain empty, but contains a definite choice of objects from which human beings may choose in an always finite decision. This sphere of freedom is threatened and secretly determined by anonymous powers determining public opinion without being controlled themselves, which produce mass psychoses, direct consumption, and the ever more intricate relations of social life. Thus both the enlargement and the narrowing of the sphere of freedom are strangely interdependent, because such things as technology, automation, and the development of social relations which enlarge the sphere of freedom at the same time also furnish the means to restrict it.

THE CHRISTIAN'S YES
TO THE ENLARGED SPHERE OF FREEDOM

In accordance with their theology of freedom Christians will have, in principle, a positive attitude to the enlarged sphere of freedom. By its very nature freedom needs an uncluttered sphere in which to realize itself, even if this implies inevitably the possibility and danger of a guilty perversion of freedom. Hence, if freedom is to be, because it alone makes possible finality and eternity, there must also be a sphere of freedom despite all danger. The subjective exercise of freedom is the demand of what ought to be. Where subjective freedom is only regarded as a possible way of producing objective reality, subjective freedom will be justified only by its object. In the nineteenth century Catholic theologians often assumed that subjective freedom was only a neutral possibility to do something, without possessing a moral claim in itself. From this it followed quite easily that only truth and goodness have rights, but not error and evil, which, on the contrary, must be prevented.

It cannot be the duty of individuals or society to take away the sphere of freedom, even in the case of wrong decisions, from other human beings. This would always be an attack on the dignity of the person and his or her freedom, which is not a means to an end (in this case the compulsory realization of something good), but part of the meaning and goal of the human person.

Any enlargement of this—though somewhat dangerous—sphere of freedom increases the chance of producing freedom. If, therefore, this sphere is enlarged, even though not without human guilt, this should not, on principle, frighten Christians. If this sphere has become larger and inevitably more dangerous they may quite happily accept it as allowed by the Lord of history. They may admit that, relatively to all human civilization and society, there was formerly perhaps more that was specifically Christian in the world. But an outwardly homogeneous Christian society as the given sphere of freedom does not necessarily imply and guarantee that the Christian ethos is really realized in faith, hope, and love and thus really produces eternity. It may also happen that such a Christianity gives the impression of a kind of drill, almost of a subtle form of brainwashing, a sociological routine which may produce a bourgeois Christianity but not Christian freedom, and which therefore remains unimportant in the sight of God. From the Christian point of view a pluralistic society may, indeed, be dangerous and harm the stock of Christianity and the church. But God alone can know whether God may not produce from this as much fruit of freely achieved eternity as in the good old days of a united Christendom; God has not told us anything about it. However that may be, we Christians have every reason to regard the enlargement of the sphere of freedom through modern developments first of all as a positive chance for Christian existence, for as free children of God we can realize the grace of freedom that generates eternal salvation only in the freedom also of the natural spirit.

125

A Christian theology of freedom can regard any determination or limitation of the sphere of freedom only either as an inevitable consequence of the exercise of freedom by others, or as a provisional educational measure for the protection of a still maturing freedom. In the second case the aim will be to train men and women for making free decisions so that they will not be enslaved by powers which manipulate this space of freedom in such a way that moral freedom can no longer make its proper decisions within this sphere.

Freedom consists first of all in the courage to accept its larger sphere despite its danger. As it is given by God it is the divinely willed chance to exercise our freedom in it. This enlargement of the social sphere of freedom is actually of Christian origin and hence not actually suspect to Christians. True, throughout the history of Christianity and of the church the Christians themselves had slowly to learn—and this process is not yet finished—what their Christianity really means; they must ask this question again and again and answer it in ever-new situations which they cannot, of course, foresee and for which they will not have ready-made answers.

Thus Christians have not always been tolerant and freedom-minded. They have persecuted each other and non-Christians, often committing dreadful atrocities, and they have often canonized forms of society that were anything but free. We may mention, for example, the principle *cuius regio, eius religio* [one's religion shall be determined by the religion of the ruler], Leo X's bull *Exsurge Domine,* directed against Luther, which condemned the view that it was a sin against the Holy Spirit to burn heretics, or the ideology of the completely ecclesiastical state. But even though this may be admitted and regretted, it must nevertheless be realized that much in the behavior of Christians was not due to Christianity but to social conditions which had not been created by Christianity and actually blocked Christian possibilities and horizons. Moreover, much of it, even though contradicting the ultimate logic of Christianity, originated as a claim to absolute validity inherent in every great historical concept of the world such as is still only too evident in militant communism.

Nevertheless, it ought at last to be stated that the passion for social and cultural freedom is principally a Christian passion, even though Christians often had to learn it from those who had abandoned Christianity. For civic freedom, after all, originated in the toleration of the various Christian denominations. Freedom was first and most radically proclaimed as the freedom of faith and its confession. The dignity of the individual person is a Western experience grounded in the Christian knowledge of human beings as children of God and their eternal value as such. Let us ask quite simply: Would the inviolable dignity of every woman and man continue to be acknowledged if it did no longer receive its force—even secretly—from this fundamental conviction? If human beings are regarded merely as a material or social factor, why should they not be used for any purpose, without their dignity being respected or even known? I certainly do not mean that only Christians respect this intangible dignity of the unique individual. What I say is that this respect is adequately understood only in Christianity and that it is actually of Christian origin.

For this reason it behooves Christians above all to respect not only the freedom of belief but freedom in itself. Otherwise Christianity would betray itself. We Christians must not be interested in freedom only insofar as it affects our own religious or even ecclesial purposes. For freedom is truly indivisible. German Catholics as well as Protestants ought to admit that under the Nazis their official representatives did not realize this sufficiently to defend the freedom of others. For the best proof of one's devotion to freedom is the readiness to grant it also to others. At this point the seemingly merely human concept of freedom receives a strangely Christian character and depth. For if we are really concerned for the freedom of others, we shall be prepared to give up part of our own freedom. We shall make this sacrifice, appearing as weak and stupid, incapable of defending ourselves, as men and women who give without receiving anything in return. This is the attitude of the Sermon on the Mount and of him who could freely have saved his life, but surrendered it to the guilty freedom of others even unto death.

3

ON REVELATION
AND THE DEVELOPMENT OF DOGMA

As we have seen in the introduction to the second chapter, Rahner's "supernatural existential" is a key concept in his developing both a transcendental theology of grace and a theology of universal revelation. For Rahner, revelation will always be God's self-disclosure in a freely given intercommunion with God's people that begins at creation. As in his attempts to open up a theology of grace beyond the more constricted, extrinsicist textbook theology of neo-scholasticism, here too Rahner depicts divine revelation within the wider content of God's offering grace and salvation to all people. He claims that if this more universally graced outreach of God to creation is to be a possibility, then revelation must have a transcendental characteristic. God's entering into the world of creation to make God's self known and loved cannot, therefore, be limited only to the history of Jews and Christians. God must in some way draw near to all God's people in the context of their particular mode of life and worship. Such revelation is said to be transcendental because it is not reducible to biblical phrases, dogmatic propositions, church pronouncements, or published statements from the best authorities whether they be saint, pope, or mystic. This is not to deny the relationship between revelation and the Bible and so-called definitive church teaching. But such Rahner prefers to call "categorical revelation." Transcendental revelation, in contrast, is Rahner's way of portraying God's breaking into our personal world, entering our consciousness, not in any objectified manner but in the encounter with our deepest self in the restlessness of a heart yearning for fulfillment in God. This is the intercommunion of God with people, making God's self known but never fully grasped, touching people in the mystery of God's son's life and death but never fully unraveling the mystery of who God is and why God loves us so.

In his own subtle way Rahner undermines the Christian imperialism that declares God's revelation to have begun only with Judaism and to have been made perfect only with the Christian church. Such theological arrogance seems to limit God's revelation to a narrow, verifiable span of history, ignoring the universal outreach to all God's people by God, father to Abraham and Jesus, but father and mother also to those who knew neither Abraham nor Jesus. Rahner insists that beyond the highlight of revelation categorized in the Jewish and Christian traditions is the wider, infinite world of God's interrelation-

ship with all creatures in all the epochs of God's creation. The selections of this section include a segment from Rahner's most detailed analysis of universal, transcendental revelation as well as one of his earliest explanations of how one expression of categorical revelation, Christian dogma, can undergo development within the church.

UNIVERSAL, TRANSCENDENTAL REVELATION AND SPECIAL, CATEGORICAL REVELATION

In the selection that follows we see clearly the setting Rahner assigns to both universal, transcendental revelation and the special, categorical revelation one associates with the Jewish and Christian covenants. In all this Rahner affirms Jesus Christ to be the criterion of what constitutes authentic revelation. Only in Jesus, Rahner observes, do we have the unsurpassable event of God's self-communication to the world. But even in the case of Jesus, Rahner does not see any warranty to claim for a Christian community that it has more than a "provisional interpretation" or an "intrinsic dynamism toward the full revelation in Jesus Christ." Every religion, he argues, engages in the process of mediating the original, unreflective, nonobjective revelation of the living God and moving it into reflective, interpretative propositions. When this is done by the mediating prophets under God's own inspiration, then we have "what is called public, official, particular and ecclesially constituted revelation." But this officially approved version of revelation can never provide believers with the totality of who God is. Churches with their Bibles and dogmatic traditions are reminded by Rahner that the high point of God's self-giving in God's historical embodiment in Christ remains unsurpassed and unsurpassable. Knowledge of God can never be boxed into the formulas and books of one church or groupings of churches.

The text that follows is from the detailed section entitled "The History of Salvation and Revelation" in Rahner's Foundations of Christian Faith *(pp. 153–61, 170–75), a translation of* Grundkurs des Glaubens: Einführung in den Begriff des Christentums *(Basic course of faith: Introduction to the idea of Christianity), published by Herder of Freiburg in 1976. Rahner mentions in volume 19 of the* Theological Investigations *that originally he wanted as sole title of the book that which is now only the subtitle:* An Introduction to the Idea of Christianity. *He mentions his fears that the book could be taken as a popular catechism rather than as his attempt to bring Christianity as a whole under its dominant idea and thereby to reflect on the ultimate unity and intelligent coherence of what is proclaimed in Christianity. His section on revelation illustrates this effort to achieve some kind of unity out of the conflicting notions of what constitutes God's self-revelation in Christ to God's church.*

As God's real self-communication in grace, ... the history of salvation and revelation is coexistent and coextensive with the history of the world and of the human spirit, and hence also with the history of religion. Because there is self-transcendence on human beings' part through God's ontological and revelatory self-communication, the history of revelation takes place wherever this transcendental history has its history, and hence in the whole history of humankind. Up to now we have postulated this history of revelation and salvation in a more a priori way, but where and how it takes place in human history and how this universal, supernatural history of revelation allows for the necessity along with itself, or better, within itself, of that history of revelation which is usually called the history of revelation in an absolute sense are two questions which we can now consider and answer together.

THE ESSENTIAL AND NECESSARY
HISTORICAL SELF-INTERPRETATION
OF SUPERNATURAL, TRANSCENDENTAL EXPERIENCE

Supernatural, transcendental experience has a history, and does not just occur again and again as embedded in history, for transcendental experience as such has a history which is identical with human history, and does not just occur at certain points in this history.

In order to see from this vantage point the relationship, the necessity, and the difference between this transcendental history of salvation and revelation and the categorical, particular, and official history of salvation, two things especially have to be taken into account. First, the categorical history of human beings as spiritual subjects is always and everywhere the necessary but historical and objectifying self-interpretation of the transcendental experience which constitutes the realization of the human being's essence. Second, this realization of the human being's essence does not take place alongside the events of historical life, but within this historical life. The categorical, historical self-interpretation of what the human being is takes place not only, and not even in the first instance, by means of an explicit anthropology formulated in propositions. It takes place rather in the whole human history, in what each person does and what he or she suffers in individual life; in what we call simply the history of culture, of society, of the state, of art, of religion, and of the external, technical, and economic mastery of nature. It is here that this historical self-interpretation of human beings takes place, and not just when the philosophers begin to do anthropology. The theoretical reflection in a metaphysical or theological anthropology which we usually call humankind's self-interpretation and self-explanation is indeed necessary. But it is nevertheless bound to this total history of humankind and is a relatively secondary moment.

This self-interpretation must be understood as taking place in genuine history, and not as a biological, deterministic evolution. It is history, and therefore freedom, risk, hope, reaching out to the future and the possibility of failure. And it is only in all of this and in this way that human beings possess their transcendental experience as event, and with it their own essential self. This essential self cannot be possessed subjectively alongside the actualization of history. Therefore this self-interpretation of transcendental experience in history is essential and necessary. It belongs to the very constitution of transcendental experience, although these two elements are not simply the same thing in an identity which is given from the outset.

If, then, history exists in this way as the necessary and objectifying self-interpretation of transcendental experience, then there is a revelatory history of transcendental revelation as the necessary and historical self-interpretation of that original, transcendental experience which is constituted by God's self-communication. This historical self-communication of God can and must be understood as the history of revelation. For this history is the consequence and the objectification of this original self-communication of God which reveals God. It is its interpretation and hence its very history. We have no choice, then, but to call the history of the explicit self-interpretation of transcendental, supernatural experience in the life of the individual and of humankind, and in the propositional, theological anthropology which follows upon this experience, we have no choice but to call it the history of revelation.

ON THE NOTION OF A CATEGORICAL
AND SPECIAL HISTORY OF REVELATION

The categorical history of revelation, in an unthematic way and through everything which takes place in human history, can indeed be the historical mediation of the transcendental, supernatural experience of God as supernatural revelation. But the history of the transcendental revelation of God will necessarily show itself again and again to be a history which is taking place in an irreversible direction toward a highest and comprehensive self-interpretation of humankind. Consequently, it will be ever more intensely an explicitly religious self-interpretation of this supernatural, transcendental, and revelatory experience of God.

From this perspective we can now say: where such an explicitly religious and categorical history of revelation as the history of transcendental revelation through God's self-communication knows itself to be willed positively and to be directed by God, and is assured of the legitimacy of this knowledge in ways which are offered by this history, there we have the history of revelation in the sense which is usually associated with this word. To be sure, this mode of the history of revelation is only a species, a segment of the universal, categorical history of revelation. It is the most successful instance of the necessary self-interpretation of transcendental revelation, or better, it is the full realization of the essence of both revelations and their single history, both transcendental and categorical revelation in the unity and purity of their essence.

Admittedly this still leaves us with a concept of the categorical history of revelation which does not simply coincide unambiguously and exclusively with the Old and New Testament history of revelation. We have not come that far yet. For what we have just given as a kind of definition of the categorical history of revelation in the narrower sense, a definition which is therefore applicable unambiguously to the Old and New Testaments, does not necessarily have to apply only to the Old and New Testaments. When we say that in the word of God which God proclaims an Old Testament prophet really satisfies the narrower definition of what we are calling the categorical history of salvation, a definition based on the fact that this history knows itself to be a history of salvation explicitly willed and directed by God, this still does not answer the question whether this has not also occurred outside the Old and New Testament history of revelation.

If the transcendental and supernatural experience of God necessarily interprets itself historically, and therefore forms a categorical history of revelation, and if this is present everywhere, then this also means that such a history is always a history of revelation which is provisional and not yet completely successful, and which is still seeking itself, and it means especially that it is a history of revelation which is permeated and made obscure and ambiguous by humankind's guilt in a situation which is co-conditioned by guilt.

Therefore the history of revelation in the usual and especially the full sense of the term is found where this self-interpretation of God's transcendental self-communication in history succeeds, and where with certainty it reaches its self-awareness and its purity in such a way that it correctly knows itself to be guided and directed by God, and, protected by God against clinging tenaciously to what is provisional and to what is depraved, it discovers its own true self.

THE POSSIBILITY
OF A GENUINE HISTORY OF REVELATION
OUTSIDE THE OLD AND NEW TESTAMENTS

This is not to say that revelation in such essential purity is found *only* within the realm of the Old and New Testaments. At least in individual salvation history, there are no reasons against but many reasons for saying that in such an individual history of salvation and revelation there are moments of history in which the divine origins and the absolute correctness of a self-interpretation of the transcendental experience of God become manifest and achieve certainty about themselves.

But also in the collective history of humankind and in the history of its religion outside the economy of salvation in the Old and New Testaments, there can be such brief and partial histories within this categorical history of revelation in which a part of this self-reflection and reflexive self-presence of universal revelation and its history is found in its purity. But usually they will lack any tangible continuity among the various moments in these partial histories as far as we can see. In a history of guilt and of false religion they will always be shot through with a history of erroneous, sinful, or merely human interpretations of this original transcendental experience which is present thematically and unthematically everywhere in history.

Whatever in fact might be the situation with regard to this possibility, in principle it need not be denied. It presupposes only that this categorical history of revelation is understood or can be understood as a self-interpretation of the revelatory and transcendental experience of God. If this interpretation is correct, it must be understood as positively willed and directed by God because of God's real salvific will. "Direction" is understood here not as adventitious and coming from without, but rather as the immanent power of this divine self-communication. As coming freely from God and as given to humankind in history, it is of course a real and genuine history whose concrete course cannot be deduced a priori from some abstract principle. Rather, just like humankind's historical self-interpretation in other areas, it must be experienced, suffered, and accepted in history itself.

Christian historians of religion do not have to understand the non-Christian history of religion outside the Old and New Testaments merely as a history of human beings' religious activity, nor merely as depraved examples of their potentialities for establishing religion. They can observe and describe and analyze the phenomena in the history of non-Christian religions without reservations, and interpret them with regard to their ultimate intentions. If these historians of religion see the God of the Old and New Testament revelation also at work in those religions, however primitive they might be or however depraved, and these things of course do exist in the history of religion, then they are in no way prejudicing Christianity's absolute claims.

Since, however, there is obviously also a history of the opposite of salvation, these historians must not overlook this history and the history which is contrary to revelation within the history of the human race and of religious phenomena. But when and where they discover the history of real and genuine and supernatural revelation, which of course cannot be complete because it can only be complete in Jesus Christ, the crucified and risen one, their findings are not to be rejected a priori and dogmatically because of Christianity's absolute claims. They are rather simply cautioned to do their work in the history of religion objectively, and to see human beings as they really are: as beings who always and everywhere stand before the claim of God's self-communication in grace, and who are always and everywhere sinners who receive this grace of God in their history and again and again allow it to become depraved through their own fault. This of course raises the question about the concrete criteria for drawing distinctions.

JESUS CHRIST AS THE CRITERION

Not until the full and unsurpassable event of the historical self-objectification of God's self-communication to the world in Jesus Christ do we have an event which, as an eschatological event, fundamentally and absolutely precludes any historical corruption or any distorted interpretation in the further history of categorical revelation and of false religion. We shall have to supply the theological foundations of this assertion in the next chapter. In Jesus Christ, the crucified and risen one, then, we have a criterion for distinguishing in the concrete history of religion between what is a human misunderstanding of the transcendental experience of God, and what is the legitimate interpretation of this experience. It is only in him that such a discernment of spirits in an ultimate sense is possible.

It is in fact also true that with regard to the actual situation of the Old Testament history of revelation too, it is only in Christ that we Christians have the possibility of making a radical distinction between the categorical history of revelation in the full sense and in its purity, and the formation of human substitutes for it and misinterpretations of it. If as historians and scientists of religion, and independently of

our faith in Jesus Christ, we tried in an impartial and purely historical way to transpose ourselves back into the Old Testament and the
religious phenomena which are attested to historically there, we would
have no ultimate criterion for distinguishing from the perspective of the
essence of God's transcendental self-communication what is a pure and
legitimate manifestation and historical objectification of this divine self-
communication and what is an abbreviated, human corruption of it. We
would also have to distinguish here more precisely (but once again this
is impossible without taking Jesus Christ into account) between what
would be legitimate there as a provisional objectification at a particular time of the transcendental experience of God, which, although it is
only a provisional interpretation, does have an intrinsic dynamism toward the full revelation in Jesus Christ, and what was really a corruption
even when measured against the Old Testament situation at the time.

THE FUNCTION OF THE BEARERS OF REVELATION

Although the possibility and the actuality of a history of salvation and
revelation which is found outside of reflexive Christianity is beyond
doubt, there still remains the possibility of allowing for a special "official" history of revelation along with a universal, categorical history
of salvation and revelation which is the self-interpretation of the transcendental, supernatural experience of God. This special history then is
really identical with the Old and New Testament history. This categorical history of revelation in the Old and New Testaments can and must be
understood as the valid self-interpretation of God's transcendental self-
communication to humankind, and as the thematization of the universal
categorical history of this self-communication, which of course does not
necessarily have to be made thematic always and everywhere in a sacral
way. Those persons who were the original bearers of such a revealed
communication from God and whom we characterize as *prophets* in the
traditional terminology are to be understood as persons in whom the
self-interpretation of this supernatural, transcendental experience and
its history takes place in word and in deed. Hence something comes to
expression in the prophets which fundamentally is present everywhere
and in everyone, including ourselves who are not called prophets.

A self-interpretation and historical objectification of humankind's
supernatural transcendentality and its history need not and may not
be explained as a merely human and natural process of reflection and
objectification. For we are dealing with the self-interpretation of that
reality which is constituted by the personal self-communication of God,

and hence indeed by God. If it interprets itself historically, then God's self-interpretation occurs in history, and the concrete human bearers of such a self-interpretation are authorized by God in a real sense. This self-interpretation is not a subsequent process, but rather is an essential, historical moment within this supernatural transcendentality which is constituted by God's self-communication. Looked at from both God's side and human beings' side, it is not a static reality, but has its own history in the history of humankind. The historical objectification and self-interpretation of God's transcendental self-communication, therefore, is governed by the same absolute and supernatural salvific will of God and by the same supernatural salvific providence as that divine self-communication through which human beings are constituted in their concrete essence, and from out of which they enter into their most real history, into the history of this transcendental self-communication, into the history of salvation and revelation.

In theological terms the "light of faith" which is offered to every person, and the light by which the "prophets" grasp and proclaim the divine message from the center of human existence is the same light, especially since the message can really be heard properly only in the light of faith. Once again, this light is nothing else but the divinized subjectivity of humankind which is constituted by God's self-communication. Of course the notion of the prophetic light implies that historical and concrete configuration of the light of faith in which the transcendental experience of God is *correctly* mediated by concrete history and its interpretation. Looked at theologically and correctly, prophets are none other than believers who can express their transcendental experience of God correctly. Perhaps as distinguished from other believers, it is expressed in the prophets in such a way that it becomes for others too the correct and pure objectification of their own transcendental experience of God, and it can be recognized in this correctness and purity.

The notion of such a special, categorical revelation as we have just outlined it and the notion of a revelatory event which takes place in a prophet and is destined for others presuppose, of course, that not absolutely everybody is the prophetic voice of such a categorical and historical self-interpretation of God's transcendental revelation through self-communication. It presupposes rather that many receive and must receive such a self-interpretation from other individuals, not because they do not have this transcendental experience of God, but because it belongs to human beings' essence that their own experience of themselves, both in the realm of the human and in the realm of grace, is realized in the history of their interpersonal communication.

A self-interpretation which really succeeds and finds a living form takes place among women and men in such a way that particular people, their experiences, and their self-interpretation become a productive model, an animating power and a norm for others. This does not relativize the prophet. For this very self-interpretation which takes place in a pure objectification is the history of the transcendental self-communication of God. For this reason it is not only a gnoseological history of pure theory, but is a reality of history itself. As existing in an interpersonal world, persons arrive concretely at their own self-interpretation, however much it comes from within and enters within, only within the self-interpretation of their interpersonal world, and by participating in and receiving from the tradition of the historical self-interpretation of those people who form their interpersonal world from out of the past and through the present into the future.

A person always forms her or his own secular self-understanding only within a community of persons, in the experience of a history which she or he never makes alone, in dialogue, and in experience which reproduces the productive self-interpretation of other people. Therefore in their religious experience, too, human beings are always interpersonal beings, and this extends to the ultimate uniqueness of their subjectivity. The historical self-interpretation of one's own religious existence is not a solipsistic affair, but takes place necessarily in and through the historical experience of the religious self-interpretation of one's own world, of one's own "religious community." Its creative and unique figures, its prophets, succeed in a special way in objectifying historically the transcendental self-communication of God in the material of their history by the power of this self-communication of God. Consequently, they succeed in making possible the self-discovery in history of transcendental religious experience for other members of such a historical, interpersonal world.

There is no real difficulty in the fact that this implies something of a fluid boundary between believing prophets and "mere" believers. Insofar as there is a question of establishing a critical norm for and the legitimacy of the success of the historical self-interpretation of the transcendental experience of God in the historical words and deeds of a prophet, there can always still be an "absolute" difference between prophets and "simple believers." Such a criterion and such a legitimacy do not belong to every such self-interpretation in each and every believer by himself or herself. In any case they cannot be established for others because "signs" do not accompany every self-interpretation, and we shall have to discuss the sense and the function of these signs as a criterion of legitimacy. Where such a self-interpretation of the transcendental, supernatural experience of God takes place, an interpretation which is legitimate and destined for many others, there we have an event in the history of revelation in the *full* and usual sense of the term. There these events have sufficient continuity among themselves, and sufficient causal connections and relationships. There individual self-interpretations, which are therefore limited in their theme and in their depth, form a unity with others, and hence form a structure which is consistent and which binds the individual interpretations together.

THE ORIENTATION TOWARD UNIVERSALITY
IN THE PARTICULAR AND SUCCESSFUL
HISTORY OF REVELATION

Perhaps we have said enough to clarify the characteristics, the relationship, and the difference between the universal, both transcendental and categorical history of revelation, and the particular, regional history of revelation. They do not exclude each other, but rather mutually condition each other. The former, the universal history of revelation, both transcendental and categorical, reaches its complete essence and its full historical objectification in the particular, regional, categorical history of revelation. This is not to say that the former history of revelation may be overlooked because the latter exists. If the particular, categorical history of revelation, in which transcendental revelation is interpreted for a spatially or temporally defined group of people, is conceivable simply because in other areas of life as well there are spatially, temporally, and culturally limited self-interpretations of humankind in particular cultures and in limited epochs, nevertheless every correct self-interpretation of humankind's supernatural transcendentality as the fundamental element in the constitution of every person's existence has a fundamental meaning for all men and women. Every correct, regionally or temporally limited historical self-interpretation of humankind's supernatural relationship to God has therefore an intrinsic dynamism toward universalism, toward the mediation of an ever more adequate religious self-understanding for all men and women, although it might not be aware of this dynamism.

To what extent this fundamentally universal determination of a regionally or temporally limited categorical history of revelation is in fact operative under God's salvific providence, and in what explicit and tangible way or in what historical anonymity this takes place, these things of course can only be learned a posteriori from history itself, and cannot be deduced in an a priori way. If the "prophets" who appear in such a particular history of salvation and the religious institutions which are thereby founded have an "authority" vis-à-vis the individual person in his or her own religious self-interpretation, then we can and must also speak of an "official" particular, categorical history of revelation....

"NATURAL" REVELATION
AND GOD'S REAL SELF-REVELATION

If God creates something other than God's self and thereby creates it as something finite, if God creates spirit which recognizes this other as finite through its transcendence and hence in view of its ground, and if therefore at the same time it differentiates this ground as qualitatively and wholly other from what is merely finite, and as the ineffable and holy mystery, this already implies a certain disclosure of God as the infinite mystery. This is usually called the "natural revelation of God," although this is a misleading term. But this leaves God still unknown insofar as God becomes known only by analogy as mystery, insofar as God becomes known only negatively by way of a preeminence over the finite, and only by mediate reference, but God does not become known in God's self by direct immediacy to God. God's ultimate and unambiguous relationship to spiritual creatures cannot be known in this way. For in this kind of a natural, transcendental relationship to God the question is still unanswered whether God wants to be for us a silent and impenetrable mystery keeping us at a distance in our finiteness, or wants to be the radical closeness of self-communication; whether God wants to confront our sinful rejection of God in the depths of our conscience and in its categorical objectifications in history as judgment or as forgiveness.

Beyond this "natural revelation," which is really the presence of God as question, not as answer, there is the real revelation of God. This is not simply given with the spiritual being of women and men as transcendence, but rather has the character of an event. It is dialogical, and in it God speaks to human beings, and makes known to them something which cannot be known always and everywhere in the world simply through the necessary relation of all reality in the world to God in human beings' transcendence. This latter is the way we know the question about God and the fact that human beings are placed in question by this mystery. Rather, presupposing the world and transcendental spirit, the real revelation discloses something which is still unknown for human

139

beings from the world: the inner reality of God and God's personal and free relationship to spiritual creatures.

We do not have to raise the question here whether we as individuals could know by ourselves and with certainty that God *can* express God's self in this way or not. Whether the *possibility* of a self-communication of God in grace could be known from human beings and their transcendence, whether they could interpret their transcendence as the realm of a possible self-communication of God in God's own self, or whether God would have said that this realm is indeed given as the condition of possibility for a relationship to the absolute mystery, but could not be fulfilled by God's self-communication without being shattered, these are all questions which we will not treat here. God has in fact revealed God's self in this way. And at least from this we know that such a revelation through God's self-communication is in itself *possible*.

This revelation has two aspects, transcendental and historical, which are distinct but belong together. Both are necessary so that revelation can exist at all. These two aspects have a certain variability in their reciprocal relationship.

THE TRANSCENDENTAL ASPECT OF REVELATION

First of all, the historical and personal revelation in word encounters the inner, spiritual uniqueness of human beings. God communicates God's self to it in God's own most proper reality as spiritual luminosity, and gives human beings in their transcendence the possibility to accept this personal self-communication and self-disclosure, to listen and to accept it in faith, hope, and love in such a way that it is not brought down to the "level" of finite creatures as such. Rather, as the self-disclosure of God in God's very self, it can really "come" into humankind's midst. For the act of hearing, the acceptance of this self-disclosure and self-communication is borne by God through God's divinization of humankind.

This revelation is God giving God's self in absolute and also forgiving closeness, so that God is neither the absolute, remote, and distant one, nor judgment, although God could be both. Consequently, in this forgiving closeness God gives God's self as the inner fulfillment of unlimited transcendentality. The absolutely unlimited question is fulfilled and answered by God as the absolute answer.

What we have described in this way is called in Christian terminology sanctifying and justifying grace as a divinizing elevation of humankind. In this elevation God gives not only something different from God's self, but God's very own self, and the act of its acceptance is borne by God. Now insofar as, first of all, this grace was offered by God to all times and to all human beings in view of and in God's absolute willing of Jesus Christ, the God-man, and insofar as it is already effective as an offer, and, as we can hope, although we cannot know for sure, is accepted at least by the majority of men and women as the final result of the free act of their whole lives; insofar as, secondly, this grace alters human beings' consciousness and gives them, as scholastic theology says, a new, higher, and gratuitous, although unreflexive, formal object, that is, gives them transcendence toward the absolute being of God as beatifying; insofar as, thirdly, at least the horizon of the human spirit as the infinite question is filled by this ineffable self-communication of God with the believing trust that this infinite question is answered by God with the infinite answer which God is, it follows that through this grace the event of free grace and of God's self-communication is already given to all times. This inner self-communication of God in grace at the core of a spiritual person is destined for all men and women, in *all* of their dimensions, because all are to be integrated into the single salvation of the single and total person. Therefore all transcendent subjectivity possesses itself not for itself *alongside* history, but *in* this very history, which is precisely the history of human transcendence itself.

THE CATEGORICAL, HISTORICAL ASPECT OF REVELATION

God's self-revelation in the depths of the spiritual person is an a priori determination coming from grace and is in itself unreflexive. It is not in itself an objective, thematic expression; it is not something known objectively, but something within the realm of consciousness. But none of this means that this a priori determination exists for itself, and that in this apriority it could only become the object of a subsequent reflection which would have nothing intrinsically to do with the apriority of grace as such. Rather God's self-gift, the gratuitously elevated determination of humankind, the transcendental revelation is itself always mediated categorically in the world, because all of humankind's transcendentality has a history. It takes place in the historical material of a person's life, but does not for this reason become simply identical with it. If, then, this supernatural determination is to take place in the concrete, and especially, if God's self-revelation in grace is to become the principle of concrete action in its objective and reflexive consciousness, and hence also in the dimension of society, then God's nonobjective and unreflexive self-revelation in grace must always be present as mediated in objective and reflexive knowledge, regardless in the first instance of whether this is an explicitly and thematically religious mediation or not.

This "mediation" has its history, and it exists within this history under God's direction, which is nothing else but the dynamism of God's transcendental self-communication toward its historical realization and mediation, and hence this mediation is itself God's revelation. The history of the mediation of God's transcendental revelation is an intrinsic moment in the historicity of God's self-disclosure in grace. For by its very nature and not only because of the nature of humankind, this self-disclosure has a dynamism toward its own objectification, since it is the principle of the divinization of the creature in all of its dimensions.

The attempt is made in every religion, at least on human beings' part, to mediate the original, unreflexive, and nonobjective revelation historically, to make it reflexive and to interpret it in propositions. In all religions there are individual moments of such a successful mediation made possible by God's grace, moments when the supernatural, transcendental relationship of human beings to God through God's self-communication becomes self-reflexive. Through these moments God creates for human beings the possibility of salvation also in the dimension of their objectivity, their concrete historicity. But just as God has permitted human beings' guilt, and this guilt has its darkening and depraving effect on all of humankind's collective and social dimensions, this is also the case in the history of human beings' objectifying self-interpretation of gratuitous revelation. It is only partially successful, it always exists within a still unfinished history, it is intermixed with error, sinful delusions, and their objectifications, and these once again codetermine the religious situation of other people.

Whenever and wherever this objectification of revelation is accomplished for a community of people and not only for the individual existence of an individual as such; when the mediating translation is accomplished in those persons whom we then call religious prophets, bearers of revelation in the full sense, and when it is directed by God in the dynamism of God's divine self-communication in such a way that it remains pure, although it mediates perhaps only partial aspects of the transcendental revelation; and when this purity of revelation in its objectification by the prophets and our own call by this objectified revelation is shown to be legitimate for us by what we call signs, then we have what is called public, official, particular, and ecclesially constituted revelation and its history, we have what we are accustomed to call "revelation" in an absolute sense.

This kind of revelation not only has the character of event and is historical insofar as it is a free decision of God, and insofar as it calls for a free, historical response on the part of every person. This revelation is also historical and particular in the sense that it does not take place everywhere in this official and, as it were, reflexively guaranteed purity. Rather, it has a special history within universal history and within the universal history of religion. Although this universal history and the history of religion themselves always remain the history of revelation, and although this particular history of revelation in its purity and as reflexively guaranteed always has a more remote or a more proximate significance for the history of everyone, the particular history of revelation still remains a moment within the universal history of salvation and revelation, although an immanent moment. In view of the genuine historicity of human beings who necessarily exist in a world of personal relationships, this is no more surprising than it is surprising that in other areas of their history there are preeminent historical events which cannot be repeated every day.

THE UNSURPASSABLE CLIMAX OF ALL REVELATION

If history is also the history of what is always unique and unrepeatable, then universal history always contains particular history, and this latter still always remains a moment within the whole universal history. Insofar as this revelation has a history because of the historicity of reflection upon God's self-gift to human beings in grace—and indeed this history is differentiated within universal history—the history of revelation has its absolute climax when God's self-communication reaches its unsurpassable high point through the hypostatic union and in the incarnation of God in the created, spiritual reality of Jesus for his own sake, and hence for the sake of all of us. But this takes place in the incarnation of the Logos because here what is expressed and communicated, namely, God, and, secondly, the mode of expression, that is, the human reality of Christ in his life and in his final state, and, thirdly, the recipient Jesus in grace and in the vision of God, all three have become absolutely one. In Jesus, God's communication to us in grace and at the same time its categorical self-interpretation in the corporeal, tangible, and social dimension have reached their climax, have become revelation in an absolute sense. But this means that the event of Christ becomes for us the only really tangible caesura in the universal history of salvation and revelation, and it enables us to distinguish a particular and official history of revelation within the universal history of revelation before Christ.

*

THE DEVELOPMENT OF DOGMA

Rahner's thoughts on the development of dogma reinforce, in a way, what he has already affirmed to be categorical revelation. Following the advent of God's becoming known in the unreflexive, nonobjective moment of an experiential intercommunion with God's people, there begins the reflexive, categorical thematizing of this in various forms including the Bible, Christian tradition, church teaching, and other forms related to the human attempt to cope with knowledge of the divine. Dogma represents the phase of a human quest to understand through a theology that can never fully grasp but must ever try to articulate and interpret this revelation. Just as there is a history of revelation, so too, for Rahner, there must also be a history of faith, of theology, and of dogma. In this, Rahner consistently points out that God's word is directed to people through the medium of historical processes. As a consequence revelation is historically conditioned. What was originally heard must be pondered and translated into words or propositions that are themselves bound to the human world of qualified conceptual expression. But, as Rahner notes, this does not mean that the presence of the Holy Spirit and God's continuing communion with humans in their unthematized, unobjectified experience of God cease with a church's de fide *declarations. God's continuing presence, impacting on the church and entering into personal relationship with God's people, inspirits a development in and a deeper penetration of the dogmatic expression of this most fundamental of mysteries, God's graced presence as Father, Son, and Spirit in the community openly proclaiming faith in God. According to Rahner, dogma develops under this inspiriting influence and not as a mere logical deduction or adaptation from an already fixated-in-time conceptual content.*

The following essay was originally published in two issues of the journal Wissenschaft und Weltbild *(Science and worldview) in 1954 and was incorporated into volume 1 of the* Schriften *in that same year. The English translation is from volume 1 of* Theological Investigations *(pp. 39–51). The essay strikes a delicate balance between arguing for a more open attitude toward dogmatic development and a deference to church authority. Rahner acknowledges that church authorities are "the court of last appeal." But he also cautions against the wrong turns away from the truth that are also a possibility, given the ever-present danger of a pseudotheological speculation and visionary deception. As he wryly comments, such dangers are not unexpected in any situation, given the human factor in the church. One must trust the Holy Spirit; and in this, as he sees it, what were thought by church authorities to be clear, unequivocal, and unsurpassable formulations of dogma give evidence, on the contrary, of genuine historical development and conditioning.*

Furthermore, he denies that there is any universally applicable formula for regulating dogmatic development to bring it more into control of ecclesiastical legislation. He offers, nonetheless, some principles for appreciating and eventually accepting such transformations within the teachings of the church said to possess "a portion of the revelation which has fallen to her share as the object of her unconditional faith." First of all, Rahner recognizes the inherent limitedness of anything finite to capture in language the infinite. But the inadequacy of human words, he adds, does not necessarily make these statements either false or half-false. In effect, the concrete historical, contingent reality of being human conditions the word of God. Second, development is necessary because human hearing of the word of God demands the medium of historical processes in which what was originally spoken must reach people of an entirely different historical situation if the word is to inspire an increased depth of faith and decisive deeds. Otherwise, dogma dies the death of monotonous abstraction. Even propositions of faith supposedly closed to any further development—and here Rahner uses the example of a seemingly etched-in-stone contention by the church that revelation was closed with the death of the last apostle—can assume an entirely different meaning. Rahner probes the formula for dogma's deeper significance to a searching believer of the twentieth century. The openness for Rahner is, of course, through the abiding presence of Christ resurrected in a fullness of revelation and through a Spirit continuing to move human consciousness to enter into living contact with the reality affirmed. Through his resurrected presence, the living Christ remains present in the church and continues to reveal his Father to countless new generations of Christians.

This essay set a pace for Rahner's later contributions to the church document Mysterium Ecclesiae, *of 1973. In this document, contrary to past magisterial pronouncements, both a hierarchy of truths and genuine history of dogmas were affirmed, although, as Rahner later commented, the assertion that the church always produced better formulas could have been said to work in another direction as well, the church's ability to generate worse formulas ("Mysterium Ecclesiae,"* Cross Currents 23, *no. 2 [Summer 1973], 192). It is obvious that Rahner wished to avoid dogmatic relativism. But at the same time, he argues convincingly the need for a sense of history, culture, and language, so that dogmatic formulations barnacled with age and ambiguity can be given new life in better, more suitable statements, faithful to the original word that was fully revealed only to the mind of the risen Lord, from whom the church derives its identity as way, truth, and life.*

Many of the church's doctrines are characterized by the fact that they have not always been present in the church and in its consciousness in faith in an expressly apprehensible form. The bodily assumption of our Lady into heaven is an example of this which touches us especially closely today. This doctrine has not always been in existence as an explicit statement; at any rate we today cannot grasp it or point to it as something in the past with a persistent identity; it seems not to have been proposed to the faith of every age with the clarity, the precision, the definiteness, and the binding character which it has today. That is to say it has—in a certain sense—"developed," it has, in a sense still to be determined, "come to be" within the course of Christian history, for when the gospel was first preached this doctrine was not to be found in its present form.

But if we are to gain a true understanding of this doctrine (and all those others which are characterized by such a "development"), we are forced to make some fundamental reflections on the meaning, the possibility, and the limits of such a "development of dogma" in general. Of course this is a heavy undertaking, because whatever the general meaning, possibility, and limits of a development of dogma may be, they cannot be deduced with the necessary exactness and precision from general theological considerations alone but must be arrived at inductively from the actual facts of such a development. In itself this is not remarkable: we discover the possible from the real. We discover the laws of development of a living thing—and of something spiritually alive too, regarded as a process of spiritual unfolding—from its actual development. But in our case this has its special difficulties; for the living spirit with which we are concerned here appears in its authentic form in a solitary instance: the unique historical fortune of the gospel of Christ under the direction of that Spirit which leads us into all truth, from the time of Christ himself to the moment when by his return faith will be transformed into the vision of God, face to face. We have here a homogeneous process of which there is just one instance. Certainly it has its laws, with which it emerged from the very beginning; it takes place according to laws promulgated at the very beginning, by which it remains bound for ever and ever and which are in force throughout the whole course of a history that has been guaranteed by the Spirit. Moreover laws certainly exist which may be observed in a section of this total process, and which can then be applied to other (later) phases and partial developments. The *perfected* law of dogmatic development however may only be laid down when the whole unique process has reached its term. And because it is a genuinely historical process, under the impulse of the Spirit of God, which never makes itself accessible without remainder to laws which can be grasped by human minds, it is never just the working out of a formula and an all-embracing law.

It is manifestly erroneous a priori to attempt to construct an adequate formula of this kind, and by this means to master the single sense of this process and combat possible "deviations" as false developments. The historical course of the development of dogma is itself the process in which its own mystery is progressively unveiled. It is in the very act of developing, and not in any prior reflection, that the living reality of the church's consciousness in faith comes progressively into a fuller possession of itself. Let us suppose that in the development of the doctrine of the assumption, for example, forms and properties of the development of dogma become apparent which cannot be demonstrated with the same clarity in other phases and sectors of this development; these properties may even clearly be of a kind which do not harmonize with the accounts of development given in the ordinary theological treatment (not of course in the authoritative pronouncements of the church). Yet this would not indicate any false development here, a "rank growth" in the development of doctrine; at most it would be a sign that the scheme proposed in the average treatment requires to be improved, qualified, or enlarged.

An anxious theologian may inquire, "How are we to get anywhere, if no adequate laws of this development can be formulated? Are we not leaving the field open to the rankest proliferations of pseudotheological speculation and callow visionary enthusiasm?" The answer is that this danger, one which is involved in all human experience, is not going to be realized for three reasons. In the first place there are of course certain laws of dogmatic development which, because they are known a priori (we shall discuss this later), may be applied to "developments" in an obvious way—though certainly with prudence—in order to determine whether they are genuine developments of the faith of the church or on the other hand contain the danger of a wrong turning. Such laws do exist, even if they can be applied only in the church and in the last resort only *by* the church itself; for applications made by individual Christians and theologians are never more than appeals to the church itself, which consequently has to be recognized as the court of last appeal. Second, just as with all living things, every advance achieved in this world of the finite, of shadows and images, always has something final about it and inevitably marks a restriction of future possibilities. The fuller and clearer truth becomes, the more strict it becomes, and more thoroughly excludes possibilities of future error. Looked at from this point of view, progress in the development of dogmas must in a certain respect become progressively slower, which is not to say that it must come to a standstill. Third, and this is the decisive point, the danger of the human factor simply remains a danger, and no precautionary measures exist which can exclude it unambiguously at the very start. Any attempt to protect oneself by human sharpsightedness against such a danger, so that it is simply not *possible* for anything to "slip through," is itself radically false. It is the promise of the Spirit and that alone which prevents the final realization of an ever-present danger.

After these preliminary remarks we have now to consider a few essential features of a Catholic doctrinal development. From what has been said it will be clear why it is impossible to propose an interpretation *merely* in terms of a universally applicable formula or indeed one which is authoritatively taught by the church. The general theory of the development of dogma is still in a rudimentary stage, because the history from which it must in large part be derived is not nearly sufficiently investigated for the purpose. All the same a few principles may be set down.

In the first place it is obvious that a revealed truth remains what it is, remains precisely "true," that is, it corresponds to reality and is always binding. What the church has once taken possession of as a portion of the revelation which has fallen to its share, as the object of its unconditional faith, is from then on its permanently valid possession. No doctrinal development could be merely the reflection of a general history of humanity, a history of civilizations containing nothing but the objectivization of the everchanging sentiments, opinions, and attitudes of a continual succession of historical epochs. Such a historical relativism is simply false, metaphysically and still more theologically. Yet all human statements, even those in which faith expresses God's saving truths, are finite. By this we mean that they never declare the *whole* of a reality. In the last resort every reality, even the most limited, is connected with and related to every other reality. The most wretched little physical process isolated in a carefully contrived experiment can only be described adequately if investigators possess the one comprehensive and exhaustive formula for the whole cosmos. But they do not possess such a formula; they could have it if and only if they could place themselves in their own physical reality at a point which lay absolutely outside the cosmos—which is impossible. This is even more true of spiritual and divine realities. The statements which we make about them, relying on the word of God which itself became "flesh" in human words, can never express them once and for all in an entirely adequate form. But they are not for this reason false. They are an *adaequatio intellectus et rei* [correspondence of the mind and the thing], insofar as they state absolutely nothing which is false. Anyone who wants to call them "half false" because they do not state everything about the whole truth of the matter in question, would eventually abolish the distinction between truth and falsehood. On the other hand, anyone who proposes to regard these propositions of faith, because they are wholly true, as in themselves *adequate* to the matter in question, that is, as exhaustive statements, would be falsely elevating human truth to God's simple and exhaustive knowledge of God's self and of all that takes its origin from God. Just because they are true, an infinite qualitative difference separates them, in spite of their finitude, from false propositions, however hard it may (even often) be in individual cases accurately to determine in the concrete where the boundary lies between an inadequate and a false statement. But because our statements about the infinite divine realities are finite and hence in this sense inadequate—that is, while actually corresponding to reality, yet not simply congruent with it—so every formula in which the faith is expressed can in principle be surpassed while still retaining its truth. That is to say, in principle at least it can be replaced by another which states the same thing, and what is more states it not only without excluding more extensive, more delicately nuanced prospects, but positively opening them up: prospects on to facts, realities, truths, which had not been seen explicitly in the earlier formulation and which make it possible to see the same reality from a new point of view, in a fresh perspective.

Now this evolution within the same truth is not, at any rate not necessarily, the play of empty curiosity; it can have an essential significance for human beings and their salvation. The human mind is not like a photographic plate, which without preference or alteration simply registers anything which falls upon it at a particular isolated moment. Rather, in order simply to understand what they see or hear, human beings must react, take up a stand, bring the new experience into connection with what they already know or have been affected by or dealt with, the whole historical sum of their experience. They must find a place for their own reality, their own lives and conduct in the order of divine truth, and direct their lives accordingly; and this is a matter of faith and love and observance, in worship, in the ordinances and the activity of the church, and in their day-to-day lives in the world. And so they can never abstract from what they are, from their ever-new, changing historical reality. For it is not just their unchangeable metaphysical "entity" which they have to insert into the economy of God's message, but their concrete, historical, "contingent" reality, their "existence" with all it includes: their talents, their particular, limited, and evolving endowments; the spirit of their time, the possibilities of their epoch; their concepts, which, granting all the fixity of metaphysical truth, are nonetheless historically conditioned; the particular task, always changing and always sharply defined, which is set them by their inescapable situation in the world—and this situation again must never be thought of as just the result of a secular historical development, but is itself the result of Christ's government of his church, as he gradually leads it, sometimes by new ways, through a changing reality to its own single truth. If human beings do all this—and they must do it, because they always have their eyes (metaphysically and theologically) on the absolute, though always from a finite historical viewpoint—no change takes place in the divine reality, nor do the true propositions concerning this reality become false; but there is a certain change in the perspective in which they see the reality through these propositions: they express this reality differently, they can state something new about it which they had not explicitly noticed before. The decisive feature of such a change is not "progress" in the sense of acquiring a sort of plus-quantity of knowledge (as though the church were somehow to become "cleverer"), but (in principle, at least) the change, the new look, of the same reality and truth, appropriate to just this age of the church: it is change in, not of, identity. By this again is not meant that the change is necessarily an entire abandonment of the earlier view or perspective; this would be a conception of change as we see it in the material and not in the spiritual realm. The mind of humanity, and even more the church, has a "memory." They change while they preserve, they become new without losing anything of the old. We today have our own philosophy, while we still philosophize with Plato and his abiding truth. And still more we have our theology, which bears the undeniable stamp of our time, while we continue to learn anew from Scripture, the fathers, the scholastics. If we fail either to preserve or to change, we should betray the truth, either by falling into error or by failing to make the truth our own in a really existential way.

Now it may at first sight seem that this formulation of the concept of a change within a single abiding truth is concerned just with what could be called "theology" as opposed to revealed faith. We should then be dealing merely with the human understanding of revelation, which as it were circles continually round this fixed point of Scripture and perhaps a few fixed data of (early) tradition too: at once removed from it and gravitating toward it. Thus we should be dealing all the time with *theology*, with something which could never become the authentic and plenary revealed word which grasps revelation itself. Such a relation between revelation on the one hand, and human understanding (always conditioned by time and situation, and striving to reach perfection) on the other, does undoubtedly exist. In relation to revelation there is such a thing as theology, the human word which seeks to express and understand the revealed; so that one can have no certain guarantee from revelation itself that the attempt has been successful. But there is question not only of a theology which evolves and revolves round the fixed point of a revealed utterance which has been pronounced once and for all. There exists not only a development of theology but also a development of dogma, not only a history of theology but also (after Christ, if only in the same Christ) a history of faith; and this for two reasons. First, the church understands its doctrinal decisions not just as "theology" but as the word of faith—not indeed as newly revealed but as the word which utters revelation itself truly and with binding force. Second, this doctrinal word can be understood within broad limits and at the same time not as a merely external, verbal modification of the original revealed propositions. On the contrary it is very often impossible to say that the new doctrinal utterance is simply the old one "differently expressed," so that individual Christians cannot invariably limit its doctrinal content a priori to what they themselves could recognize as "identical" with the corresponding declaration made previously. For example, the declarations of Nicaea and Florence on the mystery of the blessed Trinity, which are intended to be propositions of faith and not merely theological explorations, have a fixed meaning. This meaning is proposed as an object of faith, even if I myself as an individual Christian and a private theologian do not succeed in demonstrating off my own bat, that is, by the methods of philological exegesis, that these declarations say "just the same as," "only in other words," what I have been able to extract from Scripture and early tradition "by a critical study of the sources." There can of course be no question of a contradiction between the two sets of propositions, and such a contradiction could never be demonstrated historically. We shall return later to the question as to how the difference (varying in magnitude, presumably, according to the matter under consideration) between an earlier and a later pronouncement of the magisterium may more exactly be understood *objectively*. For the moment it is sufficient to establish the fact that *quoad nos* [as it relates to us], at least, that is, for the individual and his or her private theology, such a difference can and in many cases does exist: that is, that at least in this one sense *quoad nos* a development of dogma does in fact exist, as shown in the actual practice of the church when it proclaims a doctrine.

It is also relatively easy to see that a development of this kind must *necessarily* exist. God's revealing word is directed through the medium of the historical process at the *total* history of humanity (speaking generally). For this reason the historically conditioned mode in which revelation is appropriated at any time need not lie absolutely outside this revelation itself. For the real understanding of what is revealed and its existential appropriation by human beings is wholly dependent on the transformation of the propositions of faith, as they were originally heard, into propositions which relate what is heard to the historical situation of the men and women who hear; it is only then that they become propositions of faith, emerging into the real, historically conditioned world of men and women as decision and living deed. If these translating propositions are just theology and nothing more, "private interpretations" of the original propositions; if there were no guarantee that the proposition heard has been correctly understood: then on the one hand the proclamation of faith itself could only be a monotonous repetition, with a purely material accuracy, of the same propositions of Scripture (and perhaps of a limited early tradition as well); and on the other what we have understood of it, in the situation which is precisely ours, would be subjective theology—an appropriation of the faith, which is itself faith, would not come to pass.

What has so far been said is only intended to indicate briefly the fact of a dogmatic development, and offer a first approximation to an understanding of its nature. In order to grasp its nature more clearly, we shall take as our starting point a proposition which belongs to the basic pronouncements of the magisterium on faith, and which apparently points in a direction contrary to that indicated by the proposition that a development of dogma is both possible and has actually taken place.

It is a doctrine of the church, though not in the strict sense a defined one, that revelation "was closed with the death of the (last) apostle(s)" (Denzinger, *Enchiridion Symbolorum,* 2020 s.). What does this proposition mean? It would be false to interpret it as meaning more or less that when the last apostle died there was left a fixed summary of strictly drafted propositions like a legal code with its clearly defined paragraphs, a sort of definitive catechism, which, while itself remaining fixed, was going to be for ever expounded, explained, and commented upon. An idea like this would do justice neither to the mode of being proper to intellectual knowledge nor to the fullness of life of divine faith and its content. When we try to discover the profound reasons for the completeness of revelation, we begin to see how we should approach the interpretation of this proposition. To start with, revelation is not the communication of a definite number of propositions, a numerical sum, to which additions may conceivably be made at will or which can suddenly and arbitrarily be limited, but a historical dialogue between God and human beings in which something *happens*, and in which the communication is related to the continuous "happening" and enterprise of God. This dialogue moves to a quite definite term, in which first the *happening* and *consequently* the communication comes to its never-to-be-surpassed climax and so to its conclusion. Revelation is a saving happening, and only then and in relation to this a communication of "truths." This continuous happening of saving history has now reached its never-to-be-surpassed climax in Jesus Christ: God has definitively given God's self to the world. Christianity is not a phase or epoch of a history of world civilizations which could be displaced by another phase, another secular "aeon." If formerly, before Christ, something took place in history, it was and is invariably conditioned, provisional, something with its own limited range and endurance and thus leading to death and emptiness: one aeon after another. The present always dies in the future. Each age goes by in successive rise and fall, infinitely far from the true eternity which abides beyond: each carries its own death within it, from the moment of its birth: civilizations, nations, states, or intellectual, political, economic systems. *Before* Christ even God's enterprise of self-revelation to the world was "open": times and orders of salvation were created and displaced each other, and it was still not apparent how God was going at last to respond to the human answer, usually negative, to God's own initiating act: whether the ultimate utterance of God's creative word would be the word of wrath or of love.

But "now" the definitive reality is established, one which can no longer become obsolete or be displaced: the indissoluble, irrevocable presence of God in the world as salvation, love, and forgiveness, as communication to the world of the most intimate depths of the divine reality itself and of its trinitarian life: Christ. *Now* there is nothing more to come: no new age, no other aeon, no fresh plan of salvation, but only the unveiling of what is already "here" as God's presence at the end of a human time stretched out to breaking point: the last and eternally the latest, newest day. It is because the definitive reality which resolves history proper is already here that revelation is "closed." Closed, because open to the concealed presence of divine plenitude in Christ. Nothing new remains to be said, not as though there were not still much to say, but because everything has been said, everything given in the son of love, in whom God and the world have become one, forever without confusion, but forever undivided. That revelation has been closed is a positive and not a negative statement, a pure *Amen*, a conclusion which includes everything and excludes nothing of the divine plenitude, conclusion as fulfilled presence of an all-embracing plenitude.

It is further to be observed that the "closed" revelation with which we are concerned here is a revelation made to the believing church, in possession of the revealed reality itself. A sure knowledge of this reality of divine salvation can only be gained through the divine tidings and through the faith which comes from hearing and speaks in human concepts and human propositions. Any attempts to transcend this divine message—in some "religious experience" or emotive state, some experimental contact eliminating the faith which hears—so as to grasp this reality immediately and without reference to the message, is delusive and impossible, and must inevitably lead to a modernistic rationalization of Christianity. Our religion, insofar as it moves within the sphere of our intellectual and moral "consciousness," is inseparably dependent upon the announcing word. But in the aeon of Christ it is not just of the remote future that this word brings us tidings, a mere anticipatory shadow of a reality still to come, but it utters what is present. The believing church possesses what it believes: Christ, his Spirit, the earnest of eternal life and its vital powers. It cannot leave the word behind in order to grasp this reality. But no more does it possess a word about the thing instead of the thing itself. Consequently its hearing of the word and its reflection upon the word heard are not *merely* a logical activity, an attempt gradually to squeeze out all the logical virtualities and consequences of the word heard as though it were a numerical sum of propositions; they are a reflection on the propositions heard in living contact with the thing itself. This reflective consideration practiced by the church, which takes place in us as a "theological" comprehension, unfolding and clarification of the church's faith, results in "new" propositions of faith and not just theology, takes place simultaneously in the word and in the thing itself: each in the other, neither without the other. Or putting it differently, the light of faith and the assistance of the Spirit which are at work in this reflection and progressive self-achievement do not mean just a sort of supervision given by a teacher. The concern of teachers is to see that their pupils do not go astray in their calculations and deductions, so that what the pupils learn (if they proceed correctly) is due only to their own insight and logical acumen and the virtualities of their own premises. It is much more in the actual result that the light of the Spirit and of faith exert their influence: the hidden but present and posited reality takes part in its own understanding. The "unction" teaches. We find a reflected image there of what we have seen with our own eyes of the living word of truth, what we have looked upon and touched with our hands (1 John 1:1). Consequently we need not be able to isolate this light and its operation reflexively, as against other impulses by which we grow and advance in the knowledge of faith.

Even in the natural order reflection upon our mental processes never quite exhausts what are in fact the grounds and motives at work in our intellectual growth or our behavior: we always understand more by a direct and simple view of things than reflection and the detailed analysis of this intellectual vision can produce for inspection, our behavior is always more variously motivated than prior or subsequent reflection upon it can make explicit. The common man and woman, still more, in their direct apprehension of the objects of everyday life, have not reflective or theoretical awareness of the nature of their intellectual powers or of formal logic, while they do in fact make use of both. How much more true this is of knowledge in faith, and how much more it is a question of principle here! The light of faith, the impulse of the Spirit, do not permit of being isolated for inspection by a reflective process in which attention is turned back upon itself and withdrawn from the object of faith. They are the brightness which illuminates the object of faith, the horizon within which it is contained, the mysterious sympathy with which it is understood, and not properly the object directly regarded, not a sun which we can immediately contemplate. But they are present and take part in the apprehension and unfolding of the object of faith; they form the cooperating subjectivity (God's and caused by God) with which the word is for the first time understood in the act of hearing and understood ever new. Knowledge in faith takes place in the power of the Spirit of God, while at the same time that Spirit is the concrete reality believed: Spirit of the Father and of the Son, Spirit of the crucified and ascended, Spirit of the church and earnest of eternal life, Spirit of justification, holiness, and freedom from sin and death. It follows that the object of faith is not something merely passive, indifferently set over against a subjective attitude to it, but simultaneously the principle by which it is itself grasped as object. This statement of course only acquires its full significance on the assumption that the actual support given to faith under the grace of the Holy Spirit is not a merely ontological modality of the act of faith beyond conscious apprehension, but also has a specific effect in consciousness (which is not necessarily to say that it is reflectively distinguishable). This effect makes it possible to apprehend the objects of faith given through the hearing of the external announcement, under a "light," a subjective a priori under grace (the formal object), which is not available to someone without grace.

4

ON THE DOCTRINE OF GOD

How to discern and how to relate to the God who is both the holy mystery at the origins of and conferring meaning on human existence are problems that Rahner's theology addresses at nearly every turn. No single selection or any proliferation of selections within the bounds of this book can adequately embrace all the facets of Rahner's doctrine of God. Indeed, in many ways, all the selections of this book, like most of Rahner's writings, are a continual probing into the reality of God's palpable yet mysterious presence in this world and in human life everywhere.

Despite the wide variety of Rahner's approaches to the problem of God, his reflections witness to a remarkable consistency in that, whether he is writing a sermon, a meditation, a philosophical treatise, or theological analysis, his God remains as always the one who elicits the Ignatian joy of finding God in all things, and who fills the human spirit with a restless attraction that promises fulfillment only in communion with God. Hence, for Rahner, now matter how complex the analyses of God may become, this God can be appreciated only in God's graced relationships with God's creation. In an unfathomable offer of personal intimacy to God's people, God speaks the free word of God's son in their Spirit, illuminating the finite spirit of God's creatures and bringing them into the orbit of God's own transcendence. But because God remains free, autonomous, and personal, any knowledge of God goes only as far as God's free decision and the created, contingent capacity of human beings in their historical, somatic possibilities of development as humans. Hence knowledge of God, like knowledge of persons, has not only an inherent limitedness but also an infinitely expanding possibility for further growth in the knowledge and love of what Augustine called the "beauty ever ancient and ever new." The selections from Rahner's writings that follow have been chosen because they illustrate how he attempts to open up Catholic dogmatics to the wider perspectives suggested by his own Ignatian spirituality and the pastoral implications of his theological anthropology.

OBSERVATIONS ON THE DOCTRINE OF GOD
IN CATHOLIC DOGMATICS

In this essay Rahner shares his opinion of how "classic" Catholic dogmatics has analyzed the problem of God. It is, indeed, a "sharing," but it is at the same time an occasion for Rahner to explore the wider contexts and deeper implications lurking in dogmatic statements said to be unchangeable. He refuses to accept as the last word on the nature of God the metaphysical attributes that fit so well into the logical categories of neo-scholastic thought. He wishes, as he states in the beginning of the essay, to be "radical," that is, to topple the idols that stand for God and the idolatrous theories that reduce knowledge of God to ecclesiastically approved statements. He contends, rather, that God is to be found in relationships in which personal freedom and mutual giving yield not an exhaustive knowledge, but an intercommunion with "unutterable mystery." He offers cautions and "unsystematic" opinions on how dogmatics can be at once more searching and more modest—more searching, in that dogmatics should tangle with the questions posed by a pluralistic search for truth, and more modest, in that God is not identical with human speech about God.

This essay was originally a lecture given at the Institute of Hermeneutics of the Theological Faculty of the University of Marburg, on July 16, 1965, and later at the College of Philosophy and Theology of Regensburg, on December 10, 1965. It was first published in the journal Catholica *in 1966 and was incorporated into volume 8 of the* Schriften *in 1967. The English translation is from volume 9 of the* Theological Investigations *(pp. 127–44), appearing in 1972.*

There is always something dubious about methodological investigations: it is only too easy for the thing under discussion itself to slip out of sight. But we may observe further limitations in such a procedure. For several reasons we cannot undertake here a *new* and *basic* foundation for the methodology of the Catholic doctrine of God. We are really presenting only "observations." Nor is it our aim to do any more than this, in a way, for it is not our intention to propound any particular, strikingly new thesis in order to contradict what is usual in Catholic theology, or which would develop a new program, proclaim a radically new orientation, and seek once more to revolutionize theology. Nothing is further from our intention. Not only because it is contrary to the nature of Catholic theology but because it seems contrary to the reality with which we are concerned here, namely God. For if one can think of anything at all under this heading which repays constant pondering, it is clear at the outset that it would be to go sadly astray and to miss the point completely if one were to say of a particular radicalism of a system, a thesis, or an opinion—as opposed to any other system, thesis, or opinion—that "this is God, and not that"; that "this is the true experience of the true God and that is not." The true radicalism in the doctrine of God can only be the continual destruction of an idol, an idol in the place of God, the idol of a theory about God. What it cannot be is a statement about God which distinguishes God from another object on the same plane, or which distinguishes this particular way of having-to-do-with-God from any other mode of approach to God. If it tries to do this it must come under the hammer of its own principle of "destruction," for one cannot gain control of God by a wild radicalism in negative theology either, since negative theology cannot give God to us if God's self-gift had not always been present to us already.

This principle is found in the sober humility of the true relationship with God. The unique character of our relationship with God and God's existence for us is shown by the fact that when we have renounced a knowledge of God which *conquers* God by means of affirmation or negation, God does not disappear, but precisely at that point becomes committed to us; furthermore it is shown by the fact that this renunciation (ultimately the renunciation of being God) is not *one* pole in the human dialectic between yes and no, but is rooted at the very basis of this dialectic, and that God only appears when accepted simply, humbly, and unself-consciously in worship and obedience and when not torn to pieces in all the talk of reflection. Finally it is also characteristic of our relationship with God that all these considerations must be thought out in very strict terms all the same, notwithstanding the foregoing....

I intend to arrange these observations, loosely related as they are, by first presenting some remarks concerning the doctrine of God within Catholic dogmatics, chiefly as regards its scholastic form. (This is to a certain extent an issue internal to Catholic theology; however, in an age of ecumenism it may also claim to be of interest to Protestant theologians.) Then in the second part I shall append some further observations in an attempt to reach beyond the confines of this Catholic academic question.

In this *first* part I make some observations which arise from a simple glance at the *history* of this treatise in Catholic dogmatics. In line with the beginning of each of the creeds, it is an uncontested practice in Catholic theology (although it is not really as evident as it seems) that dogmatics must begin with the doctrine of God if it is to be anything like systematic in its procedure. Of course, this way of beginning in Catholic theology has been called in question to a certain extent because, since the advent of modern times and the Enlightenment, the "beginning" of so-called "fundamental theology" has been prefixed to this original "beginning." Naturally, a problem has arisen in this way which, if the unity of theology is an ultimate necessity, cannot be solved by saying that this "fundamental theology" is a discipline on its own with its own method and its own subject matter, distinct from dogmatics as the study of the *content* of dogmatics. The issue becomes even more difficult because today, on account of theology's object being seen in salvation history—which bars the way to a systematic treatment—the question of a fundamental and formal theology as the starting point for dogmatic theology has been recently raised. (Not to be confused with "fundamental theology" in the usual sense.) Furthermore there is the fact that today the problems involved in an existentially effective fundamental theology apart from and prior to dogmatics have again been seen more clearly in Catholic theology, and so the tendency is to merge the two together....

Even historically speaking, the relationship between the general doctrine of God (*De Deo uno*) and the doctrine of the Trinity is more problematical. One cannot elicit a unified conception of this relationship from a study of the history of Catholic theology. The order of the treatises which is almost universally accepted today—first *De Deo uno* [on God as one], then *De Deo trino* [on God as triune]—has probably become general custom only since Peter Lombard's *Sentences* were ousted by Thomas's *Summa Theologica*. The Apostles' Creed with its trinitarian structure would only provide a clue to solving the problem of the unity and diversity of these two treatises if one were to understand—in common with the ancient *Theós* [God] terminology—the word "God" as the Father of the trinitarian confession, and, taking a Greek kind of trinitarian theology (linear with respect to the world), to discuss in addition the whole "being" of God in the first chapter concerning the Father. It is noteworthy that Peter Lombard subsumes the general doctrine of God under his doctrine of the Trinity, which M. Grabmann, for instance, regards as one of Lombard's "chief errors." Noteworthy is also the fact that we do not yet find a clear division in the *Summa Alexandri* either, whereas Thomas, for reasons which have not yet really been explained—whether in opposition to the Arabic systems or from apologetic or pedagogic motives—clearly follows the Augustinian and Latin method: he does not treat the general doctrine of God as the doctrine of God the Father, the sourceless origin in the godhead, but, by way of anticipation, as the doctrine of the nature of God which is common to all the persons. Only after that does he commence his doctrine of the Trinity. And so it has remained in general right up to today....

Furthermore, the doctrine of God of all the more recent Catholic dogmatics always contains a section on human beings' *knowledge* of God. That may seem strange, for at a first glance the theme seems to belong rather to dogmatic anthropology. For this accepted procedure to be really substantiated, as is quite possible, it would be necessary to deepen this section of a doctrine of God so that the following were made clear: First, it is concerned with that *particular* knowledge about God which arises, in an ultimate and indissoluble unity, from that experience which grasps in an original unity human existence, creatureliness transcendentally situated in the sphere of grace and of revelation history, the consequently implied possibility of a "natural" knowledge of God, and the continual temptation to atheism in human beings' tenacious sinfulness. In this case the question of "natural" knowledge of God alone, in the terms of Vatican I, cannot occupy the center of attention, but must take its place as the reductive element within a total experience of God. And, second, it must be made clear that in this case knowledge and what is known, belief and what is believed stand in a particular, unique relationship with one another, such that the knowledge of God cannot (or can only retrospectively) be regarded as constituting a regional sphere of knowledge side by side with other regional spheres of knowledge, but is the fundamental source and ultimate horizon of all knowledge whatsoever in the unity of human existence. This knowledge of God is always there and can always be "held fast"; its conceptual interpretation is always one factor of it itself to some degree and in some form, but it is not simply identical with it. As a result of this, knowledge and what is known can only be grasped by reflection *in one*, the doctrine of God *is* dogmatic anthropology *and* the doctrine of God itself, just as, by analogy, ontology is precisely onto-logy, that is, the doctrine of being *and* also the doctrine of the knowledge of being, in an indivisible unity.

As far as the inner structure of the treatise is concerned, where the doctrine of God is distinguished from the doctrine of the Trinity, it has been customary for a long time, following the presentation of the theme of the being of God, to supply a discussion of the *attributes* of God. In such a discussion it is usual for issues to be dealt with which find a place equally well in the doctrine of creation or in the doctrine of grace, like the questions of God's foreknowledge (sovereignty) and of predestination. The discussion of God's attributes pursues an almost exclusively metaphysical, that is, not originally theological, path: we usually divide them into active and passive attributes, and the latter are again distinguished as transcendental and categorial. We shall say more about this shortly.

However, these clear and tangible features in the history of the treatise's inner structure do not supply any considerable impetus toward solving the theological issues themselves; the Catholic treatise *De Deo uno* is to some extent aware, at second hand, of the questioning or contesting of a rational knowledge of God, and against such a denial it repeats the anathema pronounced by Vatican I. But so far the reformation, the change from the technical Greek way of thought to the correct anthropocentricity of modern times, the historical shift from the question of a gracious God to the question of where and how one can find God and human beings at all (and both at the same time), the question of reconciling transcendence and historicity, transcendence from above and from past origins and transcendence from ahead in the future, the question of the interweaving of faith, hope, and love in the knowledge of God itself, the question of the constant possibility of atheistic unbelief as an internal factor of faith in God—all these have not really become a part of the history of the treatise. And to allow these issues to affect its future history would not be to deliver a mortal blow.

In the second part of this section we shall make a few more *systematic* observations (if that is not a contradiction in terms).

We have already said that in its own particular dogmatics—notwithstanding "fundamental theology" and the possibility of a formal and fundamental theology—Catholic theology places the doctrine of God at the beginning. Let us leave it so. Revelation history and salvation history (and consequently the nature of theology) as God's self-revelation, together with transcendental and "eccentric" human beings, whose fundamental vocation is to obey this self-revealing God in faith (and who can only be themselves by receiving their being from the mystery which envelops them, and would not find the true God if they only considered God from the standpoint of *ad nos* [relationship with us], i.e., by measuring the *ad nos* from our point of view instead of accepting it from God)—these two factors demand that human beings should not speak first of their own salvation, but of God. In other words they must *begin again*, and correctly this time, *after* they have finished talking about themselves and their sorry state. This time we must say that our true salvation is precisely the God who does *not* exist solely to be our salvation, and that our true salvation—which is wrought by God and not by us—disappears into God's incomprehensibility. This does not exclude, but includes the fact that all remaining dogmatics is already contained in this doctrine of God. But besides being said *in toto* in each treatise (and hence necessarily more than once, since we cannot say everything *in toto* at the same time), the whole of dogmatics must first of all be uttered as the doctrine of God so that it remains clear that we must speak of God and not, after all, of ourselves, even if this speech is only meaningful as the final sound indicating the adoring silence before God. Instead of excluding it, this way of beginning includes the fact that this very treatise, because it is theology, reflection, and not the original source of the history of faith, must not forget the origin of our real knowledge of God in Christ and must make all affirmations whatever about God in such a way as to include the experience of salvation history. Thus it will (as far as possible) strive against the danger of tacitly making an abstract metaphysical schema into the *norma non normata* [absolute norms] of what, how, and who God "can be."

The mere *sequence* of the treatises *De Deo uno* and *De Deo trino,* as if the second treatise were only supplementary to the first, and as if only the second contained affirmations going beyond metaphysics (even though of a metaphysics requiring to be confirmed and secured), is apt to obscure the concrete history of theology, that is, the two possibilities which present themselves in the orthodox conception of the doctrine of the Trinity itself, and it presupposes wrongly that the history of revelation itself followed such a sequence, that is, from the revelation of God's being to the revelation of the Trinity. One could just as well say—indeed it would be more correct to say—that the history of revelation first of all shows God as a person without origin, the Father, who has then revealed God's self (as we say in technical terms) within this relationship with the world as a self-communication, as the source of divine life processes, capable of creating persons. These life processes reveal their divine immanence characteristically in the economic trinitarian relationship of God in Christ and in God's Spirit which is given to us. So the sequence whereby the treatise *De Deo uno* precedes the doctrine of the Trinity is not *necessarily* to be seen as the result of the infiltration of philosophy. Thus the question seems to be more didactic than fundamental whether and in which order the two treatises should follow one another, or whether they should be assimilated to each other. But on the other hand it is most important, if the general doctrine of God is placed first, not to present it as though there were no doctrine of the Trinity at all (as occurs in standard Catholic dogmatics). If the creation of what is not divine is understood dogmatically at the outset as a factor and a condition for the possibility of God's absolute self-communication, in which absolute love gives its very self and not something other than itself, creation as the freely uttered word of the unfathomably incomprehensible is then seen as the beginning and the "grammar" of the divine self-expression communicated into the void. Thus it is the beginning of the trinitarian self-revelation.

It may be counted as a positive achievement of the more recent academic tradition (although the latter does not have a real understanding of itself everywhere as yet) that the study of the knowledge of God is taken as a part of the doctrine of God. For as we have already said, there is a unique relationship between this knowledge as a subjective act and what is known thereby, a relationship which essentially cannot be found elsewhere. Thus we can see a transcendental factor at work in human beings' necessary recourse to God in knowledge and freedom in respect of any object whatsoever, and this inevitably involves an implicit, nonobjective experience of God which is always unthematic and capable of being overlooked. Hence too the unique character of the religious act in general (above all with its original and integrated structure), the necessity of a total involvement flowing from the very essence of this knowledge, since the *concept* of God in this knowledge only avoids being an idol by referring to the God who, without an image of God's self, standing fundamentally over against human beings, offers a self-gift. In the same way we can understand human beings' basic constitution in the experience of God, according to which they do not experience themselves as autonomous subjects who create a subject/object relation or anticipate it in their transcendental autonomy, but are aware of themselves as the ones who are destined, consigned, and "uttered" by the inexpressible mystery.

All this means that one is justified, even obliged, to maintain the unity of the treatise on God and on the knowledge of God. Furthermore it must be made more radical so that the treatise on the knowledge of God is not only one *piece* of the whole doctrine of God but the doctrine itself, and so that it actually speaks only of God and not about ourselves, since talk about ourselves is ultimately nothing but the challenge to be silent, to adore, to hide oneself in the inexpressible mystery, which commits us to ourselves in order to commend itself to us and sustain us.... In other words we must be aware of the possibility that we must not only be silent about God, but may also speak of God (and therefore *must* speak of God). Expressed in Catholic terms this doctrine of the transcendental necessity of the priority of the experience of God and its necessary expression in explicit speaking about God (with all the dangers of conceptual idolatry) refers to a knowledge which is both transcendental *and* unavoidable and is always sustained by the offer of God's self-communication in *grace*. Consequently the doctrine of the *natural* knowability and knowledge of God is not a knowledge which appears in isolation, but one element, only subsequently isolated, in a single knowledge of God, authorized by God in its direct relation to

God, which, when it is accepted, is already faith. Needless to say, this supernatural transcendentality (if we may term it thus) of the knowledge of God must be understood from the very beginning such that it only exists in the encounter with history, and consequently not only is it always open toward salvation history and the revelation of the word but it experiences the latter as its own history.

From this it is clear that the doctrine of God cannot (and not even primarily) be concerned with making statements about God's metaphysically necessary attributes, but above all concerning the workings—maintained throughout salvation history—of God's freely adopted disposition toward human beings and the world. These two things are for the most part not clearly enough distinguished and related to one another in the official Catholic doctrine of God. God's faithfulness, mercy, love, in short the concrete relationship of God to us which we experience in the unity of the transcendental experience of grace and salvation history, and which we have to express in the doctrine of God, are not merely the theologically attested necessary "attributes" of God's metaphysical being, but considerably more. For God could deny us the very faithfulness, love, and so on which God actually shows toward us, without ceasing to be faithful and loving in a metaphysical sense. And to recognize this possibility, to confide in the marvel of the *free* love of God, is to open up the horizon within which God's attributes can really be grasped as being *divine*, that is, such that a knowledge of them does not give us any power over God. From this point it might be possible for the Catholic doctrine of God to find a way of approach toward understanding and using the Lutheran *theologia crucis* [theology of the cross]. Even less than God's attributes, God's dispositions cannot be united in a single, positive concept by us; we can only say formally, aiming at the unity of God asymptotically, *that* in God they must be one, transposed into each other in perfect harmony. For us they remain materially and positively unamenable to synthesis, and thus the way they affect us has a history (which as a result of the divine act of *self*-communication to us is the genuine history of God), and the consequent history of our response therefore neither can nor needs to consist in a metaphysical equilibrium in our attitude in respect of God's free disposition toward us. For instance we have more reason to praise God's mercy than to fear God's justice, because God has allowed grace, and not anger, to overflow, and we must not let this fact be obscured by a dialectic balancing between divine attributes of God in themselves, in an attempt to manipulate God by means of the understanding. In a similar way other themes usually treated in a doctrine of God, like God's foreknowledge, predestination, God's freedom in grace, could be liberated from an abstract formalism; it could lead to the theological counterpart of Heidegger's secularized concept of the history of being (*Seinsgeschichte*).

*

Following these semisystematic observations on the doctrine of God in Catholic dogmatics I take the liberty of adding some further unsystematic remarks more or less at random, concerning particular points arising in connection with the doctrine of God. At the very outset it is strange to be talking "about" the doctrine of God, as opposed to stating it, for in the nature of the case the affirmations of this doctrine can only refer to what is meant in a very indirect way. However, that may perhaps excuse the unsystematic nature of these remarks.

1. First of all, the following plain threefold presupposition characterizes the Catholic doctrine of God.

a. The calm and unembarrassed acceptance of the pluralistic structure of human knowledge and thus of theology too. Our knowledge has an ultimate subjective and objective unity. But so far as we think in terms of propositions, we are not standing at the focus of this unity, but are situated in a plurality of modes of knowledge. Consequently there is no formula which can say everything at the same time, no single idea from which everything else could be deduced. We are rightly always engaged in *systematizing* (however we are to understand this word more precisely), but we never *have* a system; we always know more than what we have already systematized, and this unsystematized extra in our fundamentally plural experience is not merely supplementary to what we have mastered by system, but constitutes an incommensurate challenge and threat to it and is its future corrective. God is the presupposed objective and subjective unity, but is also the God whom we can only *approach* by thought; we cannot ourselves join with God in realizing this pluralism which God established and sustains in God's creativity. It is thus clear that, as the first treatise, the doctrine of God is not complete until the end of the last dogmatic treatise. It is only possible at all insofar as we have continually exposed ourselves patiently to the claims of the many theological treatises. Hence it is also clear that we must always be aware—without letting ourselves become irritable or annoyed—that in a doctrine of God we have forgotten and omitted much that we could and should actually have known.

b. The patient desire for historical continuity in theology also applies in the case of the doctrine of God. If we wish to say something new and find what has been said of old to be inadequate, we may calmly count on finding implications of it in earlier theology. In spite of *Seins-geschichte* and the recognition that the history of theology reaches right down to a real history of revelation and a real salvation history and is not merely the playing of surface waves above the unmoved depths, the religious man or woman, the person of faith, standing in the midst of his or her history where the issue is the issue of God, already possesses the totality of what can and must be pondered upon by theology. For genuine and fundamental knowledge consists in the unreserved surrender in faith to the absolute mystery, the surrender to the self-communication of this mystery, which, though holy, yet gives itself and forgives in direct intimacy, the surrender to its inscrutable ordering of history. This being so, we cannot really proceed in a revolutionary manner, as if the men and women of old did not know the God of whom we wish to speak. We can only claim to use the speech of reflection about God in such a way that it introduces *us* better to the faith which was always there. And this we must do with the painful and sobering thought that when we have poured out our pail of knowledge into the ocean of the incomprehensible God, we have really poured it back into the ocean whence we drew it in the first place.

c. The courage to engage in metaphysics. There is no theology which does not carry on metaphysics, simply because in theology too there must be the process of thinking. I am sometimes amazed that theologians are quick to declare that a metaphysics must be false or unsuitable for theology simply because it is a matter of dispute. How can they not see that their own theology too is itself a matter of dispute, and yet they do not straightway regard this as a criterion for saying that their own theology is false? The man or woman who has not the courage to pursue a metaphysics (which is not the same as a closed system), a metaphysics which can be contradicted, cannot be a good theologian. Even when one is conscious of possessing a constantly inadequate metaphysics, it is still possible to rely on it, to use it in addressing the true God and in directing human beings toward the experience which they always have already from God. For it is human beings' inalienable blessing that their words say more and purer things than they themselves know and can enclose in their impure words, provided, that is, that their pride does not make them keep silent just because, as soon as they begin to speak about God, their words immediately sound foolish. In using words one always becomes ridiculous, even if neither the others nor oneself notices it straightway; the same is true if one uses the ancient words, the tired and rickety words of tradition.

2. It seems to me that Thomas separated the question *an Deus sit* [whether God exists] rather too much from the question *quid sit Deus* [what God is]. Of course one can ask whether there is such a thing as that which everyone calls God, without first of all explaining in greater detail what is meant thereby. Naturally, as individuals always determined by history, we would not think about God unless we had already heard of God indirectly. But if it is not to be merely a question of the existence of a mere empty cipher, the question of the existence of God must be launched as a question concerning the *real* God. And as opposed to more arbitrarily chosen objects of knowledge, which can be known as *possible* prior to a knowledge of their existence, in the case of God possibility and actuality can only be grasped in a *single* act of knowledge. Thus from the point of view of ontology, the theology of creation, the theology of grace and of existence (and all four in one) the question of God can apparently only be stated as one which has necessarily already been asked and which has the answer *in itself* and has not received it from elsewhere. Hence at the *same time* the question itself says both that God is, and also who God is. If we are not to miss God right from the very outset, the question of God must on no account be put as a question about an individual existent *within* the perspective of our transcendence and historical experience, but only as a question concerning the very ground sustaining the "question" which we ourselves "are," concerning the origin and future of this question. Consequently it already of necessity contains within itself simultaneously the answer to the questions "whether?" and "what?"

3. Naturally I cannot at this point give a sufficient answer to the question of the so-called proofs of the existence of God in themselves and as an element in a doctrine of God. However, I may be permitted to make a few observations. Usually, the Catholic dogmatic doctrine of God does not discuss these proofs as such but assumes them as a task of metaphysics which has been successfully completed. Even in the section of the doctrine of God concerned with the "natural knowability of God" it is usually said that according to dogmatic sources such proofs are possible and actually exist. But on a closer investigation one would have to say that this dogmatic doctrine of God ought itself to present these proofs, at least *in nuce* [in essence]. For can it say that there are such things without giving an idea of what is actually meant by them and what may not be meant? But can one give an idea of the essence of the proofs without actually performing them if (as is surely the case) their "essence" and their transcendental necessity—their "existence"— can only be grasped together at the same time? Furthermore, can the

proofs be understood in any other way but as one element in the single, ultimately indissoluble experience of God in faith, as that element which is present (though rejected and repressed) even to the real unbelievers insofar as their unbelief is capable of leading to their judgment and loss of blessedness? That is the real theological reason why Catholic dogmatics holds fast the possibility of the so-called proofs, the possibility of a natural knowledge of God, just as it maintains the distinction between nature and supernatural grace. But that is not to deny that this "proof of the existence of God" is absolutely *sui generis* [unique in its own kind] and cannot be calculated as an individual item of knowledge by the formal and univocal procedure used in the case of any other piece of knowledge, nor is it the application of general axioms (in themselves quite independent of any application) to a particular case. Rather it is the result of the manifestation of the very ground of all such axioms, which is and remains the ultimate mystery. In Thomas's theology and ever since, in spite of his *quinque viae* [five ways of proving God's existence], there is and can be only *one* proof: in the whole questionable nature of humankind seen as a totality, which human beings are aware of in the concreteness of their existence striking them in a perpetually novel and existential way, provided that they do not run away from it.

4. In a Catholic doctrine of God the question of atheism ought to be considered much more seriously than is actually the case as a rule. And the first question must be the "atheism" of the believer himself or herself. If there can and ought to be a Catholic doctrine *simul justus et peccator* [at the same time, a just person and a sinner], its modern historical form should be concerned with the human beings who, by virtue of the grace which they simply assume without proof, are always breaking out of their atheism into faith in God. There would have to be an exposition of the fact that theism can be the mask of a concealed atheism and vice versa, and that in this sense ultimately no one can say of herself or himself whether she or he believes in God or not, in the same way that the Council of Trent taught justification's existential hiddenness from the reflection of the individual conscience. We shall only be able to speak in justice, love, and humility of the atheists outside when atheism is admitted as the constant inner temptation of the theist, as a condition of faith.

I regard it as an oxymoron, which does not really lead us any further, when Tillich says that it is just as much atheism to affirm the existence of God as to deny it. If that were true, one would be obliged to abandon the question of God as something about which essentially nothing can be said. But the only possible absolute atheism would be if one said one could manage to leave the question of God alone to such an extent that it *did not arise* at all, and thus did not even need to be dismissed. This cannot really be disproved by a priori metaphysics but by the a posteriori historical and yet unavoidable fact that human existence actually *does* ask the question. This question can become stifled and suppressed; it may be necessary to dig for it; if it were not present already, it would be senseless to wish to inculcate it. That it can only be disproved in this way is what is really meant by scholastic theology where it says that God can only be known a posteriori. For this a posteriori point of departure is not intended to make the knowledge of God into a particular individual pursuit within the homogeneous field containing all other items of knowledge; it only says that, like their existence itself, individuals have laid upon them the transcendental necessity of being aware of themselves and of the question (in whatever form), and that this necessity is their destiny, communicated to them as the question of the freedom committed to them and of the necessary nature of this freedom. The only thing which seems to me to be correct in Tillich's statement is that, if God is included as one object in an arbitrary series of other objects (similarly demonstrable) and knowledge of God is treated like any other knowledge, *this* kind of theism is in reality atheism, because it has no understanding whatsoever of the God referred to by genuine theism. A theism of this kind would be erecting an idolatrous image upon a foundation laid and ordered by ourselves, instead of reaching God on the intractable foundation which sustains us and which is God.

5. Is God in the doctrine of God, or does it only consist of talk about God which actually conceals and drives God away? Certainly God is not identical with this way of talking; for it is *our* way of talking, and we are finite and sinful. Similarly it is *our* speech when we talk of God according to God's revelation. For we only possess this revelation as one which has reached us, which we ourselves have heard, and so too as a revelation spoken by us. And it is certainly true that there is a radical distinction in the relation of the form of what we say to the content of what is said, depending on whether we are speaking of some temporal thing within our speech horizon or of God, who is not of this nature. Our speech is indeed strange and uncanny when we are obliged to speak of God with temporal words—since we have no others. And least of all can we *compare* what we say with the One of whom we speak, since for the purposes of such comparison, that One would be present only in the terms of our speech. Strictly speaking, in theological talk as such it is not God who is present, but ourselves. But we are the ones who are spoken of, related to, and destined from the incomprehensible. And so it happens

169

that talk about God comes from God, without itself possessing God. If we *speak* of our origin and destiny in this way, and thus speak of God, it is still speech. But it speaks of what we are *as* what we are. And there we have God, as the unutterable mystery, banishing us from God and yet in God's grace promising and giving us God's self. That which we ourselves are, which gives us God, and whence we speak, does not make God subject to us, does not make theology into anthropology. On the contrary it actually makes us subject to God and yet at the same time—how can we say it in any other way?—God's children.

This nameless something which we can neither grasp nor circumscribe, which lies behind us as our perpetual creation in grace, is both revelation and mysticism; as creation it always lies behind us and as the absolute future it lies ahead of us, confronting us with the concreteness of our individual and collective history and bidding us enter in (ultimately into the love of one's neighbor); this is how it actually presents itself to us; this is how we possess God. Provided that our explicit talk of God in the dogmatic doctrine of God really comes from this source, it possesses God although it is ours, although in itself it only *refers* to its origin. Whether, when a particular person is talking, it really comes from this source or is ultimately only the moribund babblings of what was once genuine in other people, no individual can know for certain. He or she can only tremble and hope. But since human beings can believe that Jesus of Nazareth spoke in such a way because through death and resurrection he was "uttered" absolutely by God as God's word; since human beings, in loving their *neighbor*—and not, in the first instance, themselves—must believe in hope that other human beings can speak in this way; since human beings in the fellowship of Jesus believe in hope that this very speech, springing from its original source in God, is really present, they can as individuals confidently join in this speech about God, boldly entrusting their theological issue to God. They too will assuredly possess something of this genuine speech; they must not think of themselves and of their sinfulness but calmly pursue their theology and commit it to God, from whom it *can* originate. And when they have spoken they should once more be silent in adoration, drinking draught by draught the everyday cup of God-less-ness, waiting for death, giving thanks for the joy of life—that is, accepting it as sent to them in love—holding on to the *theologia viatoris et crucis* [theology of one on the way and of the cross] until at last the eternal light dawns. For the present we are held suspended in the very midst of it; even in the realm of thought we have no abiding city, even in theology we are pilgrims. But that is how it must be.

170

6. In the doctrine of God there is no real difference between the *Deus in se* [God in God's self] and the *Deus extra se* [God outside God's self]. At least since Christ and in him we are both obliged and empowered to be continually overstepping this distinction. For to communicate God's self to us *in se* is exactly what God desires. And it is the paradoxical miracle of God's love (that is, of God's self "in God's self") that God is able to do this without becoming finite and without violating our creatureliness. This process of *becoming* identical (and not just *being* identical) is the real content of salvation history, which is the history of the unchangeable God, who really can *become* something in this history, precisely because (and in the final analysis not "although") God is infinite and unchanging, the absolute power, capable of doing this.

7. Can it be said that in this age there can no longer be an alliance between theology and philosophy in a Catholic dogmatic doctrine of God? If anyone thought that there were no metaphysics in theology, the answer to this question would have to be yes. For in theology at least very accurate thought is needed; but any thought which questions and ponders itself as a whole (and how could one avoid doing this in the case of the doctrine of God, which is concerned with God and the knowledge of God, that is, the onto-logical origin of everything?) is metaphysics. For that reason it is nonsense to talk about the end of *metaphysics*, however much one may wish to say that a particular form of metaphysics has been eclipsed. So the Catholic doctrine of God will always imply and maintain a fundamental unity of theology and metaphysics, even if one would not wish to speak of an "alliance" between them. Of course, this does not answer the question as to the precise relationship between metaphysics and theology, nor the question as to how these two disciplines have come, in a historically justified manner, to separate out from one another into two independent units, although from their very nature neither of them can be or wish to be "regional" disciplines, but rather are concerned fundamentally with everything (including themselves).

The questions we have just raised will be answered sufficiently when reason and metaphysics understand that it is they which pose the open question and refer human beings back to the experience of their interior and external history, and when theology grasps the fact that it can only give God's answer—God as the answer for all time—provided that it keeps the question open. (For the question into which the answer is projected has always been answered already by God—not by us.) And both philosophy and theology—in their different ways—must understand that in answering the sinner too and humankind in general, God has granted the question. If this question were not granted, both the answer given would lack a question and the question would lack an answer, or both would dissolve together into a flat commonplace. Of course all this does not mean that the old alliance between theology and metaphysics is to remain exactly as it was before. For above all in theology the doctrine of God must not talk in terms of its *own* metaphysics, but the metaphysics which is committed to us today as our lot in history, whether through our own fault or not. The actual form of this metaphysics certainly no longer has the homogeneity, the balance of language, and of presuppositions and perspectives calmly assumed which was once the case. Consequently Catholic theology no longer has simply *one* language; it must learn many languages, and thus it probably speaks them all thoroughly badly. But it will be of the opinion, furthermore, that in being obliged to speak today in many metaphysics, it is not simply uttering propositions which oppose each other with an absolute lack of mutual understanding—like a simple yes and no—but rather that there is a *philosophia perennis* [perennial philosophy] that is *in* them, not besides them, for which one must listen sympathetically, as it cannot be distilled out. Thus a dialogue is possible with these diverse metaphysics; and theology can be expressed in their language, for theology is a human language too, and every human language which is not itself dead points, questioning, toward the unutterable mystery with which alone theology is ultimately concerned.

EXPERIENCE OF SELF
AND EXPERIENCE OF GOD

This essay was originally published in 1971 as Rahner's contribution to Urbild und Abglanz *(Archetype and reflection), a festschrift honoring Professor H. Doms of Regensburg. It was incorporated into volume 10 of the* Schriften *the following year. The English translation is from volume 13 of the* Theological Investigations *(pp. 122–32), published in 1975.*

Here Rahner develops a point of intersection between his theological anthropology and his searching, Ignatian mysticism. Although, as he states in the opening paragraph of his analysis, one can travel the separate paths of metaphysical anthropology and philosophical theology, there is an underlying unity and mutual interconnection in the reality each aspires to. We see repeated here the fundamental emphasis of Rahner's doctrine of God, namely, that one's transcendental orientation to the holy mystery of God, the inner spiritual source

*of one's knowledge and freedom, makes possible a nonthematized, uncate-
gorized experience of God. In the flow of this experience of God, the acts of
reflection, interpretation, and objectification loom only as secondary moments.
The human relationship with God is sparked by God's transcendental nearness
to the created human spirit. Put succinctly, Rahner claims that there is an original unity and intimacy between the experience of self and the experience of
God to the extent that the history of one becomes the history of the other. In
this perspective, every experience of God is at the same time an experience of
self. In Rahner's words, "The experience of self is the condition which makes it
possible to experience God." One's human transcendentality in knowledge and
freedom as one reaches toward the God of one's absolute future constitutes, according to Rahner, the basis of one's ability to accept the unconditional love of
God and to experience the genuine fellowship in which the love of neighbor as
oneself for the sake of God becomes possible. For Rahner, this is akin to the
Gospel saying that in the love of neighbor one has already discovered God. The
unity between these experiences, which comes through very forcefully in Rahner's prayers, is, Rahner claims, at the foundations of Christian faith and of a
correct understanding of the doctrine of God in Christianity.*

In view of the magnitude and difficulty of the theme under investigation,
it is impossible, within the scope of a brief study such as the present one,
to treat of more than a few particular aspects, which have been somewhat arbitrarily chosen. Experience of God and experience of the self
each constitutes themes in its own right, and in a real and fundamental sense each stands for the totality of human experience and human
knowledge, albeit each in its own special way. For when human beings,
the subjects, experience themselves as such, each is recognizing himself or herself to be that particular being which is *quodammodo omnia*
[in a certain manner, all things], not, that is to say, one particular subject among many others at the material level, but that incomprehensible
being in which the sum total of reality as such achieves realization of itself, so that the only way of fully understanding it would be to achieve
an experience and understanding of reality itself. Metaphysical anthropology, therefore, is, on any right understanding of its nature, not one
particular department or branch of science among others, but rather
that philosophy which is concerned with *the* being as such, even though
it is true that as anthropology this philosophy is attempting to understand the whole of reality from one specific point of departure, namely
from that finite subject which is, nevertheless, open to the infinite. Presumably we do not need to justify in any greater detail the proposition
that teaching about God does not constitute one particular department

or branch of science, but, regarded as teaching about God at the philosophical level, constitutes an ontology as one and total, considered from one particular aspect. But if it is true that a metaphysical anthropology and a philosophical theology constitute, each in its own way, a universal science, then there are still stronger grounds for regarding the question of the mutual interconnection and underlying unity between them once more as a question involving an inquiry into reality in all its aspects. Hence it is obvious that on such a theme, and within the scope of the present study, it is only possible to touch upon it in a few brief and inadequate remarks.

*

Let us begin by drawing attention to the terms in which the subject of this consideration has deliberately been defined: *experience* of self and *experience* of God. Thus we have avoided the terms "knowledge of God" or "knowledge of self." This should be enough to indicate from the outset that what we are treating of is that kind of knowledge which is present in every man and woman as belonging essentially to the very roots of cognition in him or her, and as constituting the starting point and prior condition for all reflexive knowledge, and for all derived human knowledge in its function of combining and classifying. We are assuming, therefore, that there is such a thing as a passive experience of this kind as a matter of transcendental necessity, an experience so inescapable, in other words, that in its ultimate structures its reality is implicitly asserted in the very act of denying it or calling it in question. In accordance with this, it must be emphasized, with regard to human beings' experience of themselves, that we are treating of this here in its initial stages as an unconscious factor in human life, one that is prior to any anthropology (at the philosophical level and as a particular department) in its reflexive and classifying functions, through both of which it exercises the further function of objectifying. Human beings' experience of themselves sustains all such objectifying anthropology, and can never fully be grasped in their findings as they reflect upon their own nature. Thus it would be justifiable to say that human beings always experience more of themselves at the nonthematic and nonreflexive levels in the ultimate and fundamental living of their lives than they know about themselves by reflecting upon themselves whether scientifically or (mainly in their private ideas) nonscientifically. The transcendental orientation of the human being to the incomprehensible and ineffable mystery which constitutes the enabling condition for knowledge and freedom, and therefore for subjective life as such, in itself implies a real, albeit a nonthematic experience of God. With regard to this experience of God we must emphasize here above all that it can be so nonthematic, so different from any theology, whether popular or scholarly (whether philosophical or revelational in character) that on the one hand the experience really is present, yet on the other, under certain circumstances, the individual concerned may be ignorant of the very word "God." An experience of God of this kind, therefore, is present from the outset in everyday life, even though the individual may be interested in everything else except God. It is also present, although it may be isolated or suppressed, in those who believe themselves to be, or will to be, atheists. We have drawn a distinction between human beings' original and nonthematic experience of themselves and of God on the one hand, and a knowledge about God and human beings in which this experience is objectified and interpreted on the other. Obviously in making this distinction we do not dispute that it is both important and inevitable that human beings must achieve a certain stage of reflexive knowledge (at least of themselves as subjects). Nor does their interpretative knowledge of their own experience constitute in its turn an element in the history of human experience in the concrete. Again when we speak of an experience of human beings and God we are inevitably using the very abstract term of "experience," yet what we mean is that concrete developing history of experience in every individual man or woman in his or her uniqueness and difference from all others, and in the whole length and breadth of an individual human life, different in every case, in which the struggle for conscious knowledge, objectified and explicitated in conscious terms, constitutes only a modest and secondary part of life. And let us further assume for our present purposes that every human experience, and so too that which we are concerned with here, contains within itself a transcendental and a posteriori element of historical development. In this sense it is both subjective and objective at the same time, so that the personal history of life in the concrete is, in virtue of this fact, precisely the personal history of the transcendentality of knowledge and freedom in the individual man or woman. Conversely the only way in which this transcendentality can really achieve its true nature is for it boldly and freely to expose itself to the experience of the undeducible historical development in its a posteriori character, without attempting wholly to detach itself from this history belonging to it by a process of reflecting upon itself.

*

If we are to speak of the experience of self *and* the experience of God, then the first point to be established is that they constitute a unity. Obviously what we mean by unity here is not simply an absolute identity. For when, in experiencing ourselves as subject, we see ourselves as "transcendental," even then this "transcendental" subject is absolutely different from that which we mean when we speak of "God." Even the most radical truth of self-experience recognizes that this subject which we are is finite, even though, precisely as such, and in its sheer transcendentality, it contains an absolute orientation toward the infinite and the incomprehensible through which it is this without being identified with it. In other words, therefore, its nature is constituted by something, and experiences itself as so constituted, which it itself must perforce refuse to identify itself with. While, therefore, experience of God and experience of self are not simply identical, still both of them exist within a unity of such a kind that apart from this unity it is quite impossible for there to be any such experiences at all. Constantly both would be lost, each in its own way. This unity implies, of course, not only that every experience of God (like every other knowledge of God) as it exists in the subject is a process in which this subject is at the same time made present to itself and experiences itself. Taken by itself such a unity would in fact still not constitute any *characterization* of the experience of God as such, for in every spiritual act of knowledge or freedom, whatever it is concerned with, the subject is made present to itself. . . . The unity between the experience of God and the experience of self is too ultimate and too all-embracing for it to consist solely in the simple fact that, as in every other "subject" of human knowledge, so too in the knowledge of God, the subject experiences herself or himself at the same time. This unity consists far more in the fact that the original and ultimate experience of *God* constitutes the enabling condition of, and an intrinsic element in, the experience of self in such a way that without this experience of God no experience of self is possible. In other words the personal history of the experience of God signifies, over and above itself, the personal history of the experience of the self. Of course the point could equally well be formulated the other way round. The experience of self is the condition which makes it possible to experience God. The reason is that an orientation to being in the absolute, and so to God, can be present only when the subject (precisely in the act of reaching out toward being in the absolute) is made present to himself or herself as something distinct from his or her own act and as the subject of that act. In accordance with this we can then likewise go on to assert: the personal history of experience of the self is the personal history of the experience of God.

All this is certainly something which cannot be said of every "subject" of experience. It is true that there is no experience of the self without the passive experience of subjects of some kind of an a posteriori character in the personal lives of the individuals concerned, subjects which are offered to individuals in the course of their lives by their environment and their social milieu. To that extent the "return" to the self necessarily also involves in all cases a "projection" into the world outside. So much is this the case that true observation of the self at the level of explicit reflection upon oneself (whether scientific or nonscientific) constitutes only a very secondary and supplementary process in the totality of the human experience of the self. Nevertheless the knowledge of a particular individual subject within the world does not constitute the necessary condition enabling human beings to experience themselves or the subject of that projection in which this experience is achieved. Yet without any experience of God, however nonthematic and nonreflexive in character, experience of the self is absolutely impossible. And hence it is, as we have said, that the personal development of experience of the self constitutes the personal development of the experience of God and vice versa.

The unity which exists between experience of God and experience of the self as here understood could of course be made clear in a process of transcendental reflection. Inevitably some of the factors involved in this have already been indicated in what we have said so far. The transcendentality of human beings in knowledge and freedom, as it reaches up to absolute being, the absolute future, the incomprehensible mystery, the ultimate basis enabling absolute love and responsibility to exist, and so genuine fellowship (or whatever other presentation we may like to make in fuller detail of this transcendentality of human beings), is at the same time the condition which makes it possible for subjects strictly *as* such to experience themselves and to have achieved an "objectification" of themselves in *this* sense all along. But this philosophical argument for the unity between experience of self and experience of God will not be pursued any further in the present context.

In place of this, attention may be drawn to a theological consideration which shows that such apparently remote and abstract lines of thought have, after all, a concrete bearing upon life. The unity between the experience of God and the experience of self is the condition which makes it possible to achieve that unity which theological tradition recognizes as existing between love of God and love of neighbor, and which is of fundamental importance for any right understanding of Christianity. In order to achieve a clearer view of this a preliminary consideration must be included at this point. The only way in which human beings achieve self-realization is through encounters with their fellow human beings, persons who are rendered present to their experience in knowledge and love in the course of their personal lives, persons, therefore, who are not things or matter, but human beings. Of course an individual experience of self on the part of the subject, taken in isolation and abstracted from the totality of the course of a human life, is conceivable in connection with an individual piece of material "subject matter." In that case "*I* come to know something" would be the formal structure of an experience of self of this kind in connection with a piece of "subject matter" which, following the custom of the philosophers of old, we conceive of, not without reason, as a material object. In reality, however, the situation is different. One's fellow human being is not any "piece of subject matter," one of many in which the experience of self can be achieved. The true, living, and concrete experience of life which is identical with the experience of self in the concrete has, in relation to its "pieces of subject matter," a structure in which not every item has an equal value. Despite the ascendancy nowadays enjoyed by the sciences orientated toward material realities, and which also include human beings as one such material reality within their area of subject matter, the experience of life is an experience of one's fellow human beings, one in which material objects are encountered as elements connected with, and surrounding concrete persons and not otherwise. Life in its full sense is in the concrete achieved in knowledge and freedom in which the "I" is always related to a "Thou," arising at the same moment in the "Thou" as in the "I," experiencing itself in all cases only in its encounter with the other person by recognizing itself to be different from that other person, and at the same time by identifying itself with that other person. The original objectivity of the experience of self necessarily takes place in the subjectivity of its encounters with other persons in dialogue, in trustful and loving encounter. Human beings experience themselves by experiencing other *persons* and not other *things*. Human beings could not achieve a self-withdrawal from a world consisting exclusively in material objects any more than they could from their own bodies, the concrete experience of which as they de facto exist also in fact presupposes an encounter with the physicality of other persons. Self-experience is achieved in the unity between it and the experience of other persons. When the latter is harmoniously achieved, the former succeeds as well. Those who fail to discover their neighbor have not truly achieved realization of themselves either. They are not in any true sense concrete subjects capable of identifying themselves with themselves, but at most abstract philosophical subjects, and human beings who have lost themselves. The subjects' experience of themselves and of the Thou who encounters them, is one and the same experience under two different aspects, and that too not merely in its abstract formal nature, but in its concrete reality as well, in the degree of success or failure with which it is achieved, in its moral quality as an encounter with the real self and with one's fellow in love or hatred. Thus the concrete relationship of the subject to himself or herself is inextricably dependent upon the factor of how a subject encounters his fellow human beings.

Now assuming all this (though this statement of ours constitutes only a cursory adumbration of it) we can now inquire into a further implication of it, one contained in the doctrine of the Bible and the church, namely that love of God and love of neighbor constitute a unity. In other words it follows from this Christian doctrine that in view of the fact that on the one hand the experience of God and the experience of self are one, and on the other that the experience of self and the encounter with our neighbor are one, that all these three experiences ultimately constitute a single reality with three aspects mutually conditioning one another. Now this also implies the converse, namely that the unity between love of God and love of neighbor is conceivable only on the assumption that the experience of God and the experience of self are one. The unity which exists between experience of self and experience of God, which at first seemed to be formulated and pointed to in purely philosophical terms, is also an implication of that principle, basic to Christianity, that love of God and love of neighbor are one. We must think of these three relationships of the subject to himself or herself, to God, and to the neighbor, not simply as separate from, and existing side by side with one another like the relationships which a single subject bears to another contingent being which she or he chances to encounter, or to the subject matter of a posteriori experience. These relationships, on the contrary, are present, as a matter of necessity, all at once, and as mutually conditioning one another, in every act of the subject endowed with intellect and freedom, whatever form this act may assume. Only if we recognize this can we say that the love of neighbor is the fullness of the Law, and that in it the destiny of humankind as a whole is decided. Only then can we say that human beings discover themselves or lose themselves in their neighbor; that human beings have already discovered God, even though they may not have any explicit knowledge of it, if only they have truly reached out to their neighbor in an act of unconditional love, and in that neighbor reached out also to their own self. In brief, among many other reasons which might be adduced for the unity of this experience, but which cannot be developed here, there is a theological one too, namely the unity between love of God and love of neighbor. This statement can be maintained in its real and radical significance only if the relationship inherent in every act posited by the subjects is extended to God and the neighbor also with the same transcendental necessity as it is to the subjects themselves, if God and the subjects' fellow human beings (their fellow human beings in principle and in general, even though this is then concentrated in the concrete other subjects whom they encounter as a matter of irreducible contingency in the course of their personal lives) constitute not particular factors confined to one area within the total scope of the experience, but are realities present as a matter of transcendental necessity opening up and sustaining the experience in its totality.

*

A further point, following from what we have said, is that the personal history of the experience of self is in its total extent the history of the ultimate experience of God itself also. The history of knowledge of God at the consciously explicitated level is merely one particular and secondary element in this. But once we go beyond considering the unity of the experience of the self in formal and abstract terms and consider it is its concrete reality, it becomes in itself an anthropological problem of the utmost obscurity. For, in accordance with our basic thesis, it must also have its effect upon the history of the experience of God and its unity. The true and full unity of the history of the experience of self cannot consist merely in the fact that subjects endowed with spiritual faculties experience themselves at every moment in their self-realization as "subject to time," that is, as in the abstract orientated toward past and future in general. The unity of the concrete history of the experience of self to which we refer—in other words, therefore, the enduring possession of one's own personal history—cannot have its basis solely in what we call, in a popular and superficial sense, our memory. This cannot be the case seeing that then there would no longer be any abiding unity in the history of the experience of the self, any identity of the subject with his or her own past in relation to the earlier occurrences in his or her life. This remains true even though we do not overlook the fact that the potential memory as upheld by the material organism in human beings (the "brain") is far greater than the total range of items which we can actualize from it at will. For only if this potential memory in human beings were present in every part of the material organism in itself alone (in a way similar to that in which the genetic code is present in every cell of the organism), something which it seems impossible to accept, could we think of the identity of the subject with his or her own past history of experience of the self, and thereby the unity of this history, as having its basis solely in this potential memory. This unity of the history of the experience of self, and the abiding identity of the subject with it, does not in any sense need in principle to be extended to all and every occurrence which has actually taken place in physical concrete fact in such a history. This is something which can never be demanded of a philosophy of the material as such, even abstracting from the question of whether a factor in the history of an individual can and must also have a permanence which cannot be lost even when it has never entered his or her awareness. A real state of belonging to the past is inherent in the material as such if it is regarded purely in itself, and to the extent that in viewing it in this way we really do see something which objectively belongs to it in itself. To that extent we can confidently conclude that there can be occurrences in human beings' history of experiencing themselves too, which at least as such totally disappear, as such no longer exist, with the result that it would be totally impossible and meaningless to assert any abiding identity of the subject with such occurrences. There is a further question, namely, over and above what we have said, how the unity of the history of the experience of self, the abiding nature of this history, and the identification of the subject with his or her own history, should be thought of in further detail as *prior to* the freedom inherent in this history. But this is a question with which we shall not concern ourselves any further in the present context.

But there is a further and special question to which we must draw attention, that namely of how the unity of this history of the experience of self is to be conceived of if, and to the extent that, it constitutes a history of freedom, in other words of the free self-interpretation of human beings. For this question is of special importance in its bearing upon the unity of the history of the experience of God. The freedom in which the history of the experience of self is achieved cannot, it is true, eliminate the identity of human beings with their own past history, in other words a unity of the history of their experience of self which is not subject to their own decision. In other words in the decree posited by human freedom human beings cannot so detach themselves from their former history that this no longer affects them in any way whatsoever, even if this freedom of the past (in "conversion," as repentance, or even as guilt) can undergo very real reinterpretations. Nevertheless freedom does introduce certain radical caesuras into the abiding unity of any such history of understanding of the self or experience of the self. So long as the single personal history of freedom belonging to the individual woman or man endures, it is exposed, for all the unity and permanence inherent in it, to the constant possibility of fresh interpretation through the exercise of human beings' own freedom. At any moment in the here and now past history may be rendered present through the freedom of human beings in the form of a free identification of the subject with it, in the form of explicit rejection of it, in the form of unconscious yet free suppression of it, in the form of culpable and lying reinterpretation, and so on. This is all a line of argument that cannot be further developed here. But in the light of our basic thesis it is immediately clear that in saying this we are also saying something of decisive importance about the history of the ultimate and basic experience of God, when we conceive of this not at the abstract and formal level but in its concrete reality. The history of the experience of self, that is, of human beings' interpretation of themselves as achieved in freedom, is *eo ipso* the history of their experience of God as well, and vice versa. The destruction of false idols, the act of attaining, or failing to attain, a state of transcendence over all reality definable in terms of particular categories and also reality as the necessary starting point for our knowledge of God, extending up to the mystery which is beyond all our conceiving or achieving, human beings' surrender of themselves, constant yet ever renewed, to the incomprehensible God, or the refusal of such surrender in a lying self-sufficiency—these and many other episodes in the history of the experience of God are *eo ipso* events directly belonging to the history of the experience of the self as such as well and vice versa.

A complete and exact table might be drawn up of the correspondences between the one history and the other, because what is in question here is simply two aspects of one and the same history of experience. Such a table, which it is of course impossible to set forth here, would be very necessary precisely today. For in this way it might be possible for modern human beings, for whom all explicit statements about God fall all too easily under ideological distrust, to have it brought home to them that whether they want it or not, in the changing history of their relationship with themselves (whether in trustful acceptance of themselves, in loss of identity, in hatred toward themselves, in love for their fellow human beings, and only in this for themselves, despite all their skeptical experience of the fragility and unreliability of finite human beings, etc.) that they have all along been living through a history of their experience of God. With such a table it would be possible constantly to translate and describe an anthropology at the existential level and also in concrete human life, primarily in the form of teaching about the experience of God and ipso facto in this in a theology. It could be shown that in the history of experience of the self the experience of the loss of identity (to the extent and in the manner in which such a thing is possible, since in fact even that which is lost still always remains present in its own way) is also (in the same sense and with the same provisos) a loss of the experience of God or the refusal to accept the abiding experience of God.

5

ON JESUS THE CHRIST, SON OF GOD

Rahner's Christology appears to be both a structuring element in his theology and spirituality as well as a far-reaching outcome of the rootedness of his reflections in theological anthropology. Rahner describes Jesus the Christ as God's Word, enfleshed in a human nature, and, therefore, as a person to be considered always in relationship with the essentially spiritual structure of all humans and in accordance with all the dynamics of human subjectivity in its historical embodiment. For Rahner, not only does the transcendent God become present in Christ but God's presence in the world inspirited by that presence also points to the meaning of life for all God's creatures become brothers and sisters of God's son. Christ reveals the infinite dignity God has bestowed upon humans, placed as they are in a communion with God's incarnate son whose own destiny is interwoven with that of all peoples.

As we have seen in the introduction to the second chapter, Rahner's essays on Christology are wide-ranging. Yet, at the core of what he says about Christ is his understanding of how Christology must itself be both congruent with human nature expressed in a person's search for meaning and transcendental in that Christ is recognized only through those human experiences and structures that are the outgrowth of a person's yearning for salvific fulfillment. Christ is in this way a definitive answer to the critical question with which God confronts people by God's presence in the man Jesus. Rahner structures his Christology into a searching, transcendental quest for what the doctrine of Christ can mean in a world that poses new, critical questions to traditional Catholic dogmatics and tends to reject the triumphalist claims of the church. Rahner acknowledges the limitations in the Catholic magisterium's more cautious, narrower approach to the questions of Jesus' uniqueness, his two natures, and his historical consciousness. But Rahner also ponders the possibility of suggesting some alternate, more cogent interpretations of supposedly finalized christological doctrines from the conciliar tradition and related catechetical assertions. These conciliar decrees are accepted by Rahner as affirmations to be taken seriously in articulating a dogmatics that is contemporary in its meaning and relevant for today's Christians. Nonetheless, he also recognizes the inherent limitations of all credal formulas and dogmatic definitions, despite their being so emphatically fixed in the Christian tradition. In his analyses he emphasizes not only the vagaries of language, the historical contexts of magisterial definitions, and the cultural conditioning that were the matrix of these decrees but also the question of how contemporary people understand and interpret their experience and, indeed, their personhood. In short, he demands that one pay attention to vital anthropological considerations in the formulation of a Christology that is faithful to what it means to be at once fully human and in communion with the divine manifest in history.

The two selections of this section by no means offer an exhaustive representation of Rahner's Christology. They illustrate, however, important features of the way he combines a transcendental Christology with a respect for the historical-existential moorings of any dogmatic assertion about the person of Jesus Christ.

DOGMATIC REFLECTIONS ON THE KNOWLEDGE AND SELF-AWARENESS OF CHRIST

This first selection, taken from volume 5 of the Schriften, *published in 1962, appeared earlier in the same year in the* Trierer Theologische Zeitschrift. *The English translation comes from the* Theological Investigations, *volume 5 (pp. 199–215), published in 1966. Rahner's essay brings out not only his respect for the human and historical in analyzing dogmatic assertions about Christ; it also shows his uncanny ability to rethink what had been simply taken for granted in a more routine Christology and to offer a new mode of interpretation more faithful both to the biblical data and the critical consciousness of contemporary believers. In this instance Rahner confronts the Catholic textbook and magisterial statements that claim that, because of the union with his divine nature, Christ's humanity enjoyed not only the beatific vision but also perfect knowledge of all things human. Hence he aims his critical firepower at the theological deduction that there was in Jesus a complete absence of ignorance of any sort or of any growth in knowledge beyond experiential perception of what was already known either divinely or intuitively. Rahner argues that such a conclusion detracts from Jesus' humanity as portrayed by all the extant historical sources, particularly in the details of his passion and death. Furthermore, such conclusions were deduced from a highly abstract, philosophical logic more at home in the idealistic anthropology of a Greek worldview. This logic insists on a God-man perfection in which nescience is rendered impossible. Likewise, Jesus' union with the divine entailed a beatific vision such that Jesus' father God was an object forever emblazoned on Jesus' human consciousness. Human suffering, doubt, learning, surprise, and even dread of being forsaken were thus effectively precluded from Jesus' experience.*

For Rahner, on the contrary, these magisterial, textbook conclusions fly in the face of the biblical data. They are, moreover, rooted in what he claims are distorted views both of human nescience and of the traditional affirmation that

Jesus had an immediate vision of God. On the former, Rahner draws on his own foundational anthropology to show that to experience ignorance and to grow in knowledge, far from being a lack of perfection, are necessary if Christ in all his freedom is ever to integrate the contingent events of history and the obscured variables in the actions of persons, the "dark ground" and continuing drama of history, into his exercise of freedom.

Concerning the latter, Rahner shifts the focus away from what had been ascribed to Jesus as beatific vision toward the more Scotist view that Jesus' nearness to the divine or his "immediacy" to his Father need not have had what neo-scholastics claim to be a "beatific effect." Without denying Jesus' immediacy of vision or his hypostatic union, Rahner suggests, instead, that one speak of a subjective union of Jesus' human consciousness with the word of God that, as a consequence, gave him not infinite knowledge of objects and of every connected historical contingency but an unobjectified awareness of his divine sonship. In other words, his immediate vision of God was nothing more than Jesus' presence to himself and to his Father as God's word in every act of his knowing and loving. According to Rahner, it is in Jesus' nature to experience a direct presence to God in a relationship that is at once intimate, unreflected, and determinative of every other spiritual activity. It is the tacit dimension in Jesus' gradual development as a human person completely attuned to his Father's inspiriting love that becomes expressed in his historical lifetime. For Rahner it is preposterous to imagine Jesus as a walking encyclopedia. Jesus was a human whose consciousness of his infinite origins and destiny needed the final passage from death to resurrection to become perfected in glory. In Rahner's essay, theological anthropology and transcendental Christology seem to merge as he cautions against the inflated, dehumanizing claims for Jesus that textbook Christology seems to have encouraged.

We must try to get as directly and as quickly as possible to the very heart of our question, and this by refraining from reminiscing on the history of dogmas and of theology. Such reminiscences could not in any case be presented with the necessary accuracy in the brief space of this essay. What will be said in no way claims to be a binding theological doctrine. It is not intended to be anything more than a conceivable theological conception which is not opposed to the declarations made by the official magisterium about our question. It is simply meant to be a theological conception which seems to make sense because it seems to prove itself to be deducible from dogmatic presuppositions which are certain, a conception which without forcing things is compatible with the historical findings of the researches made into the life of Jesus. Since we are going to propose a positive solution which does not alter anything in the declarations made by the magisterium even where these have no absolutely binding authority (that is, are not dogmatic definitions), this also saves us from discussing the question of the exact theological note given to this traditional doctrine in the declarations of the church's magisterium.

In preparing for our reflections proper, it should be stated first of all that knowledge has a multilayered structure: this means that it is absolutely possible that in relation to these different dimensions of consciousness and knowledge something may be known and not known at the same time. We state this because one gets the impression that the explanation of the knowledge of Christ usually starts with the tacit presupposition that human beings' knowing consciousness is the famous tabula rasa on which something is either written or not, so that this simple "either-or" is the only possibility with regard to the question of something being written or not written on it. Yet this does not correspond to the facts. Human consciousness is an infinite, multidimensional sphere: there is reflex consciousness and things to which we attend explicitly; there is conceptual consciousness of objects and a transcendental, unreflected knowledge attached to the subjective pole of consciousness; there is attunement and propositional knowledge, permitted and suppressed knowledge; there are spiritual events in consciousness and their reflex interpretation; there is nonobjectified knowledge of a formal horizon within which a determined comprehended object comes to be present, and this sort of knowledge is an objectified, conscious a priori condition of the object comprehended a posteriori; and finally there is the knowledge about this object itself. All this is really self-evident and yet has not been considered sufficiently when thinking about our present question. In the discussion of our problem, one has always known, of course, that there are different kinds of knowledge, and one has distinguished between infused and acquired knowledge with several subdistinctions in each of them. Yet in this connection one has always more or less explicitly looked upon these different kinds of knowledge as different ways of gaining objective knowledge, rather than regarding them really as different ways of knowing a reality, that is, one has considered them as different ways in which things come to be written on the tabula rasa of consciousness but not as totally different ways in which a reality can be present in the multidimensional space of consciousness. It cannot be our job to draw up an empirico-psychological or transcendental scheme of these different ways in which something may be present in consciousness. The point just touched on is merely meant to indicate the fact of this multiplicity of possible forms in which a reality can be present in consciousness. Our remarks were not intended to give an exact analysis of the mutually distinct ways of being conscious of something, of having knowledge or of being known—it was not our intention to analyze such basic states and conditions.

There are just two things to which we would draw further attention. First, there is among these forms of knowledge an a priori, unobjectified knowledge about oneself, and this is a basic condition of the spiritual subject in which it is present to itself and in which it has at the same time its transcendental ordination to the totality of possible objects of knowledge and of free choice. This basic awareness is not knowledge of an object, and normally one does not concern oneself with it. Reflection can never quite lay hold of this basic condition even when it makes an express effort to do so. The conceptually reflex knowledge of it, even when it is present, is never this condition itself but is always supported by it in its turn and for this reason alone never gets an adequate grasp of this basic condition. Furthermore, it is not necessary that the reflection on this basic condition should succeed; it may perhaps even be impossible, and its never quite successful exercise may depend on the external, historically contingent data of external experience, on the conceptual material offered from elsewhere, and on its historical character. Ideally, of course, the theses just formulated should be proved exactly and in detail, but this is quite impossible here. But we may get some understanding of their meaning and truth simply by reflecting on the fact that spirituality, transcendence, freedom, the ordination to absolute being found in every, even the most commonplace, act of human beings which is concerned with any indifferent matter of their biological self-assertion, are not indeed given as a theme or an object, and yet are nevertheless really conscious data. Indeed, they are the most primitive of the data of consciousness, possessing transcendental necessity, and of an all-embracing significance: a significance which nevertheless can only be caught hold of in themes or objects with the greatest effort and then only in a long history of the spirit, hidden beneath the extremely changeable history of terminology and only with very mixed success and the greatest differences of opinion as to their interpretation.

The second preparatory remark consists in a critique of the Greek ideal of the human being in which knowledge is simply the yardstick of human nature as such. In other words, a Greek anthropology cannot but think of any ignorance *merely* as a falling short of the perfection toward which human beings are orientated. Nescience is something which has simply to be overcome, it is not regarded as having any possible positive function. Anything which through nescience is not present is simply something which fails to take place, but this absence is not seen as an

opening out of space for freedom and action, which can be more significant than the mere presence of a certain reality. Living at the present
time, we cannot think as undialectically as that about knowledge and
ignorance. And we have objective reasons for this. It is impossible here
to develop the positive nature of nescience—of the *docta ignorantia*—
in every direction. We would merely draw the reader's attention to the
following fact. A philosophy of the person and of the freedom of a finite being, a philosophy of history and of decisions, could undoubtedly
show with comparative ease that the facts of challenge, of going into the
open, of confiding oneself to the incalculable, of the obscurity of origin
and the veiled nature of the end—in short, of a certain kind of ignorance—are all necessary factors in the very nature of the self-realization
of the finite person in the historical decision of freedom. It could be
shown quite easily that freedom also always demands the wisely unob-
structed area of freedom and its willingly accepted emptiness, as the
dark ground of freedom itself and as the condition making it possible.
In other words, there is certainly a nescience which renders the finite
person's exercise of freedom possible within the still continuing drama
of his or her history. This nescience is, therefore, more perfect for this
exercise of freedom than knowledge which would suspend this exercise.
There is, therefore, undoubtedly a positive will for such a nescience.
That there is a place for nescience is always already affirmed and this
precisely in the will for absolute transcendence into the infinite and incomprehensible being as such. And insofar as the nature of the spirit
is directed toward the mystery of God—insofar as all the clarity of the
spirit is founded on the ordination to the eternally incomprehensible as
such, and this even still in the *visio beatifica*, which does not consist in
the disappearance of the mystery but in the absolute nearness of this
mystery as such and in its final beatifying acceptance—it becomes once
more manifest, from the point of view of the final perfection of the spirit,
that one must be very careful when one is tempted to qualify nescience
as something merely negative in human beings' lives. Whether this consideration has any contribution to make to our subject—and if so, what
contribution—is something which will become clear only later on.

We come now very quickly to the very heart of our reflections. These
reflections are of a dogmatic kind. Hence we ask: For what reasons must
one, together with Catholic textbook theology and the magisterium, ascribe to Jesus even during his life on earth the kind of direct vision of
God which is the basis and center of the beatific vision of God enjoyed
by the blessed in heaven? If we put the question this way, it is because
we wish to indicate even in the way we put the question, that right from

the beginning one ought not to speak here of a "beatific vision." For one thing, it is far too easily taken for granted as self-evident that direct contact with God must always be beatific. Without necessarily adopting the Scotist view about the manner of beatitude, it may nevertheless be asked why absolute nearness and immediacy to God, understood as the direct presence to the judging and consuming holiness of the incomprehensible God, should necessarily and always have a beatific effect. Furthermore, is it certain that what is meant, in the tradition of theology, by the consciousness of Jesus is really intended to convey an idea of beatitude by direct union with God over and above this union itself? In view of the data provided by the historical sources regarding Christ's death-agony and feeling of being forsaken by God in his death on the Cross, can one seriously maintain—without applying an artificial layer-psychology—that Jesus enjoyed the beatitude of the blessed, thus making of him someone who no longer really and genuinely achieves his human existence as a *viator* [person on a journey]? If one may reply to these questions in the negative, then the problem occupying us at present is simply a question of determining what valid theological reasons could be brought forward to convince us that we are quite correct in attributing a direct union of his consciousness with God, a *visio immediata* [immediate vision], to Jesus during his earthly life but this without qualifying or having to qualify it as "beatific."

It will probably be possible to preface this more specific question with a preliminary reflection. We will be able to divide the possible answers basically and in accordance with the facts of the history of theology into two groups. The first group of answers (naturally of many different shades) will attribute this direct union to Jesus because, and insofar as, it starts from the principle that, even on earth, Jesus must have had all those perfections which are not absolutely incompatible with his earthly mission, especially if this perfection can be proved to be—or at least probably be—a help or a more or less necessary presupposition for his teaching authority. In this group of answers, therefore, this *visio immediata* is really an additional perfection and gift granted to Jesus, a perfection which is not ontologically bound up with the hypostatic union but which at the most is connected with it by a certain moral necessity, just as for similar reasons Christ is for instance credited with infused knowledge, and so on. This group of answers to our question is then, of course, more dependent on an appeal to the testimony of the Scriptures and of tradition than is our second group, which will be discussed in a moment. For a *legatus divinus* claiming divine authority, a prophet, is absolutely conceivable even without a *visio immediata*. Furthermore, the principle that Jesus is to be credited with all those perfections and privileges which are not incompatible with his mission (for there are such, as, e.g., freedom from suffering), finds itself faced with the question as to whether this *visio immediata*, which is practically always regarded as beatific, is not itself incompatible with the mission and life of Jesus on earth—a question which, in view of the historical evidence of the life of Jesus, could be answered in the negative only with many reservations and obscurities. Beyond this, however, one will have to say that the backing which must be found in tradition for this sort of reply does not represent too solid a prop, especially when one takes into consideration the Greek concept of self-evidence of quite a few tacit presuppositions in this tradition, presuppositions which are human and not dogmatic. If one appeals simply to the teaching of the church's magisterium, then the dogmatic theologian must be reminded of the fact that it is his or her very task to show how, and from where, the modern magisterium has taken its teaching, since it does not receive any new revelation but only guards and interprets the apostolic tradition and hence must itself have objective reasons for its interpretation of this apostolic tradition. Thus, recourse to the teaching of the church's magisterium does not suffice, especially since this doctrine has never up until now been proposed as a defined and hence binding dogma, and since its content can still be given essentially different interpretations. Even seen in this light, the first group of answers—the extrinsicist theory (to call it that)—has not a great deal to recommend it.

The second group of answers regards the *visio immediata* as an intrinsic element of the hypostatic union and hence regards it as simply given bound up in this union and as something which also cannot be abandoned. Thus in this view, it is not at all necessary to find a proper direct proof for this in the tradition of all ages. Furthermore—and this is a decisive point for our reflections—it follows in this view that this vision can be determined more exactly from the nature of the hypostatic union, in such a way that the consequences of this nature for the *visio beatifica* must also be affirmed, and whatever does not follow from it must also be denied theologically, whenever one cannot support it by any other certain and theologically binding additional tradition, which presumably will not be the case.

We must now explain the meaning of this second answer more fully and—for reasons of space—this will have to be done in as brief a speculative reflection as possible, without even attempting to find any confirmation of it in the history of theology. We start then from the axiom of the Thomistic metaphysics of knowledge according to which being, and self-awareness, are elements of the one reality which condition each other immanently. Hence, something which exists is present to itself, to the extent in which it has or is being. This means that the intrinsically analogous and inflective nature of being and of the power of being, is in absolutely clear and equal proportion to the possibility of being present to oneself, to the possibility of self-possession in knowledge, and the possibility of consciousness. Let us presuppose this axiom—without being able to develop its meaning and justification more exactly here—and let us apply it now to the reality of the *unio hypostatica* [hypostatic union]. The hypostatic union implies the self-communication of the absolute being of God—such as it subsists in the Logos—to the human nature of Christ which thereby becomes a nature hypostatically supported by the Logos. The hypostatic union is the highest conceivable—the ontologically highest—actualization of the reality of a creature, in the sense that a higher actualization would be absolutely impossible. It is the absolutely highest manner of being there is apart from God's. The only other form of being which might be comparable with it, is the divine self-communication by uncreated grace in justification and in glory, insofar as both forms of being do not come under the notion of an efficient causality but rather of a quasi-formal causality, since it is not a created reality which is communicated to a creature but the uncreated being of God. Inasmuch as the hypostatic union involves an ontological *assumptio* [assumption] of the human nature by the person of the Logos, it implies (whether formally or merely consequently need not be investigated here) a determination of the human reality by the person of the Logos and is therefore at least also the actualizing of the *potentia obedientialis*, that is, of the radical capacity of being "assumed," and hence is also something on the part of the creature, particularly since—as is stressed by scholastic theology—the Logos is not changed through the hypostatic union, and anything happening (which is the case here in the most radical way) takes place on the side of the creature. But according to the previously stated axiom of the Thomistic metaphysics of knowledge, this highest ontological determination of the created reality of Christ (that is, God in God's hypostatic, quasi-formal causality), must of necessity be conscious of itself. For, according to this axiom, what is ontologically higher cannot be lower on the plane of consciousness than what is ontologically lower. Thus, given that this self-consciousness is a property of the human reality, then this ontological self-communication of God is also—and, indeed, specially and primarily—a factor in the self-consciousness of the human subjectivity of Christ. In other words, a purely ontic *unio hypostatica* is metaphysically impossible to conceive. The *visio immediata* is an intrinsic element of the hypostatic union itself. What has just been stated is simply intended to indicate what is meant here and thus to indicate the general direction which the second group of answers tends to follow in solving the problem stated at the beginning. What we have said is not meant to imply, however, that all this would not have to be explained at much greater length and with far greater precision than we have been able to do here.

We also do not mean to imply that the recognition of the fact of the *visio immediata* as an intrinsic element of the hypostatic union could not be reached in some completely different way. It would be possible to arrive at the same conclusion, for instance, by basing oneself on the profound reflections made by Bernhard Welte in the third volume of the work on Chalcedon, under the title of *homoousios hemin* [of the same substance as we], where he shows how in an ontology of the finite spirit the hypostatic union is the most radical (gratuitous) actualization of what is implied in the nature of a finite spirit as such. After that, it is easy to see that such a hypostatic union cannot be conceived as a merely ontic connection between two realities conceived of as things, but that—as the absolute perfection of the finite spirit as such—it must of absolute necessity imply a (correctly understood) "Christology of consciousness"; in other words, it will then be easily seen that only in such a subjective, unique union of the human consciousness of Jesus with the Logos—which is of the most radical nearness, uniqueness, and finality—is the hypostatic union really present in its fullest being. If one conceives of the relationship between the hypostatic union and the *visio immediata* in this way, it is not at all necessary that the latter should always have been attested explicitly by tradition or Scripture, whereas the church's teaching on this reality acquires nevertheless a necessity and binding force which is greater than if it were proved with the help of merely morally certain arguments of convenience.

Deriving this doctrine in this way will also give us an insight into *how* this direct union of Christ's human consciousness with God is to be conceived. When we hear about Christ's direct vision of God, we instinctively imagine this vision as a vision of the divine essence present before his mind's eye as an object, as if the divine essence were an object being looked at by an observer standing opposite it, and consequently as if this divine essence were brought into Christ's consciousness from without and occupied this consciousness from without and hence in all its dimensions and layers. Once we have adopted this imaginative scheme (naturally we do not do this reflectively, but for that very reason this schematic representation determines our notion of the vision of God all the more profoundly) then we pass equally unconsciously and naturally to the thought that this divine essence offering itself and viewed in this way as an object of vision from without, is like a book or mirror offering, and putting before Christ's consciousness, more or less naturally all other conceivable contents of knowledge in their distinct individuality and propositionally formulated possibility of expression.

But then we have arrived at the problem with which we started: Can such a consciousness have been that of the historical Jesus as we know him from the Gospels—the consciousness of the one who questions, doubts, learns, is surprised, is deeply moved, the consciousness of the one who is overwhelmed by a deadly feeling of being forsaken by God? Precisely this schematic image requiring an immediate conscious union with God and forcing itself upon us as if it were self-evident is not only not demanded but is also proved to be false if we start (as we have tried to indicate briefly above) from the only dogmatic basis we have for the recognition of the fact of this conscious, direct vision of God. For it follows from this that the direct presence to God, considered as a basic condition of Christ's soul, must be thought of as grounded in the substantial root of his created spiritual nature. For this direct presence to God is the plain, simple self-awareness—the necessary self-realization—of this substantial union with the person of the Logos . . . this and nothing more. This means, however, that this really existing direct vision of God is nothing other than the original unobjectified consciousness of divine sonship which is present by the mere fact that there *is* a hypostatic union. For this consciousness of divine sonship is nothing more than the inner, onto-logical illumination of this sonship—it is the subjectivity of this objective sonship necessarily present as an intrinsic factor of the actual objective condition. But for this very reason, this awareness of sonship which is an intrinsic element of the objective sonship, must not be conceived as a being-faced-with an objectlike God to which the intentionality of the human consciousness of Jesus would then be referred as to the "other," the "object" facing it. This consciousness of sonship and of direct presence to God (which is not something merely known by starting from outside it, but consists in a direct presence to God which is at once—and absolutely identically—both the reality itself and its inner illumination) is therefore situated at the subjective pole of our Lord's consciousness. The best and objectively most correct way of understanding it is to compare its characteristic nature with the intellectually subjective basic condition of human spirituality in general. This basic condition of human beings—

194

their spiritual nature, their transcendence and freedom, their unity of knowledge and action, and their freely activated understanding of self— is consciously present in them not only when they think about it, when they reflect on it, when they form propositions about it, or weigh up the various interpretations of this reality. Whenever and wherever they are and act as spirits—in short, wherever they occupy themselves intentionally with the most commonplace external realities—this "looking away from themselves" toward external objectivity rests on this unformed, unreflective, perhaps never actually reflected knowledge about themselves; it rests on a simple self-awareness which does not "reflect" or objectify itself but which—looking away from itself—is always already present to itself by way of this apparently colorless, basic condition of a spiritual being and by way of the horizon within which all traffic with the things and notions of daily life takes place. This inescapable, conscious, and yet in a sense not-known state of being lit up to oneself, in which reality and one's consciousness of reality are still unseparated from each other, may never be reflected upon; it may be given a false conceptual interpretation; it may be—and indeed always is—attained only very inadequately and never completely; it may be interpreted from the most variant possible and impossible viewpoints, using the most assorted terminologies and systems of concepts, so that human beings may systematically tell themselves what they have already always known ("known" in that unformed attunement which is the unembraceable ground of their whole knowledge, the permanent condition of the possibility of all other knowledge, its law and gauge, and its ultimate form). This all-pervading basic condition is present and is conscious even in persons who declare that they have never noticed it.

To this innermost primitive and basic condition on which rests all other knowledge and activity, there belongs in Jesus that direct presence to God which is an intrinsic subjective element of the hypostatic "assumption" of the human spiritual nature of Jesus by the Logos. And this conscious, direct presence to God shares in the characteristics of the spiritual, basic condition of a man or woman, for it belongs to it as an ontic factor of that substantial basis whose self-presence constitutes this basic condition. This direct and conscious presence to God must not be understood in the sense of the vision of an object. This fact does not make this direct presence any the less ontically and ontologically fundamental and unsurpassable. But it means that this direct presence is the same kind of presence as is meant by the *visio immediata*, except that it excludes the element of "standing opposite" an object, an element which is usually associated with it as soon as one forms an image of "vision"; we can quite rightly speak of a vision even in this case, as long as we exclude from our notion of vision this particular element of an objective, intentional counterpole. A direct presence to God belongs to the nature of a spiritual person in the sense of an unsystematic attunement and an unreflected horizon which determines everything else and within which the whole spiritual life of this spirit is lived. This direct presence to God belongs to the nature of a spiritual person as the ground which, though not allowing us to grasp it completely in a reflex manner, is nevertheless the permanent basis for all other spiritual activities and which, on this account, is always more "there" and less objectively "there" than everything else. This presence belongs to the nature of a spiritual person as the tacit factor in self-awareness which orders and explains everything but cannot be explained itself, since a basis is always the clear but inexplicable factor. To make all this still more precise and more intelligible would require further development and proof of this doctrine of the spiritual, unformed, and nonconceptual and nonobjectified basic condition of a spirit. It would then be possible to say—and it would be more understandable—that this is also precisely the way in which we must conceive the direct and personal presence of the Logos to the human soul of Jesus. Since this more general task cannot, however, be carried out any further here, we must content ourselves with these modest pointers to a conceivable understanding of the absolutely immediate nature of the fact that the Logos is consciously communicated to the spiritual human nature of our Lord.

We must, however, explain briefly a few further conclusions to be drawn from this at least briefly outlined theory, which will lead us back to the series of problems with which we started these considerations. If we take what has just been said above about the characteristic nature of Christ's conscious, direct presence to God, and connect it up with what was said in our first introductory remark, then we may say that the basic condition of direct presence to God is not only reconcilable with, but moreover demands, a genuinely human spiritual history and development of the man Jesus. After all, this basic condition is itself of such a nature as to demand a fixed form and a spiritual, conceptual objectification, without it itself having such a form as yet, though leaving all the necessary free room for it in the a posteriori, objective consciousness of Christ. In spite of human beings' always already-given basic condition *as* spiritual beings, and in spite of the attunement (*Gestimmtheit*) which is always present in the very ground of their existence (but which has nothing at all to do with a "mood" or *Stimmung*) human beings must first "come to themselves," that is, only in the course of long experience can they learn to express to themselves what they are and what indeed they have always already seen in the self-consciousness of their basic condition. In other words, just as there is this objectively reflexive process of becoming conscious of what has always been already understood consciously but without knowing it and in an unsystematic and unobjectified manner, so it is also in the case of Christ's consciousness of divine sonship and his basic condition of direct presence to God. This consciousness in Christ realized itself only gradually during his spiritual history, and this history does not consist only, or even first and foremost, in being occupied with this or that fact of external reality but consists rather in the never quite successful attaining of what and who one is oneself, and this precisely as what and whom one always already possessed oneself in the depths of one's existence. Hence it is absolutely meaningful, and no cheap trick of a paradoxical dialectic, to attribute to Jesus at the same time an absolute, basic state of being directly present to God from the very beginning and a development of this original self-consciousness of the created spiritual nature being absolutely handed over to the Logos. For this development does not refer to the establishment of the basic state of direct presence to God but to the objective, humanly and conceptually expressed articulation and objectification of this basic state; this basic condition is not a fully formed and propositionally differentiated knowledge, nor is it an *objective* vision.

These two notions are not merely not mutually contradictory—they demand each other of their very nature. For it is in accordance with the nature of spiritual, personal history itself, and its whole content, that a basic state should tend to communicate itself to itself, and in a spiritual being the explicit knowledge of its own constitution can always understand itself only in the form of an interpretation and articulation of a basic condition which always supports it again, which can never be fully attained by it, and which consists in the most secret and innermost self-illumination of a spiritual reality. We can, therefore, speak without qualms about a spiritual and indeed religious development in Jesus. Such a development, far from denying the fact of his absolute, conscious, and direct presence to the Logos, is based on this fact and interprets and objectifies it. Such a history of the self-interpretation by spirits of their own basic condition obviously always occurs in their encounter with the whole gamut of their own external history of self-discovery in their surroundings, and in the whole history of their associating themselves with their own age. That which was always already present to itself, finds itself in this material. It is therefore absolutely legitimate to try to observe in what preestablished conceptual form and in what eventual development, to be built up without bias and a posteriori historically, this systematizing self-realization of the God-man's basic condition—of Christ's direct presence to God and of his divine sonship—actually took place from the very beginning. It is absolutely legitimate to desire to see which of the notions prescribed by his religious environment Jesus actually used in order to express slowly what he had always already known about himself in the very depth of his being. In principle, at least, such a history of his self-declaration has in no way to be interpreted merely as a history of his pedagogical accommodation, but can quite legitimately be seen also as the history of his own personal *self*-interpretation of himself to himself. For this does not mean that Jesus "discovered something" which he did not know in any way up until then, but it means rather that he grasped more and more what he already always is and basically also already knows. It is not the task of dogmatic theology (which in this question is to a certain extent a priori) but of the a posteriori research into the life of Jesus, to determine whether anything can be said in particular about this history and to determine the actual course of this history. If this research proceeds properly, it will not find anything—at least in its a posteriori materials—which contradicts such an original basic condition of absolute, direct presence to God. Perhaps it would even arrive historically at the recognition that the unity of this history of Christ's self-consciousness—its inner uninterrupted, clear, and unshakable nature—can be explained sufficiently only on the basis of this basic condition even when, historically speaking, the individual factors of the conceptual materials and of the general background of this self-consciousness can or could be derived to a larger extent from our Lord's religious environment.

What has just been said may suitably be followed by a brief remark about Christ's "infused knowledge." Gutwenger has tried to show that there is no constraining theological reason for assuming such knowledge to exist side by side with the direct vision of God and acquired knowledge. Hence it will be quite permissible, for instance, to refuse to accept Ott's qualification of Christ's having such infused knowledge as being *sententia certa* [a certain opinion]. As far as I can see, the theological discussions of Gutwenger's work have not brought forward any objections against his opinion on this particular point. If one starts from the direct presence to God taken subjectively and understands it as the ultimate basic condition of Christ's consciousness in such a way that it must of its very nature and by a historical development seek to translate itself into an objective knowledge, then it is possible to see implicit in this circumstance the factual content of what is meant by the theory of an (at least habitual) infused knowledge in Christ, and it is then possible to let the whole question rest there. For it is not necessary to conceive of the infused nature of this knowledge as something constituted by an immense number of individual *species infusae* [infused species], but it could be conceived as an a priori basis for a knowledge developing through the encounter with the world of experience.

It might be objected against the theory just outlined, that it certainly asserts that Christ's self-consciousness was radically in the direct presence of God from the very beginning, but that it also teaches that there was a proper history and development at least in the dimension of the conceptual reflection and objectification of this original basic condition, and that this necessarily implies phases in which certain objectifications, developments, and expressions of this basic condition were not yet present—in other words, that there was nescience in this sense and in this dimension. We would grant that this kind of initial nescience existed, but would absolutely deny that there are declarations by the church's magisterium or theologically binding traditions which do not allow us to accept such a nescience. In fact, it must be said that—if the doctrine of the true, genuine human nature of the son as essentially similar to our own is not to be degraded into a myth of a God disguised in a human appearance—such a historicity and "coming from beginnings" in which what was yet to come (precisely because it was historical) was not always already present, must necessarily be attributed to Jesus.

The church's doctrinal pronouncements command us to hold fast to the direct vision of the Logos by the human soul of Jesus. They do not however give us any theological instructions as to what precise concept of this vision of God we must hold. It is perfectly permissible to say that this unsystematic, global basic condition of sonship and of direct presence to the Logos includes implicit knowledge of everything connected with the mission and soteriological task of our Lord. In this way one will also do full justice to the marginal and incidental declarations of the church's magisterium which point in this direction, without having to suppose for this reason that Jesus possessed a permanent, reflex, and fully formed propositional knowledge of everything after the manner of an encyclopedia or of a huge, actually completed world history. These remarks will help us to understand what was really meant by our second introductory remark, namely, that not all or any knowledge at any moment of the history of existence is better than nescience. Thus, freedom in the open field of decisions is better than if this room for freedom were filled with knowledge of such a nature as to suffocate this freedom. It cannot simply be retorted against this consideration that the same reasoning would then have to be valid also for the proposed basic condition of direct presence to God, and that this proves our reasoning to be absolutely false, since it is impossible to show it to be valid in this dimension. For this basic condition is precisely that knowledge which, rather than cluttering up, opens up the room for freedom. For the transcendence into God's infinity (no matter how exactly it is to be conceived, that is, whether it is as in our case or as in that of Christ) is precisely in its infinity the necessary condition for freedom; the transcendental anticipation of all the possible objects of freedom is the very basis for freedom, whereas the objective perception of every individual object right down to the last detail would be the end of freedom. In this connection it may perhaps be observed, finally, that this general conception would also enable us to give a clearer explanation of the eschatological consciousness of Christ. This consciousness does not consist in the prophetic anticipation of the "last things," but consists in projecting these "last things" from what Christ knew in his basic condition of divine sonship and direct presence to God. He knows the "last things" and knows them insofar as, because, by the fact that, and in the way that he knows himself to be the son of God and to be in the direct presence of God: in this direct presence he knows them absolutely, and in the objective translation of his basic condition he knows them in the way and to the extent in which this condition can be given such a historically conditioned and a posteriori expression with regard to this particular question.

Let us close this whole consideration by formulating a kind of thesis: The dogmatic theologian and also the exegete are not permitted to doubt the binding, although not defined, doctrine of the church's magisterium which states that the human soul of Jesus enjoyed the direct vision of God during his life on earth. But to begin with, this does not mean that the exegete engaged in the work of fundamental theology must or even can positively take this theological doctrine into account. Furthermore, it is a perfectly theologically correct interpretation of this direct vision of God to understand this vision, not as an extrinsic addition to the hypostatic union, but as an intrinsic and inalienable element of this union, since—after all—it is held to be necessary to understand the hypostatic union itself ontologically and not merely ontically. It is then legitimate to be of the positive opinion that such an interpretation can understand the vision of God as a basic condition of the created spiritual nature of Jesus, a basic condition which is so original and unobjective, unsystematic and fundamental, that it is perfectly reconcilable with a genuine, human experience; there is no reason why it should not be perfectly reconcilable with a historical development, understood as an objectifying systematization of this original, always given, direct presence of God, both in the encounter with the spiritual and religious environment and in the experience of one's own life.

*

THE HISTORICAL JESUS AS A DOGMATIC PROBLEM

This second selection illustrates Rahner's respect for the scriptural foundations and historical setting of the church's christological assertions. It was originally a part of a lecture entitled "The Position of Christology in the Church between Exegesis and Dogmatics," presented to the Theological Academy of Berlin during a weekend conference, May 4–5, 1968, and published in volume 9 of the Schriften *in 1970 and, in English translation, in the* Theological Investigations, *volume 11 (pp. 189–206), in 1974. In the preliminary remarks that serve as context for his lecture, Rahner claims that history and dogmatics intersect in the man Jesus. He insists, therefore, that one accord a certain continuity between Jesus' pre-Easter history and self-understanding and the proclamation of what the church believes about Jesus, the risen Lord. Otherwise, in Rahner's opinion, Jesus himself and his death would not have any salvific connection with post-Easter faith. At the same time, Rahner cautions against an uncritical identification of Jesus' historical consciousness with what subsequent church Christology made into a confession of faith about him. Even the resurrection itself, considered as validation and status conferring enthronement, is no substitute for the essential continuity of the later Christology with Jesus' own awareness of his mission and function in God's saving history. Rahner points out that the question is complicated by the fact that the Gospels themselves express post-Easter faith. Nonetheless, he argues that the findings of exegesis regarding Jesus' self-understanding are a sufficiently discernible point of departure for the later Christology and must be connected with it for the sake of cohesion and credibility. This is the context of the selection that follows. In the last section of the lecture from which this excerpt is taken Rahner turns his attention to the issue of what is meant by the resurrection and by the apostles' experience of resurrection. There Rahner offers an interpretation of resurrection that is , he believes, faithful both to the meaning of human existence and to God's promise of eternal destiny for God's faithful people. Those who have staked their lives on God's Word find in the resurrection the validation of their trust and a reason never to give up hope in the midst of suffering. According to Rahner, God confers eternal, salvific meaning on the life and death of all people in the life, death, and resurrection of God's son.*

Before we attempt to enter directly into the question which we have just posed it may perhaps be appropriate to say something further about certain more general assumptions and broader perspectives without which it is quite impossible to answer such a question at all. The *first* point that we must bear in mind is that historical certainty and the sort of certainty which we can achieve in the concrete conditions of our human existence (if we may so express it) are two different things. And the difference between them is something which we should clearly recognize and freely take into account in our faith.

We may begin by invoking a quite simple example to illustrate what we mean by this. Someone has a mother. He has a quite specific and unique relationship to this woman. He accepts all the consequences that ensue from a relationship of this kind. Now if we were to ask him what real grounds he has for knowing that this individual, in relation to whom he behaves and acts as a son, really is his mother, whether he really has any certainty of this at the levels of natural science or metaphysics, or even merely of scientific history, then surely he would in the end be forced to answer: "At this level I have no such certainty." Certainly we can see no reasonable grounds for calling this personal conviction of his of this mother-son relationship in question. But at the same time we have never yet reflected, at the level of "scientific exactitude," upon this conviction of his. In other words we have no scientific or absolute certainty of the genuineness of this relationship. We could if we wished make a scientific problem of this relationship involving a whole range of difficult questions.

Without having to analyze this "case" in any greater detail at this point we can easily perceive in the light of an example of this kind that the two kinds of certainty are two different things: the attitude which prevails at the level of the individual's own existence in the concrete, and which involves this immanent and personal certainty, together with all the radical consequences ensuing from this on the one hand, and the process of scientifically reflecting upon the grounds and presuppositions for such an attitude of existential (*existentielle*) certainty on the other. This process of scientific reflection is important and indispensable. But it can never adequately include or replace that more ultimate and global certainty which belongs to human living in the concrete and the actual experience of this. We cannot demand this from the process of scientific reflection, because it is in principle incapable of achieving any such thing, since in any given instance the explicit content of knowledge arrived at as a result of scientific consideration is only given in an act of cognition which as such is not in its turn made the subject of reflection, and which at least in the case of those kinds of knowledge which are of existential significance, at the level of concrete human living, inevitably plays its part in influencing the actual content of the considerations involved. This difference between the certainty of science and the certainty which belongs to the ultimate dimension in which we achieve the fullness of our own existence cannot be eliminated. Individuals must learn to live with this difference. They must not use it as a weapon to destroy that other, and more ultimate certainty inherent in life itself (in our case the certainty of faith), whenever this certainty, which may be more ultimate, becomes unacceptable to them for some reason or other.

Now let us apply the insight which we have merely been able to indicate above, to our present problem. All the statements of exegesis considered as a historical science belong to the category of theoretical reflection and speculation, and of historical criticism, and here they have a legitimate place of their own. But even in this case we must not suppose for one moment that the human, global, and total conviction of Jesus Christ as the absolute bringer of salvation would not be legitimate so long as that other certainty arising from theoretically reflecting upon the historical assumptions implicit in this faith has to be qualified as a lesser certainty in terms of epistemological theory. We have in principle the right to say, "Of course in exegesis many questions remain open. There is much that continues to belong to the sphere of mere historical probability, and subject to a discussion among the exegetes which is endlessly prolonged. But this cannot and need not represent any attack upon believers in the absoluteness of their faith. For this faith is in fact based not merely upon the data of exegesis and the certainty belonging to these, but is also sustained by the experience of personal grace, by a certain interior self-assurance in the Christian understanding of existence which has never been consciously reflected upon to the full, by the totality of Christian living in the concrete, by the collective experience of Christendom, in a history extending over two thousand years. In accordance with the saying attributed to Peter in the sixth chapter of John (6:68-69) this faith can always remind itself that those who abandon the Christian faith cannot find anywhere else to go where they will be able to discover a brighter light to illumine the meaning of existence."

While on the one hand it is justifiable to ask, at the level of historical reflection, what data can be found with regard to the pre-Easter Jesus and what degree of certainty these have to offer, still on the other hand we must not assume in this that these data to which we can attain are the sole factors by which the absolute assent of faith in Jesus Christ is sustained. Now the converse of this is also true. It does not imply that this absolute assent of faith in Jesus Christ has nothing whatever to do with the data of history with which exegetical speculation is concerned. If someone came to us and proved to us positively and unambiguously that for instance Jesus himself either never existed at all or *certainly* understood himself merely as having some kind of religious mission to arouse his fellow human beings with a message which had nothing whatever to do with himself, his own person, and what he himself did, then our faith would no longer have that reality of saving history as its content, then our faith would be vain. Faith in saving history has a historical content. It cannot dispense with a content of this kind, and therefore it cannot dispense with the historical element in it either, or with the process of reflecting upon history, even though we can never adequately carry this through. At the same time, however, this faith is not born of scientific speculation alone. It would certainly be a heresy, and one which could not be tolerated within the Catholic church, if anyone sought to maintain that faith in Jesus as the Christ is absolutely independent of the historical experience and self-interpretation of the pre-Easter Jesus. But it would also be false to suppose that the content and the certainty of faith in Jesus Christ are the mere product of historical speculation as practiced in exegesis.

A *second* preliminary principle must be mentioned, which is necessary if we are to supply a reasonable answer to our basic question. It is obvious, yet still for the most part forgotten, that that utterance of God which we call God's revelation requires our own capacity to hear it for it to take place at all. To state the matter once and for all *in globo:* the statements which God addresses to us exist only in the statements which we receive with our minds. Basically speaking this is a truism, even if we take into account the fact that the revelation of God also takes place in the events of our own historical environment. For in order for these to be capable of being revelation events at all they must include an element of verbal interpretation of the purely factual element in them, and one which is not merely applied to these events from without, but is an intrinsic and constitutive element in these events themselves, necessary for them to have the status of revelation events at all.

If therefore the statements which God addresses to us exist only in statements which we ourselves formulate in our minds, then this clearly raises the problem of how we can know that these statements which we formulate in the subjectivity of our own minds are statements of God with an objectivity of their own. We cannot enter into this problem at this point in our investigations. Here we must confine ourselves to pointing out that it is merely one instance, albeit the most radical, of a general range of problems that arises in epistemological theory, that namely of how we can apprehend the objective element in reality without standing outside the subjectivity of our own acts of cognition (something which is precisely impossible). But on the basis of this special quality which belongs universally to all subjective cognition in which the objective is apprehended, we can at any rate understand that the subjectivity inherent in knowledge, and which can never be overcome, is the mode in which the objective is presented to us and not that which causes this objective element to be veiled by the merely subjectivist factors. This is also true of faith. The objectivity of the revelation of God always exists in the subjective expression of an individual, in other words in her or his "hearing," her or his "faith" which, in a very extended sense of this term, also includes the attitude of listening obediently to the message of God as brought to us by the bearer of revelation. The history of revelation and the history of faith are ultimately speaking two sides of one and the same process. The very fact that the address of God takes place in the concrete only in the mind of the individual who bears it in history means that the revelation of God is a historical process, a history such that what takes place in it is not always the same. All this is at basis a self-evident datum of Catholic dogmatic teaching, which is constantly aware of a saving history and also of a history of revelation.

It is only now, however, and after these preliminary considerations, that we arrive at a point which is especially important in its bearing upon our basic question. We have to recognize that even Jesus, as man and in his special character as the bearer of revelation, likewise utters the revelation of God to the extent that he himself in his human subjectivity hears and accepts what he has to say. And in all this, this subjectivity of his can have, and has had, in its turn, an individual history. The nature of divine revelation then is such that its ultimately basic acts take place solely in the mind of the individual who hears it. However, the process of human hearing in this sense has a collective, and even more an individual historicity of its own. And again this applies to the humanity of Jesus too, which is real and true. And in the light of all this it is not only not difficult in principle, but actually and positively necessary, to recognize that that revelation which takes place in the subjective human consciousness of Jesus and in his preaching is also a historical entity. What contemporary exegesis establishes a posteriori with regard to the self-understanding of the pre-Easter Jesus is, at basis, something which the dogmatic theologian has had to postulate all along a priori on the basis of the principles indicated above with which he or she has to work. Of course what applies throughout the history of human thought applies in this case too: we can only reflect upon and explicitate the implications inherent in our own position when a posteriori the historical situation is given, and also some concrete stimulus from without impelling us to do this. But this does not alter the fact that given these conditions we can then recognize implications of this kind *precisely as such*. Thus it is not surprising that in dealing with certain implications in the basic conception of the church's Christology with regard to the historicity of revelation, and also the historicity of the human awareness of Jesus as the bearer of revelation, we only explicitate these at that stage at which exegesis, with its a posteriori approach, discovers this historicity.

Exegesis, therefore, establishes that Jesus expressed his own understanding of himself in terms which are far from being identical with those of the later Christology of the church, and indeed not even identical with those of the Christology of the primitive community or the gospels of Paul and John. And exegesis further establishes that in expressing the significance of himself Jesus may have avoided certain terms used in the theology of his environment, indeed that he could not use them at all, even though they do subsequently reappear—albeit in altered form—in the Christology of the primitive church. Finally exegesis actually establishes that a certain historical development is to be observed in this self-understanding on Jesus' part (e.g., with regard to the fact that he came to include his own death as an integral element in this self-understanding of his). Moreover this historical development is actually such that it is wholly reconcilable with the church's dogmatic teaching to the effect that God was immediately present to Jesus in his human subjectivity (this is what the established dogmatic theology means by saying that the "vision of God" was present from the outset in the human soul of Jesus, though in order to reconcile this with the findings of modern exegesis we must understand this "vision" as consisting in a "basic content" in the human subjectivity of Jesus which was only gradually objectified, though also with complete clarity, in terms of the a posteriori material of the theology of his environment). Now all these theses or hypotheses of exegesis, strange though they may seem to us at first sight, turn out, on closer examination, but also in the light of the basic data of the Christology of the New Testament and the church itself, to be such as we should have expected.

We may therefore explicitly draw attention to the fact that the position today regarding the relationship between historical and critical exegesis and its findings concerning the self-understanding of the pre-Easter Jesus on the one hand and the dogmatic and fundamental theology of Jesus as the Christ on the other, does not, in the last analysis, represent an uneasy compromise between the two which is maintained through thick and thin in order that critical exegesis and traditional Christian faith may to some extent be able to coexist with one another. Rather, on a deeper view, the position between the two is one that we should expect on any really genuine understanding of the faith, and from a Christology which is that of the church but at the same time one that is the outcome of a process of radical self-realization. This interpretation of the current position is not invalidated by the fact that dogmatic theologians only recognize the a priori implications of their own position at the radical level when they encounter them a posteriori in the findings of exegesis. In the encounter between dogmatics and exegesis, therefore, the position is, in the last analysis, far from being as critical as is sometimes assumed, though of course this position will only gradually become clearer in the course of further discussions between exegetes and dogmatic theologians. We shall have to accustom ourselves to this situation, and it is only gradually that we can do so. But when we have achieved this we shall no longer be surprised to find that Jesus of Nazareth does not explicitly put forward a Christology of the kind maintained by the church itself. We shall achieve an ever-better understanding of the fact that while the formulations of the church's Christology remain justified and indispensable, still they are not of such a kind that it is precisely *they* which, simply as they stand, constitute that which is self-evident and clear to the utmost possible extent, while that which is presented in the New Testament as Christology, and above all as the self-understanding of the pre-Easter Jesus, is merely that which is ambiguous, "elusive," and obscure in its expression, and less developed by comparison with the firmness and lack of ambiguity in the Christology of the church. Rather we must learn to view the intrinsic convergence of the two kinds of statement in such a way that the moment we reach that point in unfolding the formulations of the church at which they become perplexing, this brings us back once more to the formulations of the New Testament, while conversely the formulations of the church have done nothing else than to take seriously, and really to investigate radically, the quite homely and simple and humanly assimilable statements of the pre-Easter Jesus and the statements about him in the New Testament. Exegesis and dogmatics are not two enemies seeking to engage in a life-and-death struggle against one another, and yet precisely still allowing one another to survive. We often express the matter by saying that one or other of the findings of modern exegesis are "still sufficient" for dogmatic Christology. But this precisely does not mean that the dogmatic theologian would "properly speaking" have expected something more from the exegete. If she or he really takes seriously the historical nature of revelation, and therefore the history of Jesus himself, she or he cannot want or expect anything more at all from the exegete.

This brings us at last to the real theme, the central question, of our considerations. We have seen that with regard to the self-understanding of the pre-Easter Jesus modern critical exegesis has isolated and established this by setting aside the interpretations superimposed upon it in the post-Easter Christology. Now as we have already said at the outset of this study, what we are seeking to establish as the basic thesis of these considerations of ours is that once we presuppose the experience of the resurrection this self-understanding of the pre-Easter Jesus as isolated and established by modern exegesis provides a sufficient basis and starting point for the dogmatic Christology of the New Testament and of the church. In other words the present-day exponents of fundamental theology and dogmatic Christology have no need to feel themselves abandoned by modern exegetes. They must not have the impression that the axioms and assumptions necessary for their work have been withdrawn from them by this exegesis. Of course it cannot be the function of the systematic theologian once more to recapitulate at this point the data yielded by modern exegesis, and which represent the "residue" (so to speak) of Jesus' understanding of himself, once the subsequent accretions of christological interpretation have been set aside. This is something which we are assuming here, and we are seeking only, to the extent that such a thing is possible within the scope of a brief study, to justify the thesis formulated above.

For this we must take as our initial starting point a really correct understanding of the church's dogmatic teaching on Christology. It is necessary to build a bridge to unite present-day exegesis, with its critical methods and findings, to that body of dogmatic teaching on Jesus Christ developed by the church which must be retained as permanently valid. And the two halves of this bridge must be projected outward from both sides at the same time—including, therefore, the side represented by systematic theology. Both departments must refuse to content themselves with any facile compromise, but rather each proceeding from its own axioms must seek to achieve a new encounter, so that a genuine and intrinsic reconciliation may be achieved between the ancient dogmatic teaching and the findings of modern exegesis. For this ancient dogmatic teaching is in fact that of the Catholic exegete too and, moreover, precisely as such. But for this purpose fresh ground will also have to be broken from the side of the systematic theologians. They too will have to think out afresh those formulations of this dogmatic teaching which, though ancient and self-evident to them, still need constantly to be subjected to fresh questioning, in order to achieve a fresh apprehension of their own essential message. This implies that dogmatic theologians must be prepared to make a fresh start on the basis of the ancient and radical statements of Christology itself as these have been defined, so as to eliminate from this Christology as they de facto conceive of it all those distortions and misunderstandings which have crept into it and which are ultimately monophysite in character.

The very manner in which systematic theologians recognize, formulate, and emphasize at a specific point within their systems these ultimate principles, and chiefly that concerning the true human nature of Jesus, entails a certain danger, and one which has not yet really and permanently been eliminated. This is the danger that at some other point, or in other connections within the same Christology, or perhaps because of the religious mentality it entails and the expressions appropriate to this, they may once more forget these principles and—if we may be permitted to formulate it in these terms—fall back into the attitude of average Christians, who all too often are still either partly or wholly monophysites, even though they know and repeat the sound and correct formulations of the catechism. In the mind of these "ordinary consumers," orthodox though they may be, a strange and unconscious line of thought all too often and too easily asserts itself, by which Jesus comes simply to be identified with God who, in some remarkable manner, uses the "humanity" of Jesus as a sort of livery which God wears, or an instrument, in order to render God's self "noticeable" to us here below.

In truth, however, the Christian dogma of Chalcedon lays down that without prejudice to what we call the hypostatic union, Jesus really and in very deed is a man. The word "is" as employed by us in the formula "Jesus is God, is the son of God, is the Logos" suggests a further "is," a further synthesis between the subject and the material content of the predicate as, for instance, when we say "Fritz is a man," asserting thereby not merely that this humanity is one with the subject Fritz, but that there is a real identity between the two. In the case of Jesus, however, his humanity is precisely not identical with God in this way, and on any right understanding of the church's dogma this is precisely not what is being maintained, but rather what is excluded. We might put to the "ordinary consumer" Christians who intend to be orthodox the following questions: "Can Jesus tremble before the incomprehensibility of God? Can he, radically thrown back upon his own feeble creaturehood, adore God as the incomprehensible? Can he go to meet a fate which is dark so far as he is concerned?" And then, even though these "ordinary consumers" have themselves all along been saying that Jesus is truly man, they will suddenly be brought up short and the "yes" which they must pronounce in reply to this question will not come easily to their lips. And yet this "yes" belongs to Catholic dogma right from the outset, and not merely to the findings of a modern exegesis. The Jesus of the Chalcedonian dogma, which was directed against monophysitism and monothelitism, likewise has a subjective center of action which is human and creaturely in kind, such that in his human freedom he is in confrontation with God the incomprehensible, such that in it Jesus has undergone all those experiences which we make of God not in a less radical, but on the contrary in a more radical—almost, we might say, in a more terrible—form than in our own case. And this properly speaking not in spite of, but rather because of the so-called hypostatic union. For the more radically any given individual is related to God existentially, and so too in his or her concrete mode of existence as a creature, the more such a creature achieves the state of self-realization; again the more radically any given individual is able to experience his or her own creaturely reality, the more united he or she must be with God.

Thus we have genuinely to eliminate from the Christology which we actually live this element of monophysitism and monothelitism (though today we should more properly call it mono-subjectivism), not merely in the explicit verbal formulations of its tenets, but in our own ultimate and uncircumscribed understanding of our religion. Once we have achieved this we shall find it all the more easy to acquire a free and uncircumscribed understanding of what modern exegesis has worked out with regard to the pre-Easter Jesus. For when we can freely allow our interest in Jesus (to put the matter somewhat paradoxically) to be in a genuine sense concentrated more on his significance for the kingdom of God and for God than on his actual status as a "person," we can recognize that in his own individual history real questions arise for him, and that he is surprised, that he achieves insights and realizations at the conceptual level about himself which are only gradually articulated and expressed, and which surprise himself. At the same time, however, we understand that these are always discovered in the process of developing an understanding of himself which is based upon that element which ultimately lies at the very roots of his existence, and which dogmatic theologians are accustomed to call the "immediate vision of God present in the soul of Jesus." The fact that this is the only way in which dogmatic theologians can do justice to the data of modern exegesis is not the sole

210

reason why they have to take into account the fact of a genuine humanity in Jesus. They *must* do this because otherwise their position would be contrary to the dogmatic teaching of Catholic theology, in other words to their own principles.

There is one point which dogmatic theologians must again and again make clear to themselves on the basis of their own principles and data. It is that however true it may be that according to these dogmatic principles Jesus constitutes a unique reality in saving history such that he must not be placed on the same level as any other prophet, religious personality, or inspiring leader, still it is also true that he must be fitted organically into a basic conception of saving history as a whole, even though in fitting him in this way we only realize his position at the supreme point of saving history viewed precisely in this way as a totality after we have achieved the a posteriori experience of Jesus. He does indeed constitute the supreme point of this saving history, unique and unsurpassable, but he is this precisely within this saving history itself. We are presenting the uniqueness of Jesus in a false light if we regard him merely as the son of God, setting him in this sense over against human beings as though initially these had nothing to do with God, or when we view him simply as a messenger from the other world of the divine, entering a world which again has nothing to do with God.

Against this the real position is that whatever place we occupy throughout the whole history of humankind, we are children of God. God never ceases to dwell and to hold sway in God's own divine nature at the innermost center of this history throughout its course in virtue of an absolute, albeit a completely free and grace-given act of self-bestowal, thereby constituting the ultimate principle and the ultimate driving force of the history of this present world. Whether we always recognize this, whether we arrive at a conceptually objectified and consciously formulated statement of this basic grace-given mystery of the world and its history or not, whether we open ourselves in faith and in love to this ultimate reality of our own existence, or alternatively incur mortal guilt by closing ourselves against it (though even then we cannot banish God and God's will to bestow grace from our world)—these are yet further questions, and ones which we shall not be treating of here. The process by which this ultimate and grace-given mystery of God's self-bestowal instilled into the very roots of human nature and into the very roots of history itself achieves its own due fullness—a process of self-realization achieved in knowledge and love—constitutes the *single* history of revelation and salvation, because the history of knowledge and the acceptance of this basic mystery of the world which consists in God's self-bestowal is itself the history of this self-bestowal of God as imparting revelation. God is not to be thought of as merely "over against" the world and its history in virtue simply of being its first "cause," untouched by the world itself and transcending it. Rather in the outward movement of God's love God has inserted God's self into the world as its innermost *entelecheia* [entelechy or actualizing principle], and God impels the whole of this world and its history toward that point at which God will be the innermost and immediately present fulfillment of our existence in the "face-to-face" presence of eternal beatitude.

Without prejudice to the uniqueness of Jesus he must be viewed in his place in this saving history which is the history of God and the world both in one. Such a view need not obscure this uniqueness of his, but it will eliminate from it that element of the exaggeratedly miraculous, the mythological, which comes to be associated with the idea of an intermediary whom God sends from another world constituted by God's own life into a merely secular world. Let us therefore take as our starting point a conception of saving history of the kind we have described; one in which God, in an act of gracious self-bestowal, is always at work from the heart and center of the world itself, and which is coextensive with the history of the world in general. Let us set clearly before our eyes the fact that a saving history of this kind, which is always the history of God's freedom and human beings' freedom, presses on toward a point at which this history of God's self-offering and the free acceptance of this in the world becomes irreversible, and manifests itself in the dimension of history in this irreversibility that belongs to it. If we approach the question in this way then, on the basis of this realization of its own significance which is achieved in saving history, we have obtained a view of that point at which Jesus stands, at which God accepts the world in such a way that God can no longer let it go, and at which the world, through this self-bestowal of God, obtains as its own gift that deed of creaturely freedom in which this freedom of the world definitely accepts God's self-offering. Then we are standing at that point at which a woman or a man, from the ultimate roots of her or his own being, signifies the definitive address of God to the world, *and at the same time* the assent of the world to this God.

Assuming that an understanding of the question has been achieved from both these perspectives, we can now apply ourselves directly to the consideration of our basic thesis. According to the findings of contemporary exegesis it can be said even today that the pre-Easter Jesus understood himself as the absolute eschatological event of salvation and the eschatological bringer of salvation.

Of course for this statement to represent the findings of modern exegesis it is not necessary for absolutely all exegetes to subscribe to it. In any historical science, in view of the complicated nature of the facts under investigation, this is something which from the outset we should not expect. In this connection we may remind ourselves once more of that difference between the relative certainty or probability of historical knowledge, even as a presupposition of faith on the one hand, and the absolute assent of faith as such on the other. What the precise terms were in which Jesus made his self-understanding real in his life, and in which he actually expressed it, whether and how far he drew upon religious ideas and concepts which were already present beforehand in his environment for expressing this significance which he saw in himself—these are questions which the dogmatic theologian can freely set aside, seeing that the exegete tells him or her that while there are indeed many particular unsolved questions and difficulties with regard to the details of the self-understanding of the pre-Easter Jesus, still it can be stated with a sufficient degree of reliability that Jesus understood himself as something more than merely some kind of preacher with a mission to arouse human beings to a sense of religion such that his message merely pointed to a relationship between God and human beings, a relationship itself already existing independently of the message pointing to it. He understood himself, rather, as one in whose message (precisely as *his*), and in whose person that which he preached was actually made present in a new and irrevocable form as a new and unsurpassable summons of God. In this sense we say that the pre-Easter Jesus (including in this concept his actual message in itself) understood himself as the eschatological event of salvation and the eschatological bringer of salvation.

The self-understanding of Jesus in this sense is something that we must take with the utmost seriousness and realize in the full depths of its significance. We must take seriously the fact that in Jesus' understanding of himself his message constitutes that which is new, that which has not always been present. At the same time, however, despite the infinity of the possibilities open to God, and the openness of history itself to that which is new, this message constitutes also that which is ultimate and unsurpassable, as well as that which is inseparable from his own person. Once we have realized all this, then we have arrived at a point of departure from which we can attain to the church's dogmatic teaching on Christology, provided only that this is not itself misinterpreted in a monophysite sense. What we call the divine sonship of Jesus of Nazareth as a metaphysical and substantial reality in fact has no further content whatever beyond what can be expressed in the affirmation: Jesus is the eschatological, that is, the unsurpassable and abiding, mediator of our relationship with God. This precisely can never signify a prophet, an inspiring religious leader, or a religious genius. For the message precisely of *these* kinds of individuals is in principle always capable of being separated from their persons and their religious works. This is because the reality to which they point in this preaching exists independently of themselves. Moreover, since they are mere human beings, existing at one isolated point in history, the truth which they proclaim always is, or always should be, expressed with the proviso that this message will be made out-of-date once those further possibilities are realized which are open to God and which also exist in history. Now if on his own understanding of himself Jesus is not one of the prophets in this sense, and if it is obvious that on any Christian understanding of God he cannot be interpreted as a demigod either, then, when the Christology of the church speaks of the unity between this event of salvation in the concrete and this mediator of salvation in the concrete—a unity involving the duality of two natures as distinct, the divine and the human—it is simply stating in different terms this self-understanding of Jesus as the eschatological bringer of salvation. The converse of this is of course likewise true.

When, therefore, exegesis emphasizes that the pre-Easter Jesus speaks in the first instance not so much of his own person but of the advent of the kingdom of God which has become quite new and actual, then this should not surprise dogmatic theologians in the light of their position either. For if this kingdom of God has come definitively, victoriously, and in the manner which can no longer be surpassed by any fresh events of salvation in his person and message, and if Jesus himself declares precisely *this* to be the case, then ipso facto he has spoken about his own person. If he has come, as we confess, *propter nos et propter nostram salutem* [for us and for our salvation], then the message he had to convey to us first and foremost was: "Your salvation is there now as judgment and grace." And if it is true that he possessed a genuinely human subjectivity, which achieves the truth most proper to it precisely at that point at which it looks away from itself to the incomprehensible God and God's love, and to humankind as sisters and brothers, and in a certain sense loses itself in both directions, then we should precisely not expect him to speak of himself in that explicitly self-reflecting manner which is employed in the dogmatic Christology of the church. We understand his true nature only when we see it as absolutely one with his function in saving history. If therefore he speaks of this function of his, ipso facto he has spoken of his own "nature." If he says that in him

God has uttered God's ultimate assent to the world in a way that is ever more unsurpassable and irrevocable, and that in virtue of this the kingdom of God is irrevocably present in the world (though at the same time it still constantly has to impose itself in history), then at basis he has already spoken more clearly of himself than if he had spoken of himself in isolation, presenting us, so to say, with a mirror image of himself by a certain process of introversion after the manner of the Christology developed by the church. Certainly this latter is inevitable and good at the retrospective stage. But it is such that even then it can only really be understood by us when we make real to ourselves in our faith what he is for us, and what has taken place through him and in him in that saving history which is our own. We must understand that a dogmatic formulation, however much it is, and continues to be, binding upon us, is not something which simply has to be defined in order that everything may be "clear." We must recognize that in the case of any dogmatic formula, in order really to understand it and make it real to ourselves in our faith, we must think back to that in which it properly originated as well. And if we realize all this then we will no longer listen to what we are told about the self-understanding of the pre-Easter Jesus with that attitude of slight mistrust and surprise with which we ask ourselves how in that case he did not express himself "more clearly" about his own significance. The true meaning of the dogmatic teaching of Christology has already been grasped (indeed it may perhaps actually be more assimilable to us in our concrete human lives in this form) when for instance we have really understood that saying of Jesus which runs: "Whatsoever you have done to one of the least of these my brethren, you have done it to me" (Matt. 25:40). There is no conceivable claim which could be more radical than this, that he himself is always and in all cases involved in the ultimate relationship between two individuals.

We have still to justify in fuller and more precise terms the thesis that the concept of a bringer of salvation in the absolute ipso facto implicitly contains the dogmatic teaching of Christology, once it has been taken with the full and radical seriousness due to it, thought out and restated in different words. At this point, however, I am compelled to refer to expositions which I have put forward elsewhere. Here therefore I may confine myself to reiterating once more this one point which I have already made: all those who are genuinely Christians will concede that the message which Jesus addresses to them is unsurpassable. We must, however, recognize the immensity of the implications ipso facto contained in this statement, for all its apparent innocuousness. For it might be said: all prophets, however much they may appear as messengers of

God with a momentous and stirring message to convey, must still retain an awareness of the fact that in this message of theirs they are forming only a single tiny drop from the boundless ocean of the eternal godhead. Furthermore they can only utter this message precisely as messengers of God so long as they submit themselves in the most radical manner to the fact that tomorrow other messengers will come who, from the boundless fullness of God, in which all eternity and the future that still lies before us are comprised, will draw some quite different message, yet one that is no less momentous and that renders the old one out-of-date. In other words every prophet must, in a true sense, allow for the fact that saving history remains open to further, unforeseeable, and sometimes revolutionary developments beyond any to which he or she can point. Nevertheless in a very real sense that one brief statement which we have just taken as our starting point, and to which every Christian subscribes, puts a definitive end to all this. Otherwise it should not be taken seriously at all. In itself and without any further addition this one brief sentence states that no single word that Jesus utters can be surpassed or invalidated in its further application to the world even by God. The message which Jesus utters through his person and through his words can be the unsurpassable and abiding word of God only if the reality that it constitutes (including in this the words that he utters and the fate that he endures) is God's own reality in the manner which we seek to express by the term "hypostatic union." Otherwise saving history would be open to further extensions into the future which would no longer stand under the law of Jesus Christ. Alternatively, if we wish to deny that this one brief sentence has the definitive finality which we have ascribed to it, we would have to subscribe to that completely distorted anthropomorphism according to which God, the infinitely wise and powerful, is thought of as breaking off the history of revelation and salvation at a certain point in a completely arbitrary manner *ab externo* [from without], even though in itself, considered as God's own history, infinite further possibilities still remained open to it. Or again we would have to postulate that through his person and his words Jesus had, after all, only expressed what is true always and everywhere, and attainable from any point in history. And this would mean that there would in truth be no history of revelation and salvation. Even taken by itself, therefore, this brief statement which we have taken as our starting point as a statement which, after all, every Christian can surely make her or his own, implicitly, but in a very true sense, contains the whole Christology of the church. Admittedly this point would require a more extensive development and justification than we can accord to it here.

Once more we may formulate our basic thesis: If Jesus understood himself to be the eschatological event of salvation in the absolute, and the mediator of salvation in the absolute, and if this self-understanding on the part of the pre-Easter Jesus can, with sufficient certainty, be recognized as present in him even by modern historical and critical exegesis, then we have found an adequate point of departure for the Christology of the church. At the same time this is not to deny, but on the contrary to imply, that in the dimension of Jesus' own conscious re-flection upon himself, this self-understanding of his can in its turn have a history of its own. And this history in itself only attained its defini-tive fullness in his resurrection. Only through this event did it become credible in a definitive sense for us.

If it is true, then, that a Christology of the church is possible on these premises, it is equally true that these premises for a Christology of the church are themselves unalterable. It is perfectly justifiable for exegetes to point out the historical problems which these premises entail. But if they go beyond this, if they seek to say, rather, that they have come to recognize with positive and unambiguous historical certainty that the realities presupposed here simply did not exist at all, then the premises of fundamental theology and dogmatic theology for the Christian faith would really be destroyed. But I believe that no exegete would claim to be able to substantiate such a position. On the contrary, even a very critical approach to exegesis, so long as it remains open to what is unique and peculiar to Jesus, will conclude that the self-understanding of Jesus presupposed here is to be affirmed.

6

ON THE HOLY SPIRIT

Although Rahner's explicit writings on the Holy Spirit are few, nearly all of his theological reflections connect in some way with the reality of God as Holy Spirit. Whether it be the inner relationships of the Trinity in God's own personhood or the manner in which the power of God courses through and comes to expression in the creation and enhancement of human personhood, for Rahner, the Holy Spirit is the essential link. The world of God's caring presence is the world Rahner claims is graced by the "sending" of the Spirit, the same Spirit that is a symbol of every facet of the interrelatedness of creator with creature, of the mode of God's immanence in human experience, and of the transcendent human orientation to the divine. The Holy Spirit is central to Rahner's explication of the core Christian doctrines of Trinity and incarnation as these in turn impact on the prime locus of the Holy Spirit's historical manifestation in the mystery of God's grace.

For Rahner, the main events of God's saving history are in reality events of the Spirit bringing people into an intercommunion with the divine source of all meaning and hope. In his theology these events reach a certain definitiveness in Pentecost with the foundation of the church as a Spirit-endowed community. He claims in this connection that Pentecost grounds the absolute trust in God's promises that the community established in Jesus' name will preach to the world. Rahner depicts the Holy Spirit, then, as the life-giving promise made in creation, incarnation, and redemption come to fruition. The church is the visible sign of God's inner love, of the presence of Jesus, and of Jesus' neverending mission to the far reaches of a sinful yet graced world. Although the church has structured itself as a hierarchically organized society, in Rahner's view it remains forever a church in the power of the Spirit and of God's sacramentalized promise to God's people. Thus in Rahner's view deference to the Spirit and to the gospel must dominate the church's self-understanding and proclamation. For the church to become more visibly the community of the Spirit of the Word made flesh Rahner emphasizes that it should also be gifted in its ecclesiastical offices. Hence he affirms his faith in the presence of the Holy Spirit abiding in the church. The Spirit guides church leaders with a wisdom capable of overcoming their occasional foolishness in matters ecclesiastical and a strength that is their fortitude in weakness. Because of this aspect of the Spirit's presence, Rahner sees ecclesiastical office and ministry as essentially charis-

matic and not merely institutional. The church is not empowered solely by the juridical and authoritarian prowess in which it often operates. And he sees no plausible reason for it to glory in its achievements with a triumphalism that is repugnant to those sensitive to Christ's example and his strictures against lead-ers who like to lord their prestige over people. Rather, God's Spirit enables the ecclesiastical to transcend itself, the human element to become more Christ-like. In sum, Rahner contends that the charismata of the Spirit, which extend beyond church officials to a gifted laity as well, keep the church with all its failings in the grace, truth, and holiness of God.

Rahner concludes, therefore, that the experience of the Holy Spirit is proper to the church in its governing and graced symbolization of God's presence in the world. But it is also the same Spirit that touches individual persons, leading them sometimes gently, sometimes brusquely, to the discovery of God in the inner moments of their being human and being in relationship, and of their graced search for meaning. The first selection of this section shows how Rahner construes the "experience of the Spirit" that becomes like a potentially mystical element in one's daily life beyond the more explicit ecclesial dimension of the human relatedness to God. The second selection illustrates Rahner's pointed warning to the church against its becoming so smugly confident in its being a manifestation of the Spirit that it would be unaware of its perennial capacity to stifle that same Spirit.

EXPERIENCING THE SPIRIT

Far from constricting the vistas of his theology of the Holy Spirit to the lim-ited perspectives of Catholic "textbook theology," Rahner seeks to discern the unrestricted movement of God's Spirit in the wider vistas of the human spirit searching for endless fulfillment in the commitment to genuine human values and in the longing for God in the myriad forms such longing takes. Rahner's theology portrays God's Spirit ranging far more widely in God's creation than many segments of the Christian ecclesial world would admit. Rahner explores the activity of the Spirit behind the gentle divine persuasion and the attraction toward the good, in the urge to love God despite a seeming inner emptiness, in one's doing one's duty in an act of generous self-sacrifice, and in many other manifestations of how God's grace enhances one's being human and shapes the image of Christ even in those who do not know Christ. Rahner calls these experiences a true encounter with the supernatural even if people outside the Christian tradition lack an explicit awareness of the fact that such urgings toward the good in whatever form are the work of God's Spirit.

In short, for Rahner, God's grace is an inspiriting of the world of God's making, stirring in people a restless drive to be fulfilled in their humanity through a variety of options and movements, all subsumed in the one funda-

mental option, the choice to accept and act out their orientation to the Holy mystery of God. Rahner's theology of Spirit has, therefore, settings as varied as the quasi-infinite concretions of God's creative, salvific outreach in human history. His overview of how God's Spirit moves the human person to be more Godlike becomes, in a way, a mysticism of everyday life. The following selection illustrates this multifaceted mode of the Holy Spirit's manifestation in human experience. Rahner's reflections here were first published as Erfahrung des Geistes *by Herder Publishing House in Freiburg, Germany, in 1977. The English translation is from part 1 of the book* The Spirit in the Church, *published in 1979 (pp. 6–31).*

At Pentecost the Spirit was given to the young church with the promise that the Spirit would always remain with the church, until the end, in all the Spirit's freedom, comfort, and power. Therefore any meditation on the Holy Spirit must think of the Spirit as the gift in which God bestows God's self on human beings.

THE TESTIMONY OF SCRIPTURE
AND THE EXPERIENCE OF THE SPIRIT

Can we say anything more precise about the Spirit? We could of course turn to the Bible and search through it for all the passages in which we read of the Spirit of the Father given through the Son to all who believe in him; of the Spirit pouring as living water from the pierced side of the crucified Jesus, a source of vitality springing into everlasting life and assuaging our thirst for eternity; of the Spirit who makes us sons and daughters and allows us to say: Abba—dear Father; of the Spirit given to us in baptism and the laying on of hands. That is the Spirit who signifies the advent of the triune God and offers us a share in God's love, truth, and freedom; in whom we all become one and in whom we all hope together; through whom we are anointed and sealed; and who with incomprehensible summoning power prays in us and with us, and in access to the Father gives us the assurance of a life that will last for ever. The Bible tells us all that and much more that is marvellous, impressive, and exalted, offering many possibilities for meditation on the Spirit, so that we are stirred to strong and courageous faith and true joy.

Believing Christians who open their hearts to this encouragement and consolation of the Bible will soon realize that they can also meditate thus today on the pentecostal mystery. It is also clear, but has to be made emphatically clear, that when we attempt to follow a somewhat different way of meditating and inquire into our own experience of the Spirit, we must still have implicit recourse to this same scriptural teaching. We would not be able so precisely to contemplate and understand our own experience (that available to all women and men in the profundity of their existence) if the Bible had not already expressly raised it to the level of personal concern.

But Scripture speaks in other than doctrinal terms of the Spirit who is given to us.

The Bible refers to our own experience of the Spirit (for instance, in Galatians and on other occasions in Paul, in John, and throughout Scripture), and therefore we are especially entitled to ask where and how we experience the Spirit in our own selves in this personal, biblical way.

INDIVIDUAL EXPERIENCES AND THE ONE
FUNDAMENTAL EXPERIENCE OF THE INDIVIDUAL

When we make this inquiry, we are of course aware from the start that experience of this kind is incommensurable with what we are otherwise accustomed to call "experience" in everyday life; especially in the sense given to the word by the physical sciences or empirical psychology. This experience of the Spirit begins at the innermost core of our existence, at its subjective pole, so to speak. It does not mean an encounter with any kind of object that confronts us from without, or the effects of such an occurrence. Apart from experiences which may be given an expressly theological interpretation in our conscious mind and in our reflection on them, there is an experience within us which is of a different nature and irreconcilable with the experiences which first come to mind when we hear the word "experience."

When we first consider the associations of the word, we might think of the givenness, the occurrence as we notice it, of individual aspects of the reality of our human and objective environment, or of individual psychological phenomena within our conscious minds, as with a localized pain, or individual thoughts with a specific content, and so on. All these individual realities become present to us one by one, as it were, *within* the overall framework of our consciousness, where they are ranked, distinguished from others, and connected to or associated with one another.

But in addition to these individual experiences of specific realities, there is another kind of experience which is outside the context of our everyday experiences as we recognize and talk about them. This is the experience of individual persons as such, who undergo all those particular experiences as their own and are responsible for them; and who are present to themselves in their original unity and oneness, even when they cannot see themselves clearly and precisely in the details of their experience, but possess themselves only in an apparently empty disposition, and when they lose themselves in the multitude of everyday experiences and seem to forget that wholeness.

My intention here is not to write a metaphysical or ontological essay on the isolated cognitive or existential nature of the fundamental experience which the individual human being has of himself or herself: a unique, original basic experience which always remains hidden behind all the specific objective experiences of that same being (though I shall return later in an appropriate context to this "transcendental" subjective nature of the human individual). At this point all I want to do is to remind you that there is a form of experience which is incommensurable with ordinary everyday encounters with specific realities, but which is no less present at all times, though in most cases we tend to ignore it. Similarly, the experience of the Spirit with which I am particularly concerned here is not to be rejected out of hand as nonexistent, merely because—like the self-givenness of the human individual—it is liable to be overlooked in all specific experience.

Of course it is possible, when one thinks one cannot properly discover this experience of the Spirit in oneself, to assert its existence so to speak authoritatively from without in terms of Scripture and church doctrine. But if we did not inquire here and now into that experience of the Spirit—however important it might be to interpret it through faith and with the aid of holy writ and thus to bring it to the light of the word—then we should run into the danger of treating everything that Scripture says about that Spirit in us as ideology or mythology, and of asking almost petulantly whether, and where exactly, all the joyous possession of the Spirit we read about in the Bible is to be found in us. There is the further danger of asking (while still accepting the authority of Scripture) whether it should not all be transferred to a dimension somewhere outside our own consciousness and our freely chosen piety.

IS THERE SUCH A THING
AS EXPERIENCING THE SPIRIT?

Is there such a thing as experience of the Spirit which on the one hand enables us to understand and legitimate the testimony of Scripture to the indwelling of the Spirit in us, and on the other hand is confirmed and affirmed by Scripture as the true word? Indeed there is.

THE TESTIMONY OF THE MYSTICS

Today as so often in the church's past it is probably appropriate to our quest to remember that there have always been mystics and enthusiastic or "charismatic" experiences and movements in the church which, in spite of their extremely diverse forms and interpretations, have been taken as experience of the Holy Spirit.

Mysticism has existed and still exists. Those graced with such an experience have reported and continue to report that (either in a sudden breakthrough or in an extended series) they experience grace, the direct presence of God, and union with God in the Spirit, in the sacred night, or in a blessed illumination, in a void silently filled by God. They say that, at least within the mystical occurrence itself, they do not doubt that they experience the direct presence of the self-communicating God as the action and actuality of God's saving grace in the depths of their existence, and that that experience is the "experience of the Holy Spirit."

But the ordinary and theological ways in which this experience has been described are most various in the history of mysticism, and this objective and verbal interpretation (dependent on ideological, cultural and philosophical, and theological modes and patterns of understanding) has been offered in very different ways.

How the question is to be answered in accordance with the elation of this Christian mysticism and its Christian interpretation of similar non-Christian mystical phenomena, especially in the East and above all in Islam and in Buddhism, and how such experience can coexist with socioecclesial and sacramental-ritual piety—are questions which do not concern us here and now.

The mystics bear witness to experience of the Spirit, and in principle there is nothing to stop us accepting all their testimonies as credible. That is the case especially when we remember that the original experience and the philosophical and theological interpretation of it are two different things, and that for that reason variety and contradiction in explanations do not discredit the original experience. On the other hand, these mystics included men and women of extreme sobriety and the finest observation, right up to Carl Albrecht in our own era—a mystic who was also a prominent doctor, psychologist, philosopher, and scientist. There certainly are people who have the courage to offer credible testimony of their experience of the Spirit.

Of course theologians of Christian mysticism have stressed the extraordinary, reserved nature of these mystical phenomena. They have done so on the one hand because they wanted (quite rightly) to emphasize the origin of these phenomena in grace, and were guided by the implicit opinion that the work of grace and that which was free from all guilt must by definition occur but seldom; and on the other hand because such unmistakable mystical phenomena usually occur with accompanying ecstatic (indeed almost parapsychological) circumstances, which can of course be very rare. It is to some extent understandable that normal Christians should treat such mystical occurrences as something that does not concern them and that they can safely ignore.

But if we isolated the mystical core-experience more exactly from such unusual peripheral phenomena as ecstasy, trance, and so on (something not possible in the present context), then it would certainly be easier to see that such mystical experiences are not events that are sadly beyond the experience of an ordinary Christian, but that the testimony that mystics offer of their experiences indicates an experience which every Christian (and in fact every human being) can make and evoke but which he or she too easily overlooks or represses. In any case it is true to say that there is such a thing as mysticism, and that it is not so very distant from us as at first we are inclined to think.

LONGING FOR THE POWER OF THE SPIRIT

Enthusiastic phenomena and movements occur among non-Catholic as well as Catholic Christians. Whether such incidents represent mystical closeness to and oneness with God in the sense of the classical, more individual, and individualist mysticism, and how we can phenomenologically and theologically classify mysticism and (earlier and present-day) enthusiasm of a more communal type, is a question which I cannot examine closely here, especially since the traditional theology of mysticism recognizes the most diverse modes and stages of mystical experience, and hence there is a possibility of arranging enthusiastical or "charismatic" experiences in a mystical hierarchy of some kind, without confusing them with the apex of mysticism: ultimate union with God in grace in the *unio mystica* [mystical union] itself.

Nevertheless there are Christian enthusiastic or charismatic movements nowadays. Their members are looking for the experience and power of the Spirit. They hold long charismatically inspired prayer meetings at which they claim to experience the workings of the Spirit even in the form of ecstatic glossolalia (or speaking in tongues), and miraculous healing. A surprising number of people believe that in such prayer meetings they experience what they think of as baptism in the Spirit: an ultimate fullness of the Spirit.

Even an objective and rational theology does not have to reject all these enthusiastic experiences out of hand, or to treat them with doubt and skepticism; that is so even when it is evident that divine fire is producing an awful lot of human smoke, when a number of American charismatic efforts do not suit European taste, when a lot of these happenings can easily be explained by a very secular psychology, and when they occur just as often outside the religious context (though there they are not subjected to any theological interpretation).

Even though a man or woman who is still following his or her pilgrim way in time and history cannot really claim that he or she is fulfilled in such charismatic movements, having received an absolutely certain and ultimate message from the Spirit (traditional theology would call this confirmation or establishment in grace and count it among the most sublime of mystical experiences), here we are certainly confronted with especially impressive, humanly affective, liberating experiences of grace which offer wholly novel existential horizons. These mold the innermost attitude of a Christian for a long time, and are quite fit (if you wish) to be called "baptism in the Spirit." They are experienced in these charismatic services as the operation of the Spirit given to the community.

CAN WE EXPERIENCE THE SPIRIT?

But—and here we reach the theme proper—what if we do not dare to call ourselves mystics, and perhaps for very different reasons cannot take any personal part in these charismatic movements and practices? Do we have any experience of the Spirit? Do we merely nod respectfully in the direction of other people's experiences which we ourselves find rather elitist? Do such people merely offer reports of a country that we have never seen and whose existence we are content to accept much as we might credit that of Australia if we have never been there?

We accept, and even confess as Christians supported by the testimony of Scripture, that we can have such an experience of the Spirit, and *must* have it as something offered to us in our essential freedom. That experience *is* given to us, even though we usually overlook it in the pursuit of our everyday lives, and perhaps repress it and do not take it seriously enough.

EXPERIENCING THE UNUTTERABLE MYSTERY

If I try to bring the reader's attention to such experiences, it seems inevitable that a few theoretical remarks on the innermost nature of

225

human knowledge and freedom should precede more practical statements about personal experience. The reader will have to excuse the summary and rather abstract nature of what I have to say in a somewhat restricted space. Only by talking about knowledge and freedom can I show and analyze the structure and specific nature of our spiritual experiences, and indicate why in our reflective, verbalizing objective minds we can easily overlook those experiences, and imagine that they do not exist at all. Therefore I request special patience and attention in considering my initial theological remarks.

We should consider human knowledge and freedom together, because in spite of the great differences between them, ultimately they have a common structure. In knowledge and freedom human beings become the very essence of transcendence. That may sound rather pretentious but it is unavoidable, and what I refer to in these terms is, in the end, the ultimate ineradicable essential structure of human beings, irrespective of whether the everyday man or woman and the empirical scientist care to notice it or not. In knowledge and freedom human beings are always simultaneously concerned with the individually characterized and specifically definable individual objects of their everyday experience and their individual sciences, *and* at the same time with something beyond all that—even when they take no notice and do not name or refer to this "something else" always present outside and beyond the ordinary. The movement of the mind or spirit toward the individual object with which he or she is concerned always aims at the particular object by passing beyond it. The individually and specifically and objectively known thing is always grasped in a broader, unnamed, implicitly present horizon of possible knowledge and possible freedom, even if the reflective mind only with difficulty and only subsequently succeeds in making this implicitly present fragment or aspect of consciousness a really specific object of consciousness, and thus objectively verbalizes it.

The movement of the spirit and of freedom, and the horizon of this movement, are boundless. Every object of our conscious mind which we encounter in our social world and environment, as it announces itself as it were of itself, is merely a stage, a constantly new starting point in this movement which continues into the everlasting and unnamed "before-us." Whatever is given in our everyday and scientific consciousness is only a minute isle (though it may be big in one sense and may be magnified by our objectifying knowledge and action, and continuously and increasingly so) in a boundless ocean of nameless mystery, that grows and becomes all the clearer the more, and the more precisely, we express our knowing and wanting in the individual and specific instance. If we tried to set a boundary to this empty-seeming horizon of our consciousness, we would find that we had already passed through and beyond that very barrier that we sought to establish.

In the midst of our everyday awareness we are blessed or damned (have it how we will) in regard to that nameless, illimitable eternity. The concepts and words which we use subsequently to talk of this everlastingness to and into which we are constantly referred, are not the original actual mode of being of that experience of nameless mystery that surrounds the island of our everyday awareness, but merely the tiny signs and idols which we erect and have to erect so that they constantly remind us of the original, unthematic, silently offered and proffered, and graciously silent experience of the strangeness of the mystery in which, in spite of all the light offered by the everyday awareness of things, we reside, as if in a dark night and a pathless wilderness. (There we are in darkness and a desert place—but one that reminds us of the abyss in whose depths we are grounded but can never plumb.) . . .

If we were to use the term "mysticism" to describe this experience of transcendence in which we always, even in the midst of everyday life, extend beyond ourselves and the specific thing with which were are concerned, we might say that mysticism occurs in the midst of everyday life, but is hidden and undeclared, and that this is the condition of the very possibility of even the most ordinary, sober, and secular everyday experience.

GOD, THE INCLUSIVE BUT ILLIMITABLE GROUND

In this unnamed and unsignposted expanse of our consciousness there dwells that which we call God. The mystery pure and simple that we call God is not a special, particularly unusual piece of objective reality, something to be added to and included in the other realities of our naming and classifying experience. God is the comprehensive though never comprehended ground and presupposition of our experience and of the objects of that experience. God is experienced in this strange experience of transcendence, even though it may not be possible to arrive at a more exact metaphysical characterization of the unity and variety between the transcendental experience of the spiritual subject in knowledge and freedom, on the one hand, and the experience of God which is given in the transcendental experience, on the other hand. This kind of definition is too difficult a philosophical undertaking and unnecessary in the present context.

227

Nevertheless, the unlimited extent of our spirit in knowledge and freedom, which is ineluctably and unthematically given in every ordinary experience, allows us to experience what is meant by God as the revealing and fulfilling ground of that expanse of the Spirit and its unlimited movement. Transcendental experience, even when and where it is mediated through an actual categorial object, is always divine experience in the midst of everyday life....

EVERYDAY EXPERIENCE AND THE EXPERIENCE OF THE SPIRIT

But even if we ignore the question whether such transcendental experience of God in the Holy Spirit could properly occur in instances of undirected absorption, in a state of consciousness void of objects of any kind, and in mystical experience for its own sake, there are in any case actual experiences in our existential history in which this intrinsically given transcendental experience of the Spirit occurs more obviously in our conscious minds: experiences in which (to put it the other way round) the individual objects of knowledge and of freedom with which we are concerned in everyday life, by their very specificity more clearly and insistently reveal the accompanying transcendental spiritual experience, in which by themselves and implicitly they indicate that incomprehensible mystery of our existence that always surrounds us and also supports our everyday awareness, and indicate it more clearly than is otherwise usual in our ordinary and banal everyday life. Then everyday reality of itself refers to this transcendental experience of the Spirit which is implicitly and apparently featurelessly there and always there.

This indication, which is always associated with our everyday reality conceived in knowledge and freedom, and more insistently brought to our attention in certain situations, can also be intrinsically given by reason of the positive nature of that categorical reality in which the magnitude and glory, goodness, beauty, and illumination of our individual experiential reality promise and point to eternal light and everlasting life. But it is already understandable that such a form of reference is most clearly experienced where the graspable contours of our everyday realities break and dissolve; where failures of such realities are experienced; when lights which illuminate the tiny islands of our everyday life go out, and the question becomes inescapable whether the night surrounding us is the absurd void of death engulfing us, or the blessed holy night which is already illumined from within and gives promise of everlasting day. When therefore I refer in the following primarily to those experiences which in this second way allow transcendental experience of God in the Holy Spirit to go forward, that does not mean that people and Christians are forbidden to let this experience of God occur in the first way, and thus to receive it. Ultimately the *via eminentiae* [way of eminence: e.g., humans are good; God is all good] and the *via negationis* [way of negation: e.g., humans are finite; God is infinite] are not two ways or two stations one behind the other on a way, but two aspects of one and the same experience (though, as I have remarked, for the sake of clarity it is quite justifiable to lay special stress on the *via negationis*).

EXPERIENCING THE SPIRIT IN ACTUAL LIFE

I can now refer to the actual life-experiences which, whether we come to know them reflectively or not, are experiences of the Spirit. It is important that we experience them in the right way. In the case of these indications of the actual experience of the Spirit in the midst of banal everyday life, it can no longer be a question of analyzing them individually right down to their ultimate depth—which is the Spirit. And no attempt can be made to make a systematic tabular summary of such experiences. Only arbitrarily and unsystematically selected examples are possible.

Let us take, for instance, someone who is dissatisfied with her life, who cannot make the good will, errors, guilt, and fatalities of her life fit together, even when, as often seems impossible, she adds remorse to this accounting. She cannot see how she is to include God as an entry in the accounting, one that makes the debit and credit, the notional and actual values, come out right. This woman surrenders herself to· God or—both more imprecisely and more precisely—to the hope of an incalculable ultimate reconciliation of her existence in which the one whom we call God dwells; she releases her unresolved and uncalculated existence, she lets go in trust and hope and does not know how this miracle occurs that she cannot herself enjoy and possess as her own self-actuated possession.

There is a man who discovers that he can forgive though he receives no reward for it, and silent forgiveness from the other side is taken as self-evident.

There is one who tries to love God although no response of love seems to come from God's silent incomprehensibility, although no wave of emotive wonder any longer supports her, although she can no longer confuse herself and her life-force with God; although she thinks she will die from such a love, because it seems like death and absolute denial; because with such a love one appears to call into the void and the completely unheard-of; because this love seems like a ghastly leap into groundless space; because everything seems untenable and apparently meaningless.

There is one man who does his duty where it can apparently only be done, with the terrible feeling that he is denying himself and doing something ludicrous which no one will thank him for.

There is a woman who is really good to another woman from whom no echo of understanding and thankfulness is heard in return, whose goodness is not even repaid by the feeling of having been "selfless," noble, and so on.

There is one who is silent although he could defend himself, although he is unjustly treated, who keeps silence without feeling that his silence is his sovereign unimpeachability.

There is a woman who obeys not because she must and would otherwise find it inconvenient to disobey, but purely on account of that mysterious, silent, and incomprehensible thing that we call God and the will of God.

There is a man who renounces something without thanks or recognition, and even without a feeling of inner satisfaction.

There is a woman who is absolutely lonely, who finds all the right elements of life pale shadows; for whom all trustworthy handholds take her into the infinite distance, and who does not run away from this loneliness but treats it with ultimate hope.

There is a man who discovers that his most acute concepts and most intellectually refined operations of the mind do not fit; that the unity of consciousness and that of which one is conscious in the destruction of all systems is now to be found only in pain; that he cannot resolve the immeasurable multitude of questions, and yet cannot keep to the clearly known content of individual experience and to the sciences.

There is one who suddenly notices how the tiny trickle of her life wanders through the wilderness of the banality of existence, apparently without aim and with the heartfelt fear of complete exhaustion. And yet she hopes, she knows not how, that this trickle will find the infinite expanse of the ocean, even though it may still be covered by the grey sands which seem to extend forever before her.

One could go on like this forever, perhaps even then without coming to that experience which for this or that man or woman is the experience of the Spirit, freedom, and grace in his or her life. For all human beings make that experience in accordance with the particular historical and individual situation of their specific lives. All human beings! But they have so to speak to dig it out from under the rubbish of everyday experience, and must not run away from it where it begins to become legible, as though it were only an undermining and disturbance of the self-evidence of their everyday lives and their scientific assurance.

Let me repeat, though I must say it in almost the same words: where the one and entire hope is given beyond all individual hopes, which comprehends all impulses in silent promise,

—where a responsibility in freedom is still accepted and borne where it has no apparent offer of success and advantage,

—where men and women experience and accept their ultimate freedom which no earthly compulsions can take away from them,

—where the leap into the darkness of death is accepted as the beginning of everlasting promise,

—where the sum of all accounts of life, which no one can calculate alone, is understood by an incomprehensible other as good, though it still cannot be "proven,"

—where the fragmentary experience of love, beauty, and joy is experienced and accepted purely and simply as the promise of love, beauty, and joy, without their being understood in ultimate cynical skepticism as a cheap form of consolation for some final deception,

—where the bitter, deceptive, and vanishing everyday world is withstood until the accepted end, and accepted out of a force whose ultimate source is still unknown to us but can be tapped by us,

—where one dares to pray into a silent darkness and knows that one is heard, although no answer seems to come back about which one might argue and rationalize,

—where one lets oneself go unconditionally and experiences this capitulation as true victory,

—where falling becomes true uprightness,

—where desperation is accepted and is still secretly accepted as trustworthy without cheap trust,

—where we entrust all this knowledge and all our questions to the silent and all-inclusive mystery which is loved more than all our individual knowledge which makes us such small people,

—where we rehearse our own deaths in everyday life, and try to live in such a way as we would like to die, peaceful and composed,

—where... (as I have said, we could go on and on):

—there is God and God's liberating grace. There we find what we Christians call the Holy Spirit of God. Then we experience something which is inescapable (even when suppressed) in life, and which is offered to our freedom with the question whether we want to accept it or whether we want to shut ourselves up in a hell of freedom by trying to barricade ourselves against it. There is the mysticism of everyday life, the discovery of God in all things; there is the sober intoxication of the Spirit, of which the fathers and the liturgy speak which we cannot reject or despise, because it is real.

LIVING AS PEOPLE OF THE SPIRIT

Let us look for that experience in our own lives. Let us seek the specific experiences in which something like that happens to us. If we find them we have made the experience of the Spirit which we are talking about. The experience of eternity, the experience that the Spirit is more than a piece of this temporal world, the experience that the meaning of human beings is not contained purely in the meaning and happiness of this world, the experience of the wager and of the trust which no longer possess any obvious ground taken from the success of this world.

From there, we can understand what kind of secret passion is alive in women and men of the Spirit and in the saints. They want to make this experience. They want repeatedly (out of a secret fear that they are caught up in the world) to ensure that they are beginning to live in the Spirit. They have tasted the Spirit. Whereas ordinary people treat such experience only as an unpleasant though not wholly avoidable disruption of normal life, in which the Spirit is only the seasoning and garnishing of another life but not of one's own, women and men of the Spirit and the saints have tasted pure Spirit. The Spirit is something they take pure and neat, as it were, no longer as a mere seasoning of earthly existence. Hence their remarkable life, their poverty, their longing for humility, their passionate wish for death, their readiness to suffer, their secret longing for martyrdom. It is not as if they were not also weak. It is not as if they did not also have continually to return to the ordinary atmosphere of everyday life. It is not as if they did not know that grace can also bless everyday life and rational action, and make them steps toward God. It is not as if they did not know that we are no angels in this life and are not expected to be. But they know that as a spirit the human being (in real existence and not merely in speculation) must really live on the borderline between God and the world, time and eternity, and they try continually to make sure that they are also really doing that, and that the Spirit in them is not only the means of a human way of life.

And if we make this experience of the Spirit, then (at least as Christians living in faith) we have already experienced the supernatural factually, even though very anonymously and perhaps inexpressibly. Probably so that we cannot veer round and should not veer round in order to see the supernatural itself. But we know if we release ourselves to this experience of the Spirit, if the tangible, tellable, and enjoyable founder, if everything sounds deathly silent, if everything has the taste of death and of downfall, or if everything disappears so to speak into an inconceivable, so to speak white, colorless, and intangible blessedness, then not only the spirit but the Holy Spirit is actually at work in us. Then the hour of the Spirit's grace has come. That is the time of the apparently strange groundlessness of our existence which we experience: the groundlessness of God who communicates God's self to us, the beginning of the coming of God's infinity, which no longer has any paths, which is enjoyed like nothingness because it is infinity. When we have cast off and no longer belong to ourselves, when we have denied ourselves and we have moved an infinite distance from ourselves, then we begin to live in the world of God, of the God of grace and eternal life.

That may seem unusual to us at first, and we are constantly tempted to take fright and return to the trustworthy and close at hand; indeed we often have to do so and should do so. Yet we should try to grow used to the taste of the pure wine of the Spirit, filled by the Holy Spirit. At least we should do so to an extent that enables us not to reject the chalice when it is proffered to us.

EVERYDAY MYSTICISM
AND THE GRACE OF JESUS CHRIST

At this point one might ask whether I have not hitherto praised a mysticism of everyday life which is not specifically Christian and directed to Jesus the crucified and risen Christ but something which could be found in all religions, and even outside any expressly religious and theological interpretation. That is a question which I cannot answer adequately here even though I can offer some indications on how it might be answered.

First: if and insofar as the experience of the Spirit I talk of here is also to be found in a mysticism of everyday life outside a verbalized and institutionalized Christianity, and therefore may be discovered by Christians in their lives when they encounter their non-Christian brothers and sisters, or in their study of religious history, Christians need not be shocked or astonished at such a revelation. It should serve only to show that their God, the God of Jesus Christ, wants *all* men and women to be saved, and offers God's grace as liberation to *all* human beings, offering it as liberation into incomprehensible mystery. Then the grace of Christ takes effect in a mysterious way beyond the bounds of verbalized and institutionalized Christendom, and even outside those bounds allows people to share in the paschal mystery of Jesus, even where people who are loyal to their conscience have not yet been reached in any convincing way by the explicit message of Christianity and have not been molded by the Christian sacraments.

Such a revelation is not only something that is not forbidden to Christians if and where they undergo it. They should even expect it, because their faith requires them to believe in the universal saving will of God, which finds a barrier only in an individual's personal mortal guilt, and even offers every human being the grace of Christ again and again throughout his or her lifetime. The grace of God which has become victorious and irreversible in human history through the history of the one who was crucified and who rose, is still the grace of Jesus Christ where it is not expressly and reflectively conceived and interpreted as such. That is not only something that Christians should opine; it is an actual part of their faith if they believe in the universal and supernatural saving will of God for all women and men, and it forbids Christians to believe that that salvific will operates for a person's salvation only if she or he has already expressly embraced Christianity.

SHARING IN THE VICTORIOUS DEATH OF JESUS

If we consider what I have already said about the human transcendental experience absolutized by the grace of God and allowed entry into the ineffable mystery of God, we see that it has something to do with the death of Jesus, irrespective of whether this is expressly conceived of or not.

Originally and ultimately, the actual and freely accepted experience of transcendence in the Holy Spirit is no matter of theoretical reason but one of the whole woman or man in the actual history of her or his life and freedom. Therefore it occurs ultimately where it is impossible to stop at some particular reality in life and treat it as final and absolute; it occurs where an ultimate autonomous urge to self-defense is surrendered in free and liberated hope with no other protection; it occurs, in short, where one dies into the incomprehensibility of God.

If Christians, by reason of their relationship with the absolute God, cannot and will not leave their historical existence open, the moment of their mystical union with God and therefore the apex of their experience of the Spirit is ultimately given not so much in a sublime mystical experience of immersion or inward communion as such, as in their death. It occurs in death though not necessarily in the moment of their medical *exitus*. Conversely, moreover, their actual existential death in certain circumstances (though not necessarily) may occur as ultimate self-abandonment, which is death indeed, in a mystical experience of immersion which cannot occur before one is dead in the usual sense of the word. Experience of the Spirit and sharing in the victorious death of Jesus, only in which the true good fortune of our death is experienced in a community of faith, are one and the same thing. In this life the chalice of the Holy Spirit is identical with the chalice of Christ. But only that man or woman drinks from it who has slowly learnt—to some extent—how to find fullness in emptiness, uprightness in downfall, life in death, and discovery in abandonment. Whoever learns these things undergoes the experience of the Spirit, of pure Spirit, and in this experience meets with the experience of the Holy Spirit of grace. For, on the whole, ultimately one reaches this liberation of the spirit only by the grace of Christ in faith. When Christ liberates the spirit, he liberates it through supernatural grace and then releases it into the life of God.

Before I close this part, I must make two points which refer back to the point at which I began, and to which I hope they have kept fairly close. I refer to the connection between the experience of the Spirit and everyday life.

EXPERIENCING THE SPIRIT IS NOT ELITIST

The experience of the Spirit I have described here has nothing to do with any elitist consciousness of being one of the elect who are set apart from the great majority of average Christians and human beings. If the foregoing is properly understood then experience of the Spirit as I have described it occurs constantly in the life of anyone who is alive to personal self-possession and to the action of freedom, and truly in control of his or her entire self. In most human lives that does not happen as meditation proper, in self-immersive inward communion, and so on, but in the warp and weft of everyday life, where responsibility, loyalty, love, and so on are practiced absolutely, and where ultimately it is a secondary question whether such behavior is accompanied by any expressly religious interpretation. That does not mean, however, that any such thematically religious interpretation is not correct and important in itself. Meditation and similar spiritual "exercises" are not to be devalued. They can be a form of training for the occasion when ultimate experiences of the Spirit (wherever they occur in life) are ordained and accepted in radical, absolute freedom. Such exercises can also (though not exclusively) afford the opportunity to experience the Spirit more clearly and reflectively. They should be grasped in the ultimate fundamental freedom of the human being so that they become a decision comprising the whole of existence and taking it into salvation.

Christianity is not elitist. If we look at the New Testament it offers details of various sublime experiences of the Spirit that can be summarized as "mystical." But all human beings who selflessly love their neighbor and experience God in that love are accorded ultimate salvation by God's jurisdiction, which is not capped by the highest ascent or deepest immersion of the mystic. Therefore the New Testament, even when it does not expressly consider the point, is of the opinion that this insurpassable salvation in the self-communicating Holy Spirit of God can occur where apparently nothing more is happening than the final bitter duty of everyday life and a solitary death. Such an ultimate experience of the Spirit can occur in the midst of everyday life in spite of all the elitist pride of the "pneumatics."

Of course when there is genuine concern for salvation, and when God is loved, when human beings learn ever more clearly that they can never come to a finally valid stop on the road of self-liberation, and when they submit to the hard though happy demands of the Sermon on the Mount, they will never refuse to take at least those expressly meditative and spiritual paths revealed to them in the ultimately inaccessible history of their lives.

EVERYDAY MISSION

When we read the letters of Paul we eventually come upon his teaching about charismata, or charisms. These are not merely identical with a possession of the Spirit and the experience of the Spirit of a man or woman justified by faith. But they do have an inward connection with that possession of the Spirit and its form of experience. They are seen by Paul as versatile, always variously distributed capacities which are never all given to one individual; they also comprise a commission to construct a Christian community. They may—like healing powers or speaking in tongues—be quite extraordinary and even spectacular in nature. But they can also be almost secular, everyday capabilities, up to the point of good cash administration of a parish or community. In a sense we can overlook the importance of these charismata for the construction of the *community*. We may say that all abilities and possibilities of Christian action, inasmuch as it is ultimately empowered, supported, and ensouled by the Holy Spirit of God, are charismata or gifts of the Spirit.

Though we must not forget that the many separated Christians have in different ways one and the same possession of the Spirit, charismata are primarily quite sober individual commissions, individual abilities, and individual offers, which make up the everydayness of individuals and their many-sided lives. Such possibilities always exceed what individuals (given the limitations of their strength and time) can actually accomplish. They have to choose and discern. If they make this choice duly (that is, in the Spirit and acting from the Spirit), then what is chosen may certainly be called "charisma" or the "will of God."

How is such a choice made? The masters of the spiritual life have thought much about and experimented with the rules for the discernment of spirits, and have showed their conviction that the discovery of what is actually right here-and-now is not *only* a matter for rational consideration and theoretical moral theology. There is no room here to recapitulate these teachings of the spiritual masters. But the fundamentals I have outlined should help me to say something very short and basic but important which unites the ultimate experience of the Spirit and the constantly new, ultimately "charismatic" individual decisions which life says have to be made. Whenever such a choice of any specific thing is not merely rationally justified and does not merely accord with the principles of Christian morality, but also (something far from obvious) does not displace or darken an ultimate openness to specific experience of the Spirit in unlimited freedom, where a Christian experiences as given a final, nonarbitrary, rationally indissoluble yet factually given synthesis of original experience and the inclination to a specific object from his or her everyday freedom, then that Christian has found the will of God. Then he or she acts not only rationally and morally but charismatically. Of course a great deal of practice and spiritual experience are necessary in order to recognize accurately occasions when an inclination to a specific object proffered by everyday life does not displace this ultimate experience of the Spirit into an apparent void freed of God, but becomes the starting point for that experience of the Spirit and offers a successful synthesis of the experience of the Spirit and everyday duties.

But the experience of such a synthesis, in which human beings leave everything for the unlimited mystery of God, in which their courageous decision "fits" the actual reality of life and the "world," is possible and comprises the whole Christian life. In such a life, with the dying Jesus, human beings leave everything in order to enter the exitless and unsignposted freedom of God *and* at the same time lovingly accept the individual everyday aspects of this world that are allotted them, in order to take them with them into that Spirit of God.

We must look for experience of the Spirit and for grace in the contemplation of our own lives. But not so that we can say, "There's the Spirit. Now I know where the Spirit blows." That is not how the Spirit is discerned. The Spirit cannot be found by laying triumphant claim to the Spirit as if it were our possession and property. We can seek the Spirit only by forgetting self. We can find the Spirit only in seeking God and surrendering self in generous outgoing love, and without returning to self. Moreover we must continually ask whether anything like that annihilating and enlivening experience of Spirit is at work in us, so that we know how far we still have to go, and how distant what we presume to call our "spiritual" life still is from real experience of the Holy Spirit.

Grandis nobis restat via. Venite et gustate, quam suavis sit Dominus! There is still a long way to go. Come and see how full the Lord is of loving kindness!

*

DO NOT STIFLE THE SPIRIT!

The following essay was originally given as a lecture in the main auditorium of Salzburg University as a feature for the celebration of the Austrian "Catholic Day," on June 1, 1962. Subtitled "Probleme und Imperative des Osterreichischen Katholikentages 1962" (Problems and imperatives of the 1962 celebration of Catholic Day in Austria), the lecture caused considerable offense among members of the Roman curia who undoubtedly took some of Rahner's remarks to be directed at them. Rahner's outspokenness here was one of the reasons behind the curial movement to silence him (for more on this see the Introduction to the present book).

In this lecture Rahner states that the church is or should be conscious of the fact that although the Spirit is projected into and belongs to the church, that same Spirit never finds adequate expression in any or all of the church's official functions and activities. In the face of Pope Pius XII's claim that the charismatic element belongs to the church's essence and must be under the sole governance of the church, Rahner observes that this attitude is indicative of the church's remaining at the level of mere theory and lacking a genuine appreciation of the charismata of the Spirit. He accuses the church of making the charisms of the Spirit ineffective in many ways, not the least of which is bureaucratic resistance due to the "faults of self-will and ossification" of the leadership and a defensiveness that tends to make the church close in upon itself. Hence

238

the title of the lecture, which is drawn from 1 Thessalonians 5:19, becomes an imperative and exhortation by Rahner to the church to be courageous and self-critical. He appeals for boldness of initiative and more self-confidence in listening to the Spirit in the search for God's authentic word in the contemporary era. In contrast, he laments the tactics of a stale, dull ecclesiastical bureaucracy pitted against the "fire and energy of the Spirit." Here he reiterates his strong conviction that the Spirit of the one who conquered the world by his death on the cross cannot be stifled.

In the midst of the extraordinary changes of the times and the increasing richness of the church's relations to an ever-increasing non-Christian world, Rahner can also decry the church's plodding reluctance to embrace fearlessly the radical moves that the Spirit seems to be urging. In this regard Rahner makes a number of exhortations. First, he calls on all Christians to adopt an attitude of caring and of conversion so that the stirrings of the Spirit can be recognized beyond official church pronouncements and beyond the mandates of its more stolid leaders. Second, he asks Christians to have the courage to take risky courses of action. In this he notes the need to reinterpret the directive "to obey the church." Such obedience, he insists, can also extend from those touched by the Spirit, the "ministered," to the "ministers" themselves, if these will only listen. And this summons up the third of his exhortations: The church needs the courage to endure the antagonisms that can arise within it in the realization that church officialdom can never fully control the charisms of the Spirit. To be sure, one must discern the true Spirit and distinguish God's call from the siren of a pseudospirit. But the church leadership must also draw unity from the plurality of charisms and opinions within the ecclesial community without losing tolerance for and appreciation of the diversity of the Spirit's impulses in the church. In effect, Rahner urges the church to love even dissidents whose contrary charisms do not make them any less one's brothers and sisters. While affirming the role of authority to appraise such movements and even to warn against them, Rahner pleads that the church take the sting out of its struggle with diversity by a spirit of love and largeheartedness.

Finally, Rahner states that if the church is not to stifle the Spirit, then it must allow the Spirit to breathe where it wills and not necessarily or solely in the directions mapped out by authorities in their initiatives, commands, and authoritarian tactics, so often tantamount to human control mechanisms over the Spirit of God. Rahner's reflections here, considered controversial at the time, were first published by the Prasidium der katholischen Aktion Osterreichs (Praesidium of Catholic Action of Austria) in 1963. With the note that the lecture might still have relevance in the post–Vatican II period, it was incorporated into volume 7 of the Schriften *in 1966. The English translation is from volume 7 of the* Theological Investigations *(pp. 72–87), published in 1971.*

In view of recent Vatican moves against dissent in the church, the essay still appears to be timely.

"Do not stifle the Spirit!" This quotation from Scripture is found in the earliest of the New Testament epistles, the First Epistle of Paul to the Thessalonians, chapter 5, verse 19, in a verse, therefore, in which the apostle is expressing his concluding exhortations to the community he has founded. If we take the verse in this sense it may seem, on the first hearing, to be expressing something obvious. Who would deliberately, obstinately, and of set purpose oppose the workings of the Holy Spirit? And if this saying is indeed addressed in the first instance to the actual community of the faithful as a whole and not to the individual with his or her personal problems of salvation, then as an exhortation it seems to be almost superfluous. Is the church not the temple of the Spirit, the body of Christ which is vivified by the Spirit of Christ? Does not the Spirit preside in this church with the power of the eschatological victory of the final age, never abandoning it, always making it the holy church? How could the church ever stifle the Spirit of God?

And yet we have only to ask ourselves what Paul actually had in mind in the concrete when he exhorted his hearers in these terms to see that his exhortation both to individuals and to the church as a whole is far from superfluous. When we first read this exhortation we should tremble at the idea that it is possible for a human being at all actually to stifle the Spirit, the burning fire of God, at the idea which the apostle presupposes, namely that we ourselves—at any rate in a very broad sense—are actually in a position to do this. If only we reflected upon this what a change it might bring about in our lives! *We* could stifle the Spirit! We could frustrate the Spirit's movements in us and in the world! The Spirit has been given into our power, made subject to the inertia of our spirit, brought under the control of our cowardice, placed at the disposal of our empty, earthly, loveless hearts! Not only are we able to be false to ourselves and to betray the dignity and destiny of our own nature. We can block the Spirit who wills ever to renew the face of the earth! We can kill the life of God in the world, render the spheres of life Godless, empty and meaningless! Furthermore what a terrible danger there must be, a danger that we are too stupid to notice! How easy it must be for us to bring it about, almost without noticing, that the flame of the Spirit is prevented by us from doing its work! How easy it must be evidently to act like this in all "good conscience" if the apostle feels himself called upon to exhort us: "Do not stifle the Spirit!"

In point of fact, if we think of the gifts of grace bestowed by the Spirit as Paul sees them which must not be brought to nothing we shall find it easy to understand that the object of Paul's exhortations is far from obvious. For such gifts of grace are first of all distributed among many in such a way that no one individual possesses them all, and that they are given as the Spirit decides, and not according to the will and pleasure of any one individual, nor even to that of the authorities in their designs. And yet how difficult it is for us to allow that another person possesses something important, something God-given, which we ourselves do not have, which we can never altogether understand; something that our own nature tells us is alien, and which perhaps seems strange and even shocking. How easily we conclude that the divine is to be identified with that which we possess, and which is accessible to us precisely because it has entered into our life. And further, for Paul these gifts are of such a nature that to the worldly individual they seem folly (1 Cor. 2:14). They can be manifested in the community in such a way that to the profane they are the occasion of derision; that those endowed with the gifts of the Spirit appear psychologically unbalanced or, to put it plainly, are out of their minds (1 Cor. 14:23). In dealing with his communities Paul presupposes that the Spirit blows everywhere, and in the most varied ways: as a Spirit of witness, of loving service, of instruction, consolation, helpful exhortation, almsgiving, understanding, compassion (Rom. 12:4-8), wisdom, knowledge, the prayer that moves mountains, the power of healing, acts of power, prophetic utterances, the discernment of spirits, ecstasies and the interpretation of utterances arising from these, service of others and leadership of the community (1 Cor. 12:4-11, 28-30). According to him the Spirit of Christ is active in a thousand forms and in no one individual are all of these present, because it is only all individuals taken together who constitute the one whole body of Christ. All must take place properly and in order (1 Cor. 14:40), but this order in the manifestations of the Spirit is an order which does not restrict these manifestations in any way, which is aware of, and acknowledges the fact that these gifts are inconceivably varied in kind, and quite incalculable. It is an order which lets the Spirit move where and as it wills; which admits neither of merely human judgment nor of any hybris on the part of the authorities in the church in seeking to reduce everything to their own plans. The order of which we are speaking does not allow such people to stifle the Spirit, the Spirit which can be uncomfortable, which always remains fresh and unfathomable, the Spirit which is that love which can be hard, which leads the individual and even the church itself in directions which they had not planned, leads them always into that which is new and unknown, that which is only seen to be in conformity with the one eternal Spirit, ancient yet ever new, when it has actually taken effect; that which the Spirit has intended, and which is beyond all human wisdom.

The church knows as part of its conscious faith that the Spirit too actually belongs to it, that the Spirit is indispensable to it. The church teaches explicitly that it is not only its own official organization, institutions, traditions, the rules of life which are permanent and im-mutable—in short that which is planned, that which can be foreseen that belong to it as the church of God. The church knows that the ele-ment of the unexpected and the incalculable in its own history does not consist solely in the incomprehensibility of the circumstances to which it is subjected *ab externo*, circumstances which it controls by applying its own internal and immutable principles to them. The church knows that the Spirit of God has been projected into its innermost nature, the living Spirit still actively present and at work in the here and now. The activity of the Spirit, therefore, can never find adequate expression sim-ply in the forms of what we call the church's official life, its principles, sacramental system, and teaching. These can never be the sole or exclu-sive forms in which the Spirit has, so to say, made itself available to the church. Pius XII has expressly laid down that not only the institutional factor, but the charismatic one too is of the church's essence. Accord-ing to Pius XII those who are charismatics in this sense are not simply at the disposal of the ecclesiastical authorities, nor are they mere recip-ients of directives. It is true that in the exercise of their charisms these charismatic individuals must submit their lives to the general "order" of Christ's church, that it is important for them not to break out of the confines of that church, which is also, though not exclusively, a church whose authority is vested in its official ministers. But even though all this is true, still the charismatics can be men and women endowed with such gifts of grace that Christ can lead and guide his church quite "directly" through them.

All this is a recognized fact. But it is a fact that is too often not recog-nized clearly enough in theory, and not acted upon vigorously enough in practice. Often the awareness of the role of the charisma of the Spirit in the church remains at the level of mere theoretic knowledge, which has of itself no charismatic vitality. This is not merely due to faults of self-will and ossification on the part of the church's authorities. There are other and weightier reasons why the truth of the Spirit and the Spirit's charisms in the church should be rendered ineffective in this way. It could be said that from this aspect it was easier to be a Christian in the early church which Paul knew. The communities were small; their standard of living was simple and easy to understand. There was a place for that which had not been planned for or foreseen, as well as for that which was the outcome of policy and design. Moreover the world in which such movements took place was for its part reliable and comprehensible. Today, on the other hand, we live in an age of industrial societies on a massive scale, an age in which the histories of all the nations have been drawn together into a unity, in which all have achieved a degree of communication with one another which, whether it be friendly or hostile, is in any case extremely real and direct; an age of automation, of cybernetics, of a demand for security which is already becoming neurotic in its intensity; an age in which the aged in the community constitute a far higher percentage of its members than in earlier times; an age in which the needs and opinions of the masses are manipulated; in which the machine has grown immensely in significance as a factor in society, for it is to a large extent inevitable that the circumstances previously mentioned should conduce to this effect. These and similar factors in the contemporary situation apply not only to society in the worldly sense, but also the social entity of the church, and they are from first to last hostile to all that is charismatic. In other words they have the effect of making it seem as though the only effective and valid factors are those which are the outcome of plan and design, that only the power of the masses has any prospect of success, that the lives even of individuals are more and more dependent upon the great social institutions of the state and its authorities, organizations, ruling officials with their official enactments, five-year plans, subsidies, and so on, all of them aids to the machinery of propaganda.

If we are honest we shall recognize that this danger in the present age is undeniably a danger for the church as well. We say that we have entered upon the age of the worldwide church. That is true. But we have also entered upon an age in which every regional movement in the church almost inevitably takes place under the eyes of the church as a whole, and in dependence upon the central machinery of the church. It is judged according to its real or supposed effects upon other countries and other areas of the church's influence. There is a danger that no such movement can hope to be taken seriously unless it very quickly wins the support of public opinion in the church throughout the world.

This is the danger that threatens the charismatic element in the church from the external situation in which it is placed. But it is intensified by the presence of a further danger, this time arising from the interior situation of the church. For even today the situation of the church is still—unhappily is still—one of defensiveness against the powers that threaten it from without, of a unity indeed, but the kind of unity that belongs to a faction closed in upon itself so that watchwords are needed to enter it. It is a situation dominated by a spirit which has been rather too hasty and too uncompromising in taking the dogmatic definition of the primacy of the pope in the church as the bond of unity and the guarantee of truth, this attitude objectifying itself in a not inconsiderable degree of centralization of government in an ecclesiastical bureaucracy at Rome, so that regulations governing the life of each and every individual are issued from the church's central ministries, and no one can be sure that, despite all intentions to the contrary, the approaching council will not have the effect of strengthening this tendency. For a council is expected to produce regulations covering a wide area of life, and it is almost impossible for it to avoid prescribing that its regulations are to apply in a univocal sense to the entire church. In short, the fact that there is a charismatic element in the institution of the church is recognized. It will not be denied by anyone. And yet because of the contemporary circumstances of the church, both external and internal, this fact fails to make its due impact both in theory and in practice.

It can be seen, then, that in general the saying "Do not stifle the Spirit" has the force not merely of an obvious and universal principle, but of an urgent imperative precisely for us in the here and now. As an exhortation, indeed, it has so urgent an application to the contemporary scene that its proclamation must take priority over that of many other principles. But precisely as a most earnest exhortation this saying applies supremely to us central Europeans in our relationships. Let us be honestly and calmly self-critical. What is the state of the church in the particular sphere to which we belong? Are not weariness and mere routine far too predominant as factors in our lives? When new "movements" arise or new enthusiasms which set us fresh goals to achieve, or seek to arouse support for new ideas, are we not all too fond of preaching balance and deliberation in applying the church's principles, instead of boldly translating them into imperatives—imperatives which are not indeed necessary everywhere and at all times, but which certainly are so for us in the here and now? Are we not all too often lacking in the courage to say an unambiguous "no" or an unambiguous "yes"? And this applies not merely to those basic principles which are immutable, and which no one seriously wishes directly to challenge or to deny, but also to those watchwords and slogans of controversy which summon us to a decision in the concrete. Do we know what to reply when someone asks: "What concrete objectives have you Christians set yourselves to achieve in the next ten years? What is it which does not yet exist, but which, according to you, must exist and which you are currently aiming to achieve? And that too not merely in eternity, but in the here and now?" Do we not all too often claim to be adopting an attitude of detachment toward the various factions, whereas our real reason is that we are unwilling to expose ourselves to any demands in the concrete? Where is the courage we need really to become engaged in the questions of the time, really to face up to them, really to feel the burden of them? Are we not all too ready to suppose, in our weariness and anxiety for peace, that our minds are already clear on all points, equipped with all the answers to all the questions—questions which are, in any case, not all that important? Among us, as in the church in general, is there not a phenomenon which might be called the "church of officialdom"? In other words is there not an intermediary class of official administrators which (almost inevitably, so far as we are concerned, and yet how dangerously!) comes between the Christians and those who are their real shepherds, really called by God to their ministry, and really responsible to God for their flocks? Is not our preaching, the expression of our Christian faith, too traditionalist in character, too secondhand? Does not far too little of it well up spontaneously from that experience of grace, that awareness of being touched by the authentic word of God, which is utterly our own, and which has its source in our innermost nature? Where in the life of the church do we find its members really initiating an "experiment" which is not smothered over right from its very inception, so that after all everything remains as it was? Let us face up to the fact that from the point of view of cultural and social history we are passing through a revolutionary change in the times, a change which we certainly do not overestimate, but rather underestimate. Let us then take this revolutionary change in all its breadth and depth as a standard by which to measure the vigor, the courage, the breadth of vision which we bring to bear upon the radical change which we ourselves are undergoing in the church. When we do this are we not compelled to fear that at this turning point of the times we have proved ourselves still more inadequate than did the church of the time when the feudal society of the eighteenth century was transformed into the society of civic liberalism of the nineteenth, or the time when the workers emerged as a new social class? Must we not say at this point that our response has been far too hesitant and lame, that we have merely allowed ourselves to be forced bit by bit by the sheer weight of the facts, and that for all this we have lagged pitifully behind the times? In a word where is that bold, powerful, creative, "self-confident" movement of the Spirit among us in the church?

There may be some who take these remarks of mine merely as so much facile criticism; who refuse a priori to let themselves be disturbed, who proceed from the tacit assumption that all must be well, since they themselves are honest men and women who do their duty even though they too know of no remedy for the ills of the time and of the church. But such people have failed to understand the true purport of what I have just been saying. These remarks of mine are not intended to lead up to the recommendation of any facile "cure-all," which according to my ideas needs only to be adopted for the church and the world ipso facto to be delivered from their ills. I too have no such prescription to offer. And it is extremely painful and bitter to put forward accusations when one does not know how to alter the state of affairs which is being complained of. Nor do these observations of mine imply that everything in every department of the church's life is in a bad state. On the contrary there is much that is filled with the Spirit and alive with divine life, love, faithfulness, patience in bearing the cross, apostolic work which is full of self-sacrifice, youthful courage, theological acumen, a determination to tackle fresh problems and much else besides of which the Spirit is the prime dispenser, so that without the Spirit none of these factors would be present in the church at all. But should all this, for which we do indeed thank God, make us blind to those other factors of which we have been speaking? Are we on this account to be excused from facing up to the real question of which of two alternatives is more characteristic for our particular age and for the church as it exists in our particular countries? These alternatives are on the one hand the average and the stereotyped, the bureaucratic and over-officialized, the stale and the dull which refuses to commit itself to any form of attack, and on the other the fire and energy of the Spirit, the charism of life that comes from heaven, though again only in the measure in which it can be permitted to exist in this world of the mediocre. However thankful we may be for the Spirit who does not forsake us even in this age, are we not still faced with the responsibility of being honestly and severely self-critical, and saying that it is through our own fault, the inertia of our own hearts, that we feel too little of the movement of the Spirit as guider of the church, and that too at a time when the impetus of the Spirit was never so sorely needed? In view of this, then, should we not all conclude in fear and trembling that evidently the saying of Paul is addressed to us not merely as a permanently valid principle, but as an imperative for our own particular time, disconcerting, accusing, shocking us out of our complacency?

But if this imperative has, in this sense, a particular application to us of the present age, then the question does become urgent for us: What must we do in order to avoid stifling the Spirit? This is a dark and difficult question. If it could ever be thought easy to answer it would be no question at all. The real answer to it is itself a factor in the movement and guidance of the Spirit, who ensures that the Spirit shall not be stifled. It can be found, in the last analysis, not by the reflexive processes of theory and speculation, but rather, at basis, through the sureness of instinct to be found in Christian living. And for this reason the poor stuttering schoolmaster can only say very little, and that in very inadequate and halting terms, on this particular question. And what that schoolmaster says, insofar as anything can be said directly and explicitly on this point, is once more only a part of the theoretic statements which, as we have pointed out, cannot be any substitute for the Spirit and for the Spirit's power and inalienable and uncontrollable grace. Only with these provisos can there be any right understanding of the few modest observations which follow.

The first thing that we could do, and do with all our hearts, would be to acquire an attitude of *caring;* of recognizing with anxiety that it is possible to stifle the Spirit. The Spirit can be stifled not indeed throughout the entire church, but still over so wide an area, and to such a terrible extent that we have to fear that judgment which begins with the house of God. And for this reason we must all face the possibility with fear and trembling that *we* could be the ones who stifle the Spirit—stifle the Spirit through that pride in "knowing better," that inertia of heart, that cowardice, that unteachableness with which we react to fresh impulses and new pressures in the church. How different many things would be if we did not so often react to what is new with a self-assured superiority, an attitude of conservatism, adopted as a defense not of the honor of God and the teaching and institutions of the church, but of our own selves, of what we have always been accustomed to, of the usual, with which we can live without daily experiencing the pain of the new *metanoia*. But if we realized, and with burning conviction, that we can also be judged for our omissions, for a general obtuseness and inertia of heart which, though indefinable, extends over all spheres of our lives, for our culpable lack of creative imagination and boldness of spirit, then we should lend a sharper ear, a keener eye, a livelier anticipation to the slightest indication that somewhere that Spirit is stirring whose inspiration is not merely confined to the official pronouncements and directives of the church, or to the holders of official positions in it. Then we should be eagerly on the watch to see whether charisms were not appearing, of which only a glimpse and a feeling can initially be obtained. Then we would not make it a condition for admitting those charisms which the Spirit wills to impart (a condition to which, however, we do not subject our own lives and activities) that such charisms must have no element of the human in them, nothing which has not yet been purified out. For this is not possible in view of the fact that even the fire of the Holy Spirit burns up from the thorn-bush of our human—all too human—nature.

The second requirement is the courage to *take risks*. Let us permit ourselves to reiterate most strongly what has just been said. We live in an age in which it is absolutely necessary to be ready to go to the utmost extremes of boldness in our attitude toward the new and the untried, to that point at which it would be, beyond all dispute, simply inconceivable for one who accepts Christian teaching and has a Christian conscience at all to go any further. In practice the only admissible "tutiorism" in the life of the church today is the tutiorism which consists in taking risks. Today, when we are struggling to solve the real problems which confront us, we should not, properly speaking, say: "How far *must* I go?" because the very nature of the situation itself absolutely compels us to go at least as far as possible. We should be asking ourselves, rather: "How far *can* we go by taking advantage of all the possibilities in the pastoral and theological spheres?" The reason is that the state of the kingdom of God is certainly such that we must be as bold as possible in taking risks in order to hold out in the manner demanded of us by God. For instance in ecumenical questions we should not ask: "What do we have to concede to our separated sisters and brothers?" but "How can we create, in every conceivable way, the conditions which make possible a fruitful encounter with them, provided only that the measures which we take are reasonable, and are in any way reconcilable with the Christian and Catholic conscience?" "How can we be sufficiently bold and unreserved in doing this, for today it is simply out of the question for us to do anything less in order to bring the unity of Christians at least one step nearer?" It appears to me that this kind of "tutiorism" should be applied to these and many other questions. In other words one should take as the motive force of one's actions the conviction that for these particular times of ours (the principle does not apply permanently to all times) the surest way is the boldest, and that the best chance to gain all, or at any rate something, is not caution, but the utmost boldness in taking risks. And if we do adopt this attitude, then there will be a radical change of policy in many of the questions now being canvassed in the church.

What is needful in order for the Spirit not to be stifled is a true and bold interpretation of what *obedience* to the church really means. It is a holy virtue. The Spirit of Christ in the church manifests itself in obedience to the established authorities of the church. That is no true Spirit of Christ which leads us outside the church of the bishops, the pope, the official ministers of the church. But it is important to recognize the truth that the work of the Spirit in the church takes effect not only through these official ministers, but through those over whom they preside as well; that the Spirit's influence also extends in the inverse direction, from the ministered to the ministers. And if this is true, then the individuals upon whom God bestows the grace, and also the burden, of charisms (and it would be better if more of the church's members would commit themselves to accepting that the Spirit might be entrusting them with such gifts and such responsibilities) have also a right and a duty to avoid simply hiding behind an attitude of dumb obedience—in truth not in the least because it is a humble attitude, but because it is a comfortable one. Rather they must speak out—proclaim what they believe to be true, for it is quite possible that this may be the truth of the Spirit of God. They must be tireless in testifying to it even in the presence of the established authorities in the church, and even when it is inconvenient or unpleasing to those "authorities," even when they themselves have to endure the sufferings of the charismatic for doing so, in the form of misunderstanding and perhaps even disciplinary action on the part of the authorities. The spirit of true obedience is present not so much where the official machinery of the church is running smoothly and without friction, not so much where a totalitarian regime is being enforced, but rather where the nonofficial movements of the Spirit are recognized and respected by the official church in the context of a universal striving for the will of God, while the "charismatics" for their part, while remaining faithful to their task, maintain an attitude of obedience and respect toward the official church. For it is God and God alone who builds the one church, shaping the true course of its history as God wills out of the materials of the multiplicity of spirits, tasks, and ministries in the church, and out of the ensuing tensions and oppositions which are so necessary. And further this course may seem quite different from the one thought out and planned in the official councils of the church's ministers, even though these are quite right and are only fulfilling their bounden duty in so planning a course for the church.

A further prior condition which is necessary if the Spirit is to become a vital force in the church is the *courage* to endure the *inevitable antagonisms* in the church which we have just mentioned. The church is not "one heart and one soul" in such a way, or to such an extent, that there can be no controversy, none of the pain of mutual misunderstandings in it. There are, in fact, many charisms in the church, and no one individual possesses them all. Nor is it given to any one individual to have all the various kinds of charisms at her or his disposal. For even though the authorities of the church are united, and even though they are at one in their care to ensure that there shall be one faith and one love in it, this does not imply that the official church exercises any real controlling power over all the charisms. On the contrary many different opinions are upheld among us Christians, and this is as it should be. We should manifest many different tendencies, and there is no necessity for each to be positively suitable for all. The sort of love that might be designed to weld all into one uniform whole would be all too easy. But in the church it is the Spirit of love who must reign, binding the many and diverse gifts in their very diversity into a unity. One who possesses this love recognizes and accepts others too according them their due value even though they are different from himself or herself, and even in cases in which he or she no longer "understands" them. The principle which is given to the church as a concomitant of the love it has to preserve in all its actions lays down that all individuals in the church must follow their own spirit, so long as it is not established beyond all doubt that they are in fact following a pseudospirit. In other words it must be presumed, until the contrary is proved, that they are orthodox in their beliefs, that they are persons of good will, and that they have a right to their freedom. To proceed from the opposite assumption would be contrary to the principle mentioned above. Moreover, while it is once more true that it rests with the official authorities and not simply with those subject to them to judge whether in the individual case it has been proved that a pseudospirit is being followed, it is no less true that those authorities themselves have the sacred duty, for which they will have to render account at the day of judgment, of examining themselves in a spirit of humility and self-criticism, to see whether such proof really has been put forward, or whether they have been over-hasty or self-willed in their judgment, judging merely by the standard of their own spirit and their own lights. Patience, tolerance, according to others their due freedom so long as it has not been proved beyond all doubt that their actions are wrong (and not the contrary of this: to forbid all personal initiatives until they have been explicitly proved to be orthodox, the subordinate sustaining the burden of proof here)—all these are specifically ecclesiastical virtues, which flow from the very nature of the church. For it is not a totalitarian organization. Such virtues are the necessary conditions for ensuring that the Spirit shall not be stifled.

It is no spirit of indifference to the church's authorities which leads us to presuppose these virtues in the authorities and to act accordingly.

On the contrary it is itself a Christian virtue. One can take for granted that there will inevitably be antagonisms in the church, for this is something inherent in its very nature as formed by the will of God. There is no need, therefore, to wait for a formal and positive expression of consent on the part of the ecclesiastical authorities for each and every enterprise in order to be able to say: "We too have the Spirit of Christ." But if anyone were to conclude from what has just been said that each and every movement in the church must be allowed to have its head, that no one should really take it upon himself or herself to appraise the movement of a different party within the church, to issue warnings against it, or to demand genuinely and in all sincerity that it should be resisted, then such a one would have misunderstood what I have just been saying. For to impose this interpretation on what has been said would be precisely to deny that the various movements, tendencies, and charismatic impulses, insofar as these are genuine, really do develop within one church, and that they must really be experienced as the counterpoise to corresponding movements, tendencies, and so on in others. Besides such a one would be maintaining by implication that no movement could develop within the church without the gift of the Spirit from above. Now this is not true. Neither the faithful in general nor the holders of official positions in the church in particular are equipped with any such a priori immunity to the innate promptings of the spirit of this world. We must therefore be able to summon up the courage or charism—for this can, in fact, precisely be a gift imparted to one particular member of the church—to say "No!" as members of the church. To take up a stand against particular tendencies and outlooks, and that too even before the actual officials of the church have been awakened to the danger which threatens. For to say "No!" in this way can be the means of rousing the official church to perform its function. But it is precisely when we do find the courage to accept these conflicts and tensions within the church, this real multiplicity of gifts and charisms, of tasks and functions, that we draw the sting from the struggle between opposing tendencies which always and inevitably do occur even within the church, that we transform that struggle into the strivings of love, and that we set the Spirit free, who would otherwise be stifled.

A further factor to be numbered among the necessary prior conditions for ensuring that the Spirit shall not be stifled is that all members of the church, whether high or low, must be convinced of the fact that of the various movements which arise and which should arise in the church, not all of them have necessarily to be initiated by the officials and authorities at their head in order to be legitimate. These authorities must be neither surprised nor reluctant to find a movement of the Spirit manifesting itself prior to any plan or design on the part of the church's official ministers. Nor must the faithful suppose that there is absolutely nothing for them to do until some directive has been issued from above. There are actions which are, under God's will, demanded by the conscience of the individual even before the starting signal has been given by the authorities, and furthermore the directions in which these actions tend may be such as are not already approved or established in any positive sense by those authorities. It would be necessary in such a case for the individual to think out afresh, and on the basis of this charismatic element in the church, what place should be accorded to "canonical approval" and to legitimatized custom *contra* or *praeter legem* [against or beyond the law].

By introducing such concepts as these the canonists leave room not merely for legitimate developments in the sphere of what is reasonable and just at the human level, but for the impulses of the Spirit as well. Those, therefore, who have the power to command in the church must constantly bear in mind that not everything that takes place in the church either is or should be the outcome of their own autocratic planning as though they belonged to a totalitarian regime. They must keep themselves constantly alive to the fact that when they permit movements to arise "from below," this is no more than their duty; it does not constitute an act of gracious tolerance on their part. They must not seek to retain all the threads in their own hands right from the first. They must recognize that the higher—and precisely the charismatic—wisdom may quite well lie with the rank and file, and that charismatic wisdom as applied to the church's official ministers may consist in the fact that they do not close their minds to wisdom of the former sort. The authorities in the church must always be aware of the fact that neither the obedience which the rank and file owe to them as a matter of duty on the one hand, nor the supreme juridical authority vested in themselves on the other renders the rank and file devoid of rights in relation to the authorities themselves. Nor does this relationship provide any guarantee that every measure adopted by the authorities in every individual case is necessarily in conformity with what is right and pleasing to God, or that they must a priori be preserved from extremely catastrophic decisions and omissions.

All must pray. All must have an anxious conscience about their own poverty and deficiency in charismatic gifts. All must be ready to pay heed to the gift of another, even when they themselves do not possess it. Obedience must not drive out the courage of self-responsibility, nor, conversely, must the courage of one's own convictions drive out obedience. We must be resolute enough to try out even the most radical projects in the recognition that in our situation, so extreme as it is, it is no longer tolerable merely to carry on prudently along the same lines as before. And if we do all this, then perhaps we may clear the ground—even to do this much would be, once more, a grace of God—for the Spirit to quicken us, this in turn being due solely to God's grace. Then we shall have no need to fear that at the judgment of God the reproach will be levelled against us that by our inertia and cowardice we have stifled the Spirit and that we were unwilling to admit it even for a moment.

In the last hundred years the proportion of Catholics relative to other denominations has in practice failed to increase. Instead, despite all the struggles of the missions, heroic as these may appear, it has remained the same. And all this even without counting the shocking extent of the apostasies within the church in the midst of the so-called Christian peoples. Even if the increase in the world population explosion, as it has been called, merely maintains its present rate, by the end of the present century, which some of us may yet live to see, there will be six or seven billion human beings—in other words twice as many as are living today. Now this increase will take place to far the greatest extent in that section of humanity which either in practice or as a result of an absolute political prohibition lives outside the Christian sphere of influence. In view of this fact it may be presumed that in the next few decades the Catholic element in the population of the world will diminish rapidly and perhaps even startlingly. This is only one of a hundred considerations which might be advanced in order to illustrate the seriousness of the global situation in which, even from a merely secular point of view, the church finds itself. This is the situation of the world, and it is also our situation in the present, because it is no longer possible for any country to stand apart as an autocracy in the circumstances of the present time. Have we the courage and hardihood to say to ourselves: "Do not stifle the Spirit!"? Have we the unshakable faith to trust, in spite of these warnings and exhortations to ourselves, that the Spirit of God will not let itself be stifled because it is the Spirit of him who has conquered the world upon the cross? With this sort of sincerity and this sort of courage let us go forward as believers to the decisions which we have to make from day to day.

7

ON THE CHURCH

Rahner's theology is fundamentally in the service of church. His writings on church are, in turn, an outgrowth of various aspects of his Christology. Just as Christ, the Word of God, is the living, human sign of his Father, so, for Rahner, the church, brought into being by Christ's life, death, and resurrection, symbolizes his continuing mission. In his presence as church Christ has never ceased to care for people with his saving word and grace. Rahner designates the church in its societal forms and sacramental life as the embodiment of the incarnate son's abiding presence in the world extending his word and love to all generations gathered in his name and even to those only "anonymously" linked to him. The church, considered as a primary locus and symbol of Christian faith, gives visibility, therefore, to God's salvific will for all people. In a broader sense, Rahner claims that "church" can include all those whose lives are touched by the grace of Christ even if they are seemingly outside the Christian fellowship and unattached to any formal religious community.

This extension of the meaning of church beyond its institutional embrace of the few to the more universal reach of God's Spirit to all peoples is one of the more daring affirmations of Rahner's ecclesiology. With all the developments from his earliest views to later, more innovative insights, he exhibits a remarkable consistency in his ecclesiological reflections. Although his earliest analyses of church cover all the corners of a more traditional, textbook ecclesiology, we find him even then addressing the more controversial but related concerns of freedom in the church, the function of the local church vis-à-vis the universal church, the role of the laity, and the issue of how non-Christian beliefs impact on the "one, true church of Jesus Christ." It is evident that, even as a young theologian, Rahner brought to ecclesiology fresh insights derived from his own creative theological anthropology.

Hence it is not surprising that the issue of individual, personal freedom in the church soon became for him a necessary counterweight to the hierarchical governing structure with its tendencies toward absolute control and the status quo. His own respect for the manifold movements of God's Spirit in the church made him equally wary of both the stifling of creative freedom and the danger of many Christians marching lockstep and thoughtlessly in sheeplike uniformity. Against these twin distortions of what church should be, he urges ecclesiastical authorities to recognize the graced uniqueness of individuals without losing sight of the common bonds of the fellowship of faith and worship that is the strength of community. One's personal charism, Rahner argues, must be nurtured by the church hierarchy if the church is to be what it claims for itself, God's word extended and made visible in human history. That is why his strongest ecclesiological critique seems directed against the dictatorial, narrow-minded tactics of a leadership not fully in touch with the Spirit and, suspicious of individual charisms, wittingly or unwittingly stifling personal initiative and free speech in the church.

Moreover, for Rahner, the significance of church has to be more than its historical embodiment in Roman Catholicism. This ecclesial openness is revealed in his later reflections encouraging Catholic church leaders to enter more seriously into the ecumenical movement and even to take practical measures, such as adapting both its dogmatics and sacramentology, to make the reunion of the Christian churches possible. Rahner also extends the meaning of church beyond the religions of Christendom. If God is the holy mystery behind every attraction toward the good and the creator of the graced search for fulfillment in all creatures, then, as Rahner observes, God's world of grace cannot be limited solely to the visible, juridical community bearing the name of Christ. In several of his writings, Rahner speaks of a more cosmic, universalized "church," in which the local church is considered the particularized, identifiable symbol of God's self-expression in somatic moments that witness to God's presence in all times and everywhere. This is the point where Rahner's "supernatural existential" (see chap. 2, above) and his notion of the "anonymous Christian" intersect. Rahner uses these concepts to justify the claim that God dwells in all God's people determining them to be in the image of his son by virtue of their created, graced orientation to the holy mystery they may never be able to call by name.

This openness to and respect for the transcendent in all people—and not just the structuration of this in a more definitive way through explicit church membership—became a major part of Rahner's contribution to the ecclesiology in process at Vatican II. His more innovative writings from this period are directed to the development of a theological understanding of the relationship between the local church and the universal church and to the exploration of divine inspiration and mandate behind the human origins of church offices. He strongly affirms the foundations in the life and teachings of Jesus for the church offices in which magisterial authority is concentrated. He also demands that one equally acknowledge the interrelationship between the charisms of officeholders and those of the ordinary faithful as each contributes to the life of the institution. The right to teach involves the duty of listening to the sources of truth within the community of the governed and even without, as in the case of other Christian churches with which the Roman church must enter into a genuine dialogue.

If there is a radical element in these writings of the Vatican II phase of his career, it lies in Rahner's seeking to open up church self-understanding and dogmatics to the inherently human dimension that is both the theater of God's guidance of the church and a reminder of its historical relativity and human limitedness. Much of Rahner's work of the conciliar years is foundational for the postconciliar thrust toward an even greater reform of church teachings and structures. His involvement in the preparatory work for the West German Pastoral Synod, which met for the first time in Würzburg in 1971 and 1972, brought his strongest feelings about reshaping the church in a more radical direction to the surface. In particular, Rahner urged the church to cease its self-glorification with all the idealistic portrayals of its link to the divine and to examine afresh its concrete anthropological fundament that is stitched into the historical, social, cultural, and political forms that are also part of its image. If the church is to be the sacrament of God's saving will for all humankind, truth compels the church to confess that God's Spirit of life ranges beyond the Roman Catholic institution as well as in it. Hence, Rahner suggests that an evangelization witnessing to God's goodness through a wide array of human services might be a more proper attitude toward non-Catholics and the non-Christian world than the attitude that leads to boasting about an increase in the size of Catholic church membership. The church is not the only setting for God's grace. As we see in the book from which the second selection of this section is taken, The Shape of the Church to Come, *Rahner, mindful of the multitudes whose church affiliation stems more from culture and custom than faith, calls for a rethinking of what membership really means. He asks that something more than routine baptism and loose, selective adherence to gospel values be invoked in designating full membership in the church.*

But that is only part of the problem that Rahner claims should occupy the church's attention if it is to be viable for the future. This church, which is so often lifeless, must be open to the Spirit of life. The church, so often turned in on itself, must reach out to promote human dignity wherever this is denied and wherever people experience oppression. The church, hierarchical and clericalized, should listen to those equally gifted by God with spiritual insights both within and without the community of believers that forms Christ's mystical body.

Rahner's ecclesiology offers a carefully nuanced balance between authority and freedom. While he concedes that the church must speak with the authority God's Spirit invests in its leadership and teaching office, this is an authority of service, not domination. Ultimately such authority must respect the various other voices that also constitute the authentic faith of the church and whose inspirited wisdom can instruct the church leadership in turn. In this way, Rahner hopes to engender a sensitivity within the church's governance to the individual freedom in which each Christian must appropriate his or her commitment in faith to the holy mystery of God. Human openness to the transcendent, which is at the core of Rahner's anthropology, entails not only a tolerance for the flawed nature of churches but also a willingness to recognize the movements of God's Spirit creating the freedom to be oneself in communion with God and to satisfy the yearning to be free in the journey toward one's beatific destiny. The two selections of this section illustrate some of these important Rahnerian contributions to conciliar and postconciliar ecclesiology along with his respect for the way in which God moves the church to become itself a seeker after truth and a promoter of harmony and personal freedom among people everywhere.

THE CHURCH: BASIS OF PASTORAL ACTION

This selection is taken from chapter 1 of Rahner's book Theology of Pastoral Action *(pp. 29–49), a translation from the German text,* Grundlegung der Pastoraltheologie als praktische Theologie *(vol. 2/1 of* Handbuch der Pastoraltheologie, *which was published in Freiburg by Herder Verlag in 1964). The English translation, published in 1968, officially launched the new series* Studies in Pastoral Theology. *Rahner and Daniel Morrissey, who adapted the text for an English-speaking readership, state in their general introduction that the volumes in the series are set in the framework of "correlation" suggested by Paul Tillich. While attempting to preserve the in-depth theological reflection on pastoral issues, the texts would also move away from a self-centered ecclesiology in order to dialogue more earnestly with the modern world. Following Tillich, they attempt to establish a correlation of God's revelation in Christ with the concrete situation that Christians address in their everyday lives. Hence they raise existential questions that, in turn, demand an interpretation of the Christian message valid for the changing world of each new generation. This is not to reduce pastoral theology to the dimensions of sociology, anthropology, or political science, disciplines through which many of these questions arise. Pastoral theology remains for Rahner a reflection in faith upon God and God's revelatory word in terms of how Christians choose to live their lives and act responsibly and compassionately on behalf of other people.*

Rahner's book, which is foundational for developing a theology of pastoral action, explores both the nature of the church as the basis of pastoral action and the interrelationship of individuals and officeholders. In that connection Rahner explores the nature of offices, charisms, and structures in the church. He does that in order to promote a commitment to action on behalf of peoples in need that is at the same time gospel-orientated and responsive to the perennial search of peoples for justice and love, forgiveness and tolerance. The selection that follows illustrates the way Rahner understands the church's vocation to be the sacrament of God's self-gift to God's people, a sacrament that has historical and social meaning. Here God's presence becomes a gift of salvation, and

257

God's church becomes both a sacrament of this presence and the means to attain salvation. For Rahner, the church is at once mystery, primal sacrament, new law of the gospel, eschatological sign, God's ever-renewed presence in history, and the point of reconciliation between the permanence of God's Spirit and a concrete embodiment of God's accepting sinful people as God's people.

The church is the historical and social presence of God's self-communication to the world in Christ. God reveals and communicates God's self ("uncreated grace"), as *sign of salvation,* the manifest word of God (speaking, spoken, and heard). This presupposes that the church both *is* and *acts.* This unity of potency and act is the distinguishing mark of personal, free, spiritual beings. In them an action reverts to the essence in which it is grounded, determines this, and by manifesting it, brings it to identity with itself, so that act and potency have their unity in diversity. The church has this kind of unity of what it is ("society") and in what it does (proclamation of the word, confession of faith, worship, life). This is the church: the eschatologically perfect self-giving of God to humanity in the historical and social domain.

For pastoral theology the whole problem is to determine precisely and comprehensively exactly what should become "present" in today's church in this way. The church is not simply an institution which follows divine instruction to seek the salvation of the individual man or woman. It is more than a useful society with divine help and a significant opinion about God and salvation. Above and beyond all else the church is the concrete embodiment of God's salvation, the presence of God (not God actually present, which would be heresy and yet remains the permanent temptation of the church). If we are to say what the church really has to do and in what activities it realizes its own nature, we must know precisely what becomes present in the church, what gives itself to men and women in the church, constituting the church as a saving presence, uniting God and human beings. A pastoral theologian cannot of course sharply separate the question of how the church at any given moment is to carry out its own specific function from the consideration of what those functions are. The first question nevertheless remains: What does become really present in the church? Only in this way can we hope to deal with the question of the church's pastoral action in today's world.

1. God gives God's self to human beings. This self-giving takes place in history, in faith and hope, and not in that immediacy of eternal life where we will possess the gift in its plenitude. It occurred definitively in Jesus Christ and irrevocably established its acceptance; it has an enduring, historical, empirical, social presence and manifestation. This is

the church—the enduring expression of Christ accepted as God's definitive gift and promise of God's self to humankind. Consequently, the authentic activity of the church is found when human beings are made open to God as God is in God's self and for us. Human beings can be opened to the absolute, nameless mystery that, uncircumscribed, immeasurable, in its own indefinability is both ground and unfathomable abyss, measure and measureless in one. God as God becomes present in the church; God is the living God, the destruction of every claim to finality on the part of anything specified or controlled, the end of all polytheistic idolatry.

The church, therefore, precisely by what it is, is an institution in conflict with anything purely institutional which claims to take the place of God. If revolution means the denial of what represents itself as definitive, then the church is a permanent revolution. For ultimately its sole purpose is to give honor to God and to save human beings by perpetually compelling them to relinquish anything which they take to be definitive, and to capitulate before the God who is possessed as true God only if really, and not merely in words, that God is confessed to transcend everything outside God, everything we can conceive. God makes our own transcendent orientation toward God a mystery to ourselves, beyond our control. The church continues to be a permanent revolution, destroying idols; it has not mistaken the whole business of religion for God (the essential temptation), and therein lies the abiding marvel of the grace promised to the church.

The church always discovers this grace with astonishment, turning it to self-criticism in serene awareness that such criticism of its own actual performance is an element in its nature, inherent in it and requiring no horizon beyond that of the church itself. The infinite horizon of all human criticism, God, gives God's self to the church in grace, with self-criticism as a form of that grace. The church confesses the God-man as the presence of God; because it understands human beings as the destroyers of all idols in virtue of their liberation by grace. The church adores in faith when it transcends the conditions its own existence implies. It adores in hope when it transcends the present into the unknown future of God the incomprehensible. It adores in love when it trusts and fervently accepts God's radical incomprehensibility as the gift of God's love. The church knows the one whom it adores only in this liturgy of adoration, because only in this way is the inexpressible present.

2. This presence of God in the church constituted by God's absolute, eschatological self-communication is, nevertheless, not inexpressible simply because in it presence and absence, acceptance or refusal

amount to the same thing. God's presence has to be experienced and accepted in its transcendental immediacy and irreducibility. Human beings, nevertheless, must consciously reflect on and conceptually objectify this presence of mystery as the ground of their being. This presence, without ceasing to be that of the abiding, ineffable mystery, has so true a dual character of the presence of God that the duality of God's presence in the church is an aspect of God in and for God's self.

God is present in the church as truth and as love. God's self-communication, which gives God as God is in God's self, comes in this double mode of presence as a mode of being of God in God's self. God remaining uncircumscribed in this presence (as the "Father") gives God's self as absolute love (in the Spirit). This double mode of God's action toward us is also the mode of God's own being. This is not the place to discuss the mystery of the two "processions" and the dogmatic theology of the Trinity. What is in question here is the clear development of the fundamental fact that Christian salvation is not just any kind of action of God in regard to human beings. It is God's self-giving which is so truly that of God that its radical nature cannot be thought of as other than it is, other than expressing this very duality of the inner-trinitarian processions. The Trinity of the economy of redemption is the immanent Trinity. *The duality of the inner-trinitarian processions forms the basis of the presence of God in the church and is therefore the basis of the nature of the church.* If the nature of the church is to be elucidated, nothing more "intelligible" or simpler will suffice.

The church is primarily the presence of God. The Father reveals himself and gives himself to be possessed as the truth uttered in the Son, and in so doing remains Father, incomprehensible mystery, mystery uttered in the Word. The church is the presence of God first and foremost as truth, the truth in which God communicates God's self. The church is both the eschatological gift of salvation and the means of salvation; it accepts the word of God in faith and confesses and bears witness to God's truth. That the church is the church of the truth heard with belief and proclaimed, a truth which is absolute mystery present to it, is essentially the first characteristic of the church and therefore of its pastoral action. It must be noted that when God gives God's self as truth, God is already salvation (light, life). God's truth must not be misconceived as a collective sum of human propositions; it is God's gracious self-giving in God's actual, real Word, who by his own reality is the basis of human beings' conceptual knowledge of revelation.

The church is primarily a gift of salvation and only consequently a means of salvation. Even the apostles had to believe first in order to be capable of becoming bearers of revelation. The only preacher who did not have to hear and believe first was Christ. The church's activity as the presence of truth must therefore always have such a form that it is evident and visible to the world that the teaching church in the accomplishment of its mission to the world listens, hears, and believes. It must be clear that the church believes during this age before the fulfillment—during the time when faith is an ever-new grace, subject to temptation, when its conceptual and intellectual element is always a means subordinated to prayerful contemplation, when without words and in a way beyond complete analysis a revelation is experienced which consists in God's self-communication in the grace of faith.

The claim of the magisterium is always an appeal to an authority present in the church of faith; it is an active functioning of the hearing faith of the church as a whole in contradistinction to the multitude of individuals as such. The faith of the whole church instructs the individuals because in its faith is the presence of the truth of God. This teaching authority is indefectible because it is the act of those in whose testimony the faith of the church as a whole receives a truly historically tangible presence of total commitment in faith. The magisterium can speak in the name of the whole church because the hearing faith of the church as a whole is indefectible. The church fulfills its nature as the presence of God's truth when it believes, lives an act of faith, remembers its faith, accepts with praise what is bestowed as God's truth. It says to God what God has said to the church, gives thanks and celebrates the anamnesis of "tradition" in which the truth is given really (although before conceptual reflection): This alone is the source of the act in which the church authoritatively teaches its own members and preaches to non-Christians. But it is clear that even here the church's activity is not identical with the acts of the official ministry. All believers in the church together constitute the one free acceptance, empowered by God's self-revelation, of the Father's self-utterance in the Word which was made flesh; they constitute the church by giving the first inner-trinitarian procession a presence in the economy of redemption, in the realm of the nondivine and its history.

How does this theology of the first believing action of the church stand in relation to the traditional classification of the church's powers into power of order (*potestas ordinis*) and power of jurisdiction (*potestas jurisdictionis*), or into the three offices of teacher, priest, and pastor? Naturally, we are concerned with the fundamental distinction in the activity of the church as a whole (the question of what the church is and does as the presence of God's self-communication), whereas these classical distinctions are those of the church's ministry or of the offices of the ministry. If, however, the traditional distinctions are really standard ones, they must reflect the nature of the church as a whole even if basically they concern the church's ministry alone. When we seek an adequate theological basis for drawing a material distinction within the one total activity of the church and consequently in the ultimately one ministry of the church, the traditional distinction between power of order and power of jurisdiction does not rule out our basic statement regarding God's self-communicating presence to God's church as truth and love. The latter is more fundamental than the former, which refers to a gradation in the order of the sacred whereby the exercise and transmission of sacred "power" is a sacramental or nonsacramental act according to the degree to which the church is involved in it.

The church's action involves the presence of God's truth and love and means a communication of the inner-trinitarian processions. We are not raising the question here as to which concrete acts of the church (in teaching, administration of the sacraments, law-making, etc.) refer to one or other of these fundamental functions. We have not even decided whether these two fundamental functions of the church can take concrete form in different acts, each of which would be an exclusive realization in the church of truth or of love. Nor is it yet clear when the activity of the church as the presence of truth has an official character, actually involves a divine right, constituting the "magisterium." The activity of the church even in this domain cannot be equated with the activity of the church's ministry, for example, its teaching capacity.

3. The second element of God's presence determining the fundamental activity of the church as a whole is the love of God. It corresponds to the second divine procession and in fact is identical with it. The church is the presence of God inasmuch as in it the Father reveals himself and gives himself to be possessed as a love which communicates itself in the Spirit. As such it remains an uncircumscribable, but accepted, mystery. Since the church is both the eschatological gift of salvation as well as the means to salvation, the church first receives God's love and then gives it to human beings in sacrament, prayer, and life; both receiving and giving belong indefectibly to the church's nature and activity, and the two in conjunction make the church holy.

The church is the presence of God's eschatologically victorious grace (love) not only in objective holiness (the efficacy of the church's means of sanctification) but also in subjective holiness, by which the church can never entirely fall from the grace of God. The bringing to accomplishment of this presence is the act of all those living in God's grace in the church. In some form they make this love present and perceptible in the church's historical and social embodiment. To accomplish that presence God's love speaks in the word of the ministry to liberate human beings' freedom to love, confessing divine love in the actual sacramental word. The accomplishment of that presence also involves active love for God and our neighbors by all Christians in whose life God's love becomes present (and *convincing*) in the world. This presence of God's love is found (as far as ministry is concerned) in the power of order, in the administration of the sacraments. A sacrament is the efficacious word of the church's (and so of God's) self-donation to the individual. There the church engages itself absolutely. The church's word never loses its character or intention of conferring God's love, even when in certain individual cases it does not possess the character of absolute commitment and so cannot be termed a sacrament in the strict sense.

But now we have a new question to consider: Are the two factors by which the church is the presence of God's self-communication to the world in Christ simply two aspects of one and the same actualization of the church? Or are they materially different acts of the church's self-realization in which God's truth acts independently of God's love? Christ has come to give human beings truth and love. His truth is love, but are they the same?

The actions of the church can be acts of the presence of truth or of love. An act of the church's teaching office, for example, is an act of one of the charisms in the church, and does not demand the presence or power of the entire church. But the function of the church as presence of divine truth has as its purpose the presence of love. And where love is genuinely practiced, truth as such is also present. Indeed the church, because it is holy, can never grasp or bear witness to God's truth in such a way as to set itself in absolute opposition to that love of which the church with eschatological necessity is the presence. Of course the church must perpetually overcome any contradiction in its life between the presence of truth and of love: Christ's truth should appear as the innermost light of love.

For God truth and love are one, but human beings, members of communities and societies, are subject to time and change. Their temporal character injects concrete, historical contingency into the church and its life. Today only *history and society can tell us about human beings and their pastoral situation, and only the existing, temporal church can attain the abiding, necessary, and divine*. The distinct actions which fill the church's life and in which God's truth and love become present can possess different degrees of intensity in different eras and societies. We might consider, for instance, the act of martyrdom, the celebration of the Eucharist, a simple congregational prayer for unity, a practical expression of Christian spirit in social action, and so on—these are all activities of the church. The official character of each is different, as is the particular grace-given commitment, or the relation between their personal Christian sign and the Christ signified in them, but all incarnate God's love for the world.

CHARACTERISTICS OF THE CHURCH

Pastoral theology seeks to express correctly in existential theological propositions not only the eschatological parousia in the church but also God's self-giving presence as truth and love. This is all the more necessary since the eschatological parousia of God in Christ, which we call the church, has to be distinguished from that self-giving of God in eternity in which God communicates God's self face to face to God's divinized creature.

Mystery

God is present in the church as mystery. God's approach does not dissolve the mystery which God is, but makes the mystery even more inescapably and sharply apparent. As the church realizes itself and becomes more and more what it should be, God, Christ, and church become more mysterious. The church cannot preach its dogmatic teaching or its moral imperatives as a diminution of or defense against God's mystery. Faith and preaching are an ever more ineluctable confrontation with God's mystery, a command to enter into believing and loving communication, a grace-given personal meeting with and transcendence of the formula, sign, or institution. Ultimately the church is not the representative of God's honor and gift of salvation for the affairs of our world. Our very God becomes present for us as mystery. God does not send a representative in order to avoid personal involvement. The *representation* simply serves to draw our attention to God's own *presence*. To draw attention in this way is God's action, which God has the church perform. The church is the action of human beings insofar as God creatively makes possible and actualizes free human action.

Primal Sacrament

If we seek a contemporary term to characterize the presence of God's self-communication to the church and through the church, and to distinguish this from God's presence in final fulfillment, "sacrament" immediately suggests itself. God is so present in the church that the church can be called the sacrament of God's self-communication; or to distinguish what we mean from the seven sacraments, we can say that the church is the most important, the primal sacrament. Naturally Christ is the primordial sacrament, God's fundamental, original sign. As the God-man he is the primordial sacrament because he is what is signified (God in God's self-communication to human beings); he is the efficacious, manifest sign of this self-communication and its acceptance by humankind, for he is human and lives as a man in time. The church is not Christ's abiding presence in the world until his return in such a way that all statements made about Christ as the primordial sacrament of salvation can apply in exactly the same way to the church. The church is not identical with Christ: it is not our goal and fulfillment in the same sense as he is. The body of Christ is distinct from him, receives from him, and serves him. Nevertheless, the church can be called the primal sacrament because, if it were not, there could be no sacraments worthy of the name. The church's own nature is ontologically prior to the seven sacraments; they are partial realizations of the church itself. The church does not simply administer the sacraments; it lives in them, finding its own fulfillment in giving the life of Christ to others.

The expression "primal sacrament" as applied to the church in many respects expresses the special mode of God's presence in the church. The church in its empirical, tangible reality is never identical with its most fundamental concern—God. The church is only a sign of God. It can never affirm that what is signified (God's grace) is present only where the sign is, that is, in the church's historical reality as doctrine, sacrament, and society. There is a grace of justification for the "non-Christian." And yet the church is *the* sign (the primal sacrament) of this grace for the whole world, the sign in which God gives God's self not simply to the church and to those in the church, but to the world and to all human beings. Also, all salvation seeks its concrete manifestation in the church. In this double sense there is no salvation outside the church. The nonidentity between sign and what it signifies relates to the church as a whole, not only to the sacramental domain in the narrower sense but also to divine truth and its human expression, to moral norm and the practice of the love of God through it, to religious law and personal existential obligation coming directly from God. In everything it is and does the church is a sign which functions by pointing away from itself to God, to God alone, to God as mystery. God must never be confused with the church. Institutionalism, legalism, clericalism, theological rationalism, objectivist sacramentalism will continually crop up somewhere in the church, when sign and signified are confused or identified in practice (if not in theory) in any dimension of the church's life.

The church is the efficacious manifest sign of the presence of God, its real symbol, containing what it signifies; by grasping the sign human beings experience what it signifies. Human beings find God's presence in faith and hope, and this search is a historically unfolding movement of men and women and the church (as their community) toward their goal, God. This movement has its counterpart in God, for God is both the goal and principle (which we call grace) of the movement toward God. The dialectic of the divine presence as goal and as inner principle characterizes God's self-giving in the church. The church is the manifest primal sign that God wills to communicate God's self to the world, and God brings about the acceptance of this gift with eschatological certainty.

In the church God is present. Anyone who culpably refuses the historical, empirical form of God's self-gift and insists instead on having God in a purely spiritual way, without God's presence in this world, fails to reach God. The question of whether there is an empirical, "sacramental" embodiment of God's self-communication and of human movement toward God, an embodiment which is nonecclesiastical and yet necessary for salvation—this problem essentially depends on a solution (ultimately a merely terminological one) of the question of the factors which constitute the church. If only those elements are taken into consideration which in the actual circumstances of history distinguish the Roman Catholic Church from others, it would have to be said that there is of course no human being whose transcendental relation to God is not mediated historically, and that this mediation (as freely accepted) is necessary for salvation. We would have to add, however, that such mediation (as really operative and not merely *in voto*) is not necessarily ecclesiastical. If, however (and this is objectively and terminologically more correct), the bond of humankind and other factors of human reality are counted among those which go to make up the church, then it can also be said that the church fundamentally exercises a sacramental function absolutely necessary for salvation even when a woman or man does not belong to it in a sociologically perceptible way.

What is the significance for pastoral theology of these ecclesiological considerations? It is apparent that the church is the concrete, tangible form and historical embodiment of the promise God addressed to all humankind. Its saving, missionary significance is not solely dependent on the number of its members. The church's missionary zeal must be based on its awareness that it conveys salvation to the world (as its necessary sign) even where men and women lay hold of salvation without having wholly understood this sign. The church is also seeking itself in its missionary activity, not only giving but receiving too when it is successful. For only if the elements of the sign of salvation which are present in all humankind were complete in the church's historical, empirical form (a goal which in this world is only imperfectly attainable), would the church be wholly what it is: the primal sacrament which announces salvation in such a way that there is no longer reference to any saving element outside itself.

*

THE SHAPE OF THE CHURCH TO COME

The title and selections of this section are taken from Rahner's book The Shape of the Church to Come *(pp. 58–60, 123–32), first published in German as* Strukturwandel der Kirche als Aufgabe und Chance *in 1972. The English translation appeared in 1974. The translator, Edward Quinn, who also wrote the introduction to the book, admits forthrightly that Rahner "is regarded as a difficult theologian." But he goes on to say that he is difficult in the way of St. Paul in that he is unafraid to make faith intelligible and challenging to his contemporaries. His struggle to find truth and meaning in the confession of faith within the church is more like Jacob wrestling with God than a Platolike jousting with ideas. Without a doubt, this text is Rahner's feistiest critique of church. It was sparked in part by his debate with a canonist, Professor Heinrich Flatten, and Cardinal Höffner at the opening of the Synod of Würzburg in 1971. Both had insisted that certain teachings of the church had to be affirmed absolutely as truths to be presupposed prior to any theological discussion. Among those listed were the teachings regarding Christ's divine sonship, resurrection, and virgin birth and that regarding the indissolubility of a validly contracted and consummated marriage. Rahner replied to Höffner that such teachings were still not all that clearly understood by people and that they could be the occasion for further scrutiny and discussion. He argued that people continue to search for the meaning of these assertions even if a church leadership proclaims them as inviolable, all the while ignoring the unanswered questions ordinary people as well as theologians might want to pose.*

Writing this book became a way for Rahner not only to continue the debate but also to point out that the Synod of German Bishops needed a focus and a clearer program. Rather than look back to the council for all its answers, Rahner advised using the council as a jumping-off platform for addressing those urgent issues the German church was to confront in the coming decades. For this reason he arranged his own remarks under three questions that for him can elicit some deeper thought and practical ideas on the future of the church: Where do we stand? What are we to do? How can the church of the future be conceived? The two selections we have made from this text bring out some of the radical questions Rahner raises not only for the German bishops but also for the church at large. These are his call for a "declericalized church" (under the question "What are we to do?") and for a "sociocritical church" (under the question "How can a church of the future be conceived?"). The latter of the two pieces issues a clear and compelling rationale for greater church involvement on behalf of the underprivileged in both developed and developing nations. Rahner's analysis of the plight of the poor in the Third World is worthy of a liberation theologian involved in the struggle. Here we find both an endorsement of the best aspects of liberation theology and a disturbing challenge to the church to do more than hide behind slogans, mouth pieties, and cajole the indifferent. He calls for nothing less than voluntary service in the name of Christ and even, where necessary, a gospel-inspired, sociopolitical commitment of church resources.

A DECLERICALIZED CHURCH

The church should be a declericalized church. This proposition is of course open to misunderstanding and must be explained. It is obvious that there are offices in the church with definite functions and powers, however these offices may be distinguished and divided, however the functions and powers transmitted to officeholders in the concrete can or must be precisely conceived. It is also obvious, in the light of the church's nature, mission, and spirit, that its offices and officeholders as such have a special character that is not shared by offices and officeholders in secular society. But this special feature comes to these offices and these officeholders as such precisely from the nature of the church as Spirit-filled community of all who believe in Jesus Christ. It does not originate in a way which would simply dissociate offices and officeholders from the church as the community of all Christians.

Office has a functional character in the church as society, even though this society with its functions (proclamation of the word, sacrament, leadership of the church's life as society) constitutes a sign of what is real in the church: the free Spirit, faith, hope, love, to which all socially institutional factors in office are orientated and at the same time are never identical with them. Hence the "hierarchy" (if we may use the term) in the real nature of the church is not identical with the hierarchy in the church's social structure. The situation in the church is really like that of a chess club. Those who really support the club and give it its meaning are the members, to the extent that they play chess well. The hierarchy of the club leadership is necessary and appropriate if and as far as it serves the community of chess players and their "hierarchy" and does not think it is identical with the latter or that it can play chess better simply in virtue of its function.

So too office is to be respected in the church; but those who love, who are unselfish, who have a prophetic gift in the church, constitute the real church and are far from being always identical with the officeholders. It is of course part of the Catholic faith that the Spirit of God in the church is able to prevent an absolute schism between those who simply possess the Spirit and those who hold office, and therefore the latter also in virtue of their social function—but only in the last resort—enjoy a certain gift of the Spirit. As soon as these obvious dogmatic truths are lived and practiced impartially and taken for granted by officeholders and other Christians, then we have what we call a declericalized church: that is, a church in which the officeholders too in joyous humility allow for the fact that the Spirit breathes where it will and that it has not arranged an exclusive and permanent tenancy with them. They recognize that the charismatic element, which can never be completely regulated, is just as necessary as office to the church: that office is never simply identical with the Spirit and can never replace the Spirit; that office too is really effectively credible in the sight of men and women only when the presence of the Spirit is evident and not merely when formal mission and authority are invoked, however legitimate these may be.

If we also remember (and this must be specially considered at greater length later) that the church of the future must grow in its reality quite differently from the past, from below, from groups of those who have come to believe as a result of their own free, personal decision, then what is meant here by declericalization may become clearer. Office will exist in a church growing from below in this way, really and not merely theoretically emerging from the free decision of faith on the part of individuals, since there cannot be a society at all without office. It can then rightly be said that this office rests on the mission from Christ and not merely on the social combination of individual believers, even though it is also true that this mission from above is included in God's gracious will to all men and women, to which the church owes its nature and existence. But this official authority will be really effective in future in virtue of the obedience of faith which believers give to Jesus Christ and his message. It will no longer be effective in virtue of powers over society belonging to office in advance of this obedience of faith, as it is today but to a constantly diminishing extent.

In this sense the authority of office will be an authority of freedom. In practice, in future, the officeholders will have as much effective authority—not merely a theoretical claim to authority—as is conceded to them freely by believers through their faith. The assumption of an authority in the church will always have to consist in an appeal to the free act of faith of each individual and must be authorized in the light of this act in order to be effective at all; in the concrete the officeholders' appeal to their authority will be a proclamation of *faith*. For it is only through this faith that authority becomes really effective; the church is a declericalized church in which the believers gladly concede to the officeholders in free obedience the special functions in a society—and thus also in the church—which cannot be exercised by all at the same time.

It is true that these official powers in the church are conferred by a special rite which we call the sacrament of Holy Order and, when they are conferred, the officeholders are also assured by God of the help of that Spirit who is with the church; but this in no way alters the declericalized conception of office in the church. In the future questions or doubts about office will no longer be effectively dismissed by appealing to the formal authority of office, but only by furnishing proof of a genuinely Christian spirit on the part of the officeholders themselves. They will gain recognition for their offices by being genuinely human and Spirit-filled Christians, ones whom the Spirit has freed for unselfish service in the exercise of their social function in the church.

We might ask now what conclusions are to be drawn from this declericalization for the officeholders' way of life in the concrete. The life-style especially of the higher clergy even today sometimes conforms too much to that of the "managers" in secular society. All the ceremony which distinguishes the officeholders even in the most ordinary circumstances from the mass of the people and other Christians and which has nothing to do with the exercise of their offices and stresses their dignity where it is out of place, might well disappear. In the very exercise of office there could certainly be much greater objectivity in judging and deciding and, particularly for outsiders, the attempt to be objective could be made more clearly visible. There is no point in being secretive. An appeal to "experience" becomes suspect when experience appears to have been conditioned from the beginning by clerical prejudices. If advisers have been consulted, we ought to be allowed to know who they were. Office loses none of its authority or dignity if the decision and the reasons for it are made public at the same time. The more secular from the nature of the case is the object of a decision, so much the more relevant are *those* reasons which can be understood even by someone who is not well versed in theology.

There must be more courage to reverse and withdraw decisions without a false and ultimately un-Christian concern for prestige and also to admit it openly if these decisions have turned out to be objectively mistaken or—humanly speaking—unjust. Reaction to criticism of decisions must be relaxed and open to enlightenment, not every time taking the form of asserting that the matter has been considered so thoroughly that the decision made is beyond all criticism. In matters also which are dogmatically and constitutionally by no means immutable, we should remember that the simple wish of a majority in the church quite legitimately counts even in advance as part of the objective substantiation of a decision. A decision to be based merely on the weight of custom must not be decked out with ideological arguments produced for the occasion by smart theologians or church functionaries: these might seem very profound, but they really convince only those who have already been convinced for a long time for other reasons of what is now propped up by subtle theological or legal arguments. The danger of self-delusion through such subsequent ideological substructures is very great in the church and it is a typical feature of false clericalism.

No damage is done to office or officeholders if the latter honestly admit uncertainties, doubts, the need of experiment and further reflection, without knowing the outcome, and don't behave as if they had a direct hot line to heaven to obtain an answer to each and every question in the church. The formal authority of offices, even when the officeholders exercise it legitimately, does not relieve them of the duty, in the light of the question before them and within really contemporary horizons of understanding, of effectively winning a genuine assent on the part of those affected by their decisions. It seems to me that Roman decrees in particular do not sufficiently take account of this principle, and therefore in such enactments too much weight is laid on Rome's formal authority. Particularly in moral theological doctrinal decisions, it cannot be claimed on the one hand that they relate to natural law which is in principle intelligible to everyone, while on the other hand invoking the merely formal teaching authority, without any adequate attempt to expound convincingly and vividly in the language of the present time the intrinsic arguments derived from the nature of the case. Many other similar and proximate and remote conclusions could be drawn from a correctly understood declericalization of office in the church. But this may suffice for the moment....

A SOCIOCRITICAL CHURCH

If we are to talk about what is the most important thing to be done in the German church of the future, then obviously the question of the church's service to the world, the social and sociocritical commitment of the church in all its members and particular groups, cannot be excluded. It is a question we approach with fear and trembling, if only because there has been so much talk about it since Vatican II and because not a few have the impression that, behind all the talk and the appeals about the world-responsibility of Christians and the church, there lies a tendency toward "horizontalism," an attempt to make the church function as a purely humanitarian institution, perhaps even as a merely secular society of the future. Radically as the nature, task, and mission of the church are distinguished from a humanism concerned only with the present world, nevertheless in the light of the nature of the church and of Christianity itself this world-responsibility is part of the church's task.

After Vatican II this is obvious. Love of God and love of neighbor in the last resort are radically dependent on each other. One is mediated by the other. But if a society has become more mobile than formerly, if for the most varied reasons it can and must be changed in order to provide the individual with the greatest possible scope for justice and freedom, then the task of Christian love of neighbor (and of the virtue of justice implicit in this) can no longer be restricted to private, personal relationships. Love of neighbor in such a society acquires also (not only!) a sociopolitical character, becomes necessarily also the will to a better society; it is not mere feeling, not only a private relationship between individuals, but is aimed at changing social institutions—or it is not what it ought to be. It is so only if it is conceived in all its fullness and in the possibilities and tasks of *all* and if its nature is not obscured as a result of individuals rushing in too quickly: for the individual can realize something of its nature within the limits of her or his gifts and opportunities only when this love is a task and a force that is "politic."

At the same time, one thing must be clear to Christians: human beings are sinners and this fact must be taken seriously also today. But, according to the teaching of Vatican II (it is obvious anyway), actual social conditions and institutions are also marked by sin. These too are sinful, at least in the sense in which according to the teaching of the

Council of Trent and particularly of the Reformed churches "concupiscence" stems from sin, tends to sin, and is the object of our constant struggle as human beings and as Christians. The sinfulness of social conditions is simply the pendant to human beings' internal, concupiscent, and combative situation. Human beings' internal situation in its disorder, its implacable pluralism, its origin from and inclination to sin, faces us again from our external social situation and is not merely an object of private introspection.

All those who simply take social conditions for granted as good must as Christians face the question whether they really think that human beings are sinners, that there is a "sin of the world," that the world is seated in wickedness; they must ask whether their retreat to a private, inner world, where alone the drama is to be played between the redeeming God of freedom, love, and justice, and sinful humankind, does not corrupt Christianity and the unity of the living and historical person at least as much as the attempt to reduce Christianity to a purely humanitarian and social commitment.

The danger of debasing Christianity by confining the struggle with sin to the wholly private sphere is imminent and menacing for two reasons. On the one hand, the institutional factor because of its coercive power and generality creates a temptation to assume that what in fact exists—because of its universality—is also morally legitimate. On the other hand, in a society which is very immobile for a variety of reasons, not working according to a plan and not changeable by a rational decision, what is morally illegitimate in itself and involved in social institutions marked by sin—even if it is felt to some extent to be illegitimate—in practice is scarcely the object of concrete verdicts and morally necessary changes, simply because little or nothing *can* be changed.

For these two reasons and because consciousness in a great church changes only slowly, the members and officeholders of the church are far from being as radically, sensitively aware as they ought to be in face of the task, imposed by Christian love, of criticizing and changing society. Otherwise the suspicion—not entirely without justification—could never arise that the church is merely a conservative power, devoted to the defense of things as they are. Because of the power of existing social realities, there is a danger—only too often realized—that clever theologians and officer-holders in the church may very readily and smartly provide the ideology necessary to justify the existing order, particularly since these theologians and officeholders—whether they are aware of it or not—belong to the privileged groups of such a society and therefore almost instinctively and unreflectingly are already convinced of the goodness of the social institutions before they begin to provide the ideological substructures.

It does not seem to me that there is sufficient concern in the church about this danger rooted in human sinfulness, particularly since very general principles on freedom, justice, and the improvement of social conditions with a small dose of criticism, which sticks to generalities, only too easily serve as an alibi for us churchgoing Christians to quiet our conscience; general declarations also by the supreme authority in the church, which can sometimes be very incisive, are in practice ignored by Christians.

If the word "revolution" does not make us think at once of blood-shed and violence, which is or can be immoral, but is understood as referring to all those vast social changes which cannot be brought about in an evolutionary way with the aid of the already institutionalized and also really functioning means in a society, and if we think of the unity and close interpenetration of all nations and societies in the modern world, then the contrast between the modern industrial nations and the underdeveloped peoples really amounts to a global revolutionary situation, even though the same cannot be said of our own society in particular. The situation is further complicated by the danger recognized today of the aimless consumer society, environmental pollution, and so on. But it cannot be said that churchgoing Christians, even including higher officeholders, take this state of affairs as seriously as it ought to be taken. We are still invoking too one-sidedly the danger of communism and of a totalitarian and authoritarian socialism and we take too little trouble ourselves to find plans and models which we could offer boldly and practically for a future society which can cope with this contemporary situation.

If Christians take seriously *as* Christians their sociopolitical task and the situations in which this must be mastered, then as individuals or groups they cannot fail to work out ideas for the future or to raise demands which will be rejected by other Christians, appealing to the same ultimate Christian principles and motivations. This sort of thing is inevitable today and was recognized as a possibility also by Vatican II. But when Christians are opposed to Christians in this way there is bound to be a great deal of bitterness. They are fighting one another while appealing to what is for both sides an absolute criterion of living. The struggle easily leads to reciprocal "moral" accusations. But to attempt to avoid this conflict simply by leaving each other in peace or merely formulating supposedly Christian principles which neither upset nor in themselves help anybody would mean that no genuine sociopolitical commitment on the part of Christians would ever be possible. The absence of conflict would however imply a betrayal of essential tasks now facing Christians.

We must therefore learn now and particularly in the church of the future to maintain the church's unity and mutual love even in this bitter struggle. This sort of thing must constantly be freshly learned and practiced. We must bring a knowledge of the realities of the situation to bear on our arguments and the latter must be intramundane and in the proper sense of the term sociopolitical. We must not invoke one-sidedly the teaching and practice of the institutional church, whose neutral attitude would then be obscured. But an internal struggle in the church in regard to these things, in the name of Christian principles, is simply unavoidable. Conflict arises in the last resort from the fact that any application of theoretical principles to concrete situations must involve some lack of reflection and must come up against things on which no adequate reflection is possible: hence the application of these principles takes different forms and the point at which it has to differ, in spite of all reflection and discussion, cannot be precisely determined.

It is of course not possible here to work out an idea of the concrete form of a future social commitment of Christians, Christian groups, and ultimately of the church's official representatives. Here we shall draw attention only to a very few points, mainly those which often seem to be forgotten in the ordinary life of our church.

It is clear, but we must insist once again, that the church, in order to become outwardly more credible, must allow the desire for freedom to become more effective in its internal life....

If we speak of Christians and the church bringing their efforts to bear on "the world outside," we are not thinking solely of the kind of spectacular declarations and demonstrations organized by student groups and others. Such efforts are justified in principle, may perhaps be required by a Christian conscience, but in particular involve questions of fact which cannot be discussed here, in the light of which one endeavor can be approved, the other questioned; nor should bishops try to prevent by administrative measures sociopolitical efforts of such groups as student parishes merely because they themselves consider the tendency objectively wrong. A student parish, for example, can certainly commit itself politically (which does not mean party politics) in a particular direction, even though this direction seems to some bishops objectively wayward, as long as the student parish does not proclaim clearly heretical fundamental principles or cease to be a community open to *all* Catholic students who want to live with it. But under these conditions such a community is also worthy of financial support by the institutional church, even if it seeks a political commitment in a direction other than that of the bishops, without of course wanting to bind every one of its members to it.

As we have said, however, this social commitment is not to be found merely in such declarations and organized efforts. The fact that there are other ways of getting involved becomes clear as soon as we recall how few Christian groups, particularly at the roots, are clearly aware of this responsibility. The question of immigrant workers, for example, stirs only a few parishes or basic groups of the church's organizations, although we must not overlook some laudable exceptions. There should be a social commitment particularly in the basic communities in the process of formation and in the living parishes to be developed in the same way.

We can have the greatest respect for the German Catholic organization for charitable works, Caritas, and its manifold institutions and activities. Caritas is certainly something of which the German church can be proud, just because it makes less noise than quite a number of other organizations which behave as if the church had hitherto done nothing in the social field. Perhaps we may leave aside the question—which might also be raised—whether such organizations as Caritas, unintentionally of course, do not sometimes work to preserve the system when it might be the time to change it, even though changing the system is not its task and even when it is difficult to draw the line between improving—with which Caritas can be concerned—and changing the system. But the question may well be raised whether this official, institutionalized Caritas does not unintentionally provide individual Christians at the roots with a clear conscience which they ought not to possess. Christians today are only too much inclined to leave to official institutions of church and state what they should do themselves and what really they alone can do by way of Christian love and the defense of justice and freedom.

Today there is certainly much to be done for people which must be done and can only be done administratively by institutions of church or state. But as a result of this institutionalization and depersonalization new needs and wants emerge: institutional security also involves compulsion. When certain persons have received from institutions all they need materially, all that to which they have a right, which they desire, they still lack what they need most of all: the person of the other human being. Here is a social task for the basic communities. This task lies in a unique way between the wholly private sphere and the interpenetration of "intimate areas" of life on the one hand and that part of social life which can be institutionalized on the other. To mention this task does not mean a retreat to pure feeling, a failure to appreciate or a distrust of specialized institutions and their tasks and achievements. But in such basic communities and in them alone can the presence or absence of what is properly human, of what cannot be departmentalized, be observed, "controlled," and thus too that singular "achievement" can be "organized" in which a person realizes himself or herself for another and does not try to make up for this by handing out material aid.

In Christian basic communities that social commitment is possible which does not appear to be social simply because it cannot be institutionalized in an act which is not related to the person performing it, but which is in fact the decisive social work: without it a person is not liberated by the institutions but would be stifled in them and their perfectionism. In the basic community there is scope for that love of the more distant neighbor which is neither mere spontaneous sympathy nor justice that cannot be institutionalized. Obviously this sort of love of neighbor in the basic communities too must be given concrete, material shape, must take the form of neighborly help, young families closely and vitally linked with one another and working for one another, assistance given quietly and taken for granted from one individual to another. But it exists only when someone gives herself or himself with the gift and the material aid does not separate one person from the other, but brings them together. Such love is possible only in these basic communities (which can be of very different kinds), because only there can the appropriate aid and personal encounter be one. For here we can really still observe whether human beings and Christians are present as such and what is required from them. People can still face quite concrete demands which hold for one individual, call for his or her personal action, and cannot be delegated to institutions.

A part of the sociopolitical commitment of Christians, their groups, and the church, which also involves their institutions, is the duty of helping the Third World. A great deal has in fact been said and written about the problem of development aid. But it is obvious that our Christians and Christian congregations are not at all clearly aware of the fundamental importance of this theme for the Christian conscience. It is more or less the same here as with the problem of environmental pollution. Experts call attention to the problem almost in despair; everyone has heard of it; all say that something must be done and halfheartedly some slight effort is made, in a way that hurts no one; then everything goes on as before, as if nothing had happened.

It is the same with the question of aid to the Third World. This aid would be in accordance with the deepest, even the material interests of the highly industrialized nations; at the same time, whether advantageous or not, it is a matter of Christian love. But far too little is done compared to what ought to be and could be done. We are not going to prove it here with figures and statistics: this has been done often enough. When concrete deeds and not merely abstract principles are required, this aid is a very difficult matter, as everything is difficult where there is a question of larger social groups, of economics, money, law, and of overcoming not merely individual, but also collective egoism with its shortsightedness. Today however, when the history of humankind has become one, when there are no longer any areas historically and socially separated from each other, we should be able to see that we are in a global revolutionary situation (which is not the same as revolution). For the social situation of this one world as a whole is characterized by such massive injustice and material peril for the greater part of humankind that it would be impossible to find any institutions capable of removing these things in an "evolutionary" way and in accordance with principles recognized on all sides in society.

Christians in this country on the whole have not yet become aware of this situation. They are all right and they are too shortsighted to see their more distant neighbor who is not all right. The will to face the problem of the Third World does not mean merely being ready to make a larger personal contribution to the funds of one of the relief organizations or to grumble a little less as a taxpayer about the amount allotted (small enough in itself) in the state's budget to development aid. For once at least we ought to go beyond all this and enter into a mental and material solidarity with those Christians and non-Christian groups which are working for radical changes in the social and economic structures in their own underdeveloped countries.

It seems to me that in this respect Latin America, for which Christianity and the church bear a special responsibility, should be of primary concern to us. If we react positively in this way to groups in Latin America who are trying as Christians to bring about far-reaching social changes, we need not be too worried here about the right abstract heading under which to describe what they are wanting to do. Revolution must not be understood either in the style of the French Revolution or of the Russian October Revolution and is certainly not something which always and in every situation is bound to be contrary to the Christian conscience or the Sermon on the Mount. Socialism would be a word to be expunged from the Christian vocabulary only if it were made clear how we are to describe the structures of that society which is clearly and

truly distinguished from a capitalism of exploitation and inhuman practices, still to be found in the world and expecting Christians to approve
or accept it, simply because we are opposed to atheistic and totalitarian
communism.

With all this we have still said almost nothing about the concrete duties and tasks of the Christian in regard to the Third World. We cannot
work out any concrete programs here. Perhaps too whatever we might
suggest with some hope of its realization would amount to no more than
the proverbial drop in the ocean. But even if this were so, even if in
this whole question we had to fear historical necessity and the practical
impossibility of really mastering the problem in the future, these circumstances do not dispense the Christian from the duty of providing at least
this drop. For instance, every Christian youth group of some size might
send—as they do in Innsbruck—every year three or even more gradu-
ates to work for a year as voluntary helpers in the developing countries;
every Christian parish might adopt some particular relief organization
in the developing countries; it might be made easier in a human and
not merely economic sense for people of color to study in our country:
these are possibilities which really cannot be called utopian.

The Christian's sociopolitical commitment inevitably involves the
question of his or her relationship to the concrete political parties. For
all the future as we can see it, it must be admitted that Christians and
the church will have to get used to the fact—if they have not already
done so—that really practicing Christians belong to different political parties. There is of course no doubt that a party program, in itself
and particularly in its practical emphasis, may sometimes be impossible
to reconcile with a Christian conscience, even though—as in all cases
of moral action—this does not imply any judgment on the subjective
state of conscience of a Christian who supports an "un-Christian" party.
It cannot however be said that a Catholic cannot vote for a particular party merely because one particular point in its program or of its
political decisions is contrary to Christian norms. For, apart from the
fact that we should have to prove that precisely this particular decision
was clearly contrary to Christian moral law, there simply are no parties which are purely Christian and whose actual conduct would never
create misgivings for a radically Christian conscience.

This thesis is not disproved by the fact that occasionally a particular offense against this Christian conscience is not clearly seen or
not seen at all in this light in a party, among ordinary people, even
by the church's officeholders, and therefore the party concerned is regarded without any misgivings by the church generally. In the light of

a Christian conscience membership of a particular party, which necessarily and inevitably consists of historically conditioned, shortsighted human beings who also represent selfish interests, can only be regarded dispassionately always as a question of the lesser evil; on this question Christians will never be agreed and this diversity of opinion is inevitably supported on all sides with a Christian motivation and cannot be forbidden to the individual Christian. We have already mentioned this.

8

ON SACRAMENT AND SYMBOL

In Rahner's theology, sacrament and symbol are intertwined. This fact dictated the pairing of the essays included in this section. Indeed, Rahner claims in the second selection, "On the Theology of Symbolic Reality," that "the teaching on the sacraments is the classic place in which a theology of the symbol is put forward in general in Catholic theology." And yet Rahner's reflections on sacrament are fundamentally an outgrowth of his Christology. The word made flesh becomes the Father's historical, symbolic presence in the world, touched irrevocably and dramatically by what have become the great mysteries of the Christian religion. Christ, the enfleshed symbol of his Father's definitive outreach to creation, conveys God's grace to people who have become brothers and sisters unto him and, in a real sense, too, children of his Father. Likewise, the church, as sacrament of Christ, stands for the indwelling of God's Holy Spirit, who, in turn, symbolizes and makes possible the continued salvific communion with Jesus Christ. Through the societal structure of church, this same Holy Spirit creates the visible signs of Christ's graced presence in the community bearing his name. It is through this historically conditioned and societally structured church that the grace of God in Christ and the continued sending of their Spirit are symbolized and made visible in sacramental tangibility. Hence Rahner uses the never-ending presence of Christ in and to his church to construct a foundation for what in Catholic tradition are the seven sacraments. Each sacramental event is viewed in this perspective as a real symbol not only of the church's reaching out to grace individuals in the significant episodes and situations of their lives—from rebirth in baptism to death—but also of how the church brings to expression in its daily mission the one privileged, primordial sacrament of God and of God's concrete offer of grace, Jesus Christ.

THOUGHTS ABOUT
THE SACRAMENTS IN GENERAL

This first selection is Rahner's introductory essay to his book Meditations on the Sacraments *(pp. ix–xvii), published in 1979, a translation of the original German text,* Die siebenfältige Gabe *(The sevenfold gift), published by Verlag Ars Sacra Josef Müller of Munich in 1974. Prior to their being brought together in one volume, the chapters of this book had appeared separately as booklets on*

the sacraments. Rahner added a chapter on religious profession and the intro-
ductory essay. He states that he intended this essay to be a help in establishing
a new groundwork for understanding the sacraments. He speaks, therefore, of
a "Copernican revolution" in the modern understanding of the sacraments in
which the grace associated with them is seen not in the more traditional, mech-
anized, "supernatural" way, totally opposed to the profane, but as God's special
self-gift that makes possible a radical opening up of human consciousness to
the immediacy of the holy mystery in individuals' everyday lives. The world it-
self and especially the human experience of freedom and choice are bound up
into the relationship the incomprehensible holy mystery of God has initiated
in creation and in the special care of God's creatures. In short, God's grace is
everywhere as an abiding existential determinant of the human spirit. Rahner
situates his sacramentology, therefore, in the interpersonal and social shape
life takes when people are encountered by Jesus Christ in concrete moments
of their lives in the believing community. The church is but the sign of Christ,
the permanent and unsurpassable symbol of God's grace conferring an infinite
fullness of meaning on human existence.

In this essay, too, Rahner hints of the new way he proposes to deal with the
ex opere operato (by virtue of the work performed) so often seen by Protes-
tant critics of Catholic sacramentology as a quasi-magical production of grace
through unerring ritual superseding any lack of faith on the part of the recip-
ient. For Rahner the opus operatum *(the work performed) is but a way of*
associating the sacraments with the irrevocable presence of Christ, and that as-
sures the church that Christ will give himself unendingly to his people in those
significant moments when individuals and the community celebrate their sacra-
mental identity in and with him. The sacraments, then, are an affirmation of
the community's faith in its continuing communion with Christ through the
specific signs in which that communion is expressed. The sacraments give visi-
bility to the way the church has been constituted the sign of Christ who as word
incarnate is himself the living sign of God's intimate nearness to God's creation.

Before turning directly to the realities of faith to be found in each of
the sacraments, we might benefit from some rather general considerations about the relationship between the sacraments and human beings
as they are today (though perhaps all of us are modern in different
degrees, because things do not happen to everybody at the same time
everywhere). I once wrote about a "Copernican revolution" in modern
human beings' understanding of the sacraments. Some people might
consider this phrase a little too dramatic, since after all there can be no
doubt that the program for this "revolution" is already laid out in the
traditional understanding of our faith. Nevertheless such a revolution
really is taking place—or at least it is already in the works.

What is the meaning of this "Copernican revolution" in the under-standing of the sacraments, in the existential realization of the sacra-mental event? To make this clear we first ask ourselves: How has the average Christian up to the present day usually felt about receiving a sacrament? A descriptive answer to this question might perhaps be: both externally and internally, human life is lived in a profane world. Christians see this profane world, and consequently themselves, as ori-ented toward God while remaining empirically profane. This world is put into the proper relationship to God by a mysterious quality called grace, which God keeps on giving, but (as far as it touches the world) in discrete quantities. We can know something about grace only from the outside, through verbal indoctrination; in its proper reality it is beyond our awareness—though that is how it sanctifies us, makes us pleasing to God, and unites us to God. The events in which this grace is imparted to us are called sacraments, which are sacred signs performed by the church.

Christians who have received a good religious education know very well that there is such a thing as the habitual, abiding grace of justifica-tion—what the catechism calls sanctifying grace. But they usually do not apply this piece of theological knowledge to the sacraments, or, if they do, they only see habitual grace as a prerequisite for receiving a par-ticular sacrament. Receiving this or that sacrament is an isolated event that happens to them; it does not come from within themselves. It gives them grace, but this remains as it were outside their experience of their own human existence, even though their knowledge of this sacramen-tally initiated grace-event, derived from sources other than their own experience, can bring about what might be called supplementary effects of consolation, of encouragement, or of impulses to do good. In my opinion, this is a pretty fair description of the traditional understanding of the sacraments.

A sacrament is thought to be a single act by which God reaches into space and time to confer grace under signs instituted by Christ. Without this grace we cannot be saved, but, because it is supernatural, it cannot be the object of "profane" awareness. Does this understanding of sacra-ment have any credible hold on our conscience? Does it correspond to the mentality of people today? I believe that one need have no scruple in answering both of these questions in the negative. There is another way to understand sacrament, which can be drawn from thoroughly tra-ditional data of theology and church teaching and which is better suited to the contemporary mentality.

"Copernican revolution" was the name we gave to the transition from the traditional concept of sacrament outlined above to the one we are now aiming at. What exactly is this new concept of sacrament? As I said, I am not thinking of some novelty, ungrounded in the traditional data of faith and theology. To that extent, it is unimportant whether we call it new or not. What I have in mind, rather, is that, if we pay attention to certain faith-insights of theology, we can understand the sacraments in a way which contrasts with the traditional understanding while remaining entirely within the bounds of orthodoxy. In order to get some preliminary idea of how this can be so, let us begin with two propositions: (1) Grace is *everywhere*, as the inmost primordial divinely implanted entelechy of world and human history. (2) Grace, in the strictest theological sense of the word, is not a particular discrete datum within consciousness—but from this it does not follow that it is a real thing beyond and outside consciousness. Instead it is the comprehensive radical opening up of a human being's total consciousness in the direction of the immediacy of God, an opening up that is brought about by God's own self-communication. Both of these propositions need a little more explanation.

Grace is everywhere as an active orientation of all created reality toward God, though God does not owe it to any creature to give it this special orientation. Grace does not happen in isolated instances here and there in an otherwise profane and graceless world. It is legitimate, of course, to speak of grace-events which occur at discrete points in space and time. But then what we are really talking about is the existential and historical *acceptance* of this grace by human freedom. Grace itself, whether in the mode of merely preceding the act, or in the mode of acceptance, or in the mode of rejection, is the inmost entelechy wherever there is spirit or mind (that is, reality's openness and self-donation to God) and wherever there is transcendentality (which is radicalized by grace to orient the creature to the immediate possession of God). God is the goal of the conscious world, inasmuch as God brings this movement out of the inmost center of this world to God's self. And this very radicalization of this movement of the conscious world out of its inmost center is called grace. Grace itself, therefore, is everywhere and always, even though a human being's freedom can sinfully say no to it, just as a human being's freedom can protest against humankind itself. This immanence of grace in the conscious world always and everywhere does not take away the gratuity of grace, because God's immediacy out of self-giving love is not something anyone can claim as his or her due. This immanence of grace always and everywhere does not make salvation history cease to be history, because this history is the history of the acceptance of grace by the historical freedom of human beings and the history of spirit coming ever more to itself in grace.

With that I have already pretty well explained the second proposition. The world and human beings contain all sorts of things that can be called gifts of grace. Good weather, which puts us in a good mood, which in turn leads to a positive affective relationship toward another human being, is an example of something that can quite meaningfully be called and be experienced as grace. But when we speak of grace as such, in a strictly theological sense, and when in this sense we say that the sacraments impart grace, we mean what theology calls "sanctifying grace" or its "increase," that is, its existentially more radical acceptance. Now sanctifying grace produces created effects in human beings, but, without taking away from that fact, at its root it is "uncreated grace." This is God imparting God's self to human beings so as to be both their goal and the inmost motive force toward this goal. Without this, human beings could never have God as *their* goal. This grace, the inmost and inclusive movement of the spirit toward God through God even to the immediacy of God (that perfect state of human existence called the vision of God), is of its essence not an objective datum of consciousness, since it is precisely the very radicality of consciousness itself in the dynamic of knowing and in freedom. And yet it is not a reality that simply transcends consciousness.

Wherever human beings, each as a totality, experience themselves in freedom and choice, wherever in hope they take on an obligation which really demands more than they can give and which cannot be justified from a worldly point of view, wherever they hope against all hope, wherever they dare to love in a way that is too costly, wherever they believe in the light although everything is dark and in meaning although everything seems to be losing its meaning, wherever they surrender and believe this surrender to be their final victory, they experience the radicalized transcendentality of the human being into the incomprehensible mystery of God. They experience grace, even though perhaps it cannot be reflected upon and verbalized and thus made into an object of thematic conceptuality. Grace is everywhere, and it is experienced, though usually not under that name. This does not necessarily mean that all human beings accept grace and thus are justified. For just as human beings can despair and hate themselves, they can also in desperate and cowardly "modesty" deny that supreme dignity which graciously orders them to the immediacy of God and which when refused still rules them in the form of judgment.

We can now take another step. We have already said that grace is given always and everywhere and is one of the abiding existential determinants of the human spirit as it de facto exists. Nevertheless, we said, grace can and does have a history. It is the history of its being freely accepted by human beings and humankind, the history of human beings' coming to themselves *as* graced and of their becoming ever more reflexly aware of it. Grace itself points us toward its goal, when it teaches us to call this process the history of revelation.

The history of the acceptance of grace can be considered here only as it occurs in individual human lives. The act of accepting the ultimate gracious dynamic toward the immediacy of God in the individual life of a human being is usually called a salutary act in faith, hope, and love. Human nature requires that such a salutary act always be mediated through a human being's taking a position toward a worldly reality (ultimately toward his or her neighbor). Human beings say their yes or no to their graced condition (their orientation toward the immediacy of God) over some worldly reality because they have this orientation consciously and freely only in a relationship to someone or something in this world. This is why their history is the history of their free relationship to their graced transcendentality, why it is salvation history.

And so in historical deeds and processes a human being's relationship to God manifests itself and becomes historically perceptible. His or her moral actions are the embodiment, the sign, of an ultimate relationship to God. These signs, in which the ultimate yes or no to God's self-communication in grace is embodied and expressed, cannot of course in most cases be interpreted with any certainty *as* signs of the salutary acceptance of grace. When a person tries to reflect on them and evaluate them, they usually remain ambiguous to say the least. Not only ambiguous of themselves but also in regard to this question: Was whatever definite orientation they do have toward God also actually intended by the person who performed them? Now such moral actions do not necessarily have to have an explicitly religious thematic. As embodiment and historical perceptibility and symbolization of the acceptance of grace, they can also occur in a situation in which, without an expressly religious thematic, a human being's freedom unconditionally obeys the absolute dictate of conscience and so, unthematically and without reflection, affirms and accepts what we call God and the radical liberation of the human being in the direction of God through God's grace.

This point will permit us to reach an understanding of the principles of what we call Christian sacraments only if we pay attention to two more things. Human actions always occur in the realm of interpersonality, they always make a difference in human relations, they always imply a communication made to others, and the interpersonal and social situation in which a person lives and deals always contributes to the shape his or her actions take. In Christ Jesus, the crucified and risen one, it has become manifest in a historically perceptible way that what has always and everywhere been brought about by grace—the salvation history of humankind as a whole—in spite of its ambivalence between salvation and eternal perdition necessitated by human beings' freedom, has entered into a stage in which this history, as the history of humankind as a whole, can no longer fall short of its goal—a goal which will be achieved infallibly but without detriment to the freedom of the individual participants in this salvation history of humanity. That is why Jesus Christ is called the primordial sacrament of salvation. By this word we mean precisely that historical event in which, as in a historical sign, God's will to save human beings, which triumphantly succeeds in its purpose in spite of all the sins of men and women and which from the beginning was implanted in the world as grace, brings about its own unmistakable historical manifestation and establishes itself in the world and not just in the transcendent will of God. The church, as the socially constituted presence of Christ in every age up to the end, can therefore rightly be called the basic sacrament of the salvation of humankind. By this we mean that it is the sign which perpetuates Christ's presence in the world, the permanent and unsurpassable sign that the gracious entelechy of the whole of history, which brings this history into God, will really be victorious in the world despite all sin and darkness and will really prevail by bringing about the completion of the world in the form of salvation rather than judgment.

Now I think we can arrive at a basic understanding of the sacraments, even though our treatment of it must unfortunately be brief. When the church as the basic sacrament, in situations of human life which are decisive for the individual or for the group, pledges itself to human beings with an absolute commitment of its being *as* the basic sacrament of salvation, and does so historically and palpably, that is, in word and deed, and when human beings in turn accept this the church's pledge of salvation and act it out as the manifestation of the acceptance of their interior grace-dynamic, then we have what we mean by the sacraments of the church. This general description of the essence of the sacraments cannot be elucidated further in this introduction. We must forgo applying it to the several sacraments of the church and showing how it leads to a historically correct understanding of the church's teaching that Jesus instituted the sacraments and by so doing conferred on them their power to give grace.

The reflections which we are going to make on the Eucharist, however, require that we emphasize or reemphasize two points. First, the starting point we took gives intelligibility to what we called the Copernican revolution in our way of looking at the sacraments. To say it once again, the sacraments are the historical manifestations of the grace which is always and everywhere at work in the world. Insofar as they participate in the primordial sacrament Christ and in the basic sacrament church, they are without doubt historical manifestations of grace which have a special character and thus differ from those always ambivalent manifestations of grace which are found in every good moral act. It is this difference, incidentally, which could be the basis for an explanation of the notion of *opus operatum* [the work that is performed]. None of this, however, alters the basic fact that the sacraments must be seen in the first place as ecclesial manifestations and historical incarnations of *that* grace which is at work everywhere in the history of humankind and manifests itself historically, though in highly diversified ways, wherever women and men are doing good and thereby in some inexpressible way striving for God in faith, hope, and love. What we see in the sacraments, therefore, is precisely the inmost being of the history of humankind in the world inasmuch as history's inmost entelechy, by being God, makes history the history of God.

Second, when we say that the most basic thing about the sacraments is that they are signs, and if, with all their historical relativity, the sacraments are ultimately signs which grace creates for itself out of its own most distinctive essence, we are not denying that these signs are *efficacious* signs. We do not think of them as mere supplementary statements expressing a reality which exists and comes to the fullness of its being just as well without such expressions. Grace is the incarnational grace of Christ, which by its nature aims at being flesh and history. By its own inner power it creates human beings' acceptance. As accepted it makes itself present in the world precisely by effecting its historically perceptible acceptance in the sacraments. And so one can quite well say that the sign is the *cause* of what it signifies just as conversely it is the *effect* of what is signified. What really matters here is this simple insight: a real understanding of the Eucharist lets us see it as the manifestation of that mysterious grace which inconspicuously governs our whole life, the celebration in the community of the church of that which wills to find its victory in the monotony and pain of daily life.

*

ON THE THEOLOGY OF SYMBOLIC REALITY

This selection is from the second part of Rahner's essay "Zur Theologie des Symbols" (On the theology of the symbol), which first appeared in 1959 as part of volume 1 of the collection Cor Jesu, *edited by Augustin Bea et al. It was integrated into volume 4 of the* Schriften *the following year and was translated into English for volume 4 of the* Theological Investigations *(pp. 235–45) in 1966. Rahner uses his theology of symbolic discourse as a structuring element throughout his writings. In part 1 of the essay excerpted here, "The Ontology of Symbolic Reality in General," Rahner claims that all beings are symbolic by their very nature because they must attain their true nature or identity by expressing themselves. Rahner adds that all self-expression is in some way symbolic expression. In fact, it is through his affirmation of the symbolic that, in part 2 of this essay, Rahner connects one's essential multiplicity of directions, choices, and possible identity to that original unity in the holy mystery of God from whom one's plurality of drives and outreach to others derives and in whom alone a person is fulfilled. Moreover, Rahner insists it is in the symbolic that a person's self-realization in the other is constituted. In symbolic discourse the stretching of one's personal potential and the deepening of one's relationship with God are articulated and enhanced. It is in this way, according to Rahner, that, enfolded in God's graced presence, people create their own self-identity and establish their communion with the other or others in and with whom their lives are bound. In the final section of the essay, Rahner examines "The Body as Symbol of the Human." From his considerations of the body as symbol of the soul by being formed as the soul's self-realization, Rahner draws implications for the foundation of devotion to Jesus' sacred heart, symbol of Jesus' love for all God's children.*

While Rahner draws his theology of the symbol from his anthropological understanding of how humans attempt to satisfy their restless drive for fulfillment, it is equally obvious that for him the symbolic nature of being human, being discursive, and being perfected imbibes its strength from the triune nature of God and the manner in which God has graced the world with God's Spirit and word. As he observes in the selection that follows, if the mystery of the Trinity is foundational for an ontology of the symbol, in any coherent theology of symbolic reality, Christology will, in turn, be the central chapter. The Logos, or Word of God, is the historical embodiment of God as triune. Through his enfleshment in a concrete human history, Christ becomes the revelatory symbol in which God, the Father of Jesus, reveals the true nature of their triune divinity. They send their Spirit of love to the church, which, in turn, becomes the symbol of Jesus' persistent presence in space and time, made visible and real in the sacraments in which the grace of God becomes historically manifest and God becomes approachable. It is because of Christ, finally, that one's relationship with the triune God will perdure through sym-

bolization even when one has been brought by God to his or her salvific destiny.

If what has been said up to this is correct, it is only to be expected that no theology can be complete without also being a theology of the symbol, of the appearance and the expression, of self-presence in that which has been constituted as the other. And in fact the whole of theology is incomprehensible if it is not essentially a theology of symbols, although in general very little attention is paid, systematically and expressly, to this basic characteristic. And again: since a simple listing of dogmatic assertions throughout the whole field of theology shows how much need it has of the concept of symbol and how much it uses it (no doubt in the most diverse acceptations and applications), the necessity of our general ontological considerations is confirmed once more from another direction.

We shall of course have to be content with a few indications. The attentive reader, especially if trained in theology, will not have failed to remark that the thought of the mystery of the *Trinity* was the constant background of the ontological considerations. The freedom of our method has already allowed us to appeal expressly to this mystery. We used it to show that a plurality in a being is not necessarily to be considered as a pointer to finiteness and imperfection, and that therefore a general ontology—which only speaks of beings strictly as such—may very properly start from the fact that each being bears within itself an intrinsic plurality, without detriment to its unity and perfection—which may eventually be supreme—precisely as the perfection of its unity. Hence an ontology confined to a particular field and likewise a theology may well ask what this means with regard to the symbolic nature of individual beings.

When we were working out the ontology of the symbol, we took no great pains to formulate it so that it would be immediately applicable to the theology of the Trinity in blameless orthodoxy. Even now we shall not try to establish expressly the convergence of this ontology and the theology of the Trinity (especially the theology of the Logos). It is enough for our purpose to point out very simply that the theology of the Logos is strictly a theology of the symbol, and indeed the supreme form of it, if we keep to the meaning of the word which we have already worked out, and do not give the term quite derivative meanings, such as the ordinary language of popular speech attributes to it. The Logos is the "Word" of the Father, his perfect "image," his "imprint," his radiance, his self-expression. Whatever answer is to be given to the question of how binding the psychological theory of the Trinity, as put forward by St. Augustine, may be—whether the Father utters the eternal Word *because* he knows himself or *in order to* know himself—two items at any rate must be retained. One, the Word—as reality of the immanent divine life—is "generated" by the Father as the *image* and *expression* of the Father. Two, this process is necessarily given with the divine act of self-knowledge, and without it the absolute act of divine self-possession in knowledge cannot exist. But if we retain these two elements, which are traditional in theology—not to give them a higher qualification—then we may and must say without misgivings: the Father is himself by the very fact that he opposes to himself the image which is of the same essence as himself, as the person who is other than himself; and so he possesses himself. But this means that the Logos is the "symbol" of the Father, in the very sense which we have given the word: the inward symbol which remains distinct from what is symbolized, which is constituted by what is symbolized, where what is symbolized expresses itself and possesses itself. We omit the question of what this means— prior to a theology of the incarnation—for the understanding of the Father and his relation to the world. If, following a theological tradition which began only since St. Augustine, one simply takes it for granted that *each* of the divine persons could set up, each for itself, its own hypostatic relationship to a given reality in the world and so could "appear," then the fact that within the divinity the Logos is the image of the Father would give the Logos no special character of symbol for the world, which would be due to the Logos alone on account of its relationship of origin to the Father. The Father could also reveal himself and "appear" without reference, so to speak, to the Son. But if one does not make this presupposition with St. Augustine, which has no clear roots in the earlier tradition and still less in Scripture, one need have no difficulty in thinking that the Word's being symbol of the Father has significance for God's action *ad extra* [outside God's inner life], in spite of such action being common to all three persons.

It is because God "must" "express" God's self inwardly that God can also utter God's self outwardly; the finite, created utterance *ad extra* is a continuation of the immanent constitution of "image and likeness"— a free continuation, because its object is finite—and takes place in fact "through" the Logos (John 1:3), in a sense which cannot be determined more closely here. But it is not our intention to go into this difficult subject here. But it has to be mentioned, even if only in passing, because we could hardly omit this link between a symbolic reality within and without the divine, since it has also been noted to some extent in tradition.

If a theology of symbolic realities is to be written, Christology, the doctrine of the incarnation of the Word, will obviously form the central chapter. And this chapter need almost be no more than an exegesis of the saying: "He that sees me, sees the Father" (John 14:9). There is no need to dwell here on the fact that the Logos is image, likeness, reflection, representation, and presence—filled with all the fullness of the godhead. But if this is true, we can understand the statement: the incarnate Word is the absolute symbol of God in the world, filled as nothing else can be with what is symbolized. The Word is not merely the presence and revelation of what God is in God's self. The Word is also the expressive presence of what—or rather, who—God wished to be, in free grace, to the world, in such a way that this divine attitude, once so expressed, can never be reversed, but is and remains final and unsurpassable.

But there are some comments to be made on the generally accepted dogmatic teaching which is here presupposed. They have not the same degree of certainty in theology, but they seem necessary if we are to have a proper understanding of the incarnation in a theology of the symbol. If we simply say: the Logos took on a human nature, considering this defined doctrine of faith as the *adequate* expression of what is meant by the dogma of the incarnation (though such a description of the hypostatic union makes no such claim), the full sense of the symbolic reality, which the humanity of the Logos represents with regard to the Logos, is given no clear expression. For if the humanity which is assumed is considered only as that well-known reality which we know in ourselves, and which is only very generally "image and likeness" of God; and if this humanity is supposed only to subsist in a static, ontic sense, that is, as "borne" and "taken on" by the Logos: then the humanity has no doubt the function of a signal or a uniform with regard to the Logos, but not in full truth the function of such a symbol as we have developed above. The Logos would make itself audible and perceptible through a reality which was of itself alien to it, had intrinsically and essentially nothing to do with it, and could have been chosen at random from a whole series of such realities. No matter how close we consider the union between the speaker and her or his means of communication—the union is in fact hypostatic—it would not change the fact that the sign and that which is signified are really disparate, and that the sign could therefore only be an arbitrary one. Or we could put it more exactly: the assumed humanity would be an organ of speech substantially united to the one who is to be made audible: but it would not be this speech itself. It itself would only tell something about—itself; it could only tell about the Word insofar as the Word used it to form words and direct actions which would divulge something about the Word by their meaning and their marvellous quality. It is not surprising that a theology with these unavowed, unconscious, but effective presuppositions should in the concrete make Jesus the revelation of the Father and his inward life only through his doctrine but not through what he *is* in his human nature. In such a position, the most that could come in question would be a revelation by means of his (virtuous) actions.

To continue on these lines, and to give greater clarity to the inexhaustible content of the truth of faith which expresses the incarnation, one could take up here the Thomistic doctrine, that the humanity of Christ exists by the existence of the Logos. But when putting forward this thesis, one should be clear that this existence of the Word is again not to be thought of as the reality which—merely because of its being infinite—could bestow existence on any thinkable "essence," as if it could offer any essence a ground of existence which in itself was indifferent to this essence rather than that or to which manner of existent being arose thereby. The being of the Logos—considered of course *as* that which is received by procession from the Father—must be thought of as exteriorizing itself, so that without detriment to its immutability in itself and of itself, it becomes *itself* in truth the existence of a created reality—which must in all truth and reality be predicated of the being of the Logos, because it *is* so. But then, starting from these Thomistic principles, we arrive at considerations and insights which show how truly and radically the humanity of Christ is really the "appearance" of the Logos itself, its symbolic reality in the pre-eminent sense, not something in itself alien to the Logos and its reality, which is only taken up from outside like an instrument to make its own music but not strictly speaking to reveal anything of him or her who uses it. However, these considerations have already been put forward in an earlier chapter on the mystery of the incarnation. We showed there that the humanity of Christ is not to be considered as something in which God dresses up and masquerades—a mere signal of which God makes use, so that something audible can be uttered about the Logos by means of this signal. The humanity is the self-disclosure of the Logos itself, so that when God, expressing God's self, exteriorizes God's self, that very thing appears which we call the humanity of the Logos. Thus anthropology itself is finally based on something more than the doctrine of the possibilities open to an infinite creator—who when creating would not however really betray *the creator's self*. Its ultimate source is the doctrine about God, insofar as it depicts that which "appears" when in God's self-exteriorization God goes out of God's self into that which is other than God. . . .

It follows from what has been said that the Logos, as son of the Father, is truly, in his humanity as such, the revelatory symbol in which the Father enunciates himself, in this son, to the world—revelatory, because the symbol renders present what is revealed. But in saying this, we are really only at the beginning of a theology of the symbol, in the light of the incarnation, not at the end. For in view of this truth, we should have to consider that the natural depth of the symbolic reality of all things—which is of itself restricted to the world or has a merely natural transcendence toward God—has now in ontological reality received an infinite extension by the fact that this reality has become also a determination of the Logos or of its milieu. Every God-given reality, where it has not been degraded to a purely human tool and to merely utilitarian purposes, states much more than itself: each in its own way is an echo and indication of all reality. If the individual reality, by making the all present, also speaks of God—ultimately by its transcendental reference to God as the efficient, exemplary, and final cause—this transcendence is made radical, even though only in a way accessible to faith, by the fact that in Christ this reality no longer refers to God merely as its cause: it points to God as to the one to whom this reality belongs as God's substantial determination or as God's own proper environment. All things are held together by the incarnate Word in whom they exist (Col. 1:17), and hence all things possess, even in their quality of symbol, an unfathomable depth, which faith alone can sound. It would be well to explain all these abstract statements in detail, by applying them to individual realities—water, bread, hand, eye, sleep, hunger, and countless other affairs of human beings and of the world which surrounds them, bears them up, and is referred to them—if one wished to know exactly what theology of symbolic reality is based on the truth that the Logos, as Word of the Father, expresses the Father in the "abbreviation" of his human nature and constitutes the symbol which communicates him to the world.

When we say that the church is the persisting presence of the incarnate Word in space and time, we imply at once that it continues the symbolic function of the Logos in the world. To understand this statement correctly, we must consider two points. One, where a reality which is to be proclaimed in symbol, is a completely human one, and so has its social and existential (freely chosen) aspect, the fact that the symbol is of a social and hence juridically determined nature is no proof that the symbol is merely in the nature of arbitrary sign and representation, and not a reality symbolic in itself. Where a free decision is to be proclaimed by the symbol and to be made in it, the juridical composition and the free establishment is precisely what is demanded by the very nature of a symbolic reality in this case and what is to be expected. A *non*-existential reality cannot express itself in this free and juridically constituted way, where the symbol is likewise a symbolic reality which contains the reality of the thing symbolized itself, because it has realized itself by passing over into the "otherness" of the symbol. This would be contrary to the nature of the non-existential reality. But exactly the opposite is true when it is a matter of something which has been freely constituted by God and which has a social structure. When such a reality renders itself present in a freely constituted symbolism formed on social and juridical lines, the process is merely what its essence demands and is no objection to the presence of a symbolic reality. But the church, even as a reality tributary to the Spirit, is a free creation of the redemptive act of Christ and is a social entity. When therefore it is constituted along juridically established lines, the result does not contradict the fact that it is the symbolic reality of the presence of Christ, of his definitive work of salvation in the world, and so of the redemption. Second, according to the church's own teaching, especially as voiced by Leo XIII and Pius XII, the church is not merely a social and juridical entity. The grace of salvation, the Holy Spirit itself, is of its essence. But this is to affirm that this symbol of the grace of God really contains what it signifies; that it is the primary sacrament of the grace of God, which does not merely designate but really possesses what was brought definitively into the world by Christ: the irrevocable, eschatological grace of God which conquers triumphantly the guilt of humankind. The church as indefectible, as church of infallible truth, and as church of the sacraments, as *opus operatum* and as indestructibly holy as a whole, even in the subjective grace of human beings—by which it is not merely object but even motive of faith—really constitutes the full symbol of the fact that Christ has remained there as triumphant mercy.

The teaching *on the sacraments* is the classic place in which a theology of the symbol is put forward in general in Catholic theology. The sacraments make concrete and actual, for the life of the individual, the symbolic reality of the church as the primary sacrament and therefore constitute at once, in keeping with the nature of this church, a symbolic reality. Thus the sacraments are expressly described in theology as "sacred signs" of God's grace, that is as "symbols," an expression which occurs expressly in this context....

In a word, the grace of God constitutes itself actively present in the sacraments by creating their expression, their historical tangibility in space and time, which is its own symbol. That the juridically established structure of the sacraments does not run counter to this view of the sacraments as symbolic realities has already been explained equivalently, when the same objection was eliminated in the question of the church as symbolic reality of the grace of God.

Further indications of the prevalent structure of Christian reality as a unity of reality and its symbolic reality must be omitted here. They can only be presented adequately when the bodily reality of the human being, and so her or his acts in the dimensions of space and time, history and society, are conceived of as symbolic realities embodying her or his person and its primordial decisions. This would be the real starting point for reaching an understanding of the historically attainable life of the church as symbolic embodiment of the Spirit of God and of the inner history of the dialogue between God's free love and human freedom. The result of this would be to show that no adequate treatise can be written *De Gratia* [on grace], unless it contributes to the theology of the symbol in the Christian history of salvation. . . .

It might be thought that *eschatology* would be the part of theology which treated of the final disappearance of the sign and hence of the symbol, in favor of a naked immediacy of God with regard to the creature—"face to face." But this would once more be a position—this time with regard to eschatology—in which the symbol is considered as an extrinsic and accidental intermediary, something really outside the reality transmitted through it, so that strictly speaking the thing could be attained even without the symbol. But this presupposition is false, and it is still false with regard to eschatology. For the true and proper symbol, being an intrinsic moment of the thing itself, has a function of mediation which is not at all opposed in reality to the immediacy of what is meant by it, but is a mediation to immediacy, if one may so formulate the actual facts of the matter. In the end, of course, many signs and symbols will cease to be; the institutional church, the sacraments in the usual sense, the whole historical succession of manifestations through which God continually imparts God's self to human beings, while they still travel far from the immediacy of God's face, among images and likenesses. But the humanity of Christ will have eternal significance for the immediacy of the *visio beata*. The incarnation of the Logos may well be considered as the indispensable presupposition for strictly supernatural grace and glory, so that the gracious freedom of God with regard to these two realities does indeed remain, but remains a freedom. And the dependence of the self-communication of God to the created spirit in glory with regard to the incarnation does not indicate a merely moral relationship, arising from the fact that the incarnate Logos once "merited" this glory for us in time. The relationship is a real and permanent ontological one. If we accept this proposition (which cannot be propounded more fully now), it implies that what has been affirmed of the symbolic function of the incarnate Logos as Logos *and* human being, also holds good for the perfected existence of human beings, for their *eschata* [last things]. Eschatology also teaches us about the symbolic reality which conveys to us the immediacy of God at the end; the Word which became flesh.

9

ON CHRISTIAN FAITH, PRAXIS, AND MARTYRDOM

Rahner's theology is permeated with reverence for the graciousness of God, who gifts creatures with faith and inspirits them to be hearers of God's word of truth and searching doers of God's will to effect good in the world. For Rahner, faith is the radical orientation of one's life to God made possible by God's prior self-communication in the tangibility of God's word and in the signs of God's loving concern for people in all phases of human history. For Rahner, this concrete immanence to God's people is epitomized most clearly in the unsurpassable embodiment of God's word in the life, death, and resurrection of Jesus Christ. Drawing on his anthropological convictions about how God has shaped and related to the human spirit, Rahner speaks of one's transcendentality to God's immediacy as a "permanent existential" in one's being human and being orientated to the holy mystery. This orientation, in turn, engenders a restlessness for spiritual fulfillment that only God can fully satisfy.

For Rahner, such faith need not be identified with the conscious choice for God made explicit in forms of religion. Nor must it be pinpointed at a dramatic moment of one's personal history or articulated clearly in a self-satisfying dogmatic analysis and objectified, baroque catechetical assertions. Faith is, rather, the graced dynamic of God's intercommunion with God's people in which one's freedom is enhanced to the point of being able to receive the divine word in all its historical contours and in all of its demands on one's time and energy. Indeed, Rahner views faith as a transcendental characteristic of the human spirit in which God stirs people to seek after the truth that gives coherence and value to their being human and being in relationships. If God is the "wholly other" to whom they are attracted and impelled, God is also, in God's trinitarian outreach as Father, Word, and Spirit, the context or horizon of the ultimate source of meaning in their lives. In Rahner's theology, God's gracious self-revelation and one's free openness to the divine presence, which is both the context and aim of one's existence, are conjoined.

In turn, Rahner construes faith as animated by what he calls one's "fundamental option," in which in all freedom human beings either lovingly yield to the holy mystery that shapes them in the image of Christ or refuse to surrender even as, ironically, they are drawn to this same mystery. In a paradoxical way Rahner declares that yielding one's aspirations to their ultimate source in

God is the catalyst of a more genuine freedom in which one is freed to be more oneself because more deeply attached to the source of transcendent meaning. Having made this option, one is led by God's Spirit into the rhythms of a life patterned after the example of God's own son. God's creative energies thus endow people with an inner dynamism of the Spirit making possible the unthinkable, their freely accepted interrelationship with the Father and with his son Jesus, the Christ, in the outpouring of their Spirit of love over all creation. Rahner attempts in his theology of faith to include all the dimensions of being human, especially the practical outcome of being orientated to the God who in Christ identifies with the least of the brothers and sisters whom God has created and cares for through the faith-inspired compassion of God's people. In two of the selections of this section we see how Rahner sets the concrete context of faith in culture, and we see also the more praxis-related dimension of his writings on how one relates faith to the call of Christians to serve people. The final selection focuses on what for Rahner is a climactic moment in the dynamic process of faith, a person's encounter with God in the moment of death. Here the person's fundamental option in faith is conjoined with the last decisive moment and high point of his or her commitment to and hope in God. In the death of the martyr Rahner sees fulfilled not only a person's faith in Christ but also the restless yearning for communion with the divine source of all beatitude.

FAITH AND CULTURE

This text, taken from the chapter "Christian Faith: The Deliverance of the World," appeared in the book Grace in Freedom *(pp. 69–77), published in 1969. It was originally part of a radio broadcast on "Faith and Culture" on Southwest German Radio, June 11, 1967, and was incorporated into the book* Gnade als Freiheit: Kleine theologische Beiträge *(Grace as freedom: Short theological essays), in 1968. Rahner uses the Pastoral Constitution on the Church in the Modern World, a conciliar text, to argue that official conciliar teaching enjoins on Christians that they not neglect their temporal duties because these impact on their duties toward neighbor and God and affect, at least indirectly, their salvation. Faith demands, moreover, that the Christian exercise responsibility for culture even though neither Christianity nor church teaching designs and defines that culture today. Rahner denies the prevailing notion that one can separate faith from one's secular, cultural life. In fact, he notes that the formation of a unified culture is a concern of the Christian churches in that Christianity strives to preserve legitimate civilizations and to promote unity among the nations through a variety of means such as education and communication.*

Much of Rahner's analysis on this point is drawn from anthropological considerations in which humans are said to share a common dignity and destiny and have, as a consequence, the right to share in the economic and cultural well-being of society. It is not difficult to detect in Rahner's assertions here a concern for greater socialization and equality in the face of the obvious gap between the haves and have-nots of prevailing national cultures. According to Rahner, faith must animate the movement to provide food and to insure peace even if the means, greater socialization or state intervention, are not always in accord with the most perfect way of life for many peoples. Faith, he says, can help bear the burdens and avoid the despair of an oppressive culture, but it must do more. Christians can infiltrate cultural structures with their faith, hope, and love and influence peoples with a sense of responsibility, thus reshaping the structures of the secular, cultural life of a society with their own "revolutionary attitudes." In effect, Rahner concludes that faith, far from becoming manipulated by society into a defense of the status quo, should move Christians, for the sake of human dignity, to call into question every structure of the secular. They are to do this on the strength of their radical conviction that God's justice will prevail. Faith thus becomes, for Rahner, a catalyst for sociocultural renewal.

Today faith and religion are often judged by their usefulness. Our contemporaries demand instinctively that faith should prove its value in the world of our experience, it should produce a better world, foster peace, mitigate or abolish social tensions, and generally make life more bearable. Otherwise, it is thought, it need not exist at all. In view of this naive prejudice we would first ask quite simply: Why must faith do all this in order to be acceptable? Is not the human being precisely the being that also has other aims? Do human beings not want truth, even if it causes suffering, beauty, even though it is useless, the holy in order to adore it? Do they not find the right relation to consumer goods and luxuries just when they are detached from them because they are aware of another sphere and selflessly worship that which is of no direct "use" to them?

We had to make this brief reservation before discussing "faith and culture." For though the sphere of culture itself belongs partly to the realm of truth, beauty, and holiness which ultimately has no need to defend itself before the court of utilitarianism, faith and its object transcend even these good things. For they are concerned with God and God's salvation, which human beings can receive only if they adore the one who is the first and last mystery of their existence in selfless hope and love.

Keeping in mind this reservation, we may now, however, discuss a positive mutual relationship between faith and culture. Without quoting too extensively we here follow particularly section two of the second chapter of Vatican II's Pastoral Constitution on the Church in the Modern World (*Gaudium et Spes* [hereafter *GS*]). For this chapter deals precisely with this subject, namely the proper development of culture and the importance of the Christian faith for this development.

We cannot here answer the question of what culture is. We can only just mention the cultural inheritance received by the individual such as scholarship, art in all its forms, morality and religion, which transcends morality and which despite its superior nature is also a cultural phenomenon, determining and being determined by the culture of a nation and an epoch. Culture may be defined as an element of tradition which helps to determine a person's surroundings and which human beings themselves not only receive and accept, but also develop through their free creative work as something that is specifically human. Such cultural work is not a luxury in which human beings indulge, because without it they could not even exist as natural beings. In this context we should like to warn against the snobbery of certain circles who imagine that natural science, technology, and social planning have nothing to do with culture, which in their view can only be created by individualistic elites. We would add to this that one must distinguish between culture such as it is and as it ought to be. For culture can be judged by critical standards: indeed, such a critical attitude which demands change is an essential element of culture itself. Further, the ideal culture, too, is no timeless entity but has itself a history in time and space, so that many ideals of culture exist beside the actual cultures. Hence we are justified in restricting our subject to the question of what the Christian faith could and should achieve for a contemporary culture such as it ought to be.

Faith demands responsibility before God also for the culture which is and remains secular. At first sight this statement seems to be valid for all time. But we should remember that a specifically secular culture exists only today, and that Christianity does not claim to design this culture directly according to the principles of the faith, let alone of the teaching office of the church. Hence there is the acute danger that believers will no longer consider this secular culture as their religious responsibility before God, but will regard it as something that interests them as human beings, but no longer affects them as Christians. The council, too, recognizes the danger (*GS* 43ff.) that Christians are only seeking "heavenly things" and think that earthly matters do not concern them and have no bearing on their salvation, because these things have become exclusively secular and human. But the council says: "The Christian who neglects his temporal duties neglects his duties toward his neighbor and even God, and jeopardizes his eternal salvation." Now the words about the temporal duties should be read within the context of the council statements about the relative autonomy of the secular culture (*GS* 59), for only thus will the sentence just quoted receive its full weight. For precisely that culture which cannot be materially given by faith and the church is nevertheless the earthly duty that determines our eternal salvation. In lonely responsibility the Christian is confronted with these secular cultural activities, and these, though not only these, are her or his Christian vocation and mission.

Unified mass culture is a Christian concern. The council document does not regard culture as the preserve of a small elite of individuals or nations who would have a monopoly on its development. It speaks quite simply of a "mass culture"; it favors the cultural development of all men and women and nations. True, it desires that most legitimate civilizations should be preserved, yet it approves of the development of "a more universal form of human culture . . . one which will promote and express the unity of the human race" (*GS* 54) and favors a powerful international organization which, despite the United Nations, does not yet exist (*GS* 84). The council wants both sexes to cooperate responsibly in this culture, and men and women of all social classes as well as all nations, whether rich or poor, to have as active a share in it as possible through education, means of communication, tourism, and so forth. The council fathers knew, of course, that there would always be differences of social status, talent, and national character, but in their view great genuine culture does not presuppose the existence of a large number of people who are poor, socially weak, and exploited. For them culture is not aristocratic and they do not favor the existence of those who, themselves without culture, make possible the culture of others. This almost socialist (to use an inexact term) characteristic of the council's idea of culture is certainly in a sense contemporary, because in former times such a program could not have been realized. Nevertheless, in the last analysis this tendency is determined by the Christian view of human beings as creatures and children of God destined for eternity. For precisely this reason every human being has the right, in principle, to share in the economic and cultural possessions of humankind. In the opinion of the council the poor have been promised the kingdom of heaven not in order that others, whether individuals or nations, should alone be and remain rich. Mass culture is not ultimately a goal to be welcomed with enthusiasm. It is fundamentally a very sober program lacking the charm of many contrasts, indeed it may be regarded as "levelling down." But such a program is a demand of contemporary Christianity, while we are not going to prejudge the sociological justification of the mostly pejorative term "mass."

The Christian faith decisively helps the individual to overcome the difficulties of the cultural situation of our time. The council document says quite freely that it is impossible to guarantee food and peaceful existence to the immense and fast-growing population of our globe without more socialization, powerful international organizations, and public intervention in the economies of individual states as well as of humankind as a whole. This greater socialization is not necessarily a good thing in itself, it is simply a necessity. It certainly involves also, though not only, new ties, very real dangers of human beings' manipulation by others, new restrictions, growing technologically planned uniformity, an ever-increasing fragmentation of human beings' work. All this is not necessarily compensated by greater freedom; but it is inevitably part of the guilt, which human beings ought not to have incurred, but which is now part of their lives. Thus the so-called progress will also ever increase or at least alter the burden of existence. Faith can help to bear the burden which the contemporary mass culture imposes on us. This does not mean that faith could be manipulated into becoming such a help. But if we unreservedly believe in God, accepting our responsibility to God and hoping in eternal life, this faith will also help us to bear the narrowness and boredom of our life, which has today become worse rather than better. This faith helps us to carry on, without despairing and trying to make up for the grayness of our present world by escaping into the idolatry of superficial pleasures. Sobriety and resigned acceptance of the inevitable are certainly virtues of contemporary human beings and their humanism. But they either do not suffice without being founded on faith, or they are already filled unconsciously with what the Christian calls faith.

According to the council, Christians have the duty to impregnate the structures of secular life with their eschatological hope (Dogmatic Constitution on the Church, art. 35; *GS* 38). This is an important statement about culture and the Christian's relation to it, for this "secular life" is actually identical with what we call culture. Now this certainly does not mean that the Christians could cause and help to establish their eschatological hope, which is the kingdom of God and ultimately God, by their cultural activities. The fulfillment of this hope which God freely gives to human history is God's own deed and grace. Yet, though the absolute future is not in human hands, precisely its hopeful expectation becomes the driving power in human beings' cultural activities: Christians hope through creating culture and vice versa. They fashion the future of the world by hoping for the absolute future. Or, to express it more cautiously: they ought to have this hope and thus also do cultural work. This includes a statement about an essential element of hope itself. This hope for eternity is realized in the constant transformation of the structures of secular life. Leaving aside the fact that "revolution" is a very vague and many-sided term, we might say:

Here Christian hope is declared to be the ground of an always revolutionary attitude of the Christian to the world. If Christianity be rightly understood and if Christians understand themselves correctly, things are exactly the opposite of what most Christians and non-Christians imagine: hope in the absolute future of God who is the eschatological salvation does not justify a fossilized conservatism which anxiously prefers the safe present to an unknown future; it is not a tranquilizing "opium for the people" in present sorrow; it is, on the contrary, the authoritative call to an ever-renewed, confident exodus from the present into the future, even in this world. Indeed, historical human beings do not realize even the ultimate transcendental structures of their nature in the abstract "interiority" of their own minds, but in communication with the world and their surroundings. And true "practice" in radical opposition to theory is not the mere execution of something planned and hence merely theoretical, but opening oneself to and risking the unplanned, so that the true possibility of what is risked appears only in this practice. True practice implies that the necessary and justifiable planning which manipulates the material world by technology, the human world by socialization, and thus human beings themselves, does not depreciate the insistent area of the unplanned. It does not reduce it to a defined residue merely waiting to be worked out. It rather increases the area in question and displays it more clearly as the result of praxis itself, since human beings, as they break down the unforeseen data, build up their own unforeseeable products. Hence in the practical risk of the unforeseen inner-worldly future human beings realize their eschatological hope by looking away from themselves to the absolute which is not in their power. It is therefore true that human beings must impress their hope on the structures of the world. This, of course, does not mean precisely that certain permanent structures of their secular world could ever be the permanent objectivization of their eschatological hope. On the contrary. Every structure of secular life both present and to come is called into question by hope, because this is the anticipation of what is not in our power, and the historical and social act of hope is realized in this calling into question, though not entirely. For Christians also accept the passing away of the "form of this world" in their individual lives, in death and the renunciation that anticipates death, and realize their hope even in them. This is anything but wild revolt. For the spirit of revolt either elevates the immediate future of the world into an absolute and thus is the opposite of hope, namely a form of pride, or else it does not hope for anything, but denies everything because it is not permanent, and thus is despair. But constant criticism also of the secular structures is one of the forms of Christian hope. For it does not hold on to anything in this life as if without it human beings would fall into an absolute void; and at the moment when they are becoming more clearly than before the masters of their world it orders them not only to let go what is taken away from them, but also actively to surrender what, in view of the infinite future of hope, they realize to be transitory and thus replaceable even in time.

It is strange that we Christians who must take the radical risk of hope in an absolute future should have acquired the reputation, among others as well as among ourselves, that our principal virtue is the will to preserve the existing order. In fact, however, the Christians as the pilgrim people of God have been given the absolute command to hope, and this includes that they must always abandon also fossilized social structures. Theoretical faith cannot simply deduce how Christians are to realize this hope despite such ever-renewed exodus, and to what they cling (as is also possible) because their hope takes away the semblance of the absolute also from the temporal future. This concrete imperative is not the result of the applied theory of the faith, just as little as faith as such changes the general promise into a special one which is grasped only by primeval hope. But this hope commands individual Christians as well as Christendom to risk these ever-new decisions between the defense of the present and the exodus into the unforeseeable future. And hope can do this, for it has already done the greater thing. Through it human beings have abandoned themselves into the eternal absolute over which they have no power. And in the power of this greater hope they also possess the lesser hope, which is the courage to change the secular structures of their lives, as the council says. The greater hope is realized in the lesser, and eternal life in the creation of ever-new forms of culture.

*

WHO ARE YOUR BROTHER AND SISTER?

The next selection is taken from the second half of the book The Love of Jesus and the Love of Neighbor *(pp. 83–98), published in 1983. The essay was reproduced from the text of an address Rahner presented on brotherhood on*

November 10, 1980, at the Catholic University of Graz on the occasion of the Diocesan Day of Recollection for the Diocese of Graz-Seckau. Originally revised for publication as the separate booklet Wer ist dein Bruder? *(Who is your brother?), by Herder Verlag of Freiburg in 1981, it was coupled with a booklet of the following year,* Was heisst Jesus lieben? *(What does it mean to love Jesus?), for the English translation bearing the title stated above. In his preface, Rahner remarks that, despite the randomness of his thoughts, he offers them here "as a gift from a brother," keeping in mind that "a communion of brothers and sisters in the church is something precious, and something to be nurtured, by one another and for one another."*

The text that follows is from the chapter on consequences and includes Rahner's "brotherly digression" in which he urges the pope to exercise the role of representative of world conscience voicing the challenge of Christ to the peoples of the world. For him, the consequences of Jesus' mandate that we enter into a reciprocal relationship between love of God and love of neighbor are, clearly, that Christians are called to an intercommunion with God and with one another. This is a communion of many dimensions, each offering practical ways in which a Christian may be neighbor to those who have become in the gospel perspective one's brother and sister in Christ. Rahner also believes that in this way parishes can be converted away from being service stations or mere administrative units within an ecclesial bureaucracy into becoming real communities of Christians inspirited by God to live with a genuine concern for each other and thus to build up a stronger church. This will be a church attuned to the command of Christ that his followers love and serve one another.

Christian love of neighbor, a Christian communion of brothers and sisters, receives an altogether new status and an altogether new value when it is lived as a concrete manner of actualizing love for God instead of being understood only as a secondary requirement and obligation imposed on us as a commandment by God. In our average Christian life, however, it looks as if what we must attend to is basically only our own salvation, through prayer, reception of the sacraments, participation in the Eucharist, and the avoidance or expiation of sin—and in the process, of course, and for the same purpose, through avoiding massive offenses against the obligation we have regarding our neighbor. But would not the Christian life look entirely different if we spontaneously and unquestioningly heard "Save your soul" as "Save your neighbor"?

When we look at the average Christian life, it would seem that the notion prevailing in the normal Christian's moral consciousness is that we have "loved our neighbor" when we have done nothing evil to him or her, and have met the objective claims he or she may justly have against us. The truth, however, is that what we are commanded by the "commandment" to love our neighbor, in its oneness with the commandment to love God, is the demolition of our own selfishness—the overthrow of the notion that love of neighbor is basically really only the rational settlement of mutual claims, that it demands only giving and taking to the mutual satisfaction of all parties. In reality, Christian love of neighbor attains its true essence only where no more accounts are kept—where a readiness prevails to love without requital—where, in the love of neighbor as well, the folly of the cross is accepted and welcomed.

When one really understands the unity of the love of God and neighbor, the latter shifts from its position as a particular demand for a delimited, verifiable achievement to a position of total fulfillment of one's life, in which we are challenged in our totality, wholly challenged, challenged beyond our capacity—but challenged in the only way in which we may gain the highest freedom: freedom from ourselves. Thus if we understand love of God and a brotherly/sisterly communion as two expressions denoting basically the same thing—and if we say "communion of brothers and sisters" rather than "love of neighbor" because this expression is less likely than the other to be misunderstood as a demand for a factual, neutral accomplishment that dispenses the heart from its last obligation—then we may safely say that with a communion of brothers and sisters, in its necessary oneness with the love of God, we have expressed the single totality of the task of the whole human being and of Christianity.

But now our expression "communion of brothers and sisters" will have to defend itself against a certain maudlin, sentimental misinterpretation. For are we not now challenged in a way calculated to throw the normal Christian consciousness into a state of considerable commotion? In consternation, must we not wonder: Have I ever, ever once, loved in such a manner that no echo, no reward, no recognition, no self-attestation or endorsement answered this love? Have I even once in my life loved with the terrible feeling that I was nothing but stupid, simply made a fool of and used?

These experiences, these tests of unselfish love, to be sure, leave something to be desired with respect to a cheery, blissful experience. But wherever a human being, in his or her love, is unable mutely and unquestioningly to bear its bitter disappointments, he or she must still wonder: Have I not confused a worldly-wise selfishness that can behave very respectably with true love that makes a human being really selfless and releases him or her to sink away into the incomprehensibility of God? Rightly understood, then, this *fraternitas,* this communion of brothers and sisters, is a very dangerous expression.

A further consequence of a genuine communion of brothers and sisters—to be sure, along with a great many others just as important—is the transcendence of a sectarian mentality in our religious subjectivity. A Munich industrialist once announced that he was leaving the church because the Bavarian bishops were seeking to add another holy day to the church calendar, and he considered this to be economically unsound. His declaration demonstrated an utter failure to grasp what Christianity and church are. Notoriously, they are only understood as a service to individual religious needs. Plainly, a communion, constitutive of church, by which we come away from ourselves, take leave of ourselves, is not yet understood. For, once more, a communion of brothers and sisters will not after all be ultimately a matter of our own utility. It will lovingly affirm the other in himself or herself, above and beyond all personal utility, and thus mold oneness and, finally, church, affirming this church even (and precisely) where it is no longer of any personal advantage to do so.

Communion within the Church

So we live in a world church. And this church is not simply tailored to our individual tastes. It does not suit the mentality of the neoindividualistic subjectivism of the twentieth century. Today there are people—Europeans in abundance, of course, but now Africans, Latin Americans, and others—whose mentality does not automatically fit in with our Western European neoindividualism, but who have the same right to a home in the one church as we have. Whether we like it or not, their mentality works in the church in such a way that we are affected by it ourselves. This may be uncomfortable for us, particularly when this foreign mentality unwittingly and naively presents itself as simply Catholic, quite as if it went without saying that it should be, when this is not the whole picture. A Polish Marian piety looks upon itself simply as part and parcel of the Catholic faith, hence as valid always and everywhere— and so it will seek to impose its validity throughout the whole church, even though it may be in many respects foreign to our own sensibilities and arouse considerable resistance on our part.

Thus if we seek to live communion in the church, this is something we shall have to deal with. After all, a communion of brothers and sisters requires precisely that we allow others the validity of their own mentality, even if that mentality is strange to us, and indeed even if it cannot, or should not, simply step forward in the name of the Catholic faith that obliges all. It is difficult to escape the impression that many of our young people today, while demanding radically more brotherly and sisterly communion in secular society, loudly protest what does not suit them in the church, quite as if in matters ecclesial it were their perfect right to continue to practice a curiously old-fashioned individualism.

A thousand things in the church do not suit us. This is perfectly plain. But why should they have to suit us? If the church had to be just precisely the way we would like it, what would everyone else do? What would the Italians do—who, perhaps fortunately for them and for us, are less exact and mulish in juridical matters than we? What would the Latin Americans do, whose Marian piety is perhaps less observant of the theoretical limits of Christology than ours? Are we not, all unawares, objectively risking a shameless individualism and selfishness, with which we seek to live in the church in such a way as baldly to arrange it to our own taste? When we feel, perhaps with some justification, that a bishop fails to "suit" us, do we still treat him as a brother, with whom we live in community for better or for worse?

Difficult as it may be for us, we live today in a concrete world church, with its historical conditions and with the limitations and tentative character of the phase through which it happens to be going at the moment. Of course it has not yet reached a later, better phase. But it is in this church that we must live. We must be prepared to abide an Italian curialism that for our brothers in Rome needs no explanation. And of course for our own part—for we, in turn, are their brothers and sisters—we too have the right to make our own desires, concerns, and troubles plainly known in this matter.

To speak frankly, quite a few German intellectuals in the church find the pope far too Polish today. But why should he not be a Pole? Why should he seek to perform the (ultimately impossible) trick of not letting his cultural origin show in his style of governing? There is simply no way for one's background not to have its concrete effects. On the other hand, to be sure, a view of things in the generosity of communion by no means obliges us to laud any and every administrative disposition a pope might make as if it were the ultimate stroke of wisdom, and the "pope fans" in the church (may we be forgiven the expression) should not take it amiss if someone else in that church, while unmistakably supporting the papacy itself, is less enthusiastic than they in these matters and honestly expresses some particular difference of opinion. This reciprocal tolerance, too, belongs to the intrachurch communion of brothers and sisters of which we have need today.

A Brotherly Digression

In this connection, we hope we may be forgiven if we inject a little something that perhaps does not pertain too strictly to our subject, but which we hope may make it easier for someone or other of our readers to come to an attitude of communion with regard to the pope and the papacy—which is not only a consequence of, but also a prerequisite for, a dogmatic conviction of the plenipotentiary prerogatives of that papacy.

It would not be difficult to imagine, in a genuine world church today, within this global world history of ours that has become such a uniform, homogeneous history now, that the office of the papacy could assume an altogether novel and positive practical function, one which it has so far exercised in no concrete way, and which we perhaps instinctively seek today and fail to find elsewhere. Here will be something we can look to the papacy for, in hope and patience, as a concrete result and expression, here and today, of what we as Catholics believe about the papacy.

Specifically: Who today but the pope represents in a certain concrete, tangible, and audible manner the world conscience of a single humanity—a humanity today more than ever living in such a necessary unity? Here the question is not the theoretical limits within which we as Catholics may ascribe such a function to the papacy as a matter of principle. Here the question is rather to what extent such a function is, or can become, actually exercised by the papacy today.

Conversely, it is not as if a factual recognition of such a function were only possible on the part of those who subscribe to our dogmatic theology of the papacy. The function of such representation could be recognized as simply factual even by those who are not Catholics in the theological sense, just as, for example, a non-Christian may find the moral impact of the World Council of Churches meaningful for the non-Christian world.

We are not maintaining, with what we are proposing here, that popes today already adequately exercise this function of effectively representing a world conscience. But the papacy, more than any other authority in the world, does factually have this potential, and perhaps its actualization could be somewhat hurried along by our patience and prayer, as well as in other ways, so that gradually the pope, whoever he may be, may assume the function of representative of world conscience as never before, and be recognized in this function in many respects even by those who do not recognize the dogmatic function of the papacy. Something of the kind seems entirely within the realm of conception and desirability: the concrete concentration and tangibility of world conscience in this way, once recognized, would be most wholesome. It cannot be supplied by the United Nations. The concentration of interests and interest differences in UN world representation does not furnish such a conscience—it stands in need of one. Whether and how today's papacy could manage to assume such a function is another question. Certainly the papacy would need to present a clear image of itself not as the patriarchate of the West, with its suffragan sees the world over, but unambiguously and right from the start as representing and supplying the principle of unity for the world church as such.

As we have said it would be, this has been a digression on an opportunity for the papacy of tomorrow, and on a hope of ours for that papacy. It is only a little parenthesis, but it does have a bearing on our question of a communion of brothers and sisters—which Christians must have with the pope, too.

CHRISTIAN MISSION OF COMMUNION

A further consequence of today's new situation for Christian communion is the fact (and this may sound rather homely) that we Christians must all have something left over for the church's world mission.

This world mission is a task to be performed in a different manner from the way it was carried out in the nineteenth century, when it exploited European expansion and colonialism for its own advantages (although it could scarcely have altogether avoided doing so). This goes without saying. Nevertheless, it is clear that today as well the world mission—evangelization everywhere—is and must be a task of the total church in a world become one. And so our Christian communion of brothers and sisters does not stop with our next-door neighbor or the other side of the back fence. It must really be worldwide now, because the concrete situation of our communion today, whether we like it or not, has become a worldwide one.

It is equally self-evident that our Christian communion must not look only to the earthly well-being of our far-away neighbor—to right and justice in secular society—but also to the salvation of this neighbor in the proper sense, to his and her access to God's unconditional and infinite self-bestowal through the historical tangibility of Jesus Christ.

311

Young Christians today seek a militant commitment to freedom and social justice all over the world, and it is well that they should. But they ought not to forget that this worldwide communion must surely not stop just where human beings' ultimate oneness begins—in God and God's grace through Jesus Christ. It may well be that an explicit public commitment to freedom and justice throughout the world today is the first, absolutely necessary step for evangelization to take. It may be that this first step is only correctly taken when it is taken selflessly, without ulterior motives, as a simple deed of human communion among sisters and brothers. But none of this excludes the duty-in-communion of every Christian to undertake explicit responsibility for world mission and evangelization. Catholics should not be ashamed of this kind of interest in world mission, not even today. Their responsibility for the entire world must not end just where the execution of the ultimate mandate of their church begins.

SOCIAL DIMENSION OF COMMUNION

A further consequence of a Christian communion of brothers and sisters as it must be implemented in today's situation consists in the insight that the very nature of this Christian communion necessarily generates a political responsibility, generates politics, and hence generates a political theology. Social, political responsibility, and our concrete perception of that responsibility—politics, then—scarcely need to be explained here. Nor need we enter into the dispute over what political theology is, whether it is necessary to have it, and how it is related to theology as a whole. Of course, when we actually come forward to take a stand for a particular political theology, or reject one, we have to say precisely what we mean by "political theology." Here, however, we may content ourselves with more simple considerations.

We have had till now a more or less static society, one which changed its actual structures very slowly, almost imperceptibly. Indeed one scarcely reflected upon the nature of this society, let alone its capacity for change or its actual changes. As a result, the tasks of Christian communion that were explicitly recognized as such were just as statically set, and hence restricted to a more or less private, or privatistic, relationship among individuals, and it was not difficult for them to remain that way. But now we live in a society that has made social and sociopolitical transformation the proper object of its very reflections and activity. We not only define our private existence in terms of a system of societal coordinates, we refuse to see that system of coordinates as fixed, and we change it. But thereby Christian love of neighbor and communion acquire a field of relevance they have never known: the field of the political, the field of responsibility for the social structures required for a life worth human living, a life that is "Christianly possible," in a society of maximal unification to this end. Today as never before, this responsibility can by no means continue to be borne by a few persons only. Today it makes its claim on everyone in a society. And the reason it weighs so heavily now, more than it did before, is that this responsibility must now be exercised in the context of a genuine choice among a multiplicity of simultaneous alternatives. It is no longer a matter of simple deductive intelligence. It is a matter of freedom, in itself and as such.

Thus politics today is no longer a matter only for "those in charge" as having an indisputable mandate from God. Today it is a matter of the responsibility of every Christian, albeit in a thousand different ways. Desirable as stability in sociopolitical structures may be, and with all due concern for the abiding validity of a basic legal structure, our new sociopolitical situation is ever one of becoming and change, and every Christian now has a political responsibility, even when the changes are occurring quietly and unobtrusively. We may therefore not allow ourselves to be deceived into thinking that the only valid Christian task is that of the defense of prevailing social structures and situations. It is perfectly possible, to be sure, for a Christian to be a conservative in some respect or other out of his or her inmost Christian convictions. He or she may be genuinely committed to the continuation of certain social realities from some basic theoretical insight, or indeed merely by virtue of a freely taken decision that is his or her own legitimate choice. In fact, a Christian may be very conservative and need not be ashamed of it. But we Christians may not act as if the dynamics of sociopolitical change were simply somebody else's business, and imagine that the defense of prevailing social structures, subject as they are (just as future structures will be) to sin, finitude, and human disappointment, is the only viable Christian task.

Presumably no one would actually espouse such a simple formula. But one easily has the impression that, subliminally, a broad undercurrent in the mentality of Christians simply assumes that we Christians are somehow automatically conservative. Has not all, or at any rate a great deal, of what has occurred since the Enlightenment first occurred in the face of bitter resistance on the part of Christians, the episcopate, or the pope? Is this simply to be explained as the fault of the novelty itself, in presenting itself tightly suited in the armor of expressions or ideologies that would inevitably and justifiably arouse Christian protest? Or does everything suddenly come clear when we consider, in Christian humility, that God's providence assigns us our special part in the cosmic concert, whose harmony is audible to God's ears alone, and that therefore we may not be allowed to protest the fact that, since the Enlightenment, the conservative counterpoint—which, after all, is also indispensable to the divine symphony of world history—has fallen to the lot of ecclesial Christianity?

Or would it not be best to leave aside all of these deep justifications of what was done sociopolitically by the church and the majority of ecclesial Christians over the past two hundred years and tell ourselves, in a spirit of self-criticism, that the church and practicing Christians in those times were not only laudably conservative, but often enough rigid and reactionary as well, and that a like mentality need not necessarily continue? If a (Blessed!) Vincent Pallotti said that Pius IX could see no further than his nose, and if we ourselves can have the impression that this pope was wiser in 1840 than in 1870 and ought not, after all, to have allowed himself to be led astray by the narrow-minded anti-clericalism of the liberals of those days so that he abandoned his earlier attitude—then are we any less "good Catholics" if we seek to learn a lesson from experiences like these, and now try to choose more cautiously and broadmindedly among the various social alternatives available today in all areas of ecclesial and social life? Are we less good Catholics if we now permit ourselves a freedom of opinion, in a spirit of tolerance of sisters and brothers, in a better way than we did before?

This is the point at which the right to have a political theology arises. Political theology is not simply a social and economic doctrine in the old style, such as we used to have in the church. Along with many another task it has taken upon itself to perform, political theology proceeds actually to interrogate theological teaching itself as to how spiritual-historical and sociopolitical systems and ideologies operate in the concrete, including this Christian social and economic doctrine itself as it has developed. This sort of questioning, bearing upon the totality of theology by way of a critique of ideology, is of itself something after the fashion of a political theology, and it legitimates it. For the rest, we need not concern ourselves with a more precise consideration of every essential aspect of the nature of this theology. We shall only say: It is yet another duty of a brotherly and sisterly tolerance to allow this theology to have its say. We may not reject it out of hand in a spirit of contentiousness that scents revolutionaries and modernists everywhere.

There are manifold instances in the nineteenth and twentieth centuries of the failure to criticize tacitly accepted social ideologies prevailing among Christians that had a disastrous effect on theology and ecclesiastical politics. Could a renunciation of the ecclesiastical state really only finally be managed under Pius XI? Did the *Non Expedit* in Italy really have to be maintained all that length of time? Was Pius X's opposition to the trade unions in Germany really necessary? Did a theological integralism under Pius X have to entail such long-term and massive effects? Could a Teilhard de Chardin really not have been dealt with in a more brotherly fashion in Rome? These are the questions that arise, along with other, similar ones, in the background of the central question of the task and the legality of a political theology (little as we may restrict this theology to the area of the internal spiritual politics of the church).

But the case may just as well be turned the other way about. Surely there are telling reasons for tolerance on the part of the representatives of a theology and a politics that deem themselves duty-bound to be on their guard against a theology and a politics in the church that seem open to the indictment of ideology and reaction. These persons and politics, too, are under the obligation of a brotherly and sisterly tolerance vis-à-vis their adversaries. And this spirit of communion includes a calm, composed patience—an ability to wait, and to hope against hope.

Today's Christian has a political responsibility. It is an entirely new one. Surely there are offices and officeholders in today's society, as also in the church, to whom everyone need not ascribe plenipotentiary sovereignty. But a communion of brothers and sisters today must be all the more strongly effective, precisely in view of the waning of an authoritarian mentality in the church's concrete style of government. Respect for the church's plenitude of authority rests on more comprehensive and more deeply rooted communion with one another than this in any case, for it is a communion through the same Lord, and one and the same grace.

COMMUNION IN THE PARISH OR LOCAL COMMUNITY

The following consequences of our basic considerations bear mainly on the second aspect of today's situation: our new opportunities for intercommunication, our new routes of access to mutually shared subjective interiority.

We can have an altogether more intensive brotherly and sisterly communion today than we could in the past, through stronger bonds of intercommunication. Even in the area of the strictly religious, a brotherly and sisterly interiority has become not only possible, but a real need and obligation. Just consider how many people there are today who yearn for a "basic Christian community," or perhaps an "integrated Christian community." In these new kinds of quasi-parishes, one strives to build communities which go beyond the ones in which so many people have only their private religious needs fulfilled, through the ministrations of the church in the Sunday liturgy, while persevering in their religious isolation from one another. In these new-style communities, people seek to bear life's burden together, in the company of one another, out of Christian motivation. Inspired by Christian ideals, people seek really to live together in brotherly and sisterly communion, to experience a oneness with one another, and actively to live out this oneness.

Of course, we must be on our guard against a certain sentimentality here—a longing for the simple life, and an inclination simply to copy the *comunidades de base* [base communities] of Latin America. When illness strikes in the rain forests of Brazil, the only person who can help may be one's nearby brother or sister in Christ, because the physician or the hospital is too far away or too expensive. Here, then, of course, is a situation of brotherly and sisterly community, and truly "being neighbor" to one another as a duty of Christian motivation, that for us in our northern countries is not a practical affair, what with our doctor and our hospital right around the corner and a pocketful of medical insurance. In other words, in our countries there are clearly many services which elsewhere in the world may well be a matter for a basic Christian community, but which here are performed by secular society, and hence which scarcely come into question as something for basic Christian communities to do. But this does not mean that a lively Christian imagination cannot discover many a task of love, communion, and self-fulfillment that a basic Christian community *can* perform among us. In an ever more anonymous and anonymously guided society like ours today, human beings are being forced to live in an ever more isolated fashion, in lonely helplessness and abandonment with respect to a good many of their needs and requirements, in which neither secular society nor today's average parish can come to their aid—needs and requirements in which neither money nor civil administration is of any avail, but only the heart of our brotherly or sisterly neighbor.

To what extent today's human beings will wish to go on living their modern individualism tomorrow, and to what extent they will voluntarily seek to be integrated into a basic community instead, is a question that has yet to be researched in these climes of ours. Presumably the problem will admit of a variety of solutions, just as in former times religious orders had very considerable differences among them, while they tend to be more uniform today. Even within a radically vital, genuine Christianity—and, to be sure, presupposing a radically vital and genuine secular society—many life-styles are possible, especially inasmuch as the Christianization of human beings' respective situations will turn out differently in a context of a secular social differentiation of these human beings, and even Christian communion does not comport a priori demands for the egalitarian life-style of everyone in the parish or community. Presumably, then, the church of the future will not be composed simply of integrated communities. But none of this alters the fact that today's situation makes greater communication possible and necessary in the religious area. We need basic communities too, and parishes must be transformed from units of authoritarian ecclesiastical territorial administration, and service stations catering to purely individualistic needs, into true communities, in which Christians live in a brotherly and sisterly fashion, united in the one Spirit who builds church.

A CONFESSING COMMUNION

The point we have just considered is surely a consequence and demand of communion that in turn implies another—a possibility we seldom see and take advantage of. We are referring to the duty of an uninhibited spirit of "joy of profession." Surely this is something that should be seen and exploited much more than it is now.

On the average, we are still religious individualists even today, and we have a very unbrotherly and unsisterly mentality. We have the idea that if there is any area of a person's life that ought to be locked up in the still, soft inwardness of the heart alone, it will be the religious area. Here, surely, we can have nothing to say to our sister and our brother. One can even gather the impression that such religious speechlessness is on the increase, even in religious orders. To be sure, there are examples of the contrary attitude, in the church as in civil life. Extraecclesial religious movements and sects surely manifest a "joy of profession." Often they exhibit an uninhibitedness and brashness that may astonish and shock even those persons who do not seek to hide the light of their own Christianity under a bushel. But by and large, a strange religious muteness permeates our society, and it prevails especially where it is not upstaged by the arresting novelty of a rare or remarkable spirit of profession on the part of a few. How many parents are embarrassed to pray with their children! Where is there an uninhibited religious dialogue today, aside from the aggressive propaganda of the religious sects? Such religious dialogue is not "in" today. We are made uncomfortable by it. We find it out of place, and "indiscreet."

Such muteness, such inexpressiveness, is basically senseless. We must of course endeavor to speak of religious things in such a way that our discourse will have some measure of intention to be understood by and be relevant to our nonbelieving fellow human beings. This is difficult, and it is something that is not sufficiently striven for in the church. The church is too attached to traditional religious formulas, absolutely and exclusively, as if without them there would be danger of obscuring or losing the very substance of its faith and belief. Another thing we must avoid is the stentorian declamation of the inwardly embittered conservative reactionary, who risks using God to defend his or her bourgeois, middle-class status quo. But we can still foster a genuine uninhibitedness in our religious speech, a brotherly and sisterly openness and joy of profession, which would bear witness to, and seek to share with others, what after all is the inmost power and brilliance of our own life.

I recall something that once happened to me at the airport in New York. There in the swirl of humanity I found myself suddenly confronting a uniformed airport employee who approached me, knelt before me in the crowd, and said, "Bless me, Father!" Of course, we need not imitate this particular example of uninhibited piety, or ostentation if you will. But a spontaneous feeling of being permitted to share something of one's ultimate Christian motivation, something of one's fears and difficulties and blessings and happiness, with one's sisters and brothers, ought to belong to Christian communion even today, a communion both possible to us and enjoined upon us.

After all, in earlier times this kind of freedom of expression did prevail among Christians. It was not only in the confessional, or on the psychotherapist's couch, that one dared go outside oneself, dared to confide in someone else, dared to entrust oneself to another. Before his conversion, Ignatius Loyola was something of a wild soldier, with his amorous adventures and excesses of anger, rather a medieval type. It once happened that, having to take the field against the French, and having no chaplain available before the battle, he confessed his sins to one of his comrades in arms. We need not imitate him in this lay confession of his (even though at times such a confession might be just as spiritual and rich in blessings as sacramental confession, given the risk of the latter of degenerating into a legalistic formality). But this little example does show that Christians once enjoyed a spiritual intercommunication of brothers and sisters that was a good deal more open than it is today. It was simply accepted in those days—far more than it is today. Why need it be automatically suspect of indiscreet religious exhibitionism today?

If Christians have an inner piety, then they may of course be allowed to communicate it, to share it with one another, to whatever degree it may be meaningful to do so. There will surely still be different styles of such "confessing intercommunication" in the future. One person will be able to be more "joyful in profession" than another. But by and large such an uninhibited joy of profession in the church today is something we hope will grow—among Christians, and on the part of Christians toward secular society.

There are still other, entirely different, neglected opportunities for brotherly and sisterly intercommunication, besides the ones on which we have been concentrating up to this point. If we still dare to ask someone to pray for us, for instance—are we still really serious about this habitual, traditional "request"? Do enlightened intellectuals, those still considering themselves Christians, really pray for their brothers and sisters? Or are our "assurances of prayers" for one another, and our requests for these prayers, no longer anything but fossil fragments from times gone by, things we keep handing on for custom's sake, but no longer seriously, from the bottom of our heart? Is a requiem Mass for a departed friend or relative, if we examine it closely and honestly, more than a traditional ceremony of the sort that will continue to exist in a religious society even when the spirit and life are long since gone out of it? Tasks like these are but a few of the things that need to be done where spirituality and love of neighbor meet in the midst of daily living. There are sure to be many others. We have only to discover them.

ON MARTYRDOM

Rahner's theological analyses of death and its conceptual correlative, eschatology, are among his most creative contributions to contemporary religious thought. For Rahner, what a person has become in life does not perish in death. Hence he insists that death, however brutal and seemingly bereft of meaning, can never be the sheer annihilation of an individual's uniqueness and self-consciousness. In facing the most basic challenge of the Christian declaration that human life, inspirited by faith, has everlasting significance even when confronted by the seeming end of it all in death, Rahner opts to affirm the dynamic process in which the human person continues to be fulfilled in God beyond the death of the body. In Rahner's perspective, death is but the climax of the human search for meaning that began with one's primal orientation to the holy mystery of God. This orientation was enhanced in the graced moments of God's salvific presence eliciting both a yearning for infinite fulfillment and in all freedom conferring the capacity for acts of love and healing so essential to growth in one's relationship with God. Hence Rahner could write in his Foundations of Christian Faith *that one's individuality "is not abolished in death but rather is transposed into another mode of existence" (p. 436). One is destined to achieve in death that fulfillment that God—in making God's self known in the pathways of human experience and in the word of God's son—has made the central force of attraction for human beings. Rahner holds that one is not drawn to the infinite, holy mystery of God in vain. Faith demands that a person cling to the affirmation that life has unconditional, eternal significance despite the obvious finiteness made so painfully evident in death.*

In fact, the reality of death becomes in Rahner's theology the spur to examine critically the grounds of a person's relentless drive for meaning beyond the material totems of personal satisfaction and despite the destruction of the physical that seems to proclaim so loudly the absurdity of faith. Rahner argues that human life is a continuum that is shaped by one's fundamental option whereby God structures the human person to posit acts in freedom that have not only a moral quality but also a lasting influence on the quality of individual existence. He singles out the moments in which human life is invested with such an enduring personal meaning that time and the apparent nullity of death are transcended. In bringing the hopes of eternity into the temporality of being human, the eternal God insinuates God's self into the fiber of one's decisions of fidelity and love for people and into the courageous commitment to enter into a Christlike solidarity with the oppressed, all signs that life in God is more powerful than death. Death for Rahner is the encounter with God in which one experiences a ratification of one's fundamental option. It is, to be sure, an end of a time but also the high point of one's self-realization in freedom and the beginning of one's total presence with and sharing in the fullness of God. Or as Rahner stated in a 1980 radio interview, three and a half years before his own death: "There can be no doubt that for theologians and their doctrine and for Christian faith, the Christ event is not an arduous restitution of the person's paradisiacal destiny, but something far superior. Hence we may safely say that . . . forgetting all evolutionary theories and speculations, . . . death may certainly be conceived as a positive event of life, as the triumph of absolute life in the dimension of the finiteness of the human person, a triumph which demonstrates that once more, even in the seeming absurdity of the person's death, God and God's eternal life are victorious" (Paul Imhof and Hubert Biallowons, eds., Karl Rahner in Dialogue *[New York: Crossroad, 1986], 246–47).*

"On Martyrdom," the essay excerpted in this section, displays Rahner's con-

fidence in God's having graciously orientated God's people to everlasting life in the face of death's grim reality. In this essay Rahner recapitulates his theology of death, but in this instance in order to emphasize his conviction that death is the act whereby persons say yes to God and thus recapitulate in their most decisive moment their life and faith. In death the depth and power of one's trust in God are revealed. Rahner points out that martyrdom discloses the nature of Christian death and the power of Christ to inspire and make possible the acceptance of death as life and God as the ultimate source and fulfillment of that life. This selection is taken from Rahner's book On the Theology of Death *(pp. 89–97, 105–13, 116–17, 121–27), which appeared in 1961 as an English translation of his* Zur Theologie des Todes, *published by Herder of Freiburg in the same year. Although the essay is over thirty years old, it still has freshness and timeliness today, given the ever-lengthening lists of Christians, both religious and laity, martyred in Central America and elsewhere for their Christlike espousal of the cause of the poor.*

Martyrdom, as it is understood today, is death for the sake of Christian faith or morals. Therefore, when speaking of death, martyrdom must also be discussed, if only as an epilogue to the larger topic. One must be careful, however, not to make the highest achievement, the most complete abandonment of self, the pure grace of the crucified, the awesome act whereby a human being is killed through criminal arrogance and from a hatred of the faith (often disguised as a service to God [John 16:2]), an object of empty words or of unthinking enthusiasm. It may be that in religious magazines the martyrs of the day are duly praised, but in doctrinal studies they are mentioned only in some remote corner of elementary theology. This subject (even after taking into account what has been written on it in earlier ages, particularly that of the fathers) does, however, provide matter for serious thought....

Martyrdom is concerned with death. Although death does not belong to the original biblical concept of the *martyrein*, of the *martyria*, or *martyrion*, we can find already in the New Testament the beginnings of a change which, as early as the second century, led to the accepted meaning: a martyr is one who, killed by powers inimical to Christ, becomes by freely accepting a beautiful testimony, a "faithful witness," to faith in Jesus Christ. Since that period, the martyr has been "a witness," a witness through death.

But the precise question is not yet answered for those who are interested in the deeper theological meaning of martyrdom. What is the fundamental connection between witness to Christ and death? Is it merely the result of the historical development of the concept, a more or less accidental and arbitrary conjunction of the two terms, "testimony" and "death," or are there some intrinsic links between them, so that they are, in fact, essentially correlated? By investigating this problem we hope that we may gain, if only vaguely, some insight into the mystery of Christian martyrdom....

Martyrdom is concerned with death. In order to understand martyrdom, death also must be understood. Thus, the mystery of death enters into martyrdom, and therefore martyrdom also partakes of the nature of mystery. One dares approach the subject of death only hesitantly. Since the hidden incomprehensibility of death is concealed from average minds, because death happens daily, such minds think that it therefore must be understandable....

It should be observed that human beings have to die their deaths in freedom. But how they die their deaths and how they understand them, depends on the decision of their freedom. Here they do not carry something imposed on them, but what they choose themselves. That is to say: in the deed of the dying existence, human beings are necessarily free in their attitude toward death. Although they have to die, they are asked how they wish to do it. For, existence conscious of itself must unavoidably see the end. It sees this end all through life, perhaps dimly and not explicitly. It may happen that it will purposely avoid looking at it, or it will simply overlook it (but still will realize it all the same). Inasmuch as human beings freely take upon themselves this existence tending toward the end, they also freely accept the movement toward the end.

Now our question is this: How do human beings understand this end toward which they freely go, since they can do nothing other than run the course of their lives in freedom? Do they run protestingly, or lovingly and trustingly? Do they view their end as an extinction, or as a consummation? Human beings usually do not express their answer to this problem in abstract statements about death, but they display without words their free conviction through the actions of their life and the deeds of their daily existence, even when they do not know explicitly that by them they interpret their death.

We shall thus have to ask what is the correct Christian interpretation of that act in our lives which is called death? Concerning this we must remember, first, that the imposed liberty has to be a free liberty. Human beings cannot be anything but free once they come to the awareness of self. That is the freedom that is imposed. Human beings may well hate this freedom; or they can refuse and reject it and pretend that it is not there at all. They may prefer to be like driftwood, and in a cowardly, lazy manner they may regard themselves as but the product of their age and environment. But their real duty is to accept their freedom willingly and without force, to love it and to have the courage to face it. And they should respond in this way to freedom in its fullest sense, since it is concerned, not only with this or that superficial aspect of life, but with life as a whole, down to its existential roots; they also ought to have a freely loving liberty, even with regard to death. They should accept death freely, and should live toward death in free liberty....

But this courageous, free liberty to die has to be, second, a liberty of abandon, that is a liberty which says yes not only to death itself, but also to its meaning, to the meaning of existence. Human beings should not hurry toward their death as toward the final end of their existence, but as toward an endless end. They should hurry not toward a death which is the consummation of emptiness, a final pouring out of life into sense-lessness, but toward a death which is the valid consummation of their existence. This, however, can be done only by faith. The eternally valid consummation in death cannot be grasped by the dying man or woman who shall die freely as something already possessed. As the high point in the passing away of all that is transitory, which alone is comprehensible, death does not fulfill existence but, in fact, seems to destroy it.

Death is a downfall, and only by faith can this downfall be inter-preted as a falling into the hands of the living God, who is called "Father." Since this positive interpretation of human beings' mortality governing their entire lives can be guaranteed, as we know from Chris-tian teaching, only by the grace of Christ (because in the present order of sinful darkness, our entire life can be mastered in a morally right way only by the grace of God), then the act performed in virtue of the grace of Christ, whereby human beings positively accept the compre-hensive sense of their existence even in face of the dark appearance of senseless death, can and must necessarily be called an act of faith. This means that there must be a surrender of the whole human be-ing from his or her uncontrollable and impenetrable existence to the incomprehensible God. Whenever human beings die in this way, believ-ing in confidence, detached from all that is particular and concrete, and with free trust that they will obtain everything, whenever human beings apparently experience a falling down into emptiness, into the fathom-less abyss, then they do something that could not have been achieved except by the grace of Christ which celebrates its victory in this very abyss of emptiness. There, human beings do not die the death of Adam, the death of the sinner who loves nothingness, autonomously disposed of, but they die the death of Christ. This is so, because only this death gained grace for us and only this death has freed our death for the real life of God. . . .

If there is such a revelatory and self-explanatory Christian death, then it must be acknowledged that in such death the concept of Christian witnessing is most perfectly realized, because in such death the consummation of Christian life is comprehensively and visibly manifested.

This death, then, would be a "beautiful death," expressing that ultimate beauty which is born of the perfect harmony between interior reality and external appearance. Such death would be the beautiful testimony (1 Tim. 6:13) in the absolute sense. Such a death, then, should be loved and desired in spite of all attendant anguish and horror—if one is really seeking true reality and its true appearance—because the true reality and its true appearance are achieved and found most fully in this death. We know that there is such a revelation of the Christian essence of death in the martyrdom of the faithful.

In order to disclose death as the act of free liberty (this was the first property of a truly Christian death), it must be a death which could have been avoided in its concrete reality. It must, then, be a death which is caused by external violence and which could have been avoided by the exercise of freedom. Only if one is able to escape it through one's own free act, can one's death be an act of liberty. If someone through his or her free act can avoid death, then what emerges as really achieved is what must be present in each Christian death, veiled and difficult to judge though it may be: the free acceptance of death. Thus is revealed the presence of that love of death which a Christian should have, and which cannot be realized by suicide. Here is fulfilled what Jesus said of his own death: "I have the power to lay down my life" (John 10:18). This is particularly true at that moment when we seem most fully under the domination of external forces: nobody takes my life; I myself lay it down. And this is exactly what does happen in the martyr's death; it is a free death. All the violence which causes it is only the effective device of God who provides the opportunity for this highest act of liberty, for this liberty which human beings cannot attain by themselves or have granted to them by any other means; for although they possess (even if not to so great a degree) liberty over their lives (whereby they can exercise their choice and by so doing choose their death), they still possess it only, as it were, in some anonymous barren manner as it is extended over their whole lives.

In that death which is violent, which could have been avoided and which is, nevertheless, accepted in freedom, the whole of life is gathered into one burning moment of ultimate freedom. Then the death of life (in its totality and freedom) enters into the death of death, in an act of complete freedom affecting the totality of life as well as life's eternal finality. The death of martyrdom is a death of free liberty. By it is disclosed what is hidden under the veil covering death's essence. By it the enigma of veiled death (Is it a death of forced freedom or free liberty?) receives a definite answer.

But when and how is death that act whereby faith is revealed? This is our second question. One might think, at first glance, that this is an easy one to answer, for where will it be more fully revealed than in that death which is entered upon as an act of free faith in the victory of Christ's death? Where will it be more fully revealed than in the death of that man or woman who dies for his or her faith in the crucified and risen Lord, that is, in martyrdom? Furthermore, it might seem obvious that martyrdom includes that quality which is essential to any death, namely, that it must be a death of faith, and not a death of mute or loud despair.

But the solution is not so simple as that. For it might be asked whether the death of a martyr is in fact exempt from the general law that every moral decision, whether undertaken for oneself or for others, remains ultimately enigmatic. Was the right thing really done? And even if it were the right thing, something objectively good, such as the fulfillment of a divine precept or of the gospel counsels, can we be certain that it was motivated from within by faith and love, and that it proceeded from the grace of God, that is from motives all beyond the observation of self and of others? Must we not humbly reply that no woman or man and no action can be disclosed as just until God has made God's own infallible judgment? Is there not then remaining, even in the case of the martyr's death, the radical problem still unanswered whether an act which is good in itself is necessarily good in execution, and whether anything will remain of the pure gold that we see when it is weighed upon God's scale?

There is the death of the fanatic, of the hero, of the sectarian and also of those many others who may die courageously and freely. Although we may pay the tribute of our respect to the shocking and unspeakable enormity which is manifested in those deaths, yet as Christians we do not attribute to them the same objective dignity and meaning which we recognize in martyrdom. At the same time, we must acknowledge that in individual cases the value of such deaths, revealed only before God, may reach even into eternal life.

Considering all this, we have to realize that the problem of the unique and revelatory quality of Christian martyrdom cannot be solved so easily. Yet upon this solution depends our understanding of how it is possible to attribute the character of an absolute testimony to martyrdom. In other words, why is a death in faith a witnessing death, a martyrdom in the eminent sense? ...

If the church must be indeed "subjectively" holy and if this holiness must appear really as a work of God's grace, then, if such an epiphany of grace exists, it must be found in martyrdom. Divine power, in order to sanctify the church and to make it appear holy, must here overcome the cleavage between human beings' existence in the eyes of God and their existence in the eyes of the world, between the suprahistorical truth and the historical appearance, between the interior spirit and the empiric fact. That which here appears—the dying with Christ in God—must manifest what really is. Here something must be done, not only by human beings who in themselves remain forever ambiguous, but by the power of God which is victorious in human weakness. Here a yes is really needed, a yes, not only to God, but as God's own word (coming from the innermost center of the human being, where nothing remains but the eternal human being and his or her God), which pierces earthly space and time, and which is the pure yes, the truth of God. When outwardly a man or woman dies in faith, death really occurs through the loving faith in the most inward truth and reality, guaranteed by that victorious eschatological grace which constitutes the church as "sacrament" of God's holiness and grace. A martyr's death is not only death through human beings' free liberty, but also the revelation of death through faith. Martyrdom is, hence, the Christian death par excellence. This death is not only, in fact, Christian death, but, moreover, it appears as such. Martyrdom discloses the essence of Christian death, the death through free faith, which character would otherwise be hidden under the veil of ambiguity which obscures all human events.

Martyrdom, thus, belongs to the essence of the church. It is to be expected, then, that there will always be martyrs in the church, for it has not only to live as a witness to the crucified Christ, but it also has to demonstrate visibly this living testimony. It is not permitted to celebrate and to make present the death of Christ only in the sacramental mystery of the holy Mass. The church itself must live it in all truthfulness. And it does live it in all those who carry the cross of Christ into the darkness of this world and who possess the secret stigmata of Christ hidden under the everyday appearance of their humanity.

If the church has to be not only internally the reality of grace, but also its visible "sacrament"—the holy sign of the intrinsic reality of grace—in this world, then also the crucified character of the church has to be continuously and repeatedly revealed in its historical life. The most conspicuous and emphatic way for this public manifestation is martyrdom....

Wherever martyrdom is celebrated in blood, there God's grace is truly victorious in the depths of reality. One could almost say that martyrdom is the only "suprasacrament" which does not admit of an obstacle in the receiver, and in which the valid sacrament always and infallibly brings forth its fruit of eternal life.

If it is asked where is the point in human life where the sign will be absolutely true and the truth absolutely signified, where is the point at which both become one, action and suffering, the commonplace and the incomprehensible, death and life, freedom and violence, the most human and the most divine, the dark sinfulness of this world and the grace of God embracing it in mercy, cult and reality—then there is but one answer: in martyrdom.

What appears here is and must be possible also in us if we are to be those who are redeemed, sanctified, who have died with Christ and have risen with him into the newness of life. However, what appears here is what we should be, what we hope we are, but what, without martyrdom, we cannot be certain of. And what is here apparently, is here also in fact. Here the sign infallibly produces what it signifies and overcomes that ambiguity and uncertainty which attach to the sacraments since they can be received unworthily. This "suprasacrament" of blood must be received worthily, or it cannot be received at all.

In martyrdom we have an indissoluble unity of the testimony and the thing witnessed, which is guaranteed by God's most gracious dispensation. Here will be consummated with absolute validity and perfection what is witnessed, the Christian existence as a triumph of the grace of God. The testimony makes present what is testified and what is testified creates for itself its justification, which is indubitable. Word and thing here become one and they are perceived in their indissoluble oneness. Of course, there could be on human beings' part mute acquiescence or empty words. From the human point of view, as may occur in the case of other voluntary deaths, it is possible to have just an empty show, just the bare shadows of the reality. But God's action in God's triumphant grace prevents such a disintegration and witnesses to human beings who have been fulfilled in order to give testimony themselves to the irresistible advent of grace in the flesh.

Church and martyrdom testify to each other reciprocally. In this verbal testimony of the church to the eschatologically victorious grace, we obtain the innermost interpretation of martyrdom. It is really what it seems to be, a really comprehensive expression of the world-conquering faith, the consummation of humankind. Martyrdom testifies to the church that in it there have been many such deaths throughout its history, and that this ultimate sacrifice has been entered upon without fanaticism or display, without theatrical pose, and under the pressure and hatred of demoniac power, and that it is loved by those who do not hate the world. This by itself testifies to the supernatural origins of the church (in the face of all those who, by the grace of God, are capable of seeing) apart from that deeper interpretation of martyrdom which is given to it anteriorly by the testimony of the church. The church, the isolated act of unique individual responsibility, the word and silent dying, hatred of the world and the love of God, death and life—they are all one here. If in the liturgy of the Mass the death of the Lord, and our own death in him, is mystically celebrated and if, in this celebration, the church in its cult reaches the summit of its own perfect self-consummation, this also applies to the death by Christian martyrdom in which the Lord continues until the end of time to suffer and to triumph "pragmatically," as Eutychius said 1500 years ago....

If any freely and willingly accepted death were, *eo ipso* [by its very nature], a morally good death, the reason would be that death comprises the totality of the human, existential self-consummation, and every such death would constitute the summit of life's moral achievement. But then the "what for?" of freely accepted death would lose all its moral significance, not only in fact and in some cases, but in principle and in all cases. This assumption would have grave consequences for the whole of morality. The intention would become divorced from the action itself. Consequently, it would not be right to canonize any freely willed death a priori and without further investigation.

But this again is only one aspect of the question. Voluntary death cannot be regarded as a morally neutral matter, which derives its significance from a particular exterior motive divorced from this death as such. Human beings have a unique feeling of reverence for that death which, though it could have been avoided, is freely accepted. How can this reverence be explained in the face of the preceding necessary observations?

Whenever someone dies freely, first of all, the whole of her or his life is present. This presence of the whole life, of the whole free spirit, commands our awe, if anything in human beings can be said to deserve our awe at all. Furthermore, death which is feared, and which is imposed by force on the unfaithful and despairing, is not even in its formal constitution the same as the death which is freely accepted. True and false freedom are not simply two activations of the same liberty in different directions and toward different objects. If freedom, as an intentional power, is specified by its object, it will be in itself different according to the different objects toward which it is directed. And it can be described through this difference, which is intrinsic to the intention itself, no matter whether such description of this reflection upon the subjective aspect of the act coming from the object intended is totally or only partially successful. If it is possible to describe the subjective act, at least in part, in its difference accordingly as it is qualified as good or evil by its subjective orientation, then, in some given case, we might also learn whether its intentional object is good or evil in fact. This in itself is not something strange at all. There must be in some way a divinely ordained preestablished harmony between the righteousness of the act and its intentional content; the materially good act in the last analysis could not be subjectively a perverse one, and vice versa....

The manner in which a human being dies shows death to be admitted and accepted in the very depths of his or her spiritual person, in that realm where abstract and theoretical statements are at stake but by a human being whose theoretical views—those precisely for which he or she dies—justify in theory what he or she does in reality.

It might be said, perhaps, that this unity between theory and practice in the acceptance of death, the one being the motive for the other, is not specifically Christian, because such deaths could be also prescribed and fulfilled on the basis of natural ethics. But looking, on the one hand, at the whole of world history, it becomes evident that this unity can be demonstrated only in Christianity (Where else is death regarded as the gate of life, and is not degraded to an accident or to an abyss of hidden despair?) and, on the other hand, the doctrine and the deed of a just death cannot be considered just a minor tenet in the religion of one who died on the cross. This hidden correspondence is not found anywhere else. It is no wonder that, looking at the whole, we find only in Christianity the free death as a historically sufficient and, in some way, historically public measure.

We can say: if such a death, according to its own proper appearance, proves itself to be a good one, a death of the blossoming, successful freedom and not a death of frustrated freedom, of an ontologically and personally crippled freedom; and, furthermore, if this death is, in fact, undergone in the presence of Christianity, for the sake of it, and in an immediately visible correspondence with its doctrines; and if this death nowhere else occurs, at least historically in this way—a fact which must have its sufficient reason—then all this can be explained only in that this good death of freedom accomplished draws its strength from that for the sake of which the man or woman dies. In other words: this death is good, because it occurs for the sake of the crucified and dead Christ....

It is no wonder that throughout the history of the church there were always Christians longing for martyrdom and praying to God for this greatest of all graces. It is no wonder that the martyrs have been the first saints of the church, not only in time—as if, by some historical accident, the apostolic church was the most persecuted one—but also objectively, because nowhere else does the indissoluble synthesis of body and soul, of sacrament and grace, of God and world appear so clearly (this is essential, inasmuch as the church is the church of the last days, i.e., eschatological), and nowhere else is this synthesis so concentrated into one, single event as in martyrdom. It is no wonder that the church in the canonization process of martyrs does not look for miracles (CJC [Code of Canon Law] can. 2116 §2). Their death in itself is God's testimony to them. It is no wonder that martyrdom, considering the number and the manner in which it is found in the church and only in the history of the church, has always been regarded as an affirmation of the strength and power of divine grace and, consequently, as a proof for the divine origin of the church.

Death, in the course of human history, has not always had the same meaning. People rightly speak of different modes of dying. There are various modes even of martyrdom, all of which are fashioned by the Spirit of God, who rules over the church and history as the Spirit pleases. Until the present, not much thought has been given to these changing modes of martyrdom in the history of the church. Perhaps we are afraid of what could be revealed to us through this startling study. What a contrast, if we compare the heaven-storming desire for death of St. Ignatius of Antioch, and the heroic, spirited, and enthusiastic death of the martyrs of the Far East in the sixteenth and seventeenth centuries, with the almost anonymous annihilation of many martyrs in our own times. But is not perhaps the martyrdom of anguish and weakness (whereby human beings are, as it were, killed before they die, through devilish modern techniques that murder the person, taking human beings completely from themselves before the life of their bodies is extinguished) an even more intense participation in the death of Christ than any other martyrdom of a more heroic appearance?

When we take Christ as the martyrs' model, it may well seem that the martyrs of our own times are closer to the Lord than any of those of the past. They are the men and women lying on the ground suffocated by their own mortal weakness, forsaken by God; or the martyrs hanging among real criminals, almost without any chance of being distinguished from them; the martyrs who are almost convinced that they are not martyrs at all; they are the men and women who are paralyzed and yet fulfill what they do not find the strength to fulfill; the martyrs who are perhaps for all their lives *ad metalla damnatus* [condemned to a lifetime in chains] and thus condemned may die an apparently normal death. Let us be clear about this; today the *metalla* need not be any particular places, for the jail may coincide with the land of godless tyranny as such.

One might almost think that Christian life can be understood only in the light of Christian death in its absolute sense, that is, in martyrdom, and that the poverty and aridity of our modern Christian existence are revealed in the discouraging fact that there is so little courage in us for such a vocation as martyrdom. Therefore, it is good for us to look to Jesus, to the source and the consummation of our faith, who, in spite of the joy that was his, and in spite of the ignominy, endured the cross (Heb. 12:2) that we might strengthen our hearts; we should pray for this grace of a faithful heart; we should look to all those who in truth and tangibly preceded us in the sign of faith as witnesses to the past and recent days of the church. Today, when we are only talking, millions are suffering for the name of Jesus. They suffer believing and enduring, unknown, and without fame, atoning also for our guilt of cowardly indifference, of our weakness of faith, of our pleasure-seeking mediocrity. They are the holocaust apart from which we live; they go the way which may suddenly become also for us the only road that leads to life; they experience the kind of vocation which, in the depths of reality, is also ours, because we also have been baptized into the death of the Lord, and we also receive in the sacrament of the altar the body which has undergone death for our sake. They are the real followers of the Lord in whom he himself suffers and dies, the images of true love, as Polycarp called them. We wish we could say today what the great Origen once said in his community: "I have not the slightest doubt that in this community there are a number of Christians—only the Lord knows them—who before him, according to the testimony of their consciences, are already martyrs, who are ready, as soon as it is asked of them, to shed their blood for Christ. I have not the slightest doubt that there are amongst us many who have already taken their cross upon themselves and have followed him" (Hom. in Num. 10:2). "Give the blood and take the spirit" is an old monastic saying. This is true also today. As the Spirit and the water of eternal life flowed from the pierced heart of the Lord, so, too, the Spirit in the church will always depend upon the readiness for martyrdom of some of its children.

And as, amidst the weakness and misery of human beings, the Spirit, through its own victorious strength, takes care that human beings' cowardly laziness should not extinguish them in the church, so the Spirit takes care also that in the church, always and forever, death should be a moving and blessed event testifying gloriously to human beings' free belief and their entry through this act of total freedom of faith, born from grace, into the infinite freedom of God.

10

REFLECTIONS ON METHODOLOGY
IN THEOLOGY

This final section contains a selection from Rahner's series of three lectures on theological methodology delivered at the International Symposium of Theologians at Montreal, Canada, August 18–22, 1969. These lectures were originally published in volume 9 of the Schriften *in 1970 and were then published in English translation in volume 11 of the* Theological Investigations *(pp. 101–14) in 1974.*

Rahner insists at the outset of his remarks that he is not doing a direct analysis of his personal theological methods but rather is offering "reflections" on theological methodology itself inasmuch as such reflections were needed for an intelligent assessment of the direction Catholic theology seemed to be taking in 1969. In the first lecture he addresses the situation in which contemporary theology had found its starting point. Here Rahner has two observations to make: (1) the present situation does not lend itself either to any sweeping analytic judgment or to rigorous scientific calculation; and (2) the situation in theology is determined to a large extent by the ecclesiastical context in which practitioners of theology must operate. On the first observation, Rahner notes that the situation of theology had been complicated "by an uncontrollable pluralism of theologies" and by a radically new stage in the development of thought. He characterizes individual theologians as "alien, alone, and isolated," because they feel themselves outside of the common grounds of the past and conditioned by a history that is both multifaceted and confusing. In view of this, it is Rahner's belief that Catholic theology could no longer remain a closed system controlled by the upholders of the religion who constrict the task of theologians to the mere defense and explication of preset, absolutized propositions.

Rahner calls, therefore, for new approaches in search of a method that involves dialogue beyond the narrower limits of the past, using the more direct approach of a creative apologetics and "indirect" methods of theological investigation that respect both God's impelling, alluring, unpredictable grace and human contingency. Here Rahner makes the extraordinary assertion that for theologians to be successful seekers after the truth, they must "be prepared again and again to incur the risk of involuntarily finding the church against [them] in [their] interpretations." Although he refuses to reduce theology to its methodology and declares it to be always more than its own hermeneutics, nevertheless, he argues that methodology, hermeneutics, and the various forms of theology are themselves themes that theology must investigate. But ultimately all theological reflections must yield in faith to the incomprehensible "greater entity" that "becomes an event" of faith.

In his second lecture Rahner searches for the rootedness of genuine theological discourse in a transcendental philosophy that raises the prior question of what conditions make it possible for a knowing person to acquire knowledge, in this case knowledge of God, God's relationships, and God's works. Rahner uses transcendental inquiry to bring into an interrelationship the subjectivity of the knower and the object to be known in such a way that they can be said to mutually condition each other. In Rahner's opinion, as stated in this lecture, awareness of the conditions that make a subject's knowledge of God possible becomes an important element in the process of knowing since such awareness and the knowledge flowing from it help to link the nature of the object to be known with its concrete historical conditioning, or the metaphysical with the experiential. In this way, he contends that one must accept the inescapable reality of one's personal history as a factor in doing theology.

Accordingly, Rahner refuses to dissipate philosophical or theological reflections into an ahistorical subjectivity, such as one found in some forms of idealistic philosophy. On the contrary, in transcendental inquiry he views the subject as a question unto himself or herself and, therefore, as one impelled to be more open to what might be communicated in the experience of an object to be known and to be loved. Hence neither human history nor the empirical dimensions of knowledge can ever be devalued in those personal transcendental reflections that by necessity are anchored in history and experience. Rahner considers the question of human subjectivity in theological methodology a reality to be reckoned with as necessary preamble to an intelligent recognition of the convergence of human factors and the holy mystery's revelatory presence in any genuine theological reflection. For Rahner, transcendental inquiry as such need not be a conscious element in the drive to understand theological assertions. Nor must it be an explicit structure within the theological-methodological enterprise searching for truth and meaning. Yet he insists it is an essential context and catalyst in the process of intelligently integrating the teachings of faith into one's life. By way of illustration, Rahner shows how transcendental theological methods can be adduced from the theology of the Trinity and, in turn, can lead to a development of a transcendental Christology. In each instance, according to Rahner, one's radical transcendental orientation to the holy mystery of God is sustained by and conjoined with God's freely offered gift of love reaching out in self-communication to the human person called to absolute immediacy and intimacy with the divine. As a result, God's history has a human history that attains its highest point with "the absolute bringer of salvation, Jesus as crucified and risen, the son of the Father."

Rahner then discusses the consequences of a transcendental approach to theological methodology. The first of these is an awareness of the limitations of transcendental inquiry itself as these are posed by human historicity and the nature of language, dialogue, and hermeneutics. Transcendental theology is not the whole of theology but an element in making intelligible the concrete nature of human historicity and the drive to know the truth at the point of intersection with God's gift of faith. The second of these consequences is that theological methodology needs transcendental inquiry in order to enrich one's understanding of God's existential presence constituting one's humanity in the giftedness of a self-communication that both determines and liberates one's personhood.

The selection we have featured here is from the final lecture of the series. Rahner says he had been tempted to entitle the lecture "Reductio in Mysterium" (Being led back into mystery). At the very outset Rahner reiterates his conviction that theological reflection begins and ends in the holy mystery of God; hence an awareness of how and why theology must become a "Reductio in Mysterium" is, he notes, a well-needed methodological pointer. He declares that to be led back to God or restored to a sense of God as the holy mystery gracing human existence and the world of creation is the positive distinguishing characteristic of theology and its most proper task. In effect, theology can be construed as the "science of mystery." For Rahner, theology must relate the multiplicity of life's sequences, experiences, and ideas to the inspiriting reality of God at once "ineffable and obscure." Beyond and at the foundations of the intelligent explication of concepts and truths of revelation and dogma, the stuff of which theology is made, is the silent presence of God. Hence Rahner concludes that theology must ultimately cope, not with the formulation of mere human words, but with the call for an "attitude of trembling and silent adoration" that in turn begets true theological creativity. The words themselves point toward the prayerful silence that Rahner claims is needed for theologians to appreciate the relativity of all theological discourse and to be themselves led to a deeper relationship with the mystery they seek to explicate.

A single phrase could be used, a title to sum up the theme of this third lecture: *reductio in mysterium.* Obviously such a theme does also constitute a special area of subject matter in theology. At the same time, however, and over and above this, it also expresses a methodological pointer for theologians, serving to warn them against falling into a certain kind of illusion, at least so far as theology is concerned. This is the illusion that the mystery of reality as such is merely that part of it which still remains obscure for the time being even though in principle it is comprehensible, a part, therefore, which is constantly being diminished as the various branches of science advance, and which is destined ultimately to disappear completely at least in the *visio beatifica*. Now this illusion, this radical misunderstanding of themselves on human beings' part, is de facto constantly asserting itself again and again in theology, and for this reason when we come to speak of the *reductio in mysterium* of all theological proposition which takes place in theology, this also constitutes a methodological guide which is of fundamental importance. Precisely today it is of the utmost importance that we shall understand the significance which theology has as *reductio in mysterium*, that is, we must understand that this *reductio* constitutes not a regrettable imperfection in theology, but rather that which is most proper to it of its very nature. Theology must be bold enough to make it clear to modern human beings that this *reductio in mysterium* is its positive distinguishing characteristic and at the same time the task most proper to it—something, in fact, which arises as a matter of transcendental necessity from the very nature of human beings themselves. If theology fails to do this, then in an age which sets a premium upon scientific knowledge, human beings will inevitably receive the impression that theology is the mere external facade for an intellectual discipline which increasingly dissolves and frees itself from theology itself.

It is all too easy for modern human beings to receive the impression that theology supplies answers of a mythological kind or otherwise unscientific answers to questions which either have no communicable meaning or which in reality will only be answered by the sciences of the day. It is all too easy for modern human beings to receive the impression that theology is a mere interweaving of ideas which are, of their nature, incapable of any verification, which remain at the level of poetical concepts and can still be upheld, at most, simply by pointing with a certain arbitrariness to those dark and subconscious levels in human beings which have not yet been illumined by the anthropological sciences and so, for the time being, are not yet really capable of being used in any constructive system of thought.

Now in reply to such an attitude on the part of modern human beings what can the theology of faith say when it sets itself resolutely to stand and to make a direct counterattack upon this attitude, that is, when it manifests its position with the utmost conscious rationality of which it is capable as a transcendental discipline? It can only assert that this reference to the absolute mystery which it involves is in fact the condition which makes all the perceptions available to the human reason possible. It can only point out that "mystery" is not merely another word for that which for the time being has not yet been comprehended and perceived, that it is both possible and meaningful explicitly to come to terms with mystery as such and in itself, so that we precisely do not have to say with Wittgenstein that we should simply be silent about anything concerning which we cannot speak clearly. Theology then is to be understood as the "science" of mystery as such (though admittedly it is this as sustained by *that* proximity of this mystery to human beings which is designated by Christians as grace and so on). Furthermore the only chance which theology has of providing for the future is for it to show itself openly and with the utmost resolution true to its own nature in this sense, and for it to refuse to conceal its true nature for fear of modern opinion. And if all this is true, then theology must not forget this nature which it has in the manner in which it is practiced from day to day among the theologians themselves either. It must understand itself not as that science which develops itself more and more in a systematic drawing of distinctions down to the last possible detail, but rather as that human activity in which human beings, even at the level of conscious thought, relate the multiplicity of the realities, experiences, and ideas in their lives to that mystery, ineffable and obscure, which we call God.

How strange it is in fact! We are accustomed to understand the history of revelation and dogma according to the conceptual model of a logically developing system in which ever-finer distinctions are drawn. There may be some element of truth in this, and it may be that those phases in the history of dogma and theology which now lie behind us can to a large extent be rendered comprehensible in terms of a conceptual model of this kind. After all even Thomas Aquinas regarded the true nature of theology as consisting in a progressive exposition in terms of concepts of this kind, and the same idea still dominates the modern interpretation of the history of theology. And yet the question may be asked whether it really does constitute the basic principle of development of the history of dogma and theology as such, or merely that of one specific epoch in it, and one which, even though it has lasted for almost two thousand years, is in our own days drawing to its close. And further, is it not possible to understand even the history of dogma and theology up to the present as a *reductio in mysterium* constantly renewed, constantly made more radical, of all theological statements, so that precisely the believer actively engaged in theology knows better than anyone else that every theological statement is only truly and authentically such at that point at which human beings willingly suffer it to extend beyond their comprehension into the silent mystery of God?

First an attempt must be made very briefly to say something about mystery as such, before we undertake the further attempt to understand theology itself as *reductio in mysterium* (in all this it is, of course, self-evident that theology as such constitutes such a *reductio in mysterium* only in a *derived* sense, since the original act by which human beings surrender themselves to the mystery is as such the act of faith). Again in defining what mystery means the declarations of the church's magisterium, and still more the general tendency in theological thinking, take as their basis that which is not mystery at all. Thus mystery is made to appear in a purely negative guise as that which has not been comprehended, that which can only with difficulty avoid giving the impression of being contradictory, and yet at the same time that which is destined to be illumined for human beings too one day, and as mystery to be dissolved at latest in the *visio beatifica*, or perhaps only at that stage. Mystery is restricted almost inadvertently to a pilgrim mode of existence here below. Thus mystery is presented under a merely negative aspect. In comparison with that which human beings can comprehend that which they recognize as mystery may be in its own objective reality for the most part or even always of greater importance for their salvation. But even so the very fact that they are still aware of it precisely as mystery makes their present knowledge of it negative by comparison with any other knowledge which they have, and still more by comparison with knowledge of this mysterious entity in itself, for they think of this as in principle possible and as something that they will later attain to, so that then this knowledge will itself dissolve the element of mystery in their earlier knowledge and in the entity that was mysterious in itself. The measure and ideal of knowledge that is applied to knowledge of mystery is that which comprehends and thoroughly sees into the object known.

In reality, however, this is not the case. The concept of mystery that is commonly accepted is false, or at any rate superficial. This is implied even by the dogmatic teaching of the abiding and essential incomprehensibility of God, which is not eliminated even in the *visio beatifica*, but on the contrary is borne in upon us in its most radical, most infinite, and most blessed form precisely there. In this statement the word "blessed" needs special emphasis. For manifestly the incomprehensibility of God as made immediately present to the creature signifies not the limit, the mere borderline showing the finitude of the beatific vision of God. Rather it is a positive element in this vision in itself, because clearly human beings can achieve the truest fulfillment of their own nature at that point, and only at that point, at which they reach beyond themselves and overstep the limitations of their own knowledge, being definitely drawn out of themselves and ecstatically attaining to the incomprehensibility of God as such, which we only truly grasp in its immediacy when it is accepted by us as that which abidingly blesses us. This in itself is sufficient to reveal every kind of comprehensive knowledge for what it really is: the knowledge appropriate to a finite reality considered as that which is provisional, part of our pilgrim mode of existence, not bestowing any blessing upon us. The dogma of the incomprehensibility of God is in itself enough to show that comprehensive knowledge is a deficient mode of knowing when measured by that knowledge which is beyond all doubt the highest, the most intensive, and that which bestows the deepest blessing upon us, that which takes place in the immediate vision of the incomprehensibility of God.

Now the same conclusion which we have been able to demonstrate on the basis of a direct dogmatic datum can also be arrived at by approaching the question rather from the standpoint of the philosophy of transcendentality. Human beings are the subject of a transcendentality that is limitless. As such they apprehend each of the objects of their knowledge and freedom in a prior awareness, itself not contained within any finite limits, of the original and infinite unity of all possible objects. Yet at the same time human beings as subjects in this sense of a transcendence that is limitless must not, even as such, be understood as the absolute subjects, for this would be God. Now if this is true then the condition which makes any individual act of cognition possible is this prior awareness of that horizon of all knowledge and freedom which is absolute. In other words it is that which, while not simply identical with the knowing subject, is the condition which makes any act of cognition on his or her part possible. It can never be known in the same way as the individual objects of cognition which are rendered intelligible and comprehensible precisely in virtue of the fact that they fall within the ambience of this horizon of all knowledge. This horizon, then, which makes knowledge possible within its ambience, this ultimate point of reference toward which all knowledge tends, is itself radically beyond all comprehension, and its incomprehensibility is such that it is not removed even when, in accordance with the Christian doctrine of the *finitum* considered as *capax infiniti* [the created capacity of finite creatures to know and love the infinite], the absolutely original cause and the ultimate goal of this transcendental awareness, prior to all knowledge, actually imparts itself directly to human beings. Indeed it is precisely at this moment that this first cause and ultimate goal really manifests itself as incomprehensible in the most radical sense. Thus the *mysterium* reveals itself as the condition which makes it possible for us to know that which is not mysterious. The relationship in which human beings stand to the *mysterium* is a primary and an ultimate datum of their own nature and their mode of existence, one of which, in their transcendence, they are constantly aware, though not as the object of their conscious thought, and one which cannot be deduced from any other datum as a secondary phenomenon. The *mysterium*, therefore, is that which alone is genuinely self-evident, and for that very reason that too which can always be overlooked and misinterpreted as a negative phenomenon belonging to the periphery of human living.

Taking the concept of the *mysterium* in the sense in which we have presented it here (though admittedly we have only given a brief indication of what we mean by it) we can now begin to understand the nature of theology as *reductio in mysterium*. The fact that Christian theology has to do with mysteries (in the plural) is something that this theology itself regards as immediately obvious. Moreover this point has been formulated still more explicitly and precisely in the official teaching of the church by Pius IX and the First Vatican Council in answer to a kind of rationalism which had come to regard every theology of revelation involving faith as constituting merely the prelude to a philosophical vision. In this official teaching of the church, however, these mysteries as such continued to be viewed in their relationship to the situation of human beings as pilgrims, and hardly any attempt was made to bring this teaching about the mystery explicitly into connection with the eternal and abiding incomprehensibility of God. And even abstracting from this point, no consideration was ever given to the strangeness of the fact that the mysteries of faith as such should be manifold. The question of whether in fact there could be many real mysteries in the strictest sense of the term such that they were really distinct from one another was hardly touched upon, if indeed it was adverted to at all. It seemed more or less obvious that this question would have to be answered in the affirmative in view of the many mysteries with which theology de facto has to deal. And yet it is perfectly possible to lay down the following thesis: there is, and there can be, only one single absolute mystery in the strictest sense of the term, namely God, and in relation to God all those aspects under which human beings with their finite knowledge have to conceive of God to themselves are specified in the same manner by this character of the *mysterium*.

The thesis can also be formulated negatively: a finite being as such can never be a *mysterium* in the strict sense of the term, but is, of its very essence, merely that which has not yet been fully understood. On any correct ontology of the relationship between being and knowledge, which ultimately speaking consists in the confrontation of a being with itself, it belongs to every finite being necessarily and of its very nature that it should be endowed with a kind of cognition appropriate to itself such that for its own cognitive powers this being cannot be a mystery to itself (apart from its radical orientation to the one mystery which is God). The reason for this is that this mode of cognition is either simply identical with the being concerned or, in virtue of its unlimited transcendentality, it offers every finite being sufficient scope for it itself to be understood within this. Every finite being, therefore, as such, and in its very nature as positive is (abstracting from its intrinsic reference to God) nonmysterious. For this reason it also constitutes as such a mere object for the sciences to investigate to the extent that these are different from theology. Just as all worldly realities are withdrawn from the sphere of the numinous through recognition of the fact that they have been created and are different from God, so too they must in themselves also be removed from the sphere of any ideologizing, that is, they must be radically submitted to the control of the sciences in the knowledge that no being accessible to the categories of human cognition can be mysterious, unfathomable, or obscure. It cannot be this except of course through and in its reference to the incomprehensible horizon of all apprehension in terms of human categories, namely God. Now this reference of which we have just been speaking (and it is this alone that renders the particular being mysterious and at the same time *non*mysterious in that special "quiddity" which is proper to *it* in itself) can be a twofold one: the reference to God as remote and the reference to God as making God's self near by an act of self-bestowal. It is the first of these two aspects that constitutes the element of mystery inherent in the world and in worldly knowledge. The second ultimately speaking constitutes (a point which we still have to develop) the whole content of the Christian mysteries.

In the light of this it is in a true sense clear that theology cannot contain as many mysteries as one wishes to ascribe to it. Basically speaking there can only be *one* mystery: God as God is in God's self. This means that theology has the task of reducing the mysteries which manifest themselves, or appear to manifest themselves, in it to this single mystery, in order thereby to avoid the danger of invoking mysteries in those areas in which all that is really needed is a more penetrating consideration, or perhaps even the "de-mystification" in some respect of a given proposition of theology. Now this process of reducing the many mysteries in theology to the single mystery which is God is not particularly difficult. The fact that God in and for God's self constitutes mystery in the strictest sense of the term and eternally—even, therefore, in the *visio beatifica*—this is a point that needs no further explanation here.

Insofar as there are propositions in theology over and above this which do constitute mystery in the strict sense, this can only mean two things: on the one hand, in accordance with what we have said, they must refer to God, while on the other, in order for them not simply to be identical with the mystery thus mentioned, even formally speaking so far as we are concerned, they must signify God in God's reference *to us*. This reference cannot simply be that which is constituted by the relationship in which God stands to the world and the individual elements in this as their creator. For abstracting from the scholastic principle that as creator God has no real relationship to the world, and that it is only the world that has the relationship to God, the content of this relationship, over and above the element of mystery in it deriving from its single point of reference, God, would be identical with the reality of the creature itself, and therefore in principle no true mystery at all.

The relationship of God to the world in which God is mystery, therefore, can only consist in the fact that it is constituted by God and not by any created reality distinct from God. In other words this means that over and above God's "intrinsic" status as mystery, God can be mystery only in virtue of a quasi-*formal* causality in which God makes not some entity different from God's self, but rather *God's self* (in God's freedom and abiding sovereignty) the specification of the creature. Let us put the same point in a different way: over and above the mystery intrinsic to God's own nature God can only be a mystery in virtue of God's self-bestowal, in which that which is bestowed is formally speaking God as mystery. Probably there is no need to spend any further time in demonstrating the point that here we have arrived at the key mysteries which are pointed to in traditional theology. For in the very meaning of this concept of God's self-bestowal both that which is designated as the hypostatic union is signified and at the same time that which is referred to as supernatural grace and *visio beatifica*. The reason is that in both of these what takes place is truly one and the same act of self-bestowal on God's part, an act which cannot be subsumed with other acts under the concept of the power of God's efficient causality as creator. This means that we are in a position to make the following assertion: that mystery which Christian faith acknowledges consists in the sheer fact that the absolute reality of God (of course understanding this as personal, loving, and grace-giving) cannot only achieve a creative confrontation with that which is other to itself, but actually wills to commit itself to, and bestow itself upon, this. Then, from the point of view of the creature we can go on to say: the mystery here consists in the fact that it truly is, in the radical sense already referred to, *capax infiniti*.

In order to clarify still further this unity which belongs to the one mystery, we would have to go on from this point to work out in detail the unity and the mutually conditioning relationship between the incarnation and the process by which the world is assimilated to God by grace, a development which we cannot undertake at this point. We may say here, however, that both of these factors constitute the free act of God, yet that at basis they constitute only one single object of the exercise of God's freedom as such. Here then we have a theology of the one mystery of God's self-bestowal upon the world with its two mutually conditioning aspects of incarnation and grace. Now if it is clear what is meant by this theology then the mystery of the Trinity is ipso facto given in such a theology and rendered intelligible as mystery. All that has to be done—and that too precisely on the basis of the concept of God's *self*-bestowal—is to show that the Trinity as present in the economy of salvation through the two *missiones* (of grace and the incarnation) necessarily embodies also the Trinity as immanent.

Once the two central mysteries of Christianity are recognized as constituting the single mystery of God's self-bestowal upon the world, then we might go on to ask in more precise terms whether other mysteries apart from these do not arise in dogmatic theology such that on the one hand they cannot be subsumed under the one mystery of the self-bestowal of the absolute mystery which is God, while on the other they can justifiably be claimed to be absolute mysteries in the true sense. In my opinion we can unhesitatingly answer this question in the negative. This opinion is based not only on a priori considerations put forward above, but also on certain a posteriori considerations in which the assertions of dogmatic theology are put to the test to see whether they can justifiably be claimed to be mysteries in the true sense without constituting an element in the mystery of God's self-bestowal and coming to be recognized as such. At most the question might be raised whether the character of mystery is not so unambiguously ascribed by tradition to transubstantiation that in this particular case we have to recognize a mystery in the strictest sense, and one that is supplementary to and distinct from the mystery of God's self-bestowal. But surely we can at least leave this question open, for it can at least be asked whether on the one hand tradition does not cling to an exaggeratedly "physical" understanding of this mystery, and on the other whether we do not have to regard the real presence of Christ as so closely bound up with the mystery of the incarnation that from the outset it is only possible to conceive of any transubstantiation at all insofar as it is related to the reality of Christ in general. Here we have only been able to indicate the

343

considerations which we feel to be relevant, yet precisely on the basis of these transubstantiation does nevertheless seem not to tell against our general thesis, namely that there is only *one single* mystery in the strict sense, that of God's self-bestowal by which God extends God's self into the dimension of that which is most interior to existence (Spirit) and into the dimension of the history of human beings (incarnation).

Now to reduce the actual statements of revelation in this way to the one single mystery has a further significance beyond that which it has for the development of a distinctive theological system as such. The true significance of this *reductio in unum mysterium* is to be found elsewhere. We are taking as our starting point the intrinsic unity and the mutually conditioning relationship between incarnation and the grace by which the world is assimilated to God, and we are not overlooking the fact that of their very nature as historical beings human beings necessarily seek for the concrete historical manifestation of that which they are as transcendental beings in their own history. This is because history is precisely that process in which the fullness of their own transcendental being is progressively made over to them. On the basis of all this, then, we can here concentrate upon the process by which human beings are endowed with grace and so assimilated to God without thereby losing sight of the single mystery of salvation in its totality. But on this basis we are compelled to state the matter as follows: that supernatural grace which has supernaturally orientated the transcendentality of human beings to the immediacy of God must not be conceived of merely as a material addition or supplement such that the only kind of knowledge which can be had of it is that which comes through indoctrination from without. Rather it is something of which human beings themselves must necessarily be aware, even though they do not consciously objectify it to themselves.

Now if and to the extent that this is true it follows that the totality of the message of the Christian faith is in a real sense already given in a transcendental experience. This does not of course make the history of revelation or the act of bearing witness to the faith, which comes from hearing, superfluous. It is precisely this history of revelation and history of faith at the social level that constitutes the historical process by which this grace-given transcendental experience, constituted and upheld as it is by the self-bestowal of God, is brought to the stage of self-realization. It is precisely in order to arrive at the most ultimate and transcendental dimension of their own nature that human beings are orientated toward their own history at both the individual and collective levels. But precisely as such this is the history of their own transcendental nature itself.

Hence it is that revelation as the transcendental experience of grace and revelation as history do not mutually contradict one another but rather are the mutually conditioning elements in one and the same event. In this sense, then, theology constitutes the *reductio in mysterium* and in fact *in unum mysterium*. But this still does not mean that what we are treating of here is merely a process of unifying and systematizing at the conceptual level the various dogmatic statements in which revelation is expressed. Equally, and in a more basic sense, we are concerned with the attempt to interpret all these various statements as a summons to that ultimate and transcendental experience of grace which is implicit in all these statements and which signifies the ultimate verification of them all.

What is meant by this is already to be perceived in Scripture itself. For theologians Scripture is indeed the absolute norm. But it is this not because the revelation imparted by God takes place originally and for the first time in these human statements as such, but rather because in them the original experience of the Spirit and of its eschatological address to human beings in Jesus Christ has been objectified in a form which has abiding validity and with a purely normative force. Measured by this original experience Scripture is in itself theology, albeit at the normative level, and even though obviously an original and basic experience of this kind never takes place without some kind of conceptual objectivation in terms of human categories. Thus the task of theology must precisely be to appeal in all the various conceptual forms in which it is objectified, to this basic experience of grace, to bring human beings again and again to a fresh recognition of the fact that all this immense sum of distinct statements of the Christian faith basically speaking expresses nothing else than an immense truth, even though one that has been explicitated throughout all the levels of humans' being; the truth namely that the absolute mystery that is, that permeates all things, upholds all things, and endures eternally, has bestowed itself as itself in an act of forgiving love upon human beings, and is experienced in faith in that ineffable experience of grace as the ultimate freedom of human beings.

So long as theology remains stuck fast at the merely conceptual level—however necessary this may be in itself—it has failed in its true mission. And if we seek to take refuge in the consoling thought that after all the statements of theology still speak constantly of God, and therefore of mystery, then it must be rejoined that this alone is not enough to avoid the danger of sticking fast in this sense. It is not only the *fides quae* [the faith which—this refers to the content of one's beliefs] that must

345

come to terms with God as mystery, but also the *fides qua* [the faith by which—this refers to the act itself of believing or trusting]. The act of faith as such in itself, and not merely its conceptual objectifications, must in some sense come to terms with the mystery as such. For this too theology (considered as a whole) should offer guidance and direction. It should constitute a "mystagogia" leading men and women to the experience of grace, and should not merely speak of grace as of a material subject which is present in human beings' lives solely through the conceptions which they formulate of it. Theology as science must certainly not be confused with kerygma, with parenesis, with the immediate utterance of the Spirit. But at the same time it must not forget either, as it all too often does, that it derives from the utterance of the Spirit and has to serve it. For unless this utterance of the Spirit and the theology deriving from it are related to the ultimate experience of the Spirit in human beings' lives, they lose their distinctive subject matter altogether.

This task of theology, then, can be defined as a *reductio in unum mysterium,* and that too in terms of its own subject matter and in the concrete circumstances in which it is currently formulated. From this very many consequences can be drawn for the practice of theology today. Here we can mention only very few of these, which we have selected at random. The propositions of theology must constantly be referred back to the single indefinable mystery and the ultimate and grace-given experience of this. In fact all of them express, ultimately speaking, nothing else than the fact that this mystery has imparted itself so as to achieve a state of absolute proximity to human beings, in which it becomes their authentic consummation and the future that lies before them. The process by which the connection between these propositions and the mystery itself is firmly established belongs to the true nature of theology as such, and this ultimately speaking constitutes the true difference between these propositions and those pertaining to the secular sphere. For these latter too do indeed express realities related to God, but in what they express the actual mystery remains unaffected and still more fails to reveal the reference latent in them to the *im*mediacy of God. This, however, is not to deny, but on the contrary once more to reiterate, that the statements of theology are different from that which they point to, even though the difference here is not self-evident, as it is in the case of statements belonging to the secular sphere. This means that theological statements have a special and peculiar theological relativity of their own, that is, their radical reference to that which infinitely transcends them, such that without this reference they become meaningless.

Now this distinctive relativity in theological statements is something constantly to be inquired into anew in a peculiar and special form of dialectic. It is one that cannot be replaced by an attitude of silent adoration, by a *theologia meditativa* [meditative theology—theology drawn from the prayer of meditation] which effectively reduces itself to silence. Nor can we express these statements in a form which suggests that the actual formulation of them in human words is the ultimate goal at which we are aiming. Rather it is the attitude of trembling and silent adoration which is intended to beget these statements, and this belongs to that deathly silence in which human beings' lips are sealed with Christ's in death. It is, therefore, a very difficult task with which theology has to cope in these statements. They must be expressed in words in order that we can arrive at the authentic silence which we need. They must be borne with in patience and hope in respect both of their necessity and of their incommensurability, in which they attempt to utter the ineffable. I believe that theology today has still very much to learn before it speaks in such a manner that human beings can achieve a direct, effective, and clear recognition of the special quality of this language.

It always remains true, then, that theological statements only authentically become such in a process in which they reach out to a point radically beyond themselves. And if this is true, then, so it seems to me, we in the church could often show ourselves far more favorable and tolerant with regard to those statements which we may be tempted to qualify as "heresies" on the grounds that they seem so inappropriate to the reality they express. This applies both to ourselves and to a magisterium in the church which may be excessively self-confident in the manner in which it does its work. Of course the church has a right and a duty to reject certain theological statements as irreconcilable with its own conviction of its faith. And indeed properly speaking those who are suspected of "heresy" in this way should not be so very resentful that their statements have been rejected provided that in these statements of theirs they too really have arrived at the *reductio in mysterium* without which their statements certainly would be heresies. This *reductio* is certainly neither prohibited nor rendered impossible by the fact that their statements have been subjected to censure. The situation today is that every statement of the church's magisterium includes an element of regulating the actual language of theology, something which, fundamentally speaking, has nothing to do with the actual reality in itself. Moreover our position today is quite different from that of earlier times. Today we have to take into account a situation in which on the one hand loyal believers and adherents of the church, with the best will in the world, cannot come to terms with specific statements of the official teaching of the church, while on the other they have not de facto simply arrived at an interpretation of such statements of their own such as could find acceptance on the part of the teaching authority of the church.

Now in this situation it is surely justifiable and necessary for the church's magisterium to show more patience and prudence than it probably brought to bear in practice in earlier times in many cases in which its authority was exercised. We must really and effectively practice theology on the basis of a *reductio in mysterium* in terms of its material content and of the actual concrete circumstances in which we practice it. We must genuinely, effectively, and radically realize the incommensurability of our own theological formulations, a point which in itself is self-evident. And if we do this, then, so I believe, we will very often find it possible to be more modest in presenting our own theology and more indulgent in considering that of others which we are tempted to qualify as heretical. Certainly we cannot hasten at will the gradual advance of history. But did not individuals on both sides already find it possible, even at the time of the Reformation, to perceive that the really fundamental positions of both sides with regard to justification, Scripture, faith, and so on, certainly did not positively contradict one another, a fact which today is, after all, conceded by both sides? I believe that in a theology which genuinely and effectively, and not merely verbally, realized its own nature as *reductio in mysterium* we of today could in many cases be more patient with so-called heresies, of course always with the proviso that the theology suspected by anyone of being heresy is intended in itself to be a *reductio in mysterium*. In fact in the theology put forward by many individuals this actually has been achieved with a notable degree of effectiveness. The theology in question must not merely be a superficial rationalism intended to preserve the individual from having to commit himself or herself to the unfathomable depths of the mystery. And of course a further proviso must be that a theology which is "under suspicion" in this sense must itself not represent any *schismatic* tendency, any attitude of arrogance in which it refuses to pay heed to the formulations of traditional theology. Rather it must in a right manner and in the right place pay due heed to the prescriptions with regard to language put forward and maintained for theology by the church's magisterium in order to preserve the unity of the church's own creed. With these provisos, however, we of today both can and should show ourselves generous, patient, and tolerant with regard to theological statements which do not immediately strike us as being "orthodox." We should adopt this attitude in view of the fact that

348

the pluralism among the theologies of today is too great for us to control or comprehend. Moreover we ourselves should have a little trust in the power of the reality itself which is being referred to, that is, in the one single mystery of the proximity of the incomprehensible God who sets all things free to come to God's self and to be drawn into God's infinitude.

SELECT BIBLIOGRAPHY

BIBLIOGRAPHIES OF WORKS
BY RAHNER

Helpful, comprehensive bibliographies of the writings of Karl Rahner can be found in the following:

Bleistein, Roman. *Bibliographie Karl Rahner, 1969–1974*. Freiburg: Herder, 1974.

Bleistein, Roman, and E. Klinger. *Bibliographie Karl Rahner, 1924–1969*. Freiburg: Herder, 1969.

Vorgrimler, Herbert, ed. *Wagnis Theologie*. Freiburg: Herder, 1979.

The following offer very useful bibliographies of Rahner's writings in English translation:

Bacik, James. *Apologetics and the Eclipse of Mystery: Mystagogy according to Karl Rahner*. Notre Dame, Ind.: University of Notre Dame Press, 1980, 143–49.

Dudley, M. "On Reading Rahner." *Scottish Journal of Theology* 37, no. 1 (1984): 81–96.

Pedley, C. J. "An English Bibliographical Aid to Karl Rahner." *The Heythrop Journal* 25, no. 3 (July 1984): 319–65; "An English Bibliographical Aid to Karl Rahner: Supplement." *The Heythrop Journal* 26, no. 3 (July 1985): 310.

AUTOBIOGRAPHICAL RESOURCES

The following books provide autobiographical data through personal interviews with Rahner:

Imhof, Paul, and Hubert Biallowons, eds. *Faith in a Wintry Season: Conversations and Interviews with Karl Rahner in the Last Years of His Life*. Translation edited by Harvey D. Egan. New York: Crossroad, 1990.

————. *Karl Rahner in Dialogue: Conversations and Interviews, 1965–1982*. Translation edited by Harvey D. Egan. New York: Crossroad, 1986.

Rahner, Karl. *I Remember: An Autobiographical Interview with Meinold Krauss*. Translated by Harvey D. Egan. New York: Crossroad; London: SCM, 1985.

SELECTED WORKS BY RAHNER

COLLECTIONS OF ARTICLES AND LECTURES

Theological Investigations, vol. 1: *God, Christ, Mary and Grace*. Translated by Cornelius Ernst. London: Darton, Longman and Todd; Baltimore: Helicon, 1961; New York: Seabury Press, 1974. Originally published as *Schriften zur Theologie* (hereafter *Schriften*), vol. 1.

Theological Investigations, vol. 2: *Man in the Church*. Translated by Karl H. Kruger. London: Darton, Longman and Todd; Baltimore: Helicon, 1963; New York: Seabury Press, 1975. Originally published as *Schriften*, vol. 2.

Theological Investigations, vol. 3: *The Theology of the Spiritual Life*. Translated by Karl H. Kruger and Boniface Kruger. London: Darton, Longman and Todd; Baltimore: Helicon, 1967; New York: Seabury Press, 1974. Originally published as *Schriften*, vol. 3.

Theological Investigations, vol. 4: *More Recent Writings*. Translated by Kevin Smyth. London: Darton, Longman and Todd; Baltimore: Helicon, 1966; New York: Seabury Press, 1974. Originally published as *Schriften*, vol. 4.

Theological Investigations, vol. 5: *Later Writings*. Translated by Karl H. Kruger. London: Darton, Longman and Todd; Baltimore: Helicon, 1966; New York: Seabury Press, 1975. Originally published as *Schriften*, vol. 5.

Theological Investigations, vol. 6: *Concerning Vatican Council II*. Translated by Karl H. Kruger and Boniface Kruger. London: Darton, Longman and Todd; Baltimore: Helicon, 1969; New York: Seabury Press, 1974. Originally published as *Schriften*, vol. 6.

Theological Investigations, vol. 7: *Further Theology of the Spiritual Life, 1*. Translated by David Bourke. London: Darton, Longman and Todd;

New York: Herder and Herder, 1971; New York: Seabury Press, 1973. Originally published as *Schriften*, vol. 7/1.

Theological Investigations, vol. 8: *Further Theology of the Spiritual Life, 2*. Translated by David Bourke. London: Darton, Longman and Todd; New York: Herder and Herder, 1971; New York: Seabury Press, 1973. Originally published as *Schriften*, vol. 7/2.

Theological Investigations, vol. 9: *Writings of 1965–67, 1*. Translated by Graham Harrison. London: Darton, Longman and Todd; New York: Herder and Herder, 1972; New York: Seabury Press, 1973. Originally published as *Schriften*, vol. 8/1.

Theological Investigations, vol. 10: *Writings of 1965–67, 2*. Translated by David Bourke. London: Darton, Longman and Todd; New York: Herder and Herder, 1973; New York: Seabury Press, 1973. Originally published as *Schriften*, vol. 8/2.

Theological Investigations, vol. 11: *Confrontations, 1*. Translated by David Bourke. London: Darton, Longman and Todd; New York: Seabury Press, 1974. Originally published as *Schriften*, vol. 9/1.

Theological Investigations, vol. 12: *Confrontations, 2*. Translated by David Bourke. London: Darton, Longman and Todd; New York: Seabury Press, 1974. Originally published as *Schriften*, vol. 9/2.

Theological Investigations, vol. 13: *Theology, Anthropology, Christology*. Translated by David Bourke. London: Darton, Longman and Todd; New York: Seabury Press, 1975. Originally published as *Schriften*, vol. 10/1.

Theological Investigations, vol. 14: *Ecclesiology, Questions in the Church, the Church in the World*. Translated by David Bourke. London: Darton, Longman and Todd; New York: Seabury Press, 1976. Originally published as *Schriften*, vol. 10/2.

Theological Investigations, vol. 15: *Penance in the Early Church*. Translated by Lionel Swain. London: Darton, Longman and Todd; New York: Seabury Press, 1977. Originally published as *Schriften*, vol. 11.

Theological Investigations, vol. 16: *Experience of the Spirit: Source of Theology*. Translated by David Morland. London: Darton, Longman and Todd; New York: Seabury Press, 1979. Originally published as *Schriften*, vol. 12/1.

Theological Investigations, vol. 17: *Jesus, Man and the Church.* Translated by Margaret Kohl. London: Darton, Longman and Todd; New York: Crossroad, 1981. Originally published as *Schriften,* vol. 12/2.

Theological Investigations, vol. 18: *God and Revelation.* Translated by Edward Quinn. London: Darton, Longman and Todd; New York: Crossroad, 1983. Originally published as *Schriften,* vol. 13/1.

Theological Investigations, vol. 19: *Faith and Ministry.* Translated by Edward Quinn. London: Darton, Longman and Todd; New York: Crossroad, 1983. Originally published as *Schriften,* vol. 13/2 and 14, selected articles.

Theological Investigations, vol. 20: *Concern for the Church.* Translated by Edward Quinn. London: Darton, Longman and Todd; New York: Crossroad, 1981. Originally published as *Schriften,* vol. 14, selected articles.

Theological Investigations, vol. 21: *Science and Christian Faith.* Translated by Hugh Riley. London: Darton, Longman and Todd; New York: Crossroad, 1988. Originally published as *Schriften,* vol. 15.

Theological Investigations, vol. 22: *Humane Society and the Church of Tomorrow.* Translated by Joseph Donceel. London: Darton, Longman and Todd; New York: Crossroad, 1989. Originally published as *Schriften,* vol. 16.

SELECTED BOOKS
IN ENGLISH TRANSLATION

Christian at the Crossroads. Translated by V. Green. London: Search Press; New York: Seabury Press, 1975. Originally published as *Wagnis des Christen,* 1974.

The Christian Commitment: Essays in Pastoral Theology. Translated by Cecily Hastings. New York: Sheed and Ward, 1963. Published in England as *Mission and Grace.* London: Sheed and Ward, 1963. Originally published as vol. 1 of *Sendung und Gnade,* 1959.

The Church and the Sacraments. Translated by W. J. O'Hara. London: Burns and Oates; New York: Herder and Herder, 1963; London: Search Press; New York: Seabury Press, 1974. Originally published as *Kirche und Sakramente,* 1961.

Encounters with Silence. Translated by James Demske. Paramus, N.J.: Newman Press, 1960; London: Burns and Oates, 1975. Originally published as *Worte ins Schweigen*, 1938.

Everyday Faith. Translated by W. J. O'Hara. London: Burns and Oates; New York: Herder and Herder, 1968. Originally published as *Glaube, der die Erde liebt*, 1966.

Foundations of Christian Faith: An Introduction to the Idea of Christianity. Translated by William V. Dych. New York: Seabury Press, 1978. Originally published as *Grundkurs des Glaubens: Einführung in den Begriff des Christentums*, 1976.

Grace in Freedom. Translated by Hilda Graef. London: Burns and Oates; New York: Herder and Herder, 1969. Originally published as *Gnade als Freiheit*, 1968.

Hearers of the Word. Translated by Michael Richards. London: Sheed and Ward; New York: Herder and Herder/Seabury Press, 1969. Originally published as *Hörer des Wortes: Zur Grundlegung einer Religionsphilosophie*, 1941. Portions of a new translation by Joseph Donceel appear in Gerald McCool's *A Rahner Reader* (see below).

The Love of Jesus and the Love of Neighbor. Translated by Robert Barr. London: St. Paul Publications; New York: Crossroad, 1983. Originally published as *Was heisst Jesus lieben?*, 1982, and *Wer ist dein Bruder?*, 1981.

Meditations on the Sacraments. London: Burns and Oates; New York: Seabury Press, 1979. Originally published as *Die siebenfältige Gabe*, 1974.

Nature and Grace: Dilemmas in the Modern Church. Translated by Dinah Wharton. London: Burns and Oates; New York: Sheed and Ward, 1964. Originally published as *Gefahren im heutigen Katholizismus*, 1950.

On Prayer. Glen Rock, N.J.: Paulist Deus Books, 1969. Published in England and Ireland as *Happiness through Prayer*. London: Burns, Oates and Washbourne; Dublin: Clonmere and Reynolds, 1958. Originally published as *Von der Not und dem Segen des Gebetes*, 1948.

On the Theology of Death. Translated by Charles Henkey. New York: Herder and Herder, 1961; New York: Seabury Press, 1973; London: Search Press, 1969. Originally published as *Zur Theologie des Todes*, 1958.

The Priesthood. Translated by Edward Quinn. London: Sheed and Ward; New York: Herder and Herder, 1973. Originally published as *Einübung priestlicher Existenz*, 1970.

The Shape of the Church to Come. Translated by Edward Quinn. London: SPCK; New York: Seabury Press, 1974. Originally published as *Strukturwandel der Kirche als Aufgabe und Chance*, 1972.

The Spirit in the Church. Translated by John Griffiths (part 1) and W. J. O'Hara (part 2). London: Search Press; New York: Seabury Press, 1979. Part 1, "Experiencing the Spirit," is from *Erfahrung des Geistes*, 1977; part 2, "The Charismatic Element in the Church," is from *Das Dynamische in der Kirche*, 1962.

Spirit in the World. Translated by William V. Dych. New York: Herder and Herder; London: Sheed and Ward, 1968. Originally published as *Geist im Welt: Zur Metaphysik der endlichen Erkenntnis bei Thomas von Aquin*, 2d ed. revised by J. B. Metz, 1957.

Spiritual Exercises. Translated by Kenneth Baker. New York: Herder and Herder, 1965; London: Sheed and Ward, 1967. Originally published as *Betrachtungen zum ignatianischen Exerzitienbuch*, 1965.

Theology of Pastoral Action. Translated by W. J. O'Hara. Adaptations by Daniel Morrissey. London: Burns and Oates; New York: Herder and Herder, 1968. Originally published as "Grundlegung der Pastoraltheologie als praktische Theologie," in *Handbuch der Pastoraltheologie*, edited by Karl Rahner, vol. 1/2, 1964.

The Trinity. Translated by Joseph Donceel. London: Burns and Oates; New York: Herder and Herder, 1970. Originally published as "Der dreifältige Gott als transzendenter Urgrund der Heilsgeschichte," chap. 5 of *Mysterium Salutis*, vol. 2, 1967.

DICTIONARIES AND ENCYCLOPEDIAS

With Cornelius Ernst and Kevin Smyth. *Sacramentum Mundi: An Encyclopedia of Theology*. London: Burns and Oates; New York: Herder and Herder, 1968.

With Herbert Vorgrimler. *Theological Dictionary*. Edited by Cornelius Ernst and translated by Richard Strachan. New York: Herder and Herder, 1965. Originally published as *Kleines theologisches Wörterbuch*, 1961.

ANTHOLOGIES OF RAHNER'S WRITINGS

The Practice of Faith: A Handbook of Contemporary Spirituality. Edited by Karl Lehmann and Albert Raffelt. New York: Crossroad, 1986.

A Rahner Reader. Edited by Gerald A. McCool. New York: Seabury Press, 1975.

SELECTED LITERATURE ABOUT RAHNER

BIBLIOGRAPHIES OF THE SECONDARY LITERATURE

Bacik, James. *Apologetics and the Eclipse of Mystery: Mystagogy according to Karl Rahner.* Notre Dame, Ind.: University of Notre Dame Press, 1980, 150–59.

Pedley, C. J. "An English Bibliographical Aid to Karl Rahner." *The Heythrop Journal* 25, no. 3 (July 1984): 319–65. Pedley arranges this listing of Rahner's writings and the literature on Rahner according to topics.

Raffelt, Albert. "Karl Rahner: Sekundarliteratur, 1979–1983." In E. Klinger and W. Wittstadt, eds., *Glaube im Prozess.* Freiburg: Herder, 1984.

Tallon, Andrew. "Bibliography of Books, Articles, and Selected Reviews, 1939–1978." *Theology Digest* 26, no. 4 (Winter 1978): 365–85.

BIOGRAPHICAL RESOURCES

The following articles and books offer helpful biographical data that provide a useful context for interpreting Rahner:

Fahey, Michael. "Presidential Address: 1904–1984, Karl Rahner, Theologian." In George Kilcourse, ed., *Proceedings of the Thirty-ninth Annual Convention: The Catholic Theological Society of America* 39 (1984): 84–98.

O'Donovan, Leo. "To Lead Us into Mystery." *America* 150, no. 23 (June 16, 1984): 453–57.

Vorgrimler, Herbert. *Karl Rahner: His Life, Thought and Works.* London: Burns and Oates, 1965; New York: Paulist Press, 1966.

———. *Understanding Karl Rahner: An Introduction to His Life and Thought.* New York: Crossroad, 1986.

BOOKS AND ARTICLES IN ENGLISH

Bacik, James. *Apologetics and the Eclipse of Mystery: Mystagogy according to Karl Rahner.* Notre Dame, Ind.: University of Notre Dame Press, 1980.

Carr, Anne. *The Theological Method of Karl Rahner.* Missoula, Mont.: Scholars Press, 1977.

Donceel, Joseph. *The Philosophy of Karl Rahner.* New York: Magi Books, 1969.

Dych, William. "The Achievement of Karl Rahner." *Theology Digest* 31, no. 4 (Winter 1984): 325–33.

Egan, Harvey D. " 'The Devout Christian of the Future Will...Be a Mystic': Mysticism and Karl Rahner's Theology." In William J. Kelly, ed., *Theology and Discovery: Essays in Honor or Karl Rahner, S.J.,* 139–58. Milwaukee: Marquette University Press, 1980.

Fiorenza, Francis. "Karl Rahner and the Kantian Problematic." Introduction to Karl Rahner, *Spirit in the World.* New York: Herder and Herder; London: Sheed and Ward, 1968.

Gelpi, Donald. *Life and Light: A Guide to the Theology of Karl Rahner.* New York: Sheed and Ward, 1966.

Kelly, William J., ed. *Theology and Discovery: Essays in Honor of Karl Rahner, S.J.* Milwaukee: Marquette University Press, 1980.

Kennedy, Eugene. "Quiet Mover of the Catholic Church: The Liberal Karl Rahner May Have Greater Impact on Catholicism Than Pope John Paul II." *New York Times Magazine,* September 23, 1979, 22–23, 64–75.

Kress, Robert. *A Rahner Handbook.* Atlanta: John Knox Press, 1982.

McCool, Gerald. *The Theology of Karl Rahner.* Albany: Magi Books, 1969.

Maquarrie, John (with comment and questions by Karl Rahner). "The Anthropological Approach to Theology." *The Heythrop Journal* 25, no. 3 (July 1984): 260–87.

Modras, Ronald. "Implications of Rahner's Anthropology for Fundamental Theology." *Horizons* 12, no. 1 (Spring 1985): 70–90.

O'Donnell, John. "The Mystery of Faith in the Theology of Karl Rahner." *The Heythrop Journal* 25, no. 3 (July 1984): 301–18.

O'Donovan, Leo. "A Journey into Time: The Legacy of Karl Rahner's Last Years." *Theological Studies* 46, no. 4 (December 1985): 621–46.

————. "Orthopraxis and Theological Method in Karl Rahner." In Luke Salm, ed., *Proceedings of the Thirty-fifth Annual Convention: The Catholic Theological Society of America* 35 (1980): 47–65.

————, ed. *A World of Grace: An Introduction to the Themes and Foundations of Karl Rahner's Theology*. New York: Seabury Press, 1980.

Roberts, Louis. *The Achievement of Karl Rahner*. New York: Herder and Herder, 1967.

Scanlon, Michael. "Systematic Theology and the World Church." In George Kilcourse, ed., *Proceedings of the Thirty-ninth Annual Convention: The Catholic Theological Society of America* 39 (1984): 13–34.

Sheehan, Thomas. *Karl Rahner: The Philosophical Foundations*. Athens: Ohio University Press, 1987.

Shepherd, William. *Man's Condition: God and the World Process*. New York: Herder and Herder, 1969.

Vacek, Edward. "Development within Rahner's Theology." *Irish Theological Quarterly* 42, no. 1 (January 1975): 36–49.

Weger, Karl-Heinz. *Karl Rahner: An Introduction to His Theology*. New York: Seabury Press, 1980.

NOTES TO THE INTRODUCTION

¹ Ronald Modras, "Karl Rahner: Moral Theology," *Theology Digest* 31, no. 4 (Winter 1984): 339. Modras cites these statistics from Eugene Kennedy's article, "Quiet Mover of the Catholic Church," *New York Times Magazine,* September 23, 1979, 22–23, 64–75.

² Leo J. O'Donovan, "In Memoriam: Karl Rahner, S.J., 1904–1984," *Journal of the American Academy of Religion* 53, no. 1 (March 1985): 130.

³ Karl Rahner, *I Remember: An Autobiographical Interview with Meinold Krauss,* trans. Harvey D. Egan (New York: Crossroad, 1985), 20.

⁴ Ibid., 26.

⁵ Ibid.

⁶ Herbert Vorgrimler, *Karl Rahner: His Life, Thought and Works* (London: Burns and Oates, 1965; New York: Paulist Press, 1966), 17.

⁷ The expression "world of grace" is used as the title of a collection of essays edited by Leo J. O'Donovan that was intended not only to be a companion piece to Rahner's *Foundations of Christian Faith* but also a general introduction to the themes and foundational principles of Rahner's theology. See Leo O'Donovan, ed., *A World of Grace* (New York: Seabury Press, 1980). On the Ignatian influence in Rahner's theology, see especially Herbert Vorgrimler, *Understanding Karl Rahner: An Introduction to His Life and Thought* (New York: Crossroad, 1986), 18–20. See also Harvey Egan, "'The Devout Christian of the Future Will...Be a Mystic': Mysticism and Karl Rahner's Theology," in William J. Kelly, ed., *Theology and Discovery: Essays in Honor of Karl Rahner, S.J.* (Milwaukee: Marquette University Press, 1980), 139–58.

⁸ Gerard Manley Hopkins, "God's Grandeur," in *Poems of Gerard Manley Hopkins,* 3d ed., rev. and enlarged by W. H. Gardner (London/New York: Oxford University Press, 1960), 70.

⁹ See Karl-Heinz Weger, *Karl Rahner: An Introduction to His Theology* (New York: Seabury Press, 1980), 22ff. See also Thomas Sheehan, *Karl Rahner: The Philosophical Foundations* (Athens: Ohio University Press, 1987), 19–54.

¹⁰ See Gerald McCool, ed., *A Rahner Reader* (New York: Seabury Press, 1975), xiii–xviii. See also McCool's essay, "Karl Rahner and the Christian Philosophy of Saint Thomas Aquinas," in Kelly, *Theology and Discovery,* 63–101.

¹¹ Robert Kress, *A Rahner Handbook* (Atlanta: John Knox Press, 1982), 2.

¹² Rahner, *I Remember,* 46.

¹³ Rahner, "Karl Rahner at 75 Years of Age: Interview with Leo O'Donovan for *America* Magazine," in Paul Imhof and Hubert Biallowons, eds., *Karl Rahner*

in Dialogue: Conversations and Interviews, 1965–1982 (New York: Crossroad, 1986), 190.

[14] Ibid., 191.

[15] Ibid.

[16] A perceptive, detailed analysis of Rahner's dissertation can be found in Francis Fiorenza, "Karl Rahner and the Kantian Problematic," introduction to Karl Rahner, *Spirit in the World* (New York: Herder and Herder, 1968), xix–xlv. See also Anne Carr, *The Theological Method of Karl Rahner* (Missoula, Mont.: Scholars Press, 1977), 59–88. See also Weger, *Karl Rahner*, 22–34, and William V. Dych, "Theology in a New Key," in O'Donovan, *A World of Grace*, 1–10.

[17] Rahner, *I Remember*, 40.

[18] Cited in Kress, *Rahner Handbook*, 3.

[19] Rahner, *Encounters with Silence*, trans. James Demske (Paramus, N.J.: Newman Press, 1960), 30–31.

[20] Rahner, "Dogmatic Reflections on the Knowledge and Self-consciousness of Christ," in *Theological Investigations* (hereafter *TI*; see Select Bibliography for publication data), 5:193–215.

[21] Rahner, *I Remember*, 49.

[22] Vorgrimler, *Karl Rahner*, 35.

[23] Kress, *Rahner Handbook*, 5.

[24] Rahner, *I Remember*, 59.

[25] Vorgrimler, *Understanding Karl Rahner*, 72.

[26] Kress, *Rahner Handbook*, 6.

[27] Ibid., 7–8.

[28] Vorgrimler, *Karl Rahner*, 44–45.

[29] Vorgrimler, *Understanding Karl Rahner*, 73.

[30] Ibid., 73–74.

[31] Kress, *Rahner Handbook*, 12.

[32] Rahner, "On Becoming a Theologian: An Interview with Peter Pawlowsky," in Imhof and Biallowons, *Karl Rahner in Dialogue*, 256.

[33] Vorgrimler, *Understanding Karl Rahner*, 75–76.

[34] Ibid., 83–85.

[35] Ibid., 76–77.

[36] Rahner, "General Preface," in Rahner, with Cornelius Ernst and Kevin Smyth, eds., *Sacramentum Mundi: An Encyclopedia of Theology* (New York: Herder and Herder; London: Burns and Oates, 1968), 1:v.

[37] Vorgrimler, *Understanding Karl Rahner*, 80.

[38] Ibid., 87.

[39] Ibid.

[40] Ibid., 87–88.

[41] See Michael Fahey, "Presidential Address: 1904–1984, Karl Rahner, Theologian," in George Kilcourse, ed., *Proceedings of the Thirty-ninth Annual Convention: The Catholic Theological Society of America* 39 (1984): 88.

[42] Rahner, "New Theological Impulses since the Second World War: Interview with Peter Pawlowsky," in Imhof and Biallowons, *Karl Rahner in Dialogue*, 263.

⁴³ Vorgrimler, *Understanding Karl Rahner*, 91–92.

⁴⁴ *TI,* 7:82 (cited in Fahey, "Presidential Address," 88).

⁴⁵ Vorgrimler, *Understanding Karl Rahner*, 148.

⁴⁶ Ibid., 150–51.

⁴⁷ Ibid., 150.

⁴⁸ Ibid., 149–51.

⁴⁹ *TI,* 20:38 (cited in Fahey, "Presidential Address," 89).

⁵⁰ Vorgrimler, *Understanding Karl Rahner*, 99.

⁵¹ Ibid., 100.

⁵² Ibid., 100–101.

⁵³ Rahner, "Church and World," in Rahner, with Ernst and Smyth, *Sacramentum Mundi,* 1:348.

⁵⁴ Rahner, "Überlegungen zum personalen vollzug des sakramentalen Geschehens," *Geist und Leben* 43, no. 4 (1970), translated in Edward Vacek, "Development within Rahner's Theology," *Irish Theological Quarterly* 42, no. 1 (January 1975): 36–49.

⁵⁵ See Rahner, *The Shape of the Church to Come,* trans. Edward Quinn (New York: Seabury Press, 1974), especially 30–31, 45ff. For an excellent analysis of this development, see Leo J. O'Donovan, "A Journey into Time: The Legacy of Karl Rahner's Last Years," *Theological Studies* 46, no. 4 (December 1985): 632–33.

⁵⁶ Cited in O'Donovan, "Journey," 636.

⁵⁷ Vorgrimler, *Understanding Karl Rahner*, 101, 104–5.

⁵⁸ Ibid., 105.

⁵⁹ Rahner, "Is Political Theology Dangerous? An Interview with Francis Alt," in Imhof and Biallowons, *Karl Rahner in Dialogue,* 234.

⁶⁰ James J. Bacik, "Karl Rahner: Finding God in Daily Life," *Contemporary Theologians* (Chicago: Thomas More Press, 1989), 16–17.

⁶¹ Harvey D. Egan, "Translator's Foreword," in Rahner, *I Remember,* 7.

⁶² Vorgrimler, *Understanding Karl Rahner*, 29.

⁶³ Ibid., 30.

⁶⁴ Cited in ibid., 30–31.

⁶⁵ See Rahner, *Shape of the Church.* On Rahner's literary productivity during his last years, see especially O'Donovan, "Journey," 621–46.

⁶⁶ Weger, *Karl Rahner,* 196.

⁶⁷ Rahner, *I Remember,* 83–84; Vorgrimler, *Understanding Karl Rahner*, 108.

⁶⁸ O'Donovan, "Journey," 624.

⁶⁹ Ibid., 626–28.

⁷⁰ Michael J. Scanlon, "Systematic Theology and the World Church," in Kilcourse, *Proceedings,* 20.

⁷¹ Ibid., 24.

⁷² *TI,* 20:143; English translation revised by O'Donovan, "Journey," 622.

⁷³ Cited by O'Donovan, "Journey," 638.

⁷⁴ Ibid., 639.

⁷⁵ Ibid., 640.

⁷⁶ Rahner, *I Remember,* 110.

[77] Cited in Fahey, "Presidential Address," 90.

[78] Cited in Vorgrimler, *Understanding Karl Rahner*, 137–39.

[79] Leo J. O'Donovan, "Orthopraxis and Theological Method in Karl Rahner," in Luke Salm, ed., *Proceedings of the Thirty-fifth Annual Convention: The Catholic Theological Society of America* 35 (1980): 47.

[80] See Rahner, "Reflections on Methodology in Theology," *TI,* 11:68–114.

[81] O'Donovan, "Orthopraxis," 48–49.

[82] Ibid., 49.

[83] Ibid.; O'Donovan refers here to Rahner's essay "Nature and Grace," in *TI,* 4:182ff.

[84] O'Donovan, "Orthopraxis," 49–50.

[85] Rahner, "Ein Brief von P. Karl Rahner," in Klaus Fischer, *Der Mensch als Geheimnis* (Freiburg: Herder, 1971), 66 (cited in Kress, *Rahner Handbook*, 26).

[86] Rahner, *Foundations of Christian Faith: An Introduction to the Idea of Christianity*, trans. William V. Dych (New York: Seabury Press, 1978), 53.

[87] Ibid., 172.

[88] Anne E. Carr, "Starting with the Human," in O'Donovan, *A World of Grace*, 19.

[89] Rahner, *The Priesthood,* trans. Edward Quinn (New York: Herder and Herder, 1973; London: Sheed and Ward, 1973), 6.

[90] Ibid., 8.

[91] Rahner, *Foundations,* 21–23. For a very lucid explanation of how Rahner understands the knowledge of God unthematically, through transcendental experience, see Dych, "Theology in a New Key," 3–6; see also Carr, "Starting with the Human," 19–22.

[92] Rahner, *Foundations,* 120.

[93] Francis Fiorenza, "Karl Rahner and the Kantian Problematic," xliv.

[94] Rahner, *Hearers of the Word*, revised by J. B. Metz, trans. Michael Richards (New York: Seabury Press, 1969), 158.

[95] Rahner, "Anthropozentric," in Josef Höfer and Rahner, eds., *Lexikon für Theologie und Kirche* (Freiburg: Herder, 1957–67), 1:634 (translated in Carr, *Theological Method,* 181).

[96] Rahner, *Foundations,* 20.

[97] Ibid., 21.

[98] Rahner, "Anthropozentric," 1:634 (translated in Carr, *Theological Method,* 181). On Rahner's study of the relationship between theology and anthropology, see especially his essay, "Theology and Anthropology," in *TI,* 9:28–45; see also Carr, *Theological Method,* 179–91.

[99] Rahner, *Foundations,* 54.

[100] On the "supernatural existential," see Rahner, "Concerning the Relationship between Nature and Grace," in *TI,* 1:297–317; Rahner, *Foundations,* 126–33; see also Carr, *Theological Method,* 109ff.; John P. Galvin, "The Invitation of Grace," in O'Donovan, *A World of Grace*, 64–75.

[101] Rahner, *Foundations,* 131.

[102] Rahner, "Theology of Freedom," in *TI,* 6:178–96.

[103] Ibid., 182, 184.

[104] Rahner, *Foundations,* 211–12.

[105] Ibid., 205.

[106] Carr, *Theological Method,* 127.

[107] Rahner, "Current Problems in Christology," in *TI,* 1:150.

[108] Ibid., 153.

[109] Ibid., 151–52.

[110] Ibid., 165.

[111] Carr, *Theological Method,* 152.

[112] Rahner, "Christology within an Evolutionary View of the World," in *TI,* 5:168.

[113] Leo J. O'Donovan, "Making Heaven and Earth: Catholic Theology's Search for a Unified View of Nature and History," in Kelly, *Theology and Discovery,* 293. O'Donovan refers to Rahner's "Immanent and Transcendent Consummation of the World," in *TI,* 10:273–89.

[114] Rahner, "Christology within an Evolutionary View," 173.

[115] Ibid., 175.

[116] Ibid., 175–76.

[117] Egan, "Devout Christian," 139–144.

[118] Rahner, *Opportunities for Faith* (London: SPCK, 1974), 123.

[119] Ibid., 125.

[120] Rahner, "The Immediate Experience of God in the Spiritual Exercises of Saint Ignatius of Loyola: Interview with Wolfgang Feneberg," in Imhof and Biallowons, *Karl Rahner in Dialogue,* 176.

[121] Rahner, *The Dynamic Element in the Church* (New York: Herder and Herder, 1964), 85.

[122] Egan, "Devout Christian," 141.

[123] Rahner, *Everyday Faith* (New York: Herder and Herder, 1968), 188 (cited in Egan, "Devout Christian," 142).

[124] Egan, "Devout Christian," 142. Egan quotes Johann B. Metz, "Karl Rahner—Ein theologisches Leben," *Stimmen der Zeit* (May 1974): 305–14.

[125] Carr, "Starting with the Human," 22.

[126] Rahner, *Foundations,* 86–87.

[127] Ibid., 87.

[128] Rahner, "Christian Humanism," in *TI,* 9:193–94.

[129] Egan, "Devout Christian," 144.

[130] O'Donovan, "Orthopraxis," 56.

[131] Rahner, "Concerning the Relationship between Nature and Grace," in *TI,* 1:310.

[132] O'Donovan, "Orthopraxis," 58.

[133] Rahner, "Karl Rahner at 75 Years of Age," 190.

[134] Ibid., 192–93.

INDEX

Adoration, 92, 347
Advent, 75–80
Anamnesis, 261
Anonymous Christian, 255
Anthropology (Christian): as basis of theological reflection, 31–62; and Christology,
47–55; and church, 257; and culture, 298–
300; and the experiential, 50; and faith,
298–300; and the fundamental option, 44–
47; humankind's self-interpretation and,
131; metaphysical, 173–74; method in theology and, 34–47; mystical, 59; objectifying
in experience, 174; pastoral implications,
156; and supernatural existential, 43–44;
and symbolic reality, 293; theological, 42,
54, 57, 170, 172; and theology of symbol,
289; transcendental, 34, 174, 177 passim
Apostles' Creed, 159
Atheism, 160, 161, 168–69, 175
Augustine, 1, 35, 43, 156, 291
Authority, 144. *See also* Church: authority
and; Freedom: authority and

Bacik, James, 24
Barth, Karl, ix
Beatific vision (*visio beatifica*), 186, 190, 296,
336, 338, 341–42
Bettschart, Oscar, 14
Blondel, Maurice, 5
"The Body as Symbol of the Human," 289
Bonhoeffer, Dietrich, viii
Buchberger, Bishop of Regensburg, 15
Bultmann, Rudolf, 16
Burns, Jean, xi

Cajetan, Cardinal, 99
Capitalism, 279
Carr, Anne, x, 50, 57
Causality, 294
Censorship (Vatican), 19–20, 22
Chalcedon, 210
Charismatic element in the church, 296
Charity. *See* Love (Christian)
Christ. *See* Jesus Christ
Christian base communities, 306–7, 312,
316–17, 318
Christian conscience. *See* Conscience
Christian life: destiny and, 302; faith and, 299;
flight from the world and, 89; individualism
and, 309, 316–17; mission and, 302; moral
consciousness and, 306–7; nurture for, 63;

a pilgrim people and, 305; prayer and, 64;
responsibility for world and, 312; vocation
and, 302
Christian perfection and martyrdom, 84
Christology, 27, 47–55; and anthropology,
47–55, 184; of Chalcedon, 210; church's
dogmatic teaching on, 208, 214–15, 217;
as developed by church, 215, 217; as
foundation of theology, 52; and the
incarnation, 292; and magisterium, 189; of
the New Testament, 206; nexus between
anthropology and church, 53; post-Easter,
208; of the primitive church, 206; salvific
fulfillment and, 184; and symbolic reality,
289; in theological methodology, 34, 47–55;
transcendental, 48–49
"Christology within an Evolutionary View of
the World," 53
Church: as action of human beings, 264;
and adaptation, 255; as anthropological
fundament, 256; and anthropology, 254;
authority and, 147, 270; and avoidance of
conflict, 274–75; as basic sacrament, 287; as
caring, 316; and charismatic element, 269;
charismatic nature of office and ministry,
218; and Christian basic communities,
276–77; and Christian conscience, 275; and
Christology, 254; as Christ's mystical body,
256; and clericalism, 270, 271; consumerism
and, 274; cosmic, universalized, 255; declericalization of, 268, 269; as destroyer
of idols, 259; doctrine of, 156–72; and
ecclesiastical politics, 315; and ecumenical
movement, 255, 256; as embodiment of
Christ's presence, 254; as embodiment of
God and the human, 266; as embodiment
of God's promise, 267; as enduring expression of Christ, 259; and environmental
pollution, 274; as eschatological sign, 258;
and Eucharist, 264; and evangelization,
256; faith of, 256; fellowship of faith and
worship, 255; freedom in, 254; and free
speech, 255; the future and, 269–79; and
God's acceptance of sinners, 258; as God's
eschatologically perfect self-giving, 258;
God's presence and, 258, 260, 262, 263,
265–67; grace and, 254, 259; and hierarchy
as service, 269; hierarchy of, 254, 255;
historical relativity of, 256; and the Holy
Trinity, 260, 261; human dimension of, 256;

and human openness to God, 259; human origins of offices, 255; and ideology of the status quo, 273; institutionalization and depersonalization of, 276; Latin America and, 278; leadership of service and, 256; and liberation, 263, 268; and liturgy of adoration, 259; local, 254, 255; and love of God, 262; and magisterial authority, 255, 262; and martyrdom, 264, 326; and migrant workers, 276; mission of Christ and, 269; as mystery, 258, 264; no salvation outside, 265; not identical with Christ, 265; not identical with officeholders, 269; and openness to the transcendent, 255, 257; as permanent revolution, 259; and personal charism, 255; as personal communion of brothers and sisters, 306–8; and political parties, 279–80; the poor and, 268, 274, 278–80; possessing what it believes, 154; power of jurisdiction, 261; power of order, 261; and praxis for future society, 274; and prayer for unity, 264; as presence of Incarnate Word, 294; as primary sacrament, 258, 265, 295; reaction to criticism, 271; representative of God's presence, 264; and revolution, 274, 278–79; and Rome's formal authority, 271; as sacrament, 21, 61, 256, 265; in sacraments, prayer, and life, 262; as saving presence, 258; salvation and, 28, 254, 258, 260, 265; and secrecy, 270; self-delusion of, 271; self-glorification of, 256; self-understanding of, 256; as sharing, 318; as sign of grace, 265; social action and, 264; social conditions and sin, 273; social embodiment and, 263; and socialism, 274, 278; and sociocritical commitment, 272; sociocritical nature of, 268; and sociopolitical commitment, 268, 274–80, 312–13; the Spirit and, 218, 255, 256, 269, 295; as spirit-filled community, 218, 268; as symbolic reality of grace, 296; as symbol of Christ's mission, 254; as symbol of universal salvation, 28; teaching and "divine right," 262; textbook ecclesiology of, 254; and tolerance, 308–10, 314–15; and tradition, 261; transcendental orientation to God, 259; and Third World, 277; truth and, 260, 261; turned in on itself, 238; and United Nations, 302, 311; and unity and diversity, 258; universal, 254, 255; versus the purely institutional, 259; visible sign of God's inner love, 218; and voluntary service, 268, 279; as witness to Christ's freedom, 17; as world church, 309, 311
"The Church: Basis of Pastoral Action," 257
Church hierarchy, 254, 255
Church office, 261, 268, 270
Concelebration of the Eucharist, 18
Confessions (St. Augustine), 35
Conscience, 71, 275, 280, 310
Consciousness, 187

Contingency, 333
Conversion to the phantasm, 7
Cor Jesu, 289
Creation, 35; and Christology, 50; and communion with God, 54; dependence on incarnation, 102; doctrine of, 160; and freedom, 45; God's communication in, 56; God's grace in, 52; God's love in, 299; God's word in, 41; as openness to the absolute, 35; orientation to God in, 35–36, 60, 174; and pain, 67; as source of knowledge of God, 86; and theological anthropology, 42
Cross, 27, 69, 80, 91, 164, 170
Culture, 299, 300, 301, 302, 303, 311
"Current Problems in Christology," 51–52

Darlap, Adolf, 16
Dasein (being-in-the-world), 7
Death, 24, 30–31, 84, 299, 319–32
de Gruchy, John, vii
Delp, Alfred, 3
de Lubac, Henri, 114–15
Despair, 305
Dessauer, Philipp, 113
Destiny, 107
"The Development of Dogma," 144–55
Dialogue between God's love and human freedom, 296
Die siebenfältige Gabe (The sevenfold gift), 281
Dissent, 31, 239
Doctoral dissertation (Rahner's), 8
Dogma: adequacy of dogmatic statements, 148–49; authoritative pronouncements of the church, 147; basis in Word of God, 148; and categorical revelation, 144; Catholic doctrinal development of, 148; caution against absolutizing, 148; Chalcedonian, 210; and church memory, 150; church practice in proclaiming a doctrine, 151; development of, 145–55; doctrine of the nature of God, 159; and ecclesiastical legislation, 145; evolution within the same truth, 149; and exegesis in Christology, 207, 210; of God and Trinity in relationship, 159; and gospel, 146; as hierarchy of truths, 145; and historical conditioning of truth, 150; and history, Jesus as intersection of, 201; history of, 144; idolatrous theories about God, 158; inadequacy of propositional truth, 149; and knowledge of God, 163; light of faith in, 154; not always present in church, 145; official Catholic doctrine of God, 164; order of divine truth, 149; and power of the Holy Spirit, 155; and proofs for God's existence, 167–68; revelation and conditioning of human understanding, 151; and sense of history, culture, and language, 145; surpassing of dogmatic formulas, 149; and talk of God, 170